The New Unionism

THE NEW UNIONISM

Employee Involvement in the Changing Corporation

CHARLES C. HECKSCHER

A Twentieth Century Fund Book

Basic Books, Inc., Publishers New York

The Twentieth Century Fund is an independent research foundation which undertakes policy studies of economic, political, and social institutions and issues. The Fund was founded in 1919 and endowed by Edward A. Filene.

Library of Congress Cataloging-in-Publication Data

Heckscher, Charles, 1949–
    The new unionism.

    "A Twentieth Century Fund book."
    Bibliography: p. 280.
    Includes index.
    1. Industrial relations—United States. 2. Trade-
unions—United States. 3. Industrial management—United
States—Employee participation. 4. Quality of work life—
United States. 5. Organizational change—United States.
I. Title.
HD8072.5.H42   1988   331.88'0973   87–47769
ISBN   0–465–05098–0

For Alexander and Fiona

CONTENTS

FOREWORD

THE American worker is living through a time of change—change in the domestic economy, dramatic advances in technology, increased foreign competition— which has brought a decline in the power and prestige of labor unions. After World War II, almost a third of the American work force was unionized; today, only a fifth is—and unionization tends to be in precisely those areas of the economy facing decline and retrenchment. These changes pose a serious challenge to both organized labor and management, because the cost of a decline in worker representation in economic decision making through unionism is all too often a loss of worker commitment, which translates into decreased productivity.

The problem facing the unions is complicated by the changes that have taken place in the labor force, that is, increases in white collar jobs, traditionally non-unionized, and a blurring of the lines between labor and management. These shifts may portend a demise of labor union power and influence. In fact, many observers claim that the age of independent trade unions and collective bargaining that began some fifty years ago with the passage of the Wagner Act is drawing to a close. The question is what will take its place.

America's social and economic health demand that a new road to labor-management cooperation be found. Charles Heckscher, now an assistant professor at the Harvard Business School, who worked with the Communications Workers of America studying innovations in worker participation in management, has examined the problem, analyzing possible responses that might be made by government, labor, and management.

In his book, he carefully probes the strengths and limitations of the New Deal system in light of the changes that have taken place in the economy, in society, and in technology over the past five decades. Then he examines the birth of a new movement, one he calls associational unionism, which opens the system of worker representation to a multiplicity of groups and interests. Heckscher suggests that by shifting the focus of labor-management relations from defense of the collective-bargaining contract to a combination of increased legal rights for employees and pressure from associations set up to influence employers through negotiations, associational unionism may be able to increase employee involvement in decision making and improve the quality of work life.

The Fund is grateful to Charles Heckscher for his penetrating examination of worker representation. His book is certain to stimulate debate on this issue, an issue that must be resolved if the American worker is to compete successfully in the world economy.

M. J. ROSSANT, *Director*
The Twentieth Century Fund
November 1987

ACKNOWLEDGMENTS

WORKING on this study has driven home the fact that knowledge is a social rather than an individual product. Let me begin by acknowledging a deep debt, which may not be immediately apparent, to Talcott Parsons and Mark Gould, whose way of looking at social systems has strongly shaped my thought. My view of worker representation has been developed in large measure through extended discussions with Fred Gordon, Chris Mackin, Bill Dickens, and Mike Howard. Michael Maccoby and Harvey Brooks supported me in my first explorations of the field and have continued to help greatly with this study. My colleagues at the Communications Workers of America (CWA) were major influences, wittingly or not, on my understanding of unions: I want particularly to thank Glenn Watts, Ronnie Straw, George Kohl, Patrick Hunt, and W. C. Button for their patience and openness. The Twentieth Century Fund gave me the necessary time to reflect on and broaden the experience I gained at the CWA.

Since this book covers many areas of knowledge that are beyond my expertise, I often had to depend on specialists to help me out. Conversations with Paul Weiler, Dan Tarullo, Karl Klare, and Alan Hyde gave me a start in the labor law arena. Larry Susskind and Lavinia Hall taught me about current developments in alternative dispute resolution. Dick Walton and Rosabeth Kanter criticized my treatment of corporations, and Charles Sabel guided me through the minefield of economics. Charles Derber gave me an overview of research on professional employees. Tom Rankin introduced me to the important innovations at Shell-Sarnia.

Many of those I have mentioned read earlier drafts of this study. Others who also gave me valuable feedback included George Lodge, Marty Manley, Thomas Rice, Mike Piore, and several anonymous reviewers; I would like to assure these last, wherever they are, that I have taken their comments to heart.

Writing is a social activity not only because it draws on many people's ideas, but also because it depends on the support of friends and family. I have been fortunate in this area, too, and I am very grateful to Lavinia and others who have helped me through the long process.

The New Unionism

CHAPTER 1

Introduction

THE American labor movement is in crisis; the evidence by now is unmistakable. For thirty years, as organized labor's share of the labor force has dropped steadily, those in and around unions have tended to downplay the problem; noting the movement's history of ups and downs, they have always predicted a rebound at any moment. But the rebound has not come: through recession and recovery, through Democratic and Republican administrations, the decline has continued unrelentingly. Today the unions' share of the private sector work force is below 16 percent—well under half its peak in 1954—and there is every indication that it will continue to shrink.[1]

These figures parallel a serious loss of political influence. Though labor has never wielded the clout attributed to it by its enemies, it has had a decent record of legislative success.[2] But not any more. In 1978 a mild attempt to tighten enforcement of the National Labor Relations Act was turned back by Congress, and there have been precious few victories since. As a business lobbyist described the situation in 1984: "The labor movement does not have the teeth, the strength, or the clout that it had even ten years ago. When labor barks, we aren't going to worry about it."[3]

Curiously, this dramatic weakening of unions has not led to a reduction in public mistrust. Even recent opinion polls show a remarkably widespread feeling that unions have "too much power."[4] Despite labor's increasing ineffectiveness, there is growing support for restrictions on the union shop, the right to strike, and other pillars of the current system. President Reagan's attack on the Air Traffic Controllers' union (PATCO), an unprecedented and successful attempt by government to decertify a body elected to represent employees, was greeted with widespread approval. "Labor unions," according to one summary of the polls, "are one of the least trusted institutions of American life."[5]

The PATCO strike, indeed, marked a turning point at which those who sought the death of the labor movement began to close in for the kill. For thirty years after World War II there had been a widespread "truce" between large employers and unions. During that time both sides spoke enthusiastically of the benefits of free collective bargaining. In the past few years, however, it has suddenly become legitimate to openly engage in antiunion activity. Illegal antiunion activity by employers, as determined by the National Labor Relations Board (NLRB), has skyrocketed, and the hiring of consultants to fend off organizing drives is now common practice.[6]

More and more companies are continuing operations during strikes by hiring replacement workers. Even the head of the NLRB, Donald Dotson, publicly attacked the institution he was pledged to defend: "Collective bargaining," he says, "means . . . the destruction of individual freedom."[7]

These events signal an enormous change in the established system of industrial relations. Yet they have aroused remarkably little *public* concern. Thirty years ago organized labor was widely seen not as a minor interest group but as a critical institution of democracy, essential in providing a balance for corporate power and in preventing employer abuses. The New Deal established unions as a pillar of its social policy. Throughout the industrialized world organized labor was considered a bulwark against despotism. Totalitarian regimes—Nazi and Communist alike—have always sought to undermine unions; even today the Reagan administration strongly protests the destruction of independent trade unions in Poland. Yet in our own country the decline of labor has gone all but unnoticed.

What has happened? Have the conditions that generated the Wagner Act in the 1930s and the labor movement as we know it been eliminated? It would be hard to argue that there is no longer a *need* for employee representation. The same polls that show such low faith in unions show even less trust in management's good intentions: almost 60 percent agree that "If there were no unions, most employers would quickly move to exploit their employees."[8] In many industries and workplaces, moreover, the need for workers' voices to be heard is clear. There are the immigrant workers in Illinois who worked with open vats of cyanide, their abusive working conditions coming to light only when one of them died;[9] workers whose plants are abruptly closed, their jobs exported to the Far East or Latin America, leaving towns decimated and families with nowhere to turn;[10] women who are subjected to sexual harassment or minorities openly baited because of their race. These workers certainly should have the means to express their concerns and needs.

Though such cases of obvious abuse have decreased in the past fifty years, they remain far more common than we would like to believe, and the weakness of unions diminishes protection against them. But the problem of worker representation extends far beyond this domain, to less familiar types of issues faced by all levels of employees—and especially by the white-collar and professional employees who are increasingly seen as the leading edge of economic growth. There are the engineers ordered to work on a transportation system they know is unsafe; we will hear more about them in chapter 8. There are middle managers, expected to show absolute loyalty to their companies, who have suddenly found in the past decade that the companies show far less loyalty to them—the pruning of management ranks has often been drastic. There are clerical workers whose jobs have been reduced to mindless machine punching by technological advances. These abuses of power, while different in type and scope from those that spawned the Wagner Act, still cause harm and generate discontent.

White-collar employees do not, however, generally seek to join unions. They view union membership as something associated with blue-collar work, adversarial bitterness, mass action, and strikes. White-collar workers tend to reject the idea of such sharp lines drawn between themselves and management. They are far more negative in their opinion of organized labor than their blue-collar counterparts.[11] They are sometimes driven toward traditional unions in the face of management intransigence—even college professors have shown considerable interest in recent years—but white-collar workers remain uneasy, straining to find structures and tactics that differ from a traditional union approach. So far, the labor movement and the policy framework that supports it are failing to meet their needs.

That there is dissatisfaction among employees is not in doubt; we will review evidence of it in chapters 4 and 12. The question is how extensive and severe it is. It has not manifested itself in violent uprisings of the sort we saw in the 1930s. Workers express themselves today more subtly, by diminishing their motivation and withdrawing their commitment from the workplace. Opinion polls and other studies show that employees give less than their full effort at work. That becomes a special concern in a period of heightened international competition. Daniel Yankelovich, who has been carefully tracking this phenomenon for the past decade and a half, summarizes his findings in this way:

> Because of a widespread "commitment gap," many high-discretion jobholders are, by their own admission, holding back effort from their jobs, giving less than they are capable of giving, and less than they are, in principle, willing to give. . . . This commitment gap has surfaced at a time when America is struggling to maintain its economic vitality in an intensely competitive world economic marketplace. . . . It is unlikely that the U.S. can revive its competitive vitality without addressing the commitment gap.[12]

The problem has been met by repeated and widespread calls for cooperation and unity—but not by effective new mechanisms of representation. Commitment comes from feeling oneself to be part of a social effort, and it vanishes when one's concerns are not dealt with. Despite their adversarial rhetoric, unions have been able to create a sense of belonging and commitment in their membership, and, thus, where unions are strong, productivity is significantly higher than in comparable nonunion companies.[13] No adequate replacement is yet in sight.

The labor relations scene, meanwhile, is frozen; in recent years there has been almost no movement and very little imagination. Efforts at direct worker participation through shopfloor discussion groups, for example, have been perceived as an attack on the system rather than as an opportunity for something really new. Most unions have resisted these efforts or have remained ambivalent, seeing them as a way of getting around union representation, and many companies have manipulated the concept for precisely that purpose.

In the legislative arena, labor has managed to stop most major assaults on the National Labor Relations Act, and its adversaries have managed to block most attempts to strengthen the Act's protections. The outcome is gridlock—a situation in which no one is satisfied, no one sees the system as working, and no one will make the first move.

This crisis has deep roots. Its origins in this country precede the Reagan administration by many years; it exists also in most other industrialized nations. Though nowhere else is the retreat of labor as complete as in this country, unions in most European nations have experienced a decline in membership and, more important, a sense of loss of direction since 1980. Their political influence has dissipated, and they are rather confusedly seeking a way to reignite enthusiasm. "We trade unionists," says Franz Steinkuhler of Germany's metalworkers in a warning that applies equally to this country, "have got to be damned careful that we don't stand there as the people of yesterday, the backward ones, while the right wing and the greens [environmentalists] are considered the creators of the future."[14]

Building an Alternative System

In this gridlocked situation it becomes increasingly fruitless to pose the problem in terms of whether unions as such are good or bad. That issue simply polarizes the debate into two equally problematic camps. It is clear that unions have performed—and, I believe, continue to perform—important functions. It is also clear from their severe decline that in their current form unions are unable to cope with major new developments. Though public sentiment increasingly calls for greater cooperation with employers, the structure and history of unions, and the legal framework that supports them, make it difficult for them to seek out new alternatives to traditional adversarial tactics. Unions have great difficulty in dealing with local shopfloor issues that cannot be reduced to contractual language. They have equal difficulty with strategic issues, like finance and technological change, which are increasingly predetermining the choices in collective bargaining.[15] They are more comfortable in challenging management than in proposing positive solutions. These limitations, which will be analyzed further in chapter 2, at one time helped a nascent labor movement to focus its energies and educational efforts, but they have now become liabilities.

To break out of the current policy deadlock, the debate must be broadened beyond the familiar attacks on and defenses of existing unions. The real issue is: What system would best and most appropriately enable employees to voice their current concerns? That is the question that forms the starting point for this study.

My chief reference point in thinking about change is the National Labor Relations Act—often known as the "Wagner Act" after its chief architect, Senator Robert F. Wagner—which has defined our approach to labor relations since the 1930s. Its solution to the bitter unrest that preceded its enactment was pragmatic and in many ways limited. First, the right to form unions was guaranteed, but only for a restricted group—those with no supervisory responsibilities.[16] Second, the decision-making process was built around adversarial negotiations. Cooperation was not actually forbidden, but it was hedged with provisions intended to maintain the autonomy of unions. Finally, these negotiations were to center on wages and working conditions: management was under no obligation to bargain on other matters.

This system has a powerful underlying logic. The essential idea embodied in the act is that worker representation involves *balancing* the power of management by building a parallel organization of workers. One behemoth, according to this logic, can best be controlled by another one. The concept requires the drawing of a series of lines to establish the field of battle: one defining workers as opposed to management, another defining the issues about which they must bargain, and a third marking legitimate tactics in the contest.

The weaknesses of this approach have become increasingly apparent in the context of rapid economic change. A balance of power is generally rigid, slow to adapt, and unable to deal with great diversity of associations and interests. These problems have shown up everywhere to a greater or lesser degree. They account, I believe, for the almost universal questioning of labor movements today.

I will argue that the limitations of the Wagner Act framework are no longer necessary—that this form of unionism, common as it is, and effective as it has been in the past, is not the only form of worker representation. It is now possible and essential to build a more flexible system for expressing the concerns of employees.

We have been through a similar transformation once before, one that provides useful lessons for the present. During the 1920s and 1930s industrial unionism as we now know it displaced an earlier form of representation—craft unionism. The 1920s was a period of crisis in the labor movement very similar to the current one:

> Unions relapsed into stagnation. . . . The symptoms were declining membership, hesitant organizing, parochial leadership, unimpressive results at the bargaining table, and the rise of dual unions. The causes were the indifference or hostility of workers to unions . . . economic concentration, craft and jurisdictional restrictions of the organizations themselves, and, perhaps most important, the antiunion practices of management.[17]

Behind this paralysis of the labor movement was a conjunction of major social forces analogous to those that are undermining unions today. The economy was shifting toward mass production; workers were being brought into large bureaucratic firms; and new movements were arising on a basis quite different from the communities that generated craft unionism. The old structures of worker representation could not cope.

Today a similar transformation is under way, involving the decline of the very mass-production organizations that originally favored industrial unionism; the bedrock of the labor movement is once again rapidly eroding. The structure of management is changing, this time from bureaucracy toward some as-yet-undefined "postbureaucratic" form. And the great movements of the past decades—especially those of equal rights for women and minorities—have again grown up outside the scope of established mechanisms.

It is these long-term transformations that have moved industrial unionism from the center to the margins of social concern. The most important problems facing unions today simply are not dealt with in the Wagner Act framework. Unions are still answering questions about raising wages and preventing supervisory abuse. Those problems have not vanished, but they have been dwarfed in the public mind by concerns about economic restructuring, technological advances, and the maintenance of continuous careers in a rapidly changing environment. The labor movement so far has no effective mechanisms for coping with these issues.

My thesis, then, is that we are approaching a new juncture, analogous to that of the 1920s and 1930s. I predict, not the end of unionism, but its reemergence in a changed form. As craft gave way to industrial unionism, so industrial unionism will, I believe, be replaced by *associational* unionism—a form more appropriate to rapid economic change, flexible systems of management, and shifting employee loyalties.

Associational unionism is foreshadowed today by a range of partial experiments involving the development by employee groups of the capacity for greater flexibility and a wider range of action. Concretely, it can be glimpsed in efforts by

8

many corporations and an increasing number of unions to establish direct worker participation on the shopfloor; in the expansion of joint committees at different levels of decision making; in the growing willingness to reduce the emphasis on fixed work rules and contractual uniformity; and in the growing assertiveness of many associations of white-collar and semiprofessional employees in response to their lack of effective voice.

These developments remain fragmentary and uncertain, at odds with the dominant system of labor relations. But they respond to essential needs of employees today, and in so doing they reveal possibilities not included in the Wagner Act framework. Most fundamentally, they break with the assumption that employee representation must be based on a balance of powerful organizations. In various ways they open the system of representation to a multiplicity of groups and interests, ranging from local worksite bodies to federations at the highest policy-making levels, and depend on influence more than on the power of confrontation for their effectiveness. These innovations show the feasibility of ongoing negotiations among many groups, thereby encouraging constructive problem solving rather than tests of strength. And they enable employee groups to respond flexibly to a range of problems, both local and strategic, rather than focusing on the defense of the collective bargaining contract.

Such moves are essential to deal with the concerns of employees today. Yet within the existing context they are also dangerous. Historically, flexibility among unions has been synonymous with weakness: the ability to check management power has come from the insistence on uniform enforcement of rules. In moving toward variable pay systems based on skill or company performance, for instance, unions risk dividing their members and losing the capacity for unified action.

To overcome these dangers requires major changes in the strategies of employee groups and in the environment that supports them. The current framework of industrial relations law and tradition, by drawing sharp lines to define the parties and their tactics, now restricts change, "freezing" action into familiar patterns. For that reason, many of the most important developments have occurred outside the traditional boundaries of the field; it is there that foundations are being laid for *systemic* change.

The most important of these developments has been the extension of employee rights by law rather than by collective bargaining. The last two decades have seen enormous activity in this area. The beginning, perhaps, was the Civil Rights Act of 1964, which gave large groups of employees recourse to the courts when they felt unjustly treated. That caused a revolution in personnel management. Since then many more acts, at both the federal and state levels, have extended similar protections to other categories of workers. And where legislative will has failed, the courts have cut deeply into the hitherto absolute doctrine that employers could fire employees for any reason, or for no reason at all. An account of these new gains in employee rights and their implications in the shifting structure of labor-management relations is given more fully in chapter 8. The new rights are still far from being extensive or systematic enough to offer a full system of representation, but they have placed important new limits on management's authority.

The new rights have not emerged in a vacuum; they result from a growing network of interest-based movements and associations that have evolved into effective mechanisms of pressure. Women's and minority groups, through the use of publicity and legal pressure, have in many respects had more important effects on corporate management than traditional unions during the past twenty years. These groups, too, now constitute powerful forces that are not integrated into the existing labor relations framework.

This growth of employee rights, which has been nearly universal in the industrialized world, drastically changes the traditional equations of labor relations. Unions often see it as a threat to their own functions, while management fears a tidal wave of litigation. In our current state of drift, these dangers are real. The current system is being eaten away piece by piece, and the replacement as yet has no coherence.

Associational unionism is the structure needed to pull together these rights and interests—now confused and fractious—into a constructive system of representation. It builds from the growing maturity and strength of interest groups and from evolving techniques of coordination among multiple groups.

The term *associational unionism* is deliberately paradoxical. Traditionally unions and associations have been seen as opposites. The former have been powerful organizations seeking to enforce claims on employers; the latter have been loose groupings providing service to individuals. But today these two poles are moving closer together. Unions, no longer able to sustain their power through the establishment of uniform contracts, are exploring ways to encourage local participation and diversity without destroying themselves. And employee associations are increasingly viewing themselves as organized pressure groups for their members' interests.

What is needed now is a unification of the two poles. A system of representation in the current environment must be *associational*, permitting a range of employee groups in shifting combinations rather than insisting on two-party confrontation; but it must also be a form of *unionism* in recognizing the need for organized pressure.

Thus, associational unionism, as I envision it:

- Must be based on universal rights guaranteed to all employees.
- Must include varied employee groupings, based on job type, organizational level, geography, and other shared interests such as gender or race.

- Must provide mechanisms of multilateral negotiation to work out agreements among these diverse claims.
- Must encompass concerns about work structure and "the quality of work life" on one hand, and about general policy issues on the other.

At the same time, it must avoid some major traps:

- It must reduce the government's role as administrative judge of disputes, encouraging instead local negotiation.
- It must *not* assume universal cooperation or harmony but must provide ways of resolving difficult disputes.
- It must *not* encourage an explosion of litigious claims to rights but must enable those concerned to work out interpretations of rights.

These requirements, when laid out in abstract terms, seem indisputable: any system that does not find a way to incorporate the growing proliferation of claims to rights can hardly hope to succeed. They also seem in many respects contradictory. It is my contention, however, that many recent innovations inside and outside the labor relations domain show the way to a reconciliation of the inherent tensions and the construction of a stable structure of associational unionism. There is a great deal of working out yet to be done, but the outlines of change are already visible.

The nature of the transition will depend considerably on the attitudes of the main parties. Management dug in its heels at the passage of the Wagner Act, fighting it tooth and nail until World War II, prolonging the turmoil and making it far more painful than it might otherwise have been. The ambivalence of the old craft unions toward the new order also complicated the process. Both unions and management have already started to repeat history, with management resisting extensions of rights and labor uncertain about the new forms of worker participation. One can only hope that this change can be carried out more peacefully than the last one.

We are still early in the process of change—still, to follow my analogy, in the drift of the 1920s rather than in the gathering momentum of the 1930s. My discussion of associational unionism, starting with chapter 7, will not aim at detailed recommendations for a new system but will merely try to sketch the main elements. We are at a point now, I believe, at which the major structural pieces of a new form of worker representation can be seen amid the welter of particular innovations and experiments, because so many of these share common dynamics and directions. The exact shape of the eventual outcome, however, will not be determined until these experiments have gone considerably further.

My focus will not be on the substantive decisions that have to be made by policymakers, either in management or in government—for example, whether we should permit the decline of our national manufacturing capacity or whether profit sharing is better than a fixed wage. I believe that no solution to these problems, no matter how technically correct, will work unless the *process* by which it is reached is seen as legitimate. If the process includes the affected parties, these and other critical decisions can build trust and consensus. Otherwise, they will tend to further fragment an already contentious society.

Though many see labor unions today as irrelevant, the issues raised by their decline are certainly not. Any organization or political system is based on cooperation, trust, and legitimacy, and these result directly from appropriate mechanisms of representation. We are not doing well in terms of cooperation and trust: our international competitiveness is threatened by our inability to develop commitment. And employee concerns are more and more often spilling out of the workplace into our courts and legislatures, which are ill-equipped to handle them. We can no longer afford to leave them to such ad hoc, inadequate forums.

PART I

THE RISE
AND DECLINE
OF THE
WAGNER ACT
FRAMEWORK

CHAPTER 2

Union History:
The Triumph of
Formal Organization

CRITICISM of the traditional structure of labor unions is easy, but finding alternatives is not. A great many variations have been tried in the past and rejected. Unions have not taken their present form by accident or stupidity; they have in fact been quite successful against great odds. As John Dunlop, the ex-secretary of labor, reminds us:

> Our collective bargaining system must be classed as one of the more successful distinctive American institutions. . . . The industrial working class has been assimilated into the mainstream of the community, and has altered to a degree the values and directions of the community, without disruptive conflict and alienation and with a stimulus to economic efficiency. This is no mean achievement in an industrial society.[1]

It would be all too easy, in seeking a way out of the current impasse, to forget these successes of the past and to repeat the failures. Any proposal for change must first deal with the burden of history.

Yet the successes of the past, while significant, were also tenuous and incomplete. There has never been a point at which the labor relations "system" has been so solidly established and accepted that we should now look back to it as a model. On the contrary, the history of unions in America is marked by a high degree of conflict and struggle—not only over particular contract issues, but over the labor movement's very identity and right to exist. The periods of relative peace and security, in which the place of labor seemed clear, have been rare and brief. Unions have "worked," not by gradually evolving toward long-term stability, but by continually finding compromises in an inherently unstable situation.

Thus the most constant theme in the history of labor is *tension*. Unions have always been fragile institutions trying to hold together contradictory forces. The current juncture is, from this perspective, a new episode in a long series of crises that have revolved around similar problems.

The Development of Collective Bargaining

Two competing visions of worker representation underlie much of the debate today, as they have for the past century or more. On the one hand, unions can be viewed as voluntary associations based on the active participation of their members; on the other, they can be seen as disciplined organizations managing a long-term battle with employers. In fact they are and must be both. Yet these poles—spontaneity vs. discipline, democracy vs. control, community vs. bureaucracy, breadth of vision vs. narrow interest—have defined many of the structural problems and changes in the labor movement since its birth.

Until the late nineteenth century the emphasis was clearly on informal community rather than on bureaucratic organization. The most important groupings of workers in the period were craft bodies, which grew out of the medieval guilds. Like the guilds, they controlled the tools and knowledge necessary for production, and they shared a rich culture that linked them closely to outside communities. The characteristic workers' associations of the nineteenth century were therefore very broad in scope, mixing local craft organizations, workingmen's clubs, and reform societies. "In the craft system," says Edward Shorter, ". . . work and leisure mingled inextricably, so that the awareness of being part of a larger community permeated the work place, and the awareness of belonging to an occupational community dominated social relations off the job."[2]

Craft organizations in this context did not act like "unions." The strength of their communal life supported a wide variety of actions that are virtually unknown today. Rather than focusing on collective bargaining, for instance, craft groups were able to set standards of fair rates that their members individually demanded from their employers. They did not often strike because they were unified enough simply to refuse to work for less than the rate agreed upon. Nor did they restrict themselves to representing members to employers: one of their most important forms of action throughout the nineteenth century was the formation of worker-owned cooperatives, continuing a centuries-old tradition of self-management.

Unskilled workers, too, behaved in very un-unionlike ways. Though they lacked shared work traditions, they had their own values based on the egalitarianism of preindustrial village and farming cultures. As they were drawn into the developing industrial sector, they carried with them their old solidarities and values that framed their responses to wage labor. The early unions of unskilled workers, such as the Knights of Labor in the 1880s, were wide ranging and dramatic compared to current labor organizations. They often had the characteristics of religious groups, involving both spiritual and social reform elements, and including secret rituals and symbols. Unskilled labor movements, when they erupted, generally expressed strongly egalitarian values and radical social reform ideals.[3]

The late nineteenth century saw the decline of these relatively communal forms of action and the rise of collective bargaining as an alternative. Collective bargaining was, by comparison with what had gone before, a quite narrow, focused, and adversarial tactic—far more reliant on formal bureaucratic organization. The question is why it emerged triumphant.

The answer lies primarily in the nature of the opposition—in transformations then underway in the organization of *management*. The decades following the Civil War saw the first development of large corporate organizations.[4] This was the period during which the railroads were built, and in which Andrew Carnegie came to control nearly the entire national steel and iron production. Management became an increasingly distinct function: skill in organization and marketing became as important as knowledge of production. The concept of bureaucracy had not yet been invented, but the reality of hierarchical organizations was already transforming the context for workers.

Craft workers employed by these organizations found themselves at an acute disadvantage. They maintained their traditional independence on the shopfloor,[5] but they no longer controlled crucial decisions such as the distribution of pay or the selection of products and markets. These decisions now lay in the hands of an "alien" management bureaucracy. The communal craft groupings were unable to organize effectively to deal with this new outside force.

In the later part of the century these underlying problems became apparent as industrialists met the growth of unions with sustained hostility. Craft unions fought many bitter battles with the new corporations—and lost. The emblematic case was the Homestead Strike of 1892. It was triggered when the Carnegie Steel Company, which had grown into one of the first great industrial empires, unilaterally announced a massive wage cut for its craft workers at Homestead, Pennsylvania. The steel union, thoroughly overmatched, tried improvised tactics, calling on the support of unskilled workers and townspeople in the area. When the company, spoiling for a battle, sent in a boatload of armed Pinkerton detectives to lock out the workers, the toll after a bloody day's battle was ten dead and scores of wounded; the union was essentially destroyed.

Such incidents increased and were characterized by extraordinary levels of violence. It was apparent that traditional job-control mechanisms of craft union-ism were no longer sufficient to battle an extremely hostile managerial class in control of effective bureaucratic organizations. Workers were suffering from a new imbalance of power, one that the sociologist Max Weber was to highlight a few decades later: "[Bureaucracy] is superior to every form of mass and even of 'communal' action. And where the bureaucratization of administration has been completely carried through, a form of power relation is established which is practically unshatterable."[6]

The distinction between bureaucracy and communal action—between formal organization and informal enthusiasm—deserves some elaboration. "Organiza-tion" (which I will use interchangeably with "bureaucracy") is characterized by:

- Action oriented to a *specific goal.*
- Limited, specialized roles defined by *function* rather than personal qualities.
- The use of *power* as the main mechanism of coordination. I will use the term "power" in a rather specific way, not as just any kind of pressure, but as the ability to *command* obedience. In an organization, issuing commands is the way most things get done.

All this is extremely familiar in business organizations, where profit is the goal and standard legitimizing a hierarchy of command.

Communal action, by contrast, is a less familiar concept in modern times. It is diffuse; it is not held together by clear goals and formal mechanisms. Instead, the "glue" is *solidarity.* That is the essential unifying principle of unions, as opposed to companies. But as any labor leader can testify, solidarity is a difficult thing to command. Indeed, communities are directed, not by commands and power, but by *influence*—that is, the ability to persuade—which derives from knowledge and past services to the group.

The main reason that organization triumphs over community is that the former can count on much stricter discipline than the latter. Commands get obeyed most of the time because they are backed up by sanctions; but influence is often disregarded because each individual may think he or she knows best. Communal action is therefore subject to factionalism and confusion of objectives. Organizations can ordinarily sustain consistent policies over a much longer period than can any voluntary grouping.[7]

As with many concepts, these two do not exist in pure form. One of the efforts of paternalistic managers, for instance, is to mix a sense of community into the bureaucratic corporation. Conversely, most communities have some kind of power structure that can be activated, at least for emergencies. Still, the differ-ence is usually clear. The nineteenth-century workers' movements, specifically, were essentially communal, making them very vulnerable to management organization. It is true that management had more "guns" than the workers, but it is also important to note that management was united and therefore able to use both guns and concessions effectively, while workers were frequently split about their goals and tactics.

The turning point came in the last decades of the nineteenth century when Samuel Gompers and others, seeking ways to end the long series of worker defeats, abandoned the social dreams and values of communal movements and accepted the fact that capitalism was here to stay. These pragmatic union leaders anticipated Weber's lesson: what was required to deal with these organizations was not communal spontaneity and enthusiasm but, rather, *counterorganizations*. They adopted the strategy of trying to meet their opponents at their own level by establishing a balance of power. The first step was the development of an effective system of internal discipline: centralized authority in the hands of international officers.[8] Second, they narrowed their goals, rejecting all grand visions of social reforms that could split their membership. Finally, they stressed tangible benefits to tie the members securely to the organization. In these ways, unions reduced their reliance on diffuse collective enthusiasm.

These changes in turn made possible the tactic of the modern strike. When based in communal movements, especially those of the unskilled workers, the strike was more like an "explosion of consciousness"[9] than a disciplined action. It often drew together whole communities and involved strong elements of radical social action. But all too often collective euphoria proved too insubstantial to sustain unity for long. When the need arose to formulate a concrete alternative to existing structures, divisions appeared among the participants.[10]

In Gompers's hands, however, the strike became something quite different—a limited, focused instrument for gaining concrete benefits. The reasoning, as far as it can be reconstructed, was this: workers *as a group* have a clear sense of their rights and obligations concerning issues of distribution and work structure. They do not have such a sense concerning the way to manage an enterprise or an economy. A movement addressing the former issues can be coherent and disciplined; one addressing the latter will disintegrate.

Furthermore, once labor accepted the existence and power of a separate management stratum, the goal had to be to reach an agreement with the "opposition." The limited strike was a way of giving the opposition something to bargain about. Though they might not have liked it, management could make compromises about wages and working conditions, but they had to fight without quarter when socialism was put on the agenda.

Although general strikes and communal outbursts were to continue into the 1920s, it was clear by the turn of the century that the strategy of the American Federation of Labor (AFL) was winning the day. The main lines of the modern structure were already drawn. The union, in Gompers's conception and the

AFL's practice, had been successfully transformed from an association into an *organization*, distinct from the old shopfloor communities and with the very limited function of dealing with management. It had successfully created a means of uniting workers for battle on issues about which they did *not* have to share a collective ideology. Political and communal aspirations of the workers' movements were shunted aside by a strict pragmatism: "We are living under the wage system," said Gompers, "and so long as that lasts, it is our purpose to achieve a continually larger share for labor, for the wealth producers . . ."[11]

> Collective bargaining in industry does not imply that wage earners shall assume control
> . of industry, or responsibility for financial management. It proposes that employees shall
> have the right to organize and deal with the employer through selected representatives
> as to wages and working conditions.[12]

The main elements of unionism down to the present were, in other words, already in place in the AFL policy. Unionism had restricted *itself* on key fronts: on the issues it would deal with; on the tactics it would employ; and on the scope of its representation. It no longer sought to establish a harmony of management and workers through cooperatives, or to transform society by mass movements. These self-restrictions had proved necessary to mold a fighting organization.

A New Crisis: The Decline of Craft Unionism

Although it established the principles of collective bargaining, the AFL structure remained a hybrid. It did not displace shopfloor craft communities; it simply placed bureaucratic organizations on top of them to deal with issues beyond the scope of the traditional groupings. Nor was the strike the only weapon. Throughout this period, and continuing until today, AFL unions wielded their control over access to trades, using apprenticeship programs and job placement as effective ways to impose terms on employers. They also adapted the old craft community to the organizational context by means of "closed shop" agreements with employers (which forbade nonmembers from taking jobs), and they frequently called on their fellows in other firms for support in sympathy strikes. Such mechanisms helped maintain craft solidarity on the shopfloor, with the workers themselves making many decisions about the structure and distribution of work, even while they accepted management's control of the broad strategic direction of production.

One more major step remained in the development of modern unions. In the first two decades of this century large business organizations grew at an unprecedented rate. It was the time of the birth of the Ford Motor Company, Standard Oil, General Electric, and other giants. These companies made the large firms of the 1880s look insignificant. Industrial employment now accelerated to a pace that drew millions of people off the farms and millions more from Europe.[13] This sudden demand for a new labor force was bound to cause strains.

Still more significant for craft unions was a structural change in industry: rather than focusing on a single type of job, entrepreneurs merged and expanded to form organizations that coordinated an enormous variety of skills and tasks into a single, coherent whole. Thus the AFL structure, in which each union represented a single craft, no longer "matched up" with the structure of industry; the unions suddenly appeared as small and divided entities within the massive new firms.

Another factor further changed the situation of workers. For the first time management, especially in these large firms, made a serious effort to bring the shopfloor organization of work within the overall hierarchy of command. Frederick Taylor, the first apostle of "scientific management," was driven almost to distraction by the sight of craft workers autonomously carrying out their jobs: he was convinced that they were all "soldiering," or slacking. Seeking to increase management's control of production, he demonstrated the possibility of breaking many jobs into bundles of very specific tasks that could be closely monitored. His general philosophy swept the ranks of large companies and has remained in force until today. The adoption of the assembly line just before World War I added the possibility of pacing the fragmented tasks by machine, reducing worker autonomy still further.

These developments burst the shell of craft autonomy, which had protected many workers from close supervision. Taylorism also had disastrous effects on the AFL unions. It made nonstrike weapons such as control of apprenticeship training much less effective by reducing the need for "intuitive" working knowledge. At the same time it also greatly reduced the effectiveness of the strike; a single craft union, however disciplined it might be, could no longer count on shutting down the firm. A hostile management could play on the parochialism of the craft structure, dividing workers and eliminating skilled jobs to maintain control.

One thing did remain constant: the level of management hostility to unions. As the workers struggled to find ways to respond to the shifts in power, they were often violently suppressed. John D. Rockefeller, for example, encouraged an antiunion program that came to a head in 1914 at a tent colony in the coal fields of Ludlow, Colorado. The company imported armed thugs from around the country to dislodge the miners, who were striking—among other reasons—for the right to shop at any store they pleased and to choose their own doctors and boarding places. The first volley of the battle killed one boy and three men. Three unarmed strikers were shot while being held prisoner, and eleven women and two children were suffocated or burned to death when the soldiers poured coal oil on the tents and set them on fire. This was just one dramatic manifestation of an era of repression in which companies regularly hired spies to infiltrate the ranks of union sympathizers, as well as armed enforcers to teach them respect.

The AFL unions, which had so recently found a way of dealing with the growth of capitalism in the nineteenth century, now found themselves once again over-matched by large manufacturing companies. The independent labor movement rapidly fell into a fragmented and weakened state. The reason was not that workers no longer had problems: this was the period in which Massachusetts had to pass a law to prevent children from working more than fifty-four-hour weeks. Nor was it that workers were acquiescent. Uprisings were frequent, to the point where many feared the specter of class war; and despite a huge pay increase to $5 a day, Henry Ford had trouble holding workers in his assembly-line factories.[14] The real problem was that workers had no organization to match the employers tactic for tactic, move for move.

In retrospect what was needed is clear. At the same time that it weakened craft unions, the spread of Taylorism had created a new social grouping of the un-skilled. The fragmentation of jobs marked off an enormous body of workers in a common situation—undivided by differing skills and sharing a hatred of the time-study men who observed their every move. The task was to weld these workers into a disciplined force, just as Gompers had done with the craft workers.

The AFL was aware of the problem but unable to act on it. While the needs of unskilled workers became more and more apparent, the unions tried to play around the edges. They professed a desire to bring unskilled workers into the ranks of labor, they often formed temporary alliances, and they sometimes joined with mass rebellions such as the 1919 general strike in Seattle, Washington. But they were neither consistent nor determined in this course and, in the end, they could not accomplish what was needed—a new ongoing organization that was capable of confronting large monopoly firms. The history of the period is full of what looks like extremely petty battles over jurisdiction by AFL unions, while around them a great movement was being ignored.

The reason for this paralysis does not lie entirely in the selfish parochialism of the leadership, though that was often a factor. There was also a rational basis for their hesitation. Craft unions rested on craft solidarity; to enter into permanent organizations with the unskilled threatened the survival and strength of those organizations. The still recent successes of Gompers's strategy made it difficult to see that another strategy was needed in new circumstances; the assumption was that they should improve on what they were doing. Thus they focused on their successes (within the old craft sectors of the economy such as construction, union strength actually grew during the 1920s), and they ignored their lack of headway in the major sectors of the economy dominated by large monopoly enterprises.

These mistakes resonate clearly in the circumstances of the 1980s. There is a strong tendency today for union leaders to fight for control over a diminishing share of union workers rather than to look for new forms of organization to draw in new sectors. There is also a tendency to assume that the solution to problems is to do more of what has already been done, only better. Thus the labor movement is again finding itself as isolated as it was during the period of the decline of craft unionism.

Industrial Unionism: Mass versus Communal Organization

Because of the AFL's resistance to change, the form of worker representation that was to prove effective in large corporations emerged outside the existing structure of organized labor. John L. Lewis became the leader of the Congress of Industrial Organizations (CIO), and in 1936, after trying to work with the old unions, led a split that was not healed until the 1950s. The CIO unions ignored craft jurisdiction and organized the workers of entire companies—steel firms, auto firms, and other large manufacturers—into one structure.

Many historians, following Selig Perlman's influential work, have stressed the continuity between the AFL and the CIO, suggesting that there was no fundamental change.[15] There is no question that the new organization drew its inspiration from Samuel Gompers: the focus on pragmatic issues of job control, the limited use of the strike, the stress on disciplined organization, were all the same. Yet, at the time, Lewis felt compelled to underline the importance of the change. Confronted by Big Bill Hutcheson, the president of the Carpenters, on the floor of the AFL convention, Lewis punched him in the jaw and led a dramatic walkout. Even Lewis did not take such risks unless the issues were serious.

What was serious was that the new unions abandoned the reliance on the worker communities that continued to be vital to the AFL. It was craft solidarity, not organizational power, that had enabled craft workers to call on their fellows in other companies for support during strikes; and by restricting access to jobs, the old craft system of apprenticeship gave the unions an additional weapon. Even during the 1920s the core AFL unions retained their old membership and, where craft employment increased, even were able to expand. The decline of the labor movement during that period was primarily a result, not of decline of the AFL, but of the relative growth of noncraft employment.

Industrial unions, by contrast, grouped together workers who had no occupational institutions of their own. Their only link was that they were all at the bottom of the hierarchy of the firm. Their solidarity was of a much weaker sort—that of a *mass* rather than of a community.

The weaknesses in this kind of solidarity were quite evident from the start: the unskilled workers were highly erratic. On the one hand, they were capable of great explosions of energy, such as the wave of general strikes that so terrified the authorities in 1919 and 1934. On the other hand, they were highly susceptible to the blandishments of employers. Within a year and a half of the massacre at Ludlow, for example, the Colorado miners joined Rockefeller in a dance to celebrate the inauguration of a company union—the Colorado Industrial Representative Plan. Almost 90 percent of the voting employees supported it.[16]

The task of pulling together such an unstable group into a cohesive organization proved much harder than the earlier problem of adding discipline to craft communities. Many previous efforts had failed. The massive uprisings before and after World War I had left few permanent marks; employers were able to outwait and outmaneuver workers. Great organizations—from the Knights of Labor in the 1880s to the Industrial Workers of the World in the early years of this century—had vanished with scarcely a trace, unable to fix and consolidate their gains. Among other things, they proved very vulnerable to ideological factionalism, frequently splitting up in disputes among the leftist intellectuals who were drawn in by the drama of the changes they were witnessing.

The response of the CIO to these challenges was to complete the organizational lessons of the old AFL. Industrial unions, compared to craft, were (and remain) relatively more centralized, hierarchical, and bureaucratic. Their tactics in dealing with employers, especially since the 1950s, have relied almost exclusively on the strike. They have developed to a high level the establishment of large-scale pattern contracts, setting uniform conditions of pay and working conditions over entire industries. They have avoided responsibility for organizing work, preferring to place restrictions on management. They manifest in a purer form the focused, reactive, rule-based approach pioneered by Gompers.[17]

These innovations did not emerge fully formed in the 1930s. That decade was characterized by upheaval and growth: between 1933 and 1941 the membership of unions tripled, with the gain coming primarily in the large mass-manufacturing corporations such as auto and steel. CIO unions were often animated by spontaneous uprisings and dramatic tactics, including the successful use of sitdown strikes by the United Auto Workers (UAW). But the move toward bureaucracy was not long delayed. During World War II the need for labor peace produced mechanisms, such as compulsory arbitration of grievances, that laid the groundwork for greater stability. In retrospect the 1950s were the high-water mark of unionism, a period during which the level of organization reached its peak and in which it briefly made sense to talk of a stable *system* of collective bargaining. It was then that industrial unions firmly established the bureaucratic structures that have since characterized them.[18]

The period of stability was, however, incomplete and astonishingly brief. During the 1960s the organized percentage of the workforce began to drop steadily, and the rate of employer unfair labor practices began once again to rise. The failure of unions to penetrate the growing service sector was already a concern to perceptive observers. By the late 1970s the whole structure was clearly starting to crumble: open antiunionism had grown acceptable again, large companies like J. P. Stevens were regularly ignoring NLRB decisions, and public opinion was increasingly viewing organized labor as self-serving and ineffective.

The Continuing Paradoxes of Union Structure

One way of summarizing this history would be as a long-term move from the associational, voluntaristic groupings of the nineteenth century toward narrower and more formal systems. Such a trend can be seen, not only in this country, but in nearly every industrialized nation. In Europe the "syndicalist" strand of activism historically stressed the value of widespread participation and popular enthusiasm, but it has everywhere been overcome by the success of formal organizational structures. Studies throughout the industrial world have found very low rates of member involvement—fewer than 5 percent regularly attend union meetings, for example—and public confidence in unions as institutions is no better in Europe than in the United States.[19] And the problem of "controlling" the membership by preventing wildcat walkouts and maintaining picket line discipline is a central concern everywhere.

Yet that tells only a part of the story. The emphasis on the bureaucracy has solved some problems, but it has also increased others. Unions are not and can never be effective *purely* as bureaucracies: *as organizations,* they are extremely weak. The number of people they can command is insignificant in the light of their opponents' strength. Before the breakup of the Bell system, for example, the Communications Workers of America represented about 500,000 members at AT&T, weighed against a management cadre of over 325,000. The total national staff of the union—those who were actually under the authority of the union's president—was slightly over two *hundred.* These 200, no matter how intrepid and well disciplined, could not make a dent on the company. A straight battle of organizations would be suicidal.

Of course, the real strength of unions lies primarily in the membership. But the members are not "inside" the organization; unlike management, union leaders cannot command them, cannot discipline them. Even more serious, the leaders' means of persuasion are limited. They cannot talk to members on work time, except under very controlled conditions (as during a grievance hearing), and they certainly have no way of bringing a group together. They can hold meetings outside of work—but few come. Or they can send out newsletters—but few read them. There is no forum in which the union can develop its case to the membership.

Thus when union leaders look to their members, there is always a major element of uncertainty. When they call a strike, it is always perfectly possible that no one will pay attention. It is also possible—and this is a less obvious but equally serious problem—that the members will pay too much attention, become worked up, and destroy the strategy that the leadership has selected for the battle. A strike generally cannot be *managed* in a bureaucratic, organized way. Even the most sober of strikes involves an element of spontaneous enthusiasm and solidarity that is foreign to formal organizations and raises the danger of fragmentation and confusion.

Unions are, in short, in the essentially contradictory situation of trying to transform the often fickle and unpredictable group emotions of a mass of members into a coherent force that can match a well-organized opponent. They are *associations trying to act like organizations.* The problem is, however, that attempts to strengthen the organizational structure often weaken the commitment of the membership, and vice versa. The resulting tensions explain many of the most common and puzzling features of union organization.

The Cooperative and the Adversarial Faces

To the "outside," which includes their own membership, unions generally portray themselves as fiercely adversarial, constantly battling management. But if that were the whole picture, open conflict would occur more frequently than it in fact does. The Industrial Workers of the World, or "Wobblies," proposed a *really* adversarial system in the first decades of this century—refusing to sign contracts with employers, rejecting all compromise with the capitalist order. The AFL at that time was frequently accused by radical groups of insufficient militancy. Its eventual triumph involved in large measure the recognition of the need to cooperate with management.

The fact is that all union leaders who survive more than one term are involved in constant cooperative deal making with management. They know they cannot simply call out the membership every time they want to ease a transfer or win a grievance. They have to work with the company—to make informal deals, trade off certain grievances for others, curtail potential strike actions. They generally understand quite well the constraints and problems of the company, and they want to create a stable, secure relationship with it.

Moreover, unions have almost always embraced cooperation when they have had the chance. The olive branch has been extended many times, even by the father of "pure and simple unionism": "Cooperation," said Gompers, "comes with development and maturity. . . . The union is just as necessary for the newer function . . . as it is for defensive and bargaining purposes."[20] Since the defeat of the Wobblies, unions have realized the obvious: they have to establish a long-term relationship with management and therefore they cannot be completely intransigent.

Thus the official ideology of American labor, which protests that unions must remain separate from and opposed to management, conceals much of the truth. As Neil Chamberlain already found in his 1948 study, unions have *in practice* assumed many functions of management, especially in the personnel area. Wherever the union/management relation is well established, unions greatly influence particular hiring, firing, and transfer decisions.

This whole set of activities, however, is largely *hidden* from the membership and, by extension, from the wider public. The leadership does not want to be held publicly responsible for them. For when cooperative deals do come out in the open, they are subject to the unstable dynamic of group emotion; the reaction is almost impossible for the union to manage. A tradeoff of grievances, for example, may be in the best interest of all concerned, but it would be hard to explain that to the people involved. Publicity can cause even the best deals to become rallying points for opponents who can generate great group emotion around charges of "selling out." So the leaders make their own judgments of what the situation demands, and they do not talk much about the details. The fear felt by local officials of seeming to be "in bed with management" thus leads to a schizophrenic attitude of public toughness and private cooperation.[21] This is the first continuing paradox of unionism.

The Problem of Internal Democracy

The second paradox of union structure lies in its internal governance: unions, although they are created by and for their members, are not very democratic institutions. It is, of course, true that union officials are constantly concerned about their electoral position; at the local level they are frequently turned out of office. Yet the public perception that union leadership is autocratic does reflect a partial truth. Free discussion of internal conflicts is rare. The leaders are reluctant to involve members too much, and for a very simple reason: when they are locked in battle with management, they cannot afford to be more democratic than their opponents. John L. Lewis perhaps put it most succinctly: "democracy, translated into modern English, [means] labor union inefficiency."[22]

One type of criticism of unions proposes that they should be opened up, that the winds of free discussion and understanding should sweep through the back rooms in which the deals are made. These proposals, as "insiders" frequently point out,[23] miss the power realities in which unions work. Too much participation is a positive danger; it opens the twin risks of fragmentation and manipulation. When workers are directly involved in the substance of decisions, they tend either to splinter or to follow the lead of management, which has far more access to the workers than do union leaders. The vulnerability of unions is further increased during negotiations, in which evidence of disunity in the ranks greatly strengthens the company's hand.

This is why liberals who essentially support labor are often disconcerted to find their proposals for internal union reform vigorously seconded by those who would destroy unions as institutions. For example, the Landrum-Griffin Act of 1959, which required certain democratic practices within unions, was pushed primarily by conservatives, leaving liberals confused about their own position. From a pragmatic perspective, such provisions for reform are a major barrier to the development of stable and effective union strategies.[24]

A parallel problem arises when—as is happening more and more frequently—employers offer workers a chance to participate directly in decisions that affect them at work. Again, direct participation by members can undermine organizational unity, and many companies are using such programs as effective devices to forestall organizing drives. Unions have therefore tended to resist such *worker* participation, favoring instead formal *union* participation through joint committees.

In practice, a difficult balance is maintained between the need to keep control of the membership and the need to mobilize support at crucial times. During "normal" periods—outside of contract negotiations—the union barely *exists* for the membership. This is a strong way of putting it, but the evidence seems to bear it out. Those few who attend union meetings typically focus on their particular gripes with management, showing little interest in issues that concern the internal workings of the union. The grievance mechanism is the only other significant point of contact with union leaders, and it appears that only a small minority use even this channel.[25]

During such "normal" periods members reciprocate the distancing attitude of their leaders by showing little loyalty to the union. Their attitude is best described by Maurice Stein: unions are "accepted as counter-bureaucracies necessary for self-protection but hardly valuable in themselves."[26] Respect for union representatives is low. A regular complaint of union officers is that the membership is unaware of what the organization is doing for them, and a UAW pamphlet directed at stewards laments, "We are not sure why members—including oldtimers—criticize the union and union officers so much."[27]

The awkward position of unions, furthermore, explains a curious and counterintuitive fact that has by now been quite solidly established: loyalty to the union and loyalty to the company are *not* normally opposed—they vary *together.* That is because the union is seen as part of the general situation, which consists of two bureaucracies balancing each other out. Workers attribute credit and blame for their feelings at work roughly equally to the two parties.[28]

When the time comes to mobilize the membership, the same types of tensions are apparent. In order to weld together diverse groups into a force that can move a large company, the union must to a large extent suppress local demands that would produce internal conflict. The material published by the UAW to guide its shop stewards through collective bargaining manifests the problem on nearly every page:

> It is doubtful if there has ever been a set of negotiations where a strain did not develop between the bargaining committee and the membership. . . . Trying to tell the members all that is happening is a worthy goal, but it won't work. . . . You lose all flexibility if you have to continuously file an accounting of what you said and they said. . . . The responsible representative does not make a demand upon management simply because a few of the loud members have insisted that he make an unreasonable demand.[29]

The sense one gets from this pamphlet, as well as from other studies of the bargaining process, is that union officials see themselves as leaders, not of a solid and committed group with a developed sense of shared interests, but rather of a movement that might fragment at any moment. Essentially, the leaders are powerless in the face of their members. Because they cannot effectively command them, they must very carefully manage the occasions on which they seek their support. Such a requirement is not compatible with open democracy.

Legalism

A third result of the paradoxical structure of unions is their emphasis on detailed rules. Unions have generally sought uniform written rights; over the years, contracts have become long and legalistic. Labor has resisted direct worker participation in the implementation of contracts, insisting instead on oversight by authorized union representatives to ensure uniformity of application. One of the most persistent charges made by management is that such rules eliminate essential flexibility in industry, leading to costly waste and inefficiency. Even many outside of management ask why such rigid uniformity is necessary.

The answer is by now familiar: local variations threaten the thin unity of the membership. It cannot be assumed that workers understand the principles behind contract language or the history of the struggle that went into it; unions have no opportunities to carry out such education. They therefore fear that hard-won gains will be given away too easily. And there is no lack of horror stories to back them up. One union I am familiar with, for example, opposed worker participation programs after management had led teams into "competitions" in which they gave up vacation time and other bargained-for rights to meet productivity standards.

An apparent solution would be to involve union officials with the membership in creating flexible rules and to make sure that basic principles were understood and not violated. The problem here is that there are simply too few officials relative to the number of members. Staff representatives typically have responsibility for hundreds of workers in dozens of work sites; they certainly cannot be involved in developing special sets of procedures for each site.

The only practical solution, then, is to operate by the letter of the law. This makes it possible for a small number of union officials to "police" the actions of a large number of management personnel, and it avoids dissension and envy in the ranks. Legalism is therefore well-nigh universal in industrial unions, and it apparently increases with time.[30]

Union Power and the Use of the Strike

For anyone who has been close to the labor movement, there are few more ironic charges than the frequently heard one that unions wield "too much power." Labor has won precious few battles in the past twenty years; in fact, since the Wagner Act it has *never* won, and several times lost, on major labor legislation. In the past few years, as we saw in the last chapter, the decline of unions has become unmistakable, their retreat threatening to become a rout. Yet according to public opinion polls, more than 60 percent of the public still believes that "unions have become too powerful and should be restricted in the use of their power by law."[31]

How to account for this perception? Paradoxically, it is the very weakness of unions that makes them seem "too strong." Their only real weapon is the strike. Strikes make a lot of noise, they injure the public, and they seem to manifest great power. Yet they are, in fact, a very poor weapon.

A strike for a union is like a sting for a bee—painful for the enemy, but often more damaging to the attacker in the end. The membership suffers the heavy cost of going without pay while the threat of losing their jobs entirely is always present. Strike funds seldom cover lost wages and only provide emergency relief to avoid the most serious hardships. For the union, a strike puts everything on the line: failure is devastating both to the leadership and to the organization as a whole. The members will exact retribution for the sacrifices they have made by turning their leaders out, and they will be reluctant to take such risks again.

At best, moreover, the strike is an extremely blunt instrument. It cannot be used often, and it can apply only to a limited range of issues. To arouse large numbers of people to the point of striking, an issue must be both *concrete*—easily identifiable—and *general*. That is why wages are so often the ostensible reason for strikes; money is a general enough issue to pull together the membership. But the real reasons for strikes almost always include other concerns: a sense of being treated unfairly, a stressful working environment, an insensitive boss. A wage victory creates a temporary sense of power and dignity that is exhilarating, but it does not get at many fundamental concerns in the long run. Rooted in particular work experiences, these issues are ill suited to a mass action.

Unions thus have to rely too heavily on a single weapon, even when it is not the most appropriate one. A strike is quite often a sign of the weakness of labor's arsenal rather than of excessive power.

There is also another, rather different, root for the perception of unions' power: the public believes that unions have too much power not only over employers and the public but also over their own members. Opinion polls show the image of union *leaders* to be far worse than that of unions themselves.[32] This, too, is bitterly ironic. Unions have almost no power at all over their members. They can fine them, and they can expel them; but a member who refuses to pay a fine or who accepts expulsion loses almost nothing. The courts and the legislature have ruled against attempts to make loss of membership grounds for loss of employment. The union is even compelled by law to represent nonmembers—perhaps people whom it has expelled for crossing picket lines—in grievance proceedings.[33]

The core of truth in the public perception, however, is that unions are fundamentally, in their origins and nature, free associations of workers. Any power or compulsion used on the membership is, from this perspective, "too much." Every effort that labor makes to discipline the troops is resented—essential though it may be for dealing with managerial organization. For example, possibly the most controversial element in the whole structure of the labor movement is the union shop, which forces new employees in certain firms to become union members; as of 1986, only 27 percent of the public approved of this provision.[34] But from labor's point of view, it is impossible to represent employees properly without the security of the union shop. If members could come and go as they pleased, labor organizations could not maintain a stable presence.

Unions, in brief, are in a constant position of balancing the need for disciplined organization against the need for member solidarity and enthusiasm; and the balancing process is an unhappy one at best. The attempt to maintain a unified and consistent position vis-à-vis management leads unions to try to centralize and control strikes and spontaneous movements, limiting the extent of direct worker participation. Conversely, the continued reliance on strikes as the ultimate weapon forces labor leaders to maintain a public stance of hostility to management, keeping their cooperative activities in the background and hidden from their members.

Variations on the Pattern

The dualism I have described is most clearly characteristic of industrial unions, especially those in the United States. The sense of community among the workers in these unions is weak, whereas their employers are large and well organized. There are, however, some variations on this theme. Craft unions, as we have seen, contrast with industrial unions in that they are supported by a live, ongoing community. Their members develop a relatively rich sense of solidarity from the fact that they must learn the job from each other rather than from management. In the most highly skilled occupations, furthermore, workers often retain their own institutions of apprenticeship and job allocation—sometimes within the union, sometimes outside it, but in either case separate from management.

Under these conditions, the split that I have described between member community and union organization is less severe: the union has more resources in dealing with its members and with management. Because the members generally share with their leaders and with each other a fairly elaborate set of educational and work experiences, there is a higher level of trust than in the industrial setting; union leaders have more personal influence in the worker culture. The stability of shared values dampens the tendency to "explosions" of passion. In dealing with management, craft unions are less exclusively dependent on the blunt and volatile weapon of the mass strike. They generally have much more labor market strength than their unskilled counterparts, and they are better able to sustain "strategic" actions requiring high levels of internal trust. For these reasons there is less pressure from both sides, and craft unions are often able to be relatively open and democratic.[35]

The case of white-collar workers is more complicated, but it follows similar patterns. White-collar workers are generally better educated, less favorably disposed to strikes, and more negative toward unions than their blue-collar counterparts. When they form groups to voice their concerns, they prefer "associations" that stress cooperation and participation. But these predispositions do not in the end determine their form of organization: the key factors, as in the other cases we have looked at, are the nature of the employee community and of the countering management organization. When management is flexible and responsive, or when workers share an underlying community (as in the case of professional groupings), white-collar employees do move toward relatively associational and participative structures. When, on the other hand, they are confronted with bureaucratic management that treats them as "outsiders," they often form unions that are traditionally militant, using adversarial tactics aimed at winning strict limits on management power—though often half against their will.[36]

Thus the split between organization and community may be muted, but it can rarely be escaped. It remains difficult today, as it has for a century or more, to combine voluntary and democratic association with effective representation in industry.

CHAPTER 3

The Public Interest: Government's Role in Labor Relations

BY FOCUSING on the internal structure of unions, I have so far avoided discussing another major factor in the development of labor organizations: the vital role played by the government. The significance of unions has not been limited to the private sphere of their own membership or their contractual relationships; unions have been centrally involved with the definition of *public* policy and social welfare. Their connection to broad political concerns is a crucial part of their history.

This has been especially true since 1935. Before then government's relation to labor had been tentative and ambiguous. The courts had generally supported employers in their claims that unions violated property rights; legislatures often leaned the other way, but with no consistent rationale. The AFL had long opposed political intervention in collective bargaining. As late as 1932 the Norris-LaGuardia Act took a radical "laissez-faire" approach, exempting this whole domain of labor-management relations from most governmental sanctions.

Three years later, however, Congress reversed itself by passing the National Labor Relations Act—the Wagner Act—to encourage the spread of collective bargaining. It limited employers' rights to intimidate union organizing drives, and it established the National Labor Relations Board to oversee the certification of unions and the process of bargaining. Quite suddenly the federal government became a major player.

From one perspective it can be said that the Wagner Act merely legitimized the system that had been established by private action over the previous fifty years. Yet that would be to severely underestimate its importance. For with the passage of the act the government in effect took responsibility for the survival of unionism; without it, the CIO would not have been possible. The organizational principles of the old AFL, which had sustained an autonomous movement in craft shops, were insufficient for the task of confronting the growing mass-production industries. Industrial unions, in attempting to organize unskilled workers, have always depended on the active protection of the state.

Every turn of labor history since the 1920s has demonstrated that fact. Before the enactment of the Wagner Act, labor was in full retreat; the intervention of the government spurred its revival. The next major advance of the movement followed World War II, when the pressures of wartime production had brought in the state still further to ensure labor relations peace. The basic compromises that shaped postwar unionism—the acceptance of union security clauses compelling workers to maintain their union membership and the development of grievance arbitration—were hammered out under the direct supervision of the War Labor Board. During the 1960s and 1970s the growth of public sector unionism likewise followed the spread of Wagner-like legislation covering government workers in many states.[1] The disastrous effects of the NLRB's antiunion "tilt" in the Reagan administration are the most recent indication that the fortunes of the labor movement are closely bound up with the favor of the state.

The Wagner Act thus made possible the transformation of unionism from a craft to an industrial base. It was also bound up with an equally important transformation within government, for it was among the first steps toward economic regulation that became characteristic of the New Deal approach to policy. Roosevelt himself came to see it as a centerpiece of his administration and as a model for defining the relation of government to corporations.

Because of the importance of this legislative action, I will use the term "Wagner Act framework" throughout this study as a shorthand term for our current system of representation: a government-supported structure based on the centrality of collective bargaining. Though the act is only one element in this system, it has been a focus for the conflicting pulls of unions and management, and it has become an increasingly crucial part of the picture.

The Wagner Act was not, of course, the last word on the subject of the government's role. The responsibility it assumed for unions was controversial then, and it is controversial now. The act's basic assumption of a strong public interest in the maintenance of collective bargaining is once again under severe attack. It is worth circling back to examine the origins of the government's involvement with labor organizations.

Political Theory and the Problem
of Private Power

The need for worker representation and the danger of oppression have troubled writers since the very origins of our capitalist system. Adam Smith, in the midst of portraying the wonders of the free market, was not blind to these concerns: "It is not . . . difficult to foresee which of the two parties must, upon all ordinary occasions, have the advantage in the dispute, and force the other into compliance with their terms. The masters, being few in number, can combine much more easily . . . [and] can hold out much longer."[2]

While political despotism was swept away by democratic revolutions through-out the Western world, the absolute power of the industrial manager remained unchallenged. The Bill of Rights limited the power of government, but its protection stopped at the walls of the factory. A person who was seen as responsi-ble enough to vote on the fate of the country was still treated at work like a child or an irresponsible servant. Albert Gallatin, secretary of the treasury under Jeffer-son and Madison, was only one among many who argued that "the democratic principle on which this nation is founded should not be restricted to the political process but should be applied to the industrial operation as well."[3]

In Gallatin's time, in an economy dominated by agriculture and small shops, the problem was not critical. The growth of private corporations in the late nineteenth century, however, brought the issue into sharper focus. For the leap in the size and power of private enterprises exposed a major weakness in the political theories underlying the modern state; in effect, corporations caused as much trouble for government as they did for employee organizations.

The entire body of classical political theory, from Thomas Hobbes to the Federalist Papers, had been based on a simple model of society in which the government had a monopoly on the use of power. Power, or what Hobbes called "sovereignty," marked off the arena of public concerns, separating it sharply from the sphere of the private individual. In the public arena of power the government had to be the unchallenged master. Any retention of sovereignty in the hands of private citizens would lead inevitably to destructive conflict and anarchy.

Hobbes, with his usual theoretical purity and intensity, denied the possibility of any associations besides the state itself. Support for the state, in his view, was based essentially on the assumption that individuals, being substantially equal in power, effectively balance each other out, sharing an interest in giving up their individual power to a body that can maintain order. But combinations of citizens would necessarily create inequalities of power, allowing the strong to dominate the weak, and thereby destroying the basis for government. This argument led Hobbes to an attack on all corporations (by which he meant, not industrial organizations, but any combination of citizens sanctioned by the state): "[C]orpo-rations," he wrote, "are as it were many lesser commonwealths in the body of a greater, like worms in the entrails of a natural man."[4]

Later theorists were less uncompromising. In this country, the Federalists believed especially that the state should not interfere with voluntary associations and contracts.[5] Still, they were very uncomfortable about what they termed the danger of "faction." James Madison's solution to this dilemma was a compromise: if you cannot do away with combinations of citizens, he suggested, the best course is to multiply them to a point at which they balance each other out. As long as the balance exists, whether among individuals or organizations, the common interest in order remains, and the state can avoid domination by any one group.[6]

Within this paradigm the role of the state is a relatively passive one, even in Hobbes's model of extreme centralization. Though the "social contract" involved the monopoly of power by the state, the purpose was not to increase collective capacity—there was, except for the exceptional case of war, no expectation that the state would actively organize people. Rather, the purpose was to free individu-als to pursue their interests without worrying constantly about being attacked. The state was to hold power in trust, as it were, not to use it. Society would be essentially stable, while the individuals within it would be in constant motion.

The extraordinary growth of industrial combinations that began after the Civil War knocked a large hole in all theories that had envisioned such a structure. Here were large entities, private and nongovernmental, that nevertheless exer-cised power in extremely obvious ways. They held their own police forces to enforce order in their domains. They broke heads, on no authority but their own. They ran towns: a number of magnates, like George Pullman in the 1880s, created model villages for their workers in which they enforced strict standards of morality and appropriate behavior. And their actions affected not just a few other individuals, as envisioned in classical theory, but large sectors of the pub-lic—the most visible of which were their workers, who were often ruled as despotically as in the most rigid monarchy. This was "faction" indeed, using power—just as Hobbes had feared—to dominate the weak and to compete with the state itself.

Furthermore, these new entities began to drive society as a whole. The un-precedented economic growth and change of the late nineteenth century de-stroyed the image of a stable society, creating an unmistakable sense that corpora-tions were setting a collective agenda. Business leaders created a dynamic vision of growing wealth and opportunity through large-scale capitalism. They justified corporations not merely as forms of private property but also as institutions necessary to the public good.

These developments clearly violated the logic of classical theory. Here was power not only claiming private status but also seeking to mobilize for a positive goal, undercutting the previous (essentially negative) conception of power. We hear a great deal today about the uncontrollable ambitions of government, but in a real sense it was corporations that first broke the pattern that had limited the power of the state. As corporations sought to justify their expansion by a new vision of societal progress, it was only natural that those who missed out on the benefits should search for alternative visions, such as socialism and populism.

Bringing corporations within the framework of classical theory and the common law therefore required some quite amazing leaps of imagination. The first move of the courts, during the nineteenth century, was to deny that corporations exercised power over their employees; instead, the courts defined corporations as free associations of voluntarily contracting members.[7] Workers, according to this theory, were free to take their labor where they wished.

The problem with this approach is that the notion of free contract does not accurately describe the employer-employee relation. The theory of contract presupposes a rough equality of bargaining power between the parties, as might be found in a society of free individuals such as had been classically envisioned. That is why there are legal restrictions on, for instance, coerced contracts or contracting into slavery. But the problem here was precisely that the corporation upset this balance. A large organization always had more mobility and more options than the workers it faced in the marketplace. Especially in relation to unskilled workers, it had an effective monopoly of an essential commodity—jobs. Thus the corporation could effectively dictate its terms, treating workers as it willed, up to the very point of rebellion. The fact that people put up with the brutality of company spies and detectives is in itself sufficient proof. Treating employment merely as a contract ignored the new realities that lay behind the contract.[8]

Even more extraordinary was an 1886 decision that waved away the whole problem by declaring that corporations were in fact not organizations at all, but merely artificial *people*.[9] The effect of this doctrine of "corporate personality," which is still very much alive today, is to protect the internal workings of corporations from governmental scrutiny. This strange doctrine is an especially clear case of trying to fit reality to theory: if legal and political theory require a society of autonomous individuals, then the solution was to declare organizations individuals—whatever empirical difficulties might lie in the way.

By dismissing the issue of power, these two legal approaches in effect removed corporations from the domain of the "public." The logical circle was closed in 1890, when the Supreme Court granted corporations the private rights of property. Today it may seem surprising that this decision was so long delayed. We have largely forgotten that for almost the whole nineteenth century the status of corporations was very much a matter of debate. Indeed, as late as 1876 the court had ruled that corporations' right of property was limited by the public interest, and that they therefore had a quasi-public character.[10]

This earlier decision, however, in addition to being anathema to business interests, was inconsistent with the deepest structure of political reasoning. The 1890 decision was at least logically consistent. Concentrations of private power are a threat to the very foundations of societal order. Rather than declare the corporations public, which was the Socialist alternative, the courts denied that the private power existed.

Not surprisingly, there were many who remained unconvinced by these feats of reasoning, recognizing power when they saw it. Judge Seymour Thompson asked in 1891 "whether the corporation is to rule the state or the state the corporation?" Forty years later Justice Brandeis was more emphatic:

> Through size, corporations, once merely an efficient tool employed by individuals in the conduct of private business, have become an institution—an institution which has brought such concentration of economic power that so-called private corporations are sometimes able to dominate the State. . . . [P]ower . . . is becoming increasingly concentrated in the hands of a few. The changes thereby wrought in the lives of the workers, of the owners and of the general public, are so fundamental and far-reaching as to lead . . . scholars to compare the evolving "corporate system" with the feudal system; and to lead other men of insight and experience to assert that this "master institution of civilized life" is committing it to the rule of a plutocracy.[11]

These "realists," however, have never solved the problem posed by Hobbes: how to control private concentrations of power. Much of the political history of this century can be seen as a series of unsuccessful attempts to establish a consistent basis for public regulation of the corporation.

In practice there have been three contrasting attempts at a resolution. Populism, during the late nineteenth century, represented one way of dealing with corporate power: to reduce it. The opposite tack was to accept the corporation but to treat it as public, a part of the state's authority. Its purest expression was the Socialist proposal to nationalize industry. But the most influential approach in the long run was a third and more complex one, which began under the banner of Progressivism. Their approach was not to attack the corporation as an entity but to seek ways to merge it into a wider conception of a national community.

This strategy also required a transformation in the role of the state, but of a different sort from that proposed by the Socialists or the apostles of regulation. Rather than absorbing the corporation into the sphere of the public, the Progressives sought to use government power to balance the corporation against other interests and to mediate among various groups. They realized that economic organization was creating disparities of power; the state, in their view, must compensate for these disparities—first by bolstering the underdog, and second by providing forums in which disputes could be solved by reason rather than by force.

In labor relations, this logic linked neatly with the emergence of the AFL. The unions, as representatives of the underdog, should (in the Progressive view) be supported by the government, and efforts should be made to bring them into harmonious relations with employers. These views began to bear fruit during the administrations of Theodore Roosevelt and Woodrow Wilson. The first goal was pursued in some early labor legislation, including the Clayton Act, which prevented the use of injunctions against labor organizations, and the Lloyd-LaFollette Act of 1912, protecting the right of postal workers to organize. The second led to the creation of a federal Conciliation Service and to two climactic conferences called by President Wilson just after World War I for the purpose of working out a program of industrial cooperation.[12]

There was always a fundamental tension in the Progressive strategy: the notion of government-sponsored cooperation was only a short step away from government-imposed harmony. Though the theory was fairly clear, it was difficult in practice to maintain the private nature of the parties when one sought to bring them all into a single "Great Community."[13] The problem was manifest in the handling of the railways. After World War I the Progressives participated in a strong effort to nationalize them and to administer them through a tripartite body of government, management, and labor. When that failed, the Railway Labor Act was passed, including provisions for government involvement in compulsory arbitration of disputes.

The AFL itself was lukewarm to governmental involvement in employment relations. Though Gompers welcomed protection from employer attacks, he did not like the idea of being folded into some political vision of harmony; and fearing the former would inevitably lead to the latter, he generally preferred to remain independent. "The stipulation of industrial relations by law," Gompers said, "does not result in industrial freedom—it only . . . substitutes a political boss for an industrial employer."[14] His skepticism about the ideal of "harmony" was probably reinforced by the failure of Wilson's conferences, where the employers refused to agree to the legitimacy of "outside" parties as representatives of their workers. Gompers and other union leaders could be pardoned for not sharing the vision of a single Great Community.

The New Deal Solution: The Balance of Power

The Wagner Act of 1935 was the great turning point in the development of labor policy. It was not primarily the creation of organized labor—certainly not a result of special interest pleading. The AFL continued its skepticism about government intervention almost to the end.[15] Only in 1933 did the American Federation of Labor come out in favor of labor legislation and even after that time there were deep divisions in its ranks. As the Wagner Act was debated in Congress, the AFL's board was debating whether it would weaken craft unions in favor of industrial unions.[16] Though labor, like President Roosevelt, eventually came out strongly in support of the Wagner bill, there is a sense that it did so largely because it could think of nothing better.

The immediate roots of the act lay, rather, in a series of conflicts in which the AFL did not play a central role, and which were the closest thing to civil war we have seen in the past century. After three years of relative quiet in the depths of the depression, workers—especially unorganized industrial workers—erupted in 1933 and 1934. In the latter year more than one-seventh of the work force was involved in strikes. San Francisco and Minneapolis witnessed massive uprisings, which triggered violent responses from the authorities. Federal militia shot, beat, and trampled largely unarmed groups, leading to dozens of deaths and hundreds of serious injuries. Employers, too, were setting up as if for a war—it is estimated from hearings before the LaFollette Committee of the Senate that American industry spent at least $80 million on antiunion agents in 1936 alone.[17]

In this crisis the evolution of government policy reached a critical point of decision. Labor legislation had not been an important part of Roosevelt's "first New Deal." The president, who was not then a great friend of unions, favored instead regulatory legislation that would place the power of government directly at the disposal of workers by setting wages and working conditions. He therefore directed his energy toward minimum wage and unemployment legislation and the establishment of basic labor standards.

The National Industrial Recovery Act of 1933, one of Roosevelt's first important initiatives, had supported both collective bargaining and direct government regulation, though in ways so vague and halfhearted that they turned out to be unenforceable. On the one hand, workers were guaranteed the right to organize independent unions in industries covered by the act; this provision unleashed a huge wave of organizing enthusiasm, but employer opposition was not visibly reduced by the timid efforts of the National Recovery Administration. On the other hand, the president was given the power directly to set wages, hours, pay, and working conditions under the act—a power that was used to maintain minimum conditions.

The course of direct regulation, however, was largely blocked. The intense opposition of the business community was made insurmountable by the Supreme Court which, during the first years of the Roosevelt administration, struck down bill after bill as infringements on the sacred rights of property. There was insufficient national consensus on a substantive vision for regulating business to take on these conservative forces in open political battle.

The Wagner Act was, in other words, born in a situation of weakness. It did not sweep the country or even the labor movement with the force of its vision. It was a compromise. The major historian of these events, Irving Bernstein, goes so far as to call it a "historical accident."[18] It is likely that it could not have passed at any time other than 1935. Indeed, the first time it was introduced—in 1934—it was defeated. When it was brought back a year later, it had gained the president's active support—and after the overwhelming Democratic gains in the 1934 elections, he could get whatever he wanted. Yet even then there is evidence that some who voted for the bill did so in the expectation that it would not survive a Supreme Court challenge.

Rather than confronting head-on the issue of setting public standards for the employment relationship, the Wagner Act encouraged the private relationship of collective bargaining. It was based on the premise, which was at least as old as Hobbes, that imbalances of private power are the primary causes of disorder, anarchy and, implicitly, of injustice. But it sought neither to do away with private corporations nor to impose direct government supervision on them. Its single-minded solution was to establish a balance of power between the organizations of employers and those of employees. The act's preamble expresses these themes succinctly:

> The denial by employers of the right of employees to organize and the refusal by employers to accept the procedure of collective bargaining lead to strikes and other forms of industrial strife and unrest. . . . Experience has proven that protection of the right of employees to organize and bargain collectively safeguards commerce from injury . . . by encouraging practices fundamental to the friendly adjustment of industrial disputes . . . and by restoring equality of bargaining power between employers and employees.[19]

The act sought to reduce the role of government to an absolute minimum. It accepted totally the private nature of the parties. Because government regulation of employment, of the type favored by Roosevelt, constituted a public claim on the actions of the parties, any hint of regulation was carefully avoided: "When the employees have chosen their organization [said Senator Walsh during the debates on the act] . . . all the bill proposes to do is to escort them to the door of their employer and say, 'Here they are, the legal representatives of your employees.' What happens behind those doors is not enquired into, and the bill does not seek to enquire into it."[20]

But the act went further: it not only rejected direct regulation in the public interest, it denied to the government even a role as harmonizer. Though in many respects it drew heavily on the Railway Labor Act, it did not pick up the mechanisms of compulsory arbitration that had been among its centerpieces. Nor did it even establish a federal role in the mediation of disputes.

The act really did only one thing: it guaranteed the right of workers to form unions and bargain collectively. Everything else in its short text supported that limited goal. Employers were forbidden to engage in five specific practices, such as firing union sympathizers, which would interfere with the right to organize. And the NLRB was created to enforce these prohibitions and oversee the employees' choice of a union.

It was a severe, almost minimalist conception. Its guiding principle was the idea of a fair fight. All the act purported to do was to establish rules of the game, enabling unions to meet employers on an equal basis. It sought to solve the problem of corporate power by restoring the balance of power.[21] The only difference from the classic paradigm was that this time the balance was not among individuals, but among organizations.

The brilliance of the solution was that it required very little substantive agreement. Its various supporters shared no common vision of the roles of corporations and workers in society; they ran the gamut from Communists to Wilsonian liberals to hard-nosed "business unionists."[22] They agreed only that corporations had excessive power that needed to be checked. All parties could plug their own hopes and aspirations into the collective bargaining framework, without trying to thrash out a prior political consensus.

The act took not the slightest step in the direction of centralized planning. It did, of course, invade the private rights of corporations by restricting certain antiunion practices. But these restrictions were so specific and focused that the Supreme Court found it possible—with a considerable nudge from Roosevelt's court-packing threat—to accept them as less than a fundamental attack on property. The transition was further eased by the fact that Wagner's approach claimed merely to stabilize and generalize a structure that had been worked out by unions and companies during a half-century of private struggles; its main lines, as we have seen, were entirely in accord with AFL policy. Thus it succeeded, at least in appearance, in carrying off a paradox—it asserted an active role for the state in maintaining private autonomy.

The Development of Labor Law

The apparent simplicity of the Wagner Act has proved, in retrospect, deceptive. If there had been consensus even on its one basic principle—the encouragement of collective bargaining—the story might have been different. It was, however, clear almost from the start that the act had failed to resolve the tensions that had generated it. Employers continued to resist it, frequently ignoring the rulings of the NLRB. A *Fortune* magazine poll of businessmen in 1939 found that over 40 percent still favored outright repeal.[23] Perhaps more surprising, the AFL turned hostile in the late 1930s because it felt the NLRB was favoring industrial unions at the expense of craft unions. In the postwar period resistance to the act produced two major pieces of legislation—the Taft-Hartley Act of 1947 and the Landrum-Griffin Act of 1959—which added often conflicting requirements. Decisions of the courts and the NLRB have added layers of interpretation that have further altered its original thrust. The Wagner Act framework has now grown exceedingly rickety, so heavily patched with inconsistent pieces that its original aims have been largely obscured.

The development of the Wagner Act, in other words, has not been a matter of working out the few basic principles it embodied. Instead it has been continuously buffeted by contrary forces. A description of its functioning, like that of unions' internal structures, must therefore be essentially a story of how the contradictions were, for a relatively brief time, held in check—a story of ongoing tension rather than of graceful evolution.

The Contradictory Functions of Regulation

Perhaps what is most notable about the role of the government in the Wagner Act framework, and most difficult to understand, has been its sheer *extent.* The act, as we have seen, was justified in part as a way to leave the initiative in the hands of private parties rather than government. There is little in its language that forces anyone to do anything, and it proposes merely to protect some simple employee actions. Its supporters, down to the present day, moreover, praise the way in which the labor relations system has remained "private," frequently adding scornful criticisms of the more active government role in many European nations.

Yet to listen only to these justifications of the present structure would be to accept a very inaccurate view of the labor relations system. One would scarcely imagine that there exists an enormous and intricate body of laws and regulations governing it. Nor would one expect to find that unions orient themselves as strongly as they do to the permissions and exclusions of those laws. Though the labor movement in this country has historically been suspicious of intellectuals, few unions nowadays do without a large and sophisticated legal staff; indeed, the current president of the Mineworkers—an organization that has long had a public image of brawling, government-be-damned militancy—is himself a lawyer. The legal profession is important because labor rarely ventures outside the framework of protections established by the Wagner Act and its later interpretations. Unions gauge almost every action in terms of the patterns established by courts and legislatures. These have determined, among other things, which issues must be negotiated, how one must bargain (in order to avoid a charge of "bad faith"), who will be represented by the union, what information must be supplied by management, and when strikes are permitted. A network of laws thus reaches deeply into the supposedly "private" union-management relation.

The Wagner Act had hoped to escape such entanglement by avoiding the regulation of "substance." It made no attempt to decide which employment practices were legitimate and which were not. The act sought only to preserve a formal balance between parties by regulating "process," making sure the opponents were well balanced.

There is a conceptual problem in this approach, however, which was obscured in the debates over the act, and which undermined its implementation. The idea of a balance of power is empty except with reference to its results; it is not a goal in itself, but only a means toward goals. When the ends are vague, procedural regulations can pile up to infinity without clarifying anything; they quickly become a disjointed parody of bureaucracy. That is precisely the condition of labor law today.

The confusion about the definition of a "balance" is now quite visible. Large segments of the public feel, on the one hand, that unions are too powerful because they have driven wages too high for international competitiveness. According to the polls, those people favor further restrictions on labor. On the other hand, many of these same people feel that unions are too weak with respect to stopping health and safety violations in the workplace. A proper point of balance, in other words, cannot be determined abstractly: what matters is whether the balance produces good results. The Wagner Act essentially avoided stating what those results might be. Lacking a public consensus or clear political definition of the governing values justifying the Wagner Act, the agencies responsible for interpretation—the NLRB and the courts—have proceeded in a highly pragmatic way to develop rules by taking one dispute at a time. The network of regulations has grown by accretion rather than by methodical coherence, which accounts for the second striking thing about the government's role, after its surprising pervasiveness: its scattered and inconsistent nature.

Not even the most fervent supporters of the Wagner Act framework would claim today that it has produced a clear, widely understood, or coherent system of industrial governance. The original illusion of clarity has been buried under a huge and still-growing mound of particular compromises and deals. The deal making has gradually made the structure more and more opaque and confusing to those outside its boundaries—including, in most cases, the workers and line managers who are supposed to be the main parties involved. They have found themselves increasingly excluded by a cadre of "professionals"—managerial labor-relations staff, union officials, and outside arbitrators and experts—who are the only ones able to understand the Byzantine maze of rules and agreements on which the labor relations order rests.

If there is a theme in all this rule making, it is the same one that marks the whole history of labor law: the tension between private rights and the public interest in collective bargaining. Interpretations of the law have favored sometimes one side, sometimes the other. The main outcome is confusion.

Collective Bargaining and the Corporate Right of Property

The Wagner Act had proposed to encourage collective bargaining while preserving the private rights of property that had been granted to corporations by law. This has proved in practice to be impossible: the two aims have clashed time and time again. It is continually necessary to choose between a perspective that emphasizes the private rights of the corporation and one that emphasizes its public duty to engage in collective bargaining, justifying governmental intervention in firms' internal affairs.

Examples of the tension are legion. Protecting the right of workers to organize entailed restricting management's right to fire and discipline. It also limited what they could say; in early decisions, the NLRB forbade companies from speaking against unions during organizing campaigns. And in order to pursue the vision of a balance of independent organizations, the act prevented employers from establishing their own internal bodies of worker representation, or "company unions." Though these were all mild and eminently fair restrictions when viewed from the balance-of-power perspective, they appeared as intolerable burdens when seen from the viewpoint favored more by business, that corporations were private associations protected by the fundamental right of property.

While at first the balance-of-power view was dominant, leading to significant incursions on the management realm, later developments have often tended toward the opposite direction. There have been a great many shifts in judicial opinion concerning, for example, employers' right to hire replacements for strikes or the conditions under which union organizers are permitted to enter company property. The Supreme Court has often tried explicitly to create a "balance" by manipulating these factors, yet it has also forbidden the NLRB to consider the relative power of the parties as a basis for its rulings.[24]

These inconsistencies are symptoms of the fact that two quite different principles are at work. On the one hand, the Wagner Act sought to limit corporate power; on the other, the fundamental basis of that power—the private rights of corporate property—remained untouched. The Supreme Court would like to believe that the rights of management rest in the private right of property rather than in its public function. The Wagner Act, however, forces the Court to examine whether the outcomes of its determinations disturb the balance of power sought by public policy. It has not resolved this difference in standards.

Unions: Private or Public Agencies?

A similar ambivalence marks the relation between government and unions. Here the intention of the Wagner Act was to preserve unions' status as private associations, but subsequent developments have entwined the state not only in unions' relations to management but also in their functioning. For the act protects only a certain kind of association—one that represents a majority of people in a bargaining unit determined by the state. When the NLRB chooses the bargaining unit, the sense of shared interests and community among the members is only one of a long list of criteria that it considers; the requirements of management and the public receive at least equal weight.

The need for an exclusive representative agent followed inevitably from the strategy of establishing a balance of power. "Collective bargaining," wrote one of those involved in framing the Wagner Act, "presupposes a united front on the part of employees. . . . The whole idea . . . [is] agreements between an employer and a united front of employees."[25] It was thought to be impossible to maintain stability if workers could associate in any combination they wanted, perhaps ending up with many divided units. But the Wagner Act clearly put the government in the business of *conferring legitimacy* on chosen bodies; it made government, in fact, partly responsible for the *creation* of unions as organizations.

The effects of this provision may be made clearer by an analogy: suppose a group wanted to form a club of bird watchers in its state; and suppose the government said, "No, you cannot do that exactly—your club must be made up only of robin watchers, and they have to be from within your city, *and* you must win the support of a majority of that group in order to be allowed to function at all." The group's natural reaction might be, "Who's running this club—us, or the government?"

That question has been asked frequently in the labor relations field—first by the unions themselves, especially those of the craft-oriented AFL. The NLRB's early decisions on bargaining units generally favored industrial unions, comprising an entire factory or firm, over craft units that included only particular categories of workers. The AFL cried foul, and during the late thirties almost torpedoed the struggling NLRB by its protests.

But the same question has also been asked by conservatives who believe the government should not be in the business of running this particular club. From within classical theory, which still frames the conservative view, the state's support of unions simply creates a Madisonian "faction" in its own midst—or, still worse, a feudal "monopoly" with immunities not granted to other citizens.[26]

They are infuriated by the fact that the government not only allows but actively promotes and puts its resources at the disposal of a special-interest group, enabling it to maintain control over labor markets in many sectors and firms. And the point cannot be denied—even in the most positive conception of the Wagner Act, its goal *was* to use the state to bolster union "monopoly" power. The only difference is that in the positive view of the Wagner Act this "monopoly" was justified as a *response* to excessive corporate power.

The structure of exclusive representation is closely tied to another element of the system that arouses particular controversy—the union shop. If one organization is to have the right to represent all workers in a unit, it seems to make sense to require that they all be members of that organization. From the perspective of bolstering union power, it is even essential that such unity be maintained. But it is not necessary to be strongly antiunion to feel that there is something contradictory about the government compelling people to join a private association.[27]

The view that unions are a state-created monopoly rather than a private association has justified many of the restrictions and attacks they have suffered since World War II. The Taft-Hartley Act of 1947 limited the use of the union shop. A decade later, the Landrum-Griffin Act placed numerous requirements on the *internal* functioning of unions, such as the need for membership meetings and internal due process. These ran clearly against Senator Walsh's view, cited earlier, that the state should avoid intrusion into the private status of the parties. The courts, beginning in the 1940s, began to impose on unions the duty of "fair representation" of all people in the bargaining unit, *whether or not they were members of the union,* on the grounds that it is by the government's choice that a single labor organization negotiates for all workers in that unit. "While . . . a union is essentially a private organization," wrote Justice Murphy in the Supreme Court opinion that established this duty, "its power to represent and bind all members of a class or craft is derived solely from Congress."[28] Therefore, he argued, it is a public institution that is subject to scrutiny of its internal functioning.

Thus the Wagner Act's claim merely to support private associations of workers has splintered along at least two flaws: on one side the argument that government should not be in the business of "picking" representative associations; and on the other, the argument that if it does, it is responsible for regulating and controlling them.

Peace versus Justice

A final recurring tension goes back to the basic purpose of the Wagner Act. The *explicit* goal, as stated in the preamble, is the achievement of labor peace:

"[T]he refusal by some employers to accept the procedure of collective bargaining," it says, "lead[s] to strikes and other forms of industrial strife or unrest."[29] But as a definition of the public interest, that is grossly insufficient to support the act's structure. If peace is what is wanted, collective bargaining is certainly not the simplest way to achieve it. The 1920s, when employers resisted collective bargaining with all their power, were quite calm, whereas periods of great struggle, such as the two postwar strike waves or the sitdowns of the 1930s, have often come when unions were gaining strength.[30]

The focus on peace in the Wagner Act was in fact somewhat disingenuous: it was a way of getting past the scrutiny of the Supreme Court, which had rejected or gutted many labor laws in the past. The real objective of the act's sponsors involved a conception of *justice*—the idea that despotism, even of a benevolent and peaceful sort, was abhorrent to the nation. Leon Keyserling, for example—an aide to Wagner and a primary drafter of the bill—was vehement in arguing that its foundation was not the protection of commerce and property, but rather the advance of "the rights of man."[31] These opinions, however, were too controversial to be a public part of the act; they remained buried in memos and drafts.

The failure to confront the controversial issue of the *purpose* of collective bargaining, however, has left the door open for restrictive interpretations. The most important example is the increasing limitation of the right to strike. Though strikes may be conceived of as private disputes, the courts have seen them also as public disruptions and have sought to limit their effects on industrial peace. Now the strike is, of course, the key weapon of unions, especially industrial unions. The promotion of peace therefore generally tends to unbalance the power relationship.

Since about 1940 changes in law and court interpretations have consistently narrowed the permissible use of economic weapons by banning most sympathy strikes, slowdowns, and stoppages during the life of a contract.[32] The net effect of these and other rulings has been to confine the strike to a narrow channel, making it highly formal and predictable. These rules tend to favor the employer—who can prepare for such eventualities by stockpiling and moving work—at the expense of workers, whose most effective weapon is often surprise.

A second and related example of the effect of these rulings is the state's role in establishing arbitration as a pillar of the industrial relations structure. Labor relations commentators in this country almost unanimously reject the government-run forms of arbitration found in many other nations, on the grounds that these interfere unduly with the private interests of the parties and create rigidity. They point proudly to our system of private arbitration, which is performed by individuals selected jointly by union and management, as an important feature that limits the encroachment of government. That is true, so far as it goes; but it ignores the fact that government actions have been crucial in encouraging this

49

type of arbitration. It was the War Labor Board during World War II that by frequently requiring a system of private grievance arbitration to reduce conflict set the pattern for postwar developments; and the courts have steadily pushed to extend the reach of this structure as an alternative to frequent strikes.[33]

The Outcome: Limited Corporatism

The close relationship between labor and government, like the bureaucratic structure of unions, is virtually universal. Indeed, in nearly every other industrial nation the labor movement's ties to the government are far more open and acknowledged than in the United States. In most cases a major political party has been closely allied to the central union federation, to a degree almost inconceivable in this country. The policies of the Social Democrats in Sweden and Denmark and the Labor Party in England, for example, have been shaped primarily by labor—union and party membership are formally linked. The countries that have gone farthest in this direction, moreover, are those with the highest levels of unionization—Sweden with nearly 90 percent, Denmark with over 70 percent, and West Germany with 40 percent. These are systems that best exemplify the concept, considerably developed in Europe, of "corporatism."[34]

Corporatism involves an acceptance of the idea that the development of unionism is a political matter with public consequences: it connects unions to the broader direction of policy. The United States is one of the few countries to shy away from that position, to emphasize the private nature of labor relations. Yet paradoxically, the impact of regulatory rules is far greater in this country than in nations that are more open about the public role. We are almost unique in asking the government to define bargaining units and to certify exclusive representatives.

The structure in the United States can be characterized as a type of limited— or even of "hidden"—corporatism.[35] Just as unions have largely kept their cooperative activities under the table, so government has been reluctant to come into the open with its role. Yet the system is nevertheless corporatist in the sense that it follows the universal pattern of close government involvement in the creation of a tripartite labor relations order. In the United States, as in other countries, unionism depends on the support of the state. It is *limited* because that support has been kept as low-keyed as possible, obscured behind a façade of formal impartiality.

In comparative terms, it is true, our structure is quite decentralized and privatized. Nevertheless, those who by using a European standard wonder why we have no corporatism miss an important point.[36] There has been and continues to be a strong pull *toward* corporatism, and many of its features have been reproduced by other means. Although we do not have centralized wage bargaining, for example, the informal system of "pattern bargaining" (under which the major auto contracts set standards for the rest of the economy) has had, until recently, much the same rationalizing effect. The United States labor movement, while rejecting close ties with any political party, in practice has been a central part of the Democratic coalition that dominated politics from the New Deal until 1980. And even though our labor relations system is strike-prone, the strikes have become more predictable and controlled.

Most important, the close dependence of unions on the protective shell provided by the state results in a pronounced tendency toward bureaucracy and legalism; a primary task of union leaders at all levels is to master the intricacies of the NLRA and its interpretations. There is a clear reluctance on the part of unions to challenge the boundaries set by the legal structure. Though unions are not *prohibited* from, say, seeking to organize middle managers, the fact that the law would not *support* them in the effort is sufficient to rule out this possibility. To put it another way: earlier I described unions as torn between needing to act like organizations in order to effectively counter management, and like associations in order to mobilize their members; the government has, on the whole, reinforced the organizational side and downplayed the associational nature of unions. This effect of government intervention is perhaps clearest in the circumstance of wildcat strikes not authorized by the union hierarchy. Wildcats focus, as it were, the conflict between organized discipline and the membership's associational enthusiasm. Increasingly courts have compelled union officials to use their power to end spontaneous walkouts, putting union leaders in an extremely difficult situation.

A similar consequence flows from many other state actions. The Wagner Act reduces the need for strikes, especially strikes for recognition, thus requiring less frequent calls on member solidarity. Also, as we have seen, the courts have restricted the permissible scope and timing of strikes. In return, the government has given unions, *as organizations,* certain positive rights that strengthen their hand both against management and over their own members. Unions have gained exclusive legal bargaining rights for work units; neither members nor management can break that jurisdiction into different pieces. And rather than relying primarily on worker solidarity to resist management attacks, unions can handle many of them by legal appeals to the NLRB and the courts.

These legal elements follow from the basic strategy of the Wagner Act, which was to confer enough power on unions to balance and stabilize relations with corporate organizations. But the logic goes beyond the particulars of this act—it appears, to a greater or lesser degree, in all the countries of the industrial world.

Government, when it enters into the labor relations game, tends always to seek simplicity, to narrow the actors down to a few identifiable, responsible centers of power. The vagaries of mass action are as unsettling for government as for management and unions; these three organizational players understand each other and often act in a symbiotic way to consolidate each others' bureaucracies.

The fact that the role of government in this country remains largely hidden, however, is not without costs. It means that the rules dominate the spirit—there is no forum for the building of public agreement or shared vision. Indeed, the NLRB avoids public involvement or debate in its proceedings. Unlike most regulatory agencies, it holds no hearings. It once had a research staff that pushed for conceptual coherence, but that was seen as too controversial. The researchers were accused of Communist influence, and the staff was dissolved: the NLRB is resolutely unreflective, and the framework as a whole continues to develop by patchwork additions.

The Wagner Act's effort to support a private system of representation has proved, in short, a temporary and inadequate solution. As private organizations, unions are not strong enough anywhere in the world to match the power of employers on an equal basis. They are and must be, in essence, a public response to the problem posed by concentrations of private power in corporations. Those countries that have confronted that problem openly have produced strong systems of worker representation (though not, as I will argue later, without problems). The United States, which has tried to avoid the issue, has produced a weak system. It is therefore not surprising that the Wagner Act framework has failed to grow and adapt in the present period of complex social change, leading to a crisis that threatens to sweep it away altogether.

CHAPTER 4

The Current Crisis

THE WAGNER ACT framework, as developed through court interpretations and NLRB actions in the past fifty years, is not only unwieldy and confusing in concept; it is now in serious disarray in practice. The dramatic loss of membership during the past decade has touched every major category of the unions, including public-sector, manufacturing, and service workers.[1] Although opinion polls report a general sense that unions are needed to prevent employer abuse, they also reflect strong criticisms of *actual* unions and their leaders. The evidence includes these findings:

- The proportion expressing "a great deal of confidence" in organized labor and its leaders stood at 10 percent in 1987—lower than the average for any other institution mentioned in the surveys.
- When people were asked whether the country would be better off if certain groups had more influence, labor came in last of seven: by a six-to-one margin, respondents said that the country would be worse off with more labor influence.
- The percentage rating the system of organized labor as "basically sound" has dropped well below a majority and is still falling—to 46 percent in 1981, and further to 42 percent in 1983.
- Those with more education, and those with white-collar or technical jobs, have especially low opinions of unions: the college-educated and professionals are over- whelmingly negative.[2]

Certainly there is something seriously wrong. The Wagner Act supported the extension of unions and collective bargaining throughout the economy; that vision became something like a reality during the 1950s, but it is so no longer. The vast majority of workers either have no representation at all or they have it through some other mechanism.

What is even less clear is the nature of the problem. One view is that the concept of the Wagner Act is essentially sound and that the problem comes only from a failure of enforcement. The solution, in this analysis, is to pass some relatively simple reforms of labor law that will add to the NLRB's enforcement powers. The alternative view is that the problems are much deeper than that—that they concern major changes in the environment that require new structures and strategies for the labor movement. The first perspective suggests that the decline of labor is temporary, that it will rebound as it always has before; the second sees the need for a significant transformation of the system of representation.

The former view is, of course, the easiest for the labor movement to accept, because it requires the least amount of internal change. In the late 1970s this was the basis of a major campaign by the AFL-CIO for the reform of labor laws. The goal was quite modest: not to extend new protections to unions, but simply to achieve adequate enforcement of the existing NLRA framework. The reforms were intended to deal with the alarming increase in employer activities that were already illegal under the act. The bulk of the proposals, therefore, aimed to make enforcement swifter and punishments more severe. The proposed legislation, in effect, did no more than to reaffirm a basic commitment to the Wagner Act framework.

It was a shock, then, when a Democratic Congress and a Democratic president failed to pass the Labor Law Reform Act of 1977–78. That shock, in turn, was mild compared to the election, three years later, of Ronald Reagan, who quickly moved the government even further away from active support of unions. Labor's response once again indicated its underlying dependence on the state. While organizing efforts continued to lag, the AFL-CIO put a huge effort into the Democratic presidential campaign in 1984 in the hope of reversing these political defeats.

The failure of that political initiative has finally shaken the belief that the problems of the labor movement are easy to resolve. The period since the Mondale defeat has certainly seen more intense soul-searching than has any in the past thirty years. Yet many labor leaders continue to feel that at bottom the problems are temporary, not fundamental; that they are experiencing a pendulum swing, not a shift of basic patterns; that the fabric of unionism is sound and will survive the current attacks. While they make statements about the need for new strategies, their real hope still rests on the possibility of out-waiting Reagan, passing needed labor law reform, and thereby stimulating a new wave of growth.

This "labor law reform" strategy is based on the belief that the current problems lie *within* the labor relations system—that the cause is merely an unbalancing of the order, and the solution is to rebalance it. There is much evidence, however, for an alternative view: that the problem lies *outside,* in major societal changes that have altered the entire "fit" between the labor relations system and its environment. It is true, for example, that corporate management has grown more openly antiunion in the past decade; but it is also true that this change is only a minor piece of a much larger and very painful transformation affecting the basic structures of corporations. It is true that there has been an adverse political environment since 1980; but it is also true that the political troubles of labor began well before, and go far deeper than, the policies of the Reagan administration. From "inside" the Wagner Act system, the Reagan NLRB and antiunion employers appear to be the key villains, but from "outside" they are only offshoots of larger trends. In that case the quest for solutions requires a broader perspective.

The Transformation of the Economic Environment

It is clear, first of all, that we are going through a period of major economic restructuring. One recent book by Michael Piore and Charles Sabel has character-ized the current changes as marking a "second industrial divide," parallel to the great transformation of the late nineteenth century.[3] Others have popularized a more cautious term: the "postindustrial" economy[4]—a negative concept that indicates that we have moved out of familiar territory but have not yet defined what it is we are entering.

Piore and Sabel are referring especially to the shift away from mass manufac-turing, which has dominated the United States economy throughout this century. Anything that can be stabilized, routinized, and deskilled can be done more cheaply overseas. Meanwhile, the sophisticated markets of developed countries demand more than the mass production of black telephones and standardized cars. Increasingly, therefore, what is left here is *specialty* production, which requires rapid changes and high levels of flexibility. "Mini-mills" producing special-purpose steel, for example, are replacing giant forges, and the domestic garment industry is looking to high fashion for its salvation rather than to standardized clothing. Piore and Sabel call the emerging form of production "flexible specialization":

> Flexible specialization is a strategy of permanent innovation: accommodation to ceaseless change rather than an attempt to control it. This strategy is based on flex-ible—multi-use—equipment; skilled workers; and the creation, through politics, of an industrial community that restricts the forms of competition to those favoring innovation.[5]

This, however, is only one of a series of interrelated changes that have transformed the economic context. Perhaps the most dramatic recent shock has been the opening of international markets. The entry of nations with lower standards of living into markets traditionally dominated by U.S. firms has produced major dislocation, including absolute declines in employment in our formerly core manufacturing sectors. Our balance of trade, especially for manufacturing, has plummeted into the red, and many observers have expressed fears of a permanent loss of American competitiveness.[6]

This process has been greatly accelerated by a quite sudden internationalization of capital markets. The difficulty of moving capital across political boundaries, which used to restrict the growth of industry in the poorer nations and help to hold it in place in the "advanced" countries, has been all but erased by deregulation and improvements in communication. Thus in an effort to meet the challenge from abroad, American manufacturers are simply investing in ventures overseas. Basic steel, garment, and auto production are carried on increasingly in Asia and Mexico, and it seems likely that much microelectronics manufacturing will follow.[7]

The movement of capital also seems to have accelerated within this country. The wave of mergers during the past decade exceeds anything seen at least since the 1950s, if not the 1920s. Plant closings have devastated many communities that depend on the employment provided by a large company.[8] Such companies, meanwhile, have frequently moved away from their focus on a single industry toward greater diversity and flexibility. US Steel has renamed itself "USX" because it has acquired so much nonsteel business. The "X" can be taken to symbolize the uncertainty of an economy in flux.

Technological change, in particular the application of computers to production, is yet another part of the new picture. The current burst of automation is already revolutionizing both blue-collar and white-collar work by introducing robots and increasing the data-handling capacity of computers. Whether these changes will lead to a long-term loss of jobs or merely a shift in the composition of labor demand cannot yet be predicted from the evidence.[9] What is indisputable, however, is that these changes are causing tremendous displacement for workers in the present, and unions are at a loss to respond to the repeated waves of innovation.

Finally, there is the overall shift from manufacturing to services. This is a somewhat quieter and longer-term change than the others previously cited. As a proportion of total employment, services passed manufacturing around 1890; however, it is only recently that the former have become the main driving force of the economy. In the past few years, both the balance of trade and employment trends have been negative for manufacturing but positive for services. There is considerable controversy about the meaning of this change—whether the new jobs are less skilled or lower-paying than the old, for instance—but no doubt at all that it poses a formidable challenge for the labor movement.

Indeed, the whole transformation threatens the assumptions on which unions have been built. The Wagner Act framework was created out of the "first industrial divide"; its major elements are closely connected to the structure of mass production industry. Pattern bargaining for wages, the insistence on detailed contractual rules, the restriction of issues in collective bargaining, the focus on blue-collar workers, the emphasis on the strike—in fact, the whole balance-of-power model itself—draw their effectiveness from their adaptation to that context. As the economic transformation proceeds, therefore, it steadily erodes the effectiveness of these traditional union strategies.

Wages

Unions' ability to raise income has always depended primarily on "taking wages out of competition" by establishing a consistent pattern throughout an industry. That strategy depends on being able to organize substantially all the workers in the industry into a unified force that can halt production through strikes. It also appears to depend on a certain level of prosperity and growth among the employers: the major study of union wage gains in recent years concluded that they come mostly through the reduction of excessive levels of profit among monopoly firms.[10]

But those conditions no longer exist widely. International competition has often grown most sharply in heavily unionized industries; that has meant a new emphasis on cost cutting and austerity among formerly "monopoly" companies. It has also meant that no single union can hope to draw together the bulk of the relevant work force. Unlike companies, unions have been largely unable to cross national boundaries—the requirement of membership solidarity sharply limits the possibility of international organization.

Unions' organizing targets have been further fragmented by the diversification of the scope of individual companies: the Steelworkers now face companies involved in oil exploration, banking, and dozens of other industries along with steel production. The proportion of blue-collar, semiskilled workers, the traditional backbone of labor, is shrinking rapidly, to be replaced by white-collar employees who are less easy to pull together in a mass organization. And the rate of change is such that whole industries may wither away or change in form during the normal three-year period between negotiations. Collective bargaining cannot cope, and is not coping, with such a situation.

Furthermore, the increasing mobility of capital has added a trump card to the hands of employers. In industry after industry the threat has been made to move plants or to close them entirely if unions insist on wage increases. The choices faced by a union in this circumstance are grim: to give in or to go down fighting. Calling the bluff rarely works, because the threat is rarely a bluff.[11]

Moreover, while unions have been ineffective even in standard collective bargaining, the factors that have had *major* effects on workers' standard of living have increasingly moved beyond the unions' scope. Decisions on trade and investment policy have a tremendous impact on compensation, with consequences that are likely only to grow. If foreign competition is allowed to increase unchecked, and if American companies can freely invest abroad, then wages will be driven down toward the level of the foreign countries—many of which pay about 20 percent of our standard wage.[12] Possible alternatives include either massive unemployment or the growth of new industries, requiring large shifts in skills and in the location of the work force.

The combination of these factors has already had a dramatic effect on the standard of living of American workers. From 1973 to 1986 average real weekly earnings dropped by almost 15 percent; among men aged twenty-four to thirty-four, they fell by 26 percent.[13] This is the kind of problem that the Wagner Act framework was originally designed to encompass, but that framework is no longer able to cope with the economic factors that are eroding income.

Yet paradoxically, another consequence has been the decline of support for labor in the population at large; labor has been painted into the corner of the "special interests." In its preamble the Wagner Act assumed explicitly that wage increases won in bargaining would benefit the economy as a whole by increasing purchasing power. But during the 1970s wage growth was linked with two major evils—inflation and the inability to compete in international markets. Given these conditions, it appeared that gains by small groups of unionized workers were harmful to the country as a whole. This has been a major factor in the redefinition of unions as private interests rather than as public movements.

Contractual Rules

The tendency of unions to seek detailed rules and written procedures fits well with the needs of mass production management. Mass production, more than any other economic activity, requires stability and predictability of relations among large numbers of people. Once the assembly line starts moving, dissension anywhere in its course has extremely costly consequences. Arbitrary actions by supervisors cause just such dissension. It is therefore in management's interest, as well as that of unions, to establish clear rules and procedures for dealing with workers. In fact, a major study of labor relations in 1960 reached the conclusion— surprising at first, but sensible on reflection—that unions had forced companies to adopt more effective managerial policies in spite of themselves.[14] The detailed work rules of union contracts were a good match for the strictly defined job processes of the Taylorized assembly line.

This central element of representation in a mass production system no longer fits the economic conditions. The emphasis of management, in both manufacturing and service industries, has shifted toward *flexibility* and *innovation*. Detailed work rules are, in these conditions, a terrible obstacle to the ability of a company to position itself rapidly, to adapt to the subtle shifts of a mature market system.

Management hostility to unions has come to focus increasingly on this issue. There are many companies that avoid unionization not because of wage considerations—they are willing to pay the union scale—but because they want the flexibility to change work patterns rapidly and between contracts. It is this nonunion sector that has taken the lead in the recent trend toward increasing worker participation and reducing bureaucratic hierarchy.[15] This puts unions in a perplexing situation: should they oppose employee involvement by sticking to their focus on uniform rules? This dilemma is insoluble within the old system.

Limited Scope

The mass production system allowed a fairly sensible carving up of "territory" between management and unions. When major strategic changes were relatively infrequent and slow to be implemented, unions could avoid dealing directly with strategy, focusing instead on controlling its direct consequences for the workers. In 1955, when union membership was at its height, George Meany reiterated a distinction drawn from Gompers: "Those matters that do not touch a worker directly, a union cannot and will not challenge. These may include investment policy, a decision to make a new product, a desire to erect a new plant so as to be closer to expanding markets, etc. . . . But where management decisions affect a worker directly, a union will intervene."[16]

The courts, as we saw, have enshrined this distinction in the NLRA framework by defining a sphere of "mandatory subjects of bargaining," restricting state support of collective bargaining to the "direct" issues described by Meany.

In a more specialized economy, however, strategic planning becomes such a central part of managerial action that such distinctions are meaningless. Shifts in investment strategy, product mix, and plant location are no longer exceptional events but are increasingly the primary road to profits. The effects on workers, in the form of job loss and obsolescence of skills, are not merely "direct" but drastic. And by the time the precise consequences become clear to the union, the time for effective action has passed. The "two-stage" process, in which management makes decisions on economic grounds and the decisions are then reviewed for human implications by the union, has been overwhelmed by the need for rapid response.

The Strike

The insufficiency of the strike as the primary worker weapon has become increasingly visible in the changed circumstances. In a mass production system, major management decisions tended to affect large numbers of workers over long periods of time. It was therefore possible (though not necessarily easy) to develop a common understanding and position among the membership and to mobilize for mass action. Furthermore, it was reasonably effective to wait until the expiration of a three-year contract, when the strike became available as bargaining leverage, and then deal with crucial issues. Compared to the present, management organization was elephantine—ponderous, massive, and powerful—and the strike was an adequate elephant gun.

But as strategic adaptability becomes more economically critical, the strike becomes less appropriate as a tactic. We saw earlier that an effective strike issue—one that can mobilize large numbers of workers—must be at the same time *general* and *concrete;* that is, it must be immediately visible to a mass of members. Some changes fit this category, especially major technological shifts that transform an entire industry, such as containerization in shipping or the move from letterpress to offset in printing. But, increasingly, change comes in the form of a large number of systems, each with different effects on the work force.

Researchers at the Sloan School of Management have documented a number of such cases. Within the rubber industry, for example, they found that different firms responded to competition in radically different ways: some by aggressive cost cutting, some by diversification into other industries, some by concentrating on high-quality "niches."[17] The effects of these strategies on the workers were enormous but complex. For many the strategic choices meant the loss of jobs; for others they produced increased work; for still others they dramatically changed the nature of the skill requirements. Yet despite the important consequences of strategic changes, their very diversity has meant that these are not "strikeable" issues. Their different effects tend to divide a union's membership rather than uniting it, and their complexity makes it difficult to find a central rallying point.

Even if mass action can be generated as a credible threat, it often comes too late to do much good. Given advance warning, management can more and more effectively use its new flexibility to shift production and prepare for a strike. Its vulnerability generally lies in the fragility of the change process—it can be best attacked *at the moment* of change. Once a strategic plan has been set and the forces marshaled behind it, unions' attempts to react become increasingly futile. The strike, in these circumstances, is like using the trusty old elephant gun to fight off a swarm of wasps: it makes a lot of noise, but it does not stop the attack. Or, to view it another way, it deals only with the symptoms of change rather than the root causes: the managerial decisions that set in motion the varied processes eventually felt by the workers.

The decline in the effectiveness of the strike has been demonstrated with increasing frequency. In 1983 nearly 100 percent of AT&T's work force walked off the job for more than three weeks; thanks to modern technology, phone users scarcely noticed. Until 1982, airlines never tried to fly during work stoppages; now they do so routinely. Many workers in the steel industry have found that strikes simply hasten the closing of plants and the permanent loss of jobs. It has become so easy to break strikes that companies sometimes encourage them. "In many situations," says a representative of the Boilermakers, "the strike weapon has actually become the strongest weapon in the employer's arsenal. . . . Union busters commonly advise employers to create strike situations as a means of hastening the objective of a union-free workplace."[18]

To the extent, then, that the economy moves from mass production to services and "flexible specialization" in an international marketplace, established patterns of worker representation break down. They do so partly because the balance of power has been upset. This is the starting point of those who recommend a strategy of labor law reform—strengthening the sanctions supporting the Wagner Act framework. Nevertheless, that strategy misses the mark because it underestimates the magnitude of the economic transformation. First, since the new imbalance is tied to the ability of capital to cross national boundaries, legislation in any one country is powerless to stop it without choking off international trade. Second, and more important, the balance-of-power model is increasingly inappropriate to a "post-industrial" economy.

The structure of a balance of power has fundamental limitations that are becoming increasingly apparent. It is not, by nature, a self-regulating system that can adapt to environmental changes. Rather, it is stabilized only by a sequence of tests of strength that produce concrete compromises. It works moderately well under two conditions: when the number of parties is small and when the rate of change is slow. In those circumstances, the players can become thoroughly familiar with each other's strengths and weaknesses. They have learned by experience what is worth trying and how far they can push. On that basis they can establish a tenuous stability in their relations.

The preceding essentially describes the situation of the American labor movement in the halcyon days of the 1950s and 1960s. The parameters of the labor relations system were set in a few great conflicts. For example, the strike against General Motors in 1946 established that management would not tolerate union involvement in price setting, but was prepared to make concessions on wages. Similarly, the steel industry experienced a series of enormous conflicts during this period, which fixed pragmatic principles for dealing with technological advances and wage increases. The patterns set in these great trials then spread through the economy to other players who were anxious not to fight the same battles over again. "Pattern bargaining" thus imposed de facto centralization on a theoretically decentralized system.

However, an economic structure that stresses flexible responsiveness to differentiated markets violates both of the conditions necessary for its stability. First, the pace of change has become too rapid to be controlled by empirical tests of strength. In fact, it throws the system into a vicious circle. As the "understanding" that had been based on the resolution of past conflicts is undercut, mistrust grows, and as it grows, the possibility of reaching new understandings is further reduced. An effective system of representation would have to discuss the full range of strategic considerations in order to build in the interests of all parties; but that would take the unions into the realm of "managerial prerogative," which is solidly protected by law and tradition. It would also take them away from their power base in the membership's willingness to strike.

Second, it has become more difficult to limit the game to a few players. As the patterns break apart, there are more and more individual agreements to be negotiated. In the telephone industry, for example, what was only a few years ago a single contract with AT&T has been fragmented into dozens of agreements with the deregulated operating companies. This development, too, threatens to overload the system by requiring too many different agreements to maintain stability.

Unions, well aware of this danger, have fought the trend fiercely, arguing that breaks in the pattern leave no standards for determination of wages. They have been driven back steadily, however, both by the insistence of employers and also by increasing differentiations within their own memberships. For the economic change is not the only problem. As in the 1920s, it has brought with it a transformation of the communal base of the union movement.

A New Work Force?

The economic environment is the first major prop of the Wagner Act system to have shifted. The second, closely intertwined with it, involves the attitudes and expectations of the work force—both those workers currently represented by unions and also those who are outside the boundaries of organized labor.

The nature of the unions as a form of worker representation has been shaped in crucial ways by the particular nature of the *solidarity* that gives them life. We saw earlier how the shift from craft communities to the mass unity of semiskilled workers caused a crisis in the labor movement, producing the split between the AFL and the CIO.

Where traditional craft or industrial communities remain, one still finds evidence of the same attitudes that drove the great events of labor history. The solidarity of adversarial "toughness" has been shaken, but it often reemerges when collective action is required. Thus the United Steelworkers local at Homestead, Pennsylvania—the location of a pivotal confrontation of the nineteenth century described in chapter 2—dealt with concession pressures and layoffs in 1985 by electing a militant who advocated disruptive tactics to put pressure on management. "The general feeling," said one official, "is: if the end is coming . . . I want to go down with dignity."[19] Those who remain wedded to classic images of labor are inspired by such displays of solidarity and see in them the seeds of potential revival.

But the base of community underlying the militant posture is steadily eroding. The toughness of the industrial labor movement has always depended principally on the semiskilled operatives. In the 1960s, nearly two-thirds of these workers were organized. They were the backbone of the great "pattern-setting" unions, especially those in auto and steel. But they have also been the ones hardest hit by the economic transformations of the past thirty years. In that time they have declined from about 35 percent of the work force to scarcely 20 percent.[20]

The shrinking of their core industries and jobs has not only reduced the absolute numbers of operatives, but also produced a new mood of uncertainty and defensiveness that has further undermined their militance. Victor Reuther, who fought the battles of the 1930s in helping to create the United Auto Workers, laments that "it would have been unthinkable in those days for the breaches in solidarity to occur that we see today—people seeking overtime while their union brothers and sisters are on layoff."[21] The ultimate form of disloyalty to the labor movement—scabbing, or crossing picket lines—has become common again even in the strongest blue-collar areas. In this context the toughness of the workers at Homestead now seems based more in desperation than in a shared vision.

The other main support of the American labor movement, crafts workers, has also been in decline, indeed for a much longer period. The rise of the assembly line in the 1920s was the first crushing blow to the autonomy of the traditional skilled worker. The spread of computer technology now looks like the second blow. Many of the old jobs that continued to be taught in long apprenticeships have been reduced to routine or eliminated by silicon chips. Machinists are a major recent example: this proud community has been in the vanguard of worker movements all over the world, protected from employer retaliation by their control of a very difficult and crucial skill. Recently, however, "numerically controlled" machine tools, which can be programmed by engineers half a world away, have begun to cut this foundation out from under them. Similarly, many highly technical diagnostic tasks in telecommunications, which used to take years to master, are now performed by computers—the VDT screen describes the breakdown and orders a repair worker to plug in a new module.[22] There remain some bastions of craft autonomy, such as the construction trades, which are still capable of powerful displays of traditional unionism, but they can no longer support a growing movement.

These traditional sectors have been replaced by white-collar workers—a category that has increased since 1950 from 36 percent of the labor force to well over 50 percent, compared to less than 25 percent currently in blue-collar jobs (operatives and craft). "White-collar," of course, is a very loose grouping; it includes everyone from highly paid professionals to clericals who earn far less than their unionized blue-collar counterparts. This tremendous diversity should make one cautious about generalizations. Nevertheless, the common use of a single category does reflect real similarities in the way these employees perceive themselves.

This group immediately poses a problem for the Wagner Act framework because it does not fall clearly on either side of the crucial line between "management" and "workers." When the act was passed, that line was intuitively obvious: "scientific management" was based on a structure in which relatively few managers detailed procedures for large numbers of semiskilled operatives. Now the middle layers have grown to a point at which they are neither part of the policy-making center nor do they merely carry out commands from above. They refer to themselves by a label that has no place in labor law—as "employees." In legal terms, some of them are "exempt employees" and some "nonexempt" (from coverage by the Wagner Act). The extreme awkwardness of the categorization reflects the arbitrariness of the line that is drawn.

Unions have not had much success with this sector. The percentage of private sector white-collar workers who are union members is extremely low—below 8 percent—and rapidly dropping. Their attitudes toward organized labor, as revealed in survey data, are highly negative.[23] Many of the large unions have tried in recent years to extend their reach to these growing sectors of the work force, but their success has so far been indifferent. The UAW's campaign to sign up the white-collar workers in their industry has largely fizzled. The story of the Newport News shipyard, where the Steelworkers won an important victory in 1977, exemplifies the problems. There the engineers broke tradition by leading the organizing efforts—but within seven years this group had decided it was too uncomfortable in an organization of steelworkers and had decertified the union.[24]

Some union representatives blame the white-collar workers for lack of solidarity. "They think of themselves," says one organizer, "as more individualistic and thus above engaging in collective actions, and they are more afraid."[25] But such accusations have a familiar ring. During the period of the AFL's decline, and before the new structure of industrial unionism had been consolidated, it appeared to many that workers had lost the solidarity that had produced the heady movements of the nineteenth century. In 1932 Louis Adamic, in an article titled "The Collapse of Organized Labor," complained: "The average working stiff is too indifferent and sour, or selfish . . ." to support unions.[26] He was wrong: it was only two years later that the solidarity of semiskilled workers emerged in full force and generated a type of organization to fit. Given the experience of the 1930s, one should ask whether the problem among white-collar workers is truly one of a *lack* of solidarity—or one of a *new form* of solidarity that is not adequately addressed by existing structures.

Certainly the white-collar sectors lack some of the bases for the solidarity that has held together blue-collar movements. Outside the workplace, they rarely have their own institutions for education or communication; they rely primarily on their employer for these functions. This is in sharp contrast to crafts workers, as we have seen, but it is also different from semiskilled workers. These, as they entered the work force in large numbers with the rise of mass production, brought with them many shared standards from common preindustrial communities. The growth of industrial unions was fueled in almost every nation by first- and second-generation immigrants to the cities, who often sustained their distinct languages and newspapers.[27] No comparable phenomena give the white-collar groups a sense of shared values.

Nor are white-collar employees clearly marked off *inside* the workplace. Mass production factories brought together huge numbers of blue-collar workers in areas that were physically separated from management. By deliberately aiming to program their every move, Taylorism further accentuated the line between the controllers and the controlled; the hated time-study man did much to stimulate solidarity. A whole array of symbols, from time clocks to separate parking lots and cafeterias, has developed to remind workers that they are outside management.

For the white-collar workers, however, the lines are less visible. Many of them work more closely with their bosses than with each other, and very few see large numbers of their peers in the workplace. And the symbolism of status, starting with the white collar itself, consistently reinforces the feeling of being a part of the managerial order. Their direct experiences do not support mass unity in opposition to the company.

It is therefore not surprising that their ambitions are linked less to the success of their peer group and more to their individual progress in the hierarchy. They hope, not for a general improvement of their "group" relative to others, but to escape from that group and move on. Though data on this point are fragmentary, they build a consistent picture. Surveys conducted by the Opinion Research

Corporation over the past two decades have shown, among clerical workers, a level of dissatisfaction with advancement opportunities that has grown rapidly toward crisis proportions.[28] Daniel Yankelovich and his colleagues have documented the rise of an ethic of "self-development" at work, visible in polls throughout the industrialized world and centered in white-collar occupations.[29] And an elegant study by Philip Selznick in 1969 showed that the concept of equity shifts dramatically, with increasing education and status, from "equal treatment for all" toward "recognition of individual abilities."[30] These studies are consistent with hundreds of interviews I have conducted in various companies, in which the most persistent and emotional complaints among these workers have consistently involved inequities in the promotion system.[31]

It is, however, not attitude but behavior which is the critical test. White-collar employees, while resisting unionization, do not reject the idea of collective representation; they merely tend toward *different* forms of organization and action from those established by the production workers of the 1930s and supported by the Wagner Act. The most typical form of organization in these categories is the association. Professional, technical, and managerial groups have always tended to band into such groupings to define their collective identity. In recent years, other white-collar layers have often done the same. Groupings of clerical workers, especially women, have grown up in informal structures outside the labor movement—typified by the success of Nine to Five, a women's organization advocating changes in the workplace, which has spread out to hundreds of local networks around the country.

An association is different from a union in several important ways. It tends to be decentralized and participative, minimizing the role of bureaucratic structure. Rather than placing demands on the employer, it emphasizes services to the membership ranging from insurance plans to intellectual networking to "consciousness-raising." And when pressing collective interests, it usually makes use of publicity rather than such direct action as a strike.

Moreover, when white-collar employees do form a union, its structure, while tighter than that of an association, often differs in these same basic ways from the classic model of an industrial organization. White-collar unions do very un-unionlike things:

- It is common for them to bargain only minimum wage levels, allowing for the operation of individual negotiations above that standard.
- They often encourage supplementary forms of participation outside the bargaining framework, and they have generally proved more open than blue-collar unions to worker problem-solving groups and other forms of employee involvement.
- They frequently downplay the emphasis on seniority; their focus is on finding fair and consistent ways to reward merit.
- They rarely seek detailed specification of work rules.

66

- They minimize the use of the strike and emphasize publicity and lobbying.
- They are relatively decentralized—even small units frequently insist on administrative independence and have their own bylaws.[32]

These characteristics of white-collar organizations seem to indicate a distinct type of consciousness or solidarity. Mass action and adversarial toughness are not their "natural" forms of behavior. Their principle of grouping seems to be more specific. White-collar employees resist defining themselves as communities based on the traditional markers of industrial unionism: opposition to an employer and attachment to a diffuse status or class. For white-collar workers these boundaries are more fluid, because they see themselves as mobile and developing. When they band together, it is for relatively specific purposes and interests. This kind of community produces more flexible, less bureaucratic organizations than industrial unions.

Several forces, it is true, can push white-collar workers toward more "standard" forms of union structure. That is because organizations are only partly dependent on the consciousness and desires of those who form them; they are also shaped by the pressures of the environment. The more bureaucratic and confrontational the employer, the more the organizations of employees will fall into adversarial and centralized patterns. When they are treated as an inferior mass, white-collar workers are quite capable of showing militance, striking and picketing in traditional fashion. It is nevertheless true that, given the chance, they will gravitate toward more associational types of action.[33]

Once we focus on their relation to management, however, it becomes apparent that there are at least two major groups hidden under the "white-collar" rubric. On the one hand are those employees who appear to be losing status: clericals, many sales and service workers, and others whose traditionally quasi-managerial status is eroding. On the other hand are those—sometimes called "knowledge workers"—who exercise a great deal of autonomy and "professional" judgment on the job.[34]

The jobs of those in the first group are coming to resemble those of blue-collar, semiskilled workers. As Harry Braverman has persuasively argued, the techniques of Taylorism are only now being applied to many clerical jobs.[35] And since he wrote, the advance of computer technology has made it possible to pace and monitor these jobs as closely as any assembly line. A secretary, in the classic image, provided personal service for one or at most a few people. Today, however, clerical workers are being rapidly moved into "word-processing centers," often resembling factory floors, where they are handed work randomly as it comes down the "line" and are measured on their rate of keystrokes-per-minute.[36]

Such groups form a substantial proportion of the work force—perhaps 20 percent—and seem to be growing, though not rapidly.[37] Their rate of unionization is low, partly because companies have fiercely resisted organizing drives, partly because unions have been slow to target this sector, and partly because the workers retain aspects of traditional white-collar consciousness, seeing themselves as part of the managerial structure.

But both the attitude of unions and the self-image of these workers are changing. This, at any rate, is the expectation and the hope of those who remain firm adherents of traditional unionism. They see white-collar workers, insofar as they hold the attitudes I have described, as victims of illusions, which are being progressively stripped away by the continuing degradation of their status and work. Furthermore, these workers have been drawn primarily from sectors of the population that share a common class position in the society at large, clearly marked off by cultural symbols: women, blacks, and youth. The basis for mass solidarity is "overdetermined" by factors both inside and outside the workplace, as it was for the semiskilled entrants into the work force in the first part of this century.

Thus, although clerical workers have in the past shared in the general white-collar aspirations described here, the picture for the future is less clear. To the extent that management pursues a strategy of deskilling these jobs, those aspirations are likely to fade as they are consistently frustrated, to be replaced by a class consciousness and militancy more in tune with traditional union structures. In that case something very like industrial unionism, with perhaps minor differences in style, is likely to develop. This will be prevented only if management adopts different approaches to these jobs (a possibility that will be examined in chapter 5).

That is one side of the white-collar world. The other is composed of those who, by contrast, have retained a considerable level of skill and autonomy within the overall management structure. Once again a comparison to the 1920s is in order. The growth of mass production then created a dominant category of semiskilled employees, people who did more than brute physical labor but whose skills were not complex enough to require apprenticeships. Today, the new dominant category might be called *semiprofessionals*—administrators, technicians, engineers, sales representatives (though not, for the most part, sales clerks), supervisors, teachers (elementary and secondary), nurses, and the like. These are *professionals* in that their work requires creative thought rather than routine activity; they are not closely controlled and monitored. But they are *semi* in that their status is bound up with their place in a particular company, not with universal standards that go beyond that firm. Unlike true professionals, they lack their own prestigious educational institutions and societies; and unlike the semiskilled, they do not share enough as a class to provide a separate base of solidarity.[38]

Semiprofessionals are not expected, like workers, merely to follow orders, to turn off their minds when they come in to their jobs, nor to apply traditional craft skills. They are expected to *use their intelligence and creativity in the service of organizational goals.* They neither merely determine policy nor merely carry it out: they bridge the familiar line.

Many in this group are called "managers." But they are not managers in the traditional sense of being part of the elite inner circle that governs the business. The idea of management as privileged and trusted depends on its being a small and homogeneous group, at least relative to the mass of workers. The middle management layers, however, are no longer either small or homogeneous: they constitute well over 10 percent of the work force, and their numbers have been rising rapidly since World War II. Nor are they just managers, in the sense of coordinating real production; to an increasing extent, as mass manufacturing declines, knowledge work is a direct part of the firm's product. Under the circumstances companies are taking another look at their policies toward this category of employees. Their salaries are no longer a negligible part of the payroll. They are an important controllable cost, central to the fluctuating fortunes and strategies of their firms.[39]

Semiprofessionals, including such middle managers, now constitute more than one-third of the work force. That is more than either the white-collar semiskilled (about 20 percent) or the traditional blue-collar (about 22 percent).[40] Furthermore, the numbers appear to be increasing more rapidly than in either of the other categories. Between 1975 and 1982 they grew six times as fast as the white-collar semiskilled, while the number of blue-collar workers actually declined.[41] Of the ten occupations projected to increase most by 1995, eight are clearly semiprofessional, including all the top five: paralegals, computer programmers, systems analysts, medical assistants, and data-processing equipment repairers. Clerical and low-level service workers, by contrast—on whom many unions are placing a great deal of hope—are now growing, and are projected to continue growing, at a much slower pace.

In a word, the semiprofessionals are hot. It is their skills that are driving the economy, and their occupations are gaining prestige from association with technological advances. Yet they are not in control. Though many of them actually fall within the traditional managerial hierarchy, they are as distant from the managerial functions of setting strategy as they are from blue-collar tasks.

That tension places them in an exceptionally important position for the labor movement. Historically, the major steps in the assertion of employee rights have always come from groups precisely like this one—workers who have been at the center of new economic sectors, who feel the sense of excitement that comes from involvement in creation and growth, yet who do not control their destinies. That describes textile workers during the eighteenth and nineteenth centuries, who throughout the West were among the first to assert their unified strength; the railroad workers and the construction crafts that drove the AFL during the late nineteenth century; the machinists early in this century; the auto and steel workers who were the core of the CIO during the mass-production revolution of the 1920s and 1930; and the truckers in the immediate postwar period.[42] And it describes the semiprofessionals today.

Yet these employees do not join unions. They manifest in a very strong form an associational type of solidarity, based almost entirely on deliberate groupings of people who share *particular* concerns. While both craft and mass solidarity are reinforced by a network of institutions that cut through the workplace—these categories are defined not only by their job titles but by their clothing, their neighborhoods, and their speech—the semiprofessionals are much less distinct from management in every respect. Nor do they expect to stay long in their present situation—their plans involve moving on. Their groupings, therefore, have a more specific character. They *associate* around problems at work but they may well not associate outside work; and when different issues become salient, they may seek to associate in a different pattern. They are not based in lasting communities, but they form shifting *communities of interest.*

Though this type of consciousness is often seen as individualistic, it has a strong moral component that goes beyond individual ambition. The sense is not simply that "I" should get ahead, but that the standards for getting ahead should be fairly and equally enforced. Semiprofessionals' associations, and their unions when they form unions, tend to focus heavily on developing evaluation systems that are based on public standards and that reward merit as defined by their common values.[43] It is a kind of group unity, of solidarity—but less concrete than that of traditional unionism.

If associational solidarity is in fact a distinct form, it should not be surprising that it causes problems for unions. There is an obvious problem of style: semiprofessionals and white-collar workers in general often speak of being put off by the "cigar-chomping types" from the traditional sectors. But beyond this is a further and more profound issue. The associational solidarity of semiprofessional workers challenges fundamental union structures. The whole industrial relations order, as we saw earlier, was built around the basic concept of a line between management and workers. The CIO based its strategies on this consciousness of difference, and the law later enshrined it as one of the principal components of the Wagner Act framework. From it flow the stress on adversarial tactics, the importance of the strike weapon, and the emphasis on seniority rather than on performance standards.

For these new workers, then, something more than a bolstering of unions is needed. A form of worker representation that fits their situation would need to be structured differently from industrial or craft unions. In an important development, management is now trying to structure a system in which knowledge workers participate without the intervention of outside institutions, and it is having significant success, at least in the short run (see chapter 5). If independent worker organizations were to take up the challenge of restructuring their groups, however, they would need to develop some new answers to the old problem of how to hold together a communal movement in the face of an organized opponent.

The Political Climate: Interest Groups and the Crisis of Regulation

The third institution that has shaped labor—in addition to mass-production industry and worker communities—is the liberal political coalition that emerged from the New Deal. Given the absolute dependence of industrial unions on government protection and support, the current disarray of the Democrats is ominous. The future of unions depends in part on whether the political changes of the 1980s are temporary or permanent.

What have the liberals delivered for labor in the past? First and foremost, of course, they delivered the Wagner Act, which emerged from the general euphoria surrounding the Democratic advances in 1934. In the reactionary tide of the 1950s they were unable to prevent the partial reverses embodied in the Taft-Hartley Act; but President Kennedy began the move to extend labor legislation to the public sector, and this move was taken up by Democratic governors in many states. Lyndon Johnson helped with the last labor law victory, which was the extension of the NLRA to hospital workers in 1964. Meanwhile, the Warren court produced many decisions extending union rights.[44] All of these moves were critical to the growth of the labor movement.

Reciprocally, the labor movement was an important part of the coalition that advanced liberal social legislation. The AFL-CIO was active in promoting the War on Poverty and the civil rights laws of the 1960s. The political image of labor is captured in a Harris survey question, with which 76 percent of the population agreed in 1976: "Most unions in the United States have been good forces, working for such things as national health insurance, higher unemployment compensation, better social security, minimum wage laws, and other social needs."[45]

The unraveling of these ties began long before 1980. During the 1970s it became clear first in the courts, then in the Democratic party, that the support unions had come to expect from government was eroding. Beginning about 1970 a rapid-fire succession of Supreme Court decisions turned against the unions: the protection of strikers was weakened, access of organizers to company property restricted, the use of injunctions against strikes restored, and major groups of employees excluded from protection by the NLRA.[46] The withdrawal of Democratic party support, meanwhile, was most clearly signaled by defeat of the Labor Law Reform Act of 1977.

It also became evident in this period that labor was experiencing strained relations with other liberal groups. The image of hard-hatted construction workers marching down Wall Street in support of the Vietnam War drove a deep wedge into formerly solid alliances. The AFL-CIO, furthermore, began to have trouble with the consequences of some of the social legislation it supported. Women and minorities who took advantage of the Equal Employment laws found themselves opposing union provisions for protection of seniority rights. Environmental activists clashed with labor organizations that feared that regulations would cost them employment. Liberals in the foreign policy arena continued to find themselves on the opposite side of the fence from the AFL, whose hawkish anticommunism has deep roots, including the desire to keep defense industry jobs.

The Growth of Interest Associations

Not all groups with claims against corporations have shared in the decline of unions during the past two decades. If we ask, What groups have had the most impact on corporations during that time? the answer is certainly not unions; it is, rather, new interest associations. The most significant changes in the management of employee relations since 1960 were forced, not by advances in collective bargaining, but by the Equal Employment Opportunity Act. The regulations that drew the most ire from business came, not from the Labor Department, but from the newly created agencies for environmental protection and consumer affairs. Just when corporate management might have been rejoicing in the critical decline of their principal adversary, they instead felt themselves to be embattled by attacks from a host of new and less identifiable opponents. As one major business institute summarized a meeting of top public relations executives: "It has become very evident to us at the Conference Board that the restoration of business credibility is the number-one issue in the minds of most executives. . . . They realize that business . . . has lost favor with the public at large. . . . The lack of credibility leads to one-sided legislation and regulation."[47] If these executives had been given to wry insight, they might have longed for the good old days when unions were strong—on the grounds that they were better off with one large organizational opponent that they could deal with in a responsible way than with the hydra-headed and elusive foes called public opinion and public interest associations.

What was happening was a phenomenon on the societal level that was similar to what was troubling unions internally: the growth of *associational* groupings—environmental, consumer, and rights groups—deliberately formed around issues rather than reflecting traditional communities. They even seem to be grounded in the same people: the semiprofessionals, or knowledge workers.[48] These associations are not trying to be *organizations* in the sense that unions are. They seek no centralized discipline over their memberships, and they avoid tactics that require coordinated action. They rely on two weapons of a different nature: the effects of publicity and the enforcement of private rights through the courts.

These interest associations have made demands on corporate organizations that have not been a part of labor's agenda, and they made substantial gains in a brief period of time (from about 1960 to 1980). Viewed from a wider perspective, they are, in a sense, descendants of the labor movement. Production workers had been the group first and most obviously affected by the growth of corporate power between the Civil War and the depression, and so they became the center of action for all those who feared that power and wanted to subject it to public accountability. With the maturing of economic organization, however, many others have found themselves affected by corporate power, both as employees and in other capacities; and these people have slowly begun to articulate their own demands on that system. As that has happened, the position of labor unions in the political spectrum has changed significantly. No longer alone in challenging corporations, they have become only *one* among a galaxy of interest groups with different and often conflicting claims.

This new context, moreover, has done more than lessen the relative importance of the labor movement—it has overloaded the whole political compromise that had been reached between labor and the government. Labor had been the *first* associational group to lay a claim to state support. As long as there was only one, it was possible to justify that support within the framework of maintaining a balance of power. But since a host of new players has entered the game, that framework has become increasingly unwieldy.

The growing interest associations cannot rely purely on volunteer effort. They have turned to the government, as labor did in the 1930s, to provide the power needed to counter corporations effectively. We saw in chapter 3 how much difficulty the government had in finding a legitimate way of intervening in the single case of unions, how it struggled to *appear* low-key while in fact playing a very active role in the labor relations system. The same tension developed again during the 1970s in relation to the other interests, but this time the tension was magnified by the sheer number of claims the state was asked to enforce. The Wagner Act's direct intrusions on the managerial domain were minor compared to those of the Equal Employment Opportunity Commission or the Environmental Protection Agency (EPA). To bring the state's power to bear on the full range of issues raised by interest associations would require an unprecedented extension of government activity.

Declining Confidence in Organizations

There were signs of trouble from the very beginning. The rise of interest associations was closely linked to a dramatic decline in public confidence in the major organizations of society. Between 1959 and 1967 the percentage of people who saw "big government" as the greatest threat to the nation (according to Gallup polls) rose from 14 percent to nearly 50 percent. In the decade between 1965 and 1975, measures of public confidence in the leaders of the military, major companies, the executive branch, the Congress, and labor *all* declined by 50 percent or more, and they have stayed at that low level up to the present.[49] This shift in public opinion has been an extraordinary one, massive and unusually stable as polls go—and ominous for all the partners in the limited corporatist compromise.

The strains have crystallized in the attack on interest groups and on government regulation. This has been a prime source of the paralysis of the Democrats and the rise of Reaganism. Both political parties have agreed since the Carter years that government has overextended its regulatory grasp, that it has been overwhelmed by the competing claims of interest groups, and that it has failed to define the proper relation of public administration and private autonomy. The difference is that the Reagan administration has a relatively untroubled view of the solution—to largely do away with regulation. However, the Democrats, believing that there is still a need to provide the protections that historically have been afforded by government, are casting about confusedly for a new approach.[50] Their association with protection of interests put the Democrats in a serious bind in the 1984 election and made it doubtful whether increased support from the labor movement was more of a help than a liability.

The Democrats' uncertainty makes for bad politics, but it actually reflects the underlying ambivalence of public opinion more closely than the Republican solution. Surveys consistently reveal a strong pattern that seems at first sight paradoxical: the respondents support *regulation* of business, but they oppose *government* regulation. Here, for example, are two 1976 Harris survey questions about the proposal for a Consumer Protection Agency:

Adding another government bureaucracy, no matter how well intentioned, will lead to more red tape, spending more tax money, and won't give the consumer more protection.

Sixty-two percent agreed with that. The other question reads:

> Such an agency is long overdue, for the individual consumer needs help in making his complaints heard and in getting better quality and safer products and services.

Though this question seems to take the opposite position from the first, 60 percent agreed with it as well.[51] The difference is that the first question stresses the involvement of government, while the second focuses on the need for protection of the public.

A similar contradiction exists on the subject of interest groups. Polls show considerable support for groups like "consumer activists" and "environmental activists," but hostility to the involvement of government—and other big organizations—in enforcing these interests.[52] In the case of unions, one pair of national survey items highlights the pattern: between 1972 and 1976 the proportion who said unions have too much influence rose by 8 percent, but the proportion who said *workers* have too *little* influence also rose by a similar amount.[53]

There is only one way to make sense of these paradoxes of the polls. During the past twenty years there has been a decline in public support for large organizations in general and an increased sense of the need to protect individuals and associations from them. People (large majorities of people) do not trust business and see it as a self-interested and powerful bureaucracy.[54] But neither do they approve of setting up further large and powerful bureaucracies—government and labor—to control it. They increasingly see all of these organizations as a power clique that acts in its own self-interest rather than in the public interest.[55]

Philip Harter's critique of the "expert model of administration" defines the problem well:

> [The] process does not allow actual participation, in the sense of sharing in the ultimate decision, that normally provides the legitimacy for political decisions. Nor is there a political consensus that would cause the body politic to have faith in the integrity of the agency decision. . . . Thus there is a crisis of legitimation with regulation. . . . This crisis is apparent in the frequency of judicial review, in the frequency of criticism in publications of virtually all the interest groups, and from a simple inquiry of any participant.[56]

Unions have been caught up in these developments; whatever their own failings, they are also in the grip of forces beyond their control. Because they are large and bureaucratic, and because they are heavily dependent on support by the state, they are swept away in the general reaction against government regulation and bigness. In political terms, they are part of a wider problem. It may be cold comfort, but it is extremely significant that public confidence in other institutions has dropped nearly as much as that in unions; for it means that defining the problem merely from the perspective of the labor relations system misses the bigger picture. The government's special relation to labor is no longer justifiable; all the other interests want a similar cut, with the result that the whole unwieldy structure crumbles in a tangle of litigation and separate squabbles. What once seemed a politically reasonable way to increase worker influence now has become too hot to handle.

If that is accurate, then the hope of achieving direct political gains for unions—especially through labor law reform—is a slim one indeed. Labor law reform is, in effect, an attempt to strengthen unions by increasing the regulatory role of the government. But given the existence of many independent interest associations, every attempt by labor to strengthen its own position inevitably increases the hostility of the others, multiplies the conflicting demands on the state, and further damages the public perception of both labor and government. The only way out would be to restore simplicity to the picture by rebuilding a unified *coalition* of interests. But that coalition cannot be built simply around labor's agenda.

The basic issue appears to go far beyond any particular mistakes or strategies of the U.S. labor movement. Its depth is revealed by the fact that it is taking much the same form throughout Europe. Even in countries where the links between political parties and unions have been much stronger than in the United States, those ties have been weakening for the past decade. Social-Democratic parties (the European analogue of our Democratic party) are on the defensive almost everywhere, and—of still greater relevance—they are seeking to distance themselves from their labor allies. Unions, and in particular unions' political activities, fare at least as badly in opinion polls elsewhere as they do in this country. The legislative extensions of union rights in the 1960s and 1970s seem to have generated a lasting reaction.[57]

That leaves no simple solution, either to the immediate problems of the labor movement or to the larger problem of government policy. The Wagner Act, as we saw, was in part aimed at making private corporations responsive to the public good. The balance-of-power approach accomplished that in part but has turned out, it seems, to be a temporary solution. It was adequate to an earlier phase of corporate power but not to a more complicated situation in which many groups feel its effects. While it might be possible to maintain a balance of power among two or three organizations, it is quite impossible to do so among a large number of interest associations.

In that case, the fundamental political issue that underlay the Wagner Act debate—"whether the corporation is to rule the State or the State the corporation"—is thrown back into the policy arena, and the implications for a democratic order are as profound as they were in the 1930s. There are public claims on corporate power—not just from blue-collar workers, nor even just from employees, but now from many other groups as well—which are not being dealt with adequately within the present framework. The Reagan response, essentially opposed to both unions and regulation, represents a reaction against the previous decade's stumbling attempt to stretch the traditional framework to fit the new circumstances. But simply insisting once again on the private rights of corporations does not solve the problem of how to prevent private concentrations of power from overwhelming the public interest.

The Restrictive Role of Labor Law

What I have referred to as the "Wagner Act framework" seemed sensible under the conditions of the 1930s. Large corporations had called into being massive groups of production workers, like the physicists' image of action and reaction—it seemed natural to weld those masses into organized bodies that could face off with management on an equal level. The limitations of the balance of power, which I alluded to earlier—its brittle nature and the fact that it works only when there are few parties and high stability—were not central at that time.

The context of the Wagner Act by now has been transformed in every major aspect: in the essential nature of the economy, of the work force, and of public expectations of government. It should not be surprising that its institutions seem out of touch with current realities, just as the previous form of management has apparently lost its effectiveness. There are needs that are not being met: for effective representation of diverse white-collar employees; for increased strategic flexibility without bitter conflict or abuse of power; for a reduction of government's role as regulatory overseer; for recognition of the claims of multiple interests on management. All of these can be summarized in the need for a better way to build agreement. At present, conflicts are too often resolved by one-sided imposition of terms (generally by management or government) or by brittle and inflexible contract language that sustains mutual antagonism rather than by building commitment. Some sort of evolution is clearly needed to get beyond these limitations.

It is a final irony in this complex pattern of change, however, that while some unions and companies have been exploring different conceptions of worker participation, the Wagner Act itself has become more of a barrier to progress than a help. By the encrustation of later amendments and court interpretations, the legislation has hardened into a restrictive framework that fixes old principles rather than encouraging the exploration of new ones.

Until recently unions for the most part set limits on themselves. Gompers's contribution to strategy was to reject grand dreams of worker control, focusing around a sharply defined set of issues and tactics in the pursuit of visible goals. Industrial unions raised some new issues, but with few exceptions have continued to respect basic limits. They have avoided encroachment on broad matters of managerial strategy; they have rejected any drive for "codetermination"—representation on company boards or other top-level organs; and they have stuck closely to their base in the blue-collar working class.

The Wagner Act assumed this limited form of representation. In its original form, however, it did not for the most part enforce these restrictions: its language was vague and general. It is only in the past twenty years, as these limits have made less and less sense, that the courts and the NLRB have drawn the limits more precisely—effectively blocking or hindering many potentially constructive moves by the labor movement to expand the form of representation.

The first limitation has involved the *people* represented by unions. The line between management and workers, though traditionally respected, was not explicitly drawn in the Wagner Act. It began to enter the law only after a few groups of supervisors had unionized during World War II: the Taft-Hartley Act excluded them from protection by the NLRA. Nothing was said, however, about any other groups—including middle managers, technicians, indeed the whole world of semiprofessional workers.[58]

Nothing was said, that is, until the 1970s, when these categories had grown to a point at which they rendered the whole concept of a "line" irrelevant in many contexts. It was then that the Supreme Court insisted on drawing it more sharply and exclusively. It ruled in 1974 that the NLRA did not cover anyone who had the authority to "formulate and effectuate management policies by expressing and making operative the decisions of the employer."[59]

What that decision says, strictly speaking, is that any employee who has the discretion to *think* on the job, to use judgment in interpreting commands—anyone, that is, whose job has not been reduced to mindless routine—is excluded from the framework of representation. The resulting problems are most clearly highlighted by the Court's *Yeshiva* decision six years later.[60] Faculty members at a private university were ruled to be "managerial" because they operated in a collegial manner and could make effective recommendations to the administration regarding policy matters. One would think that the fact that they sought to unionize indicated that their influence was not entirely effective; however, the fact that salary schedules, tenure, teaching load, and fringe benefits were all determined at the administrative level was not sufficient for the Court.

The key point, however, is that the decision shows an inability to incorporate the role of professionals (or, for that matter, semiprofessionals), in the present system of worker representation. The Court argued that the very fact that professors exercise discretion and judgment means they cannot be permitted an *independent* basis of representation—it requires that they give their "undivided loyalty" to the administration of the school. It pretended, in other words, that a sharp line can be drawn between those who hold responsibility and those who do not. That line may have made practical sense in the mass production system, where a relatively small proportion of managers made a deliberate effort to remove all judgment from the shopfloor; it makes no sense in an economy that increasingly revolves around "knowledge work," or in industries in which every employee is expected to be creative and involved. Thus the decision narrows the range of the NLRA framework so far that it is unable to deal with the current changes in the economy.[61]

The second limitation of the labor relations order has been in the *tactics* used by unions. These have traditionally been restricted to an adversarial approach— with the proviso, as we saw in chapter 2, that much cooperation goes on "under the table." In recent years many unions have been pressured by their members and by employers to explore participatory programs that encourage workers to take responsibility for decision making. The *Yeshiva* decision, however, discourages this trend. The more workers gain a *direct* voice in determining their working conditions, the more likely they are to be considered managerial employees. Thus the decision reinforces the suspicions of union officials and tends to steer them back to traditional tactics.[62]

Even within the adversarial framework, the strength of unions has been limited by its foundation in the mass strike. We have seen that as economic forces encourage the substitution of flexible specialization for mass production, the strike becomes increasingly clumsy and ineffective. Unions could represent their members far more effectively, in many cases, by more subtle tactics: public relations campaigns, partial strikes that hit particularly vulnerable spots, brief strikes that catch the employer unawares, work slowdowns, or actions involving only small groups who are affected by a particular problem. All of these, however, have been prohibited or severely restricted by court decisions. Employees who criticize their companies in public lose their protection from dismissal because they have violated their obligation of "loyalty." Strikes during the term of a contract have been ruled out in most cases. Partial withdrawals of work are unprotected.[63] Almost the only remaining *legal* action within the present framework is, in fact, the mass strike at the expiration of the contract. This restriction continues to channel union activity away from needed innovations.

The third limitation is in the *issues* dealt with by the collective bargaining system. In the language of the Wagner Act the system was to deal with "rates of pay, wages, hours of employment, or other conditions of employment. . . ." Though that seems vague, it was grounded on the by-then solidly established position, expressed clearly by Gompers, that unions would leave strategic decisions to management and attempt to control only the consequences for workers.

We have seen that the growing importance of strategic flexibility in the modern economy has made this position increasingly difficult to sustain; by the time the effects are felt, it is too late to do anything about them. Furthermore, this approach fixes an adversarial relation, since unions carry no responsibility for the decisions they are contesting.

In recent years a few unions have sought to gain a voice in new areas, such as technological change and plant location, which have dramatic effects on their members. Though this would seem to be a necessary step for an effective system of representation, the legal system has discouraged the unions at every turn. It has done so by narrowing the scope of issues it imposes on the employer to provide information for and to bargain prior to acting. For a time it seemed that the law might expand to encompass the changed circumstances: in view of the fact, for example, that subcontracting was increasingly affecting workers' jobs, the Supreme Court moved that issue into the realm of mandatory subjects of bargaining in 1964.[64] That, however, was the high-water mark; subsequent decisions have tended the other way. The clearest instance is a 1981 decision that ruled that companies had no obligation to bargain—or even to provide advance notice of—the closure of part of their operations. Plant closings have, to say the least, a significant effect on workers' "conditions of employment"; but the Court's position was that "the harm likely to be done to an employer's need to operate freely in deciding whether to shut down part of his business for purely economic reasons outweighs the incremental benefit that might be gained through the union's participation in making the decision."[65] Once again the line drawn by the Court reflects practices that once made sense, but in the present circumstances it amounts to reducing the NLRA framework to a purely marginal status, ineffective in representing workers in the most important issues of the day.

This paradox—the "hardening" of the Wagner Act just as flexibility and change are urgently called for—reflects a state of confusion. There is general agreement that the law is not working, but no agreement at all on a vision for shaping it to the new circumstances. As the consensus that created the Wagner Act has disintegrated, the only remaining consensus, even among labor's friends, is that it is better to hold onto it than to plunge into an unknown void. This is a brittle and defensive stance, and it leads to the separation of law from reality.

In effect, the NLRA has been reduced to a shell. The Wagner Act built that shell around a living labor movement, following its contours but protecting it from employer attacks. The initial plausibility of Wagner's logic stemmed precisely from the fact that the act stayed close to the social movements that produced it. But as the needs for employee representation have changed, the focus has remained on the shell rather than on the living form within. The labor relations order has become increasingly opaque, understandable only to its practitioners. The result, finally, is that most workers are no longer adequately represented.

The view embodied in the efforts at labor law reform—that the only need is for a *strengthening* of the shell—ignores the changes that have gone on around and within it. Though the Wagner Act framework does remain vital for the protection of the most disadvantaged workers, including white-collar employees experiencing deskilling and lowered pay, it is now too narrow to mobilize wide support. Fundamental changes in the political coalition that produced the original act have made it unlikely that its framework can be further extended. Even if that could be done, it would still fail to meet the economic and social needs of large sectors of the work force; for the decline of mass production and the rise of a large semiprofessional sector with associational solidarities have undercut the original assumptions. Finally, the NLRA has proved too limited to serve the purpose of bringing the private power of employers under public accountability. For all these reasons, more is needed than better enforcement of existing law; there is need for significant changes in the scope and shape of the system of representation.

PART II

EXPLORATIONS:
NEW FORMS OF
ORGANIZATION AND
REPRESENTATION

CHAPTER 5

Managerialism:
Participation
Without Unions?

ONE OF the clearest indications of the depth of change today is the profound transformation taking place in management structures and practices. The upheaval in major corporations both demonstrates the importance of new economic and social forces and indicates, at least in outline, a coherent response. That response, which I will call "managerialism," strikes at the very heart of the Wagner Act framework, for it involves extensive worker participation in decision making, a major change in the strict bureaucratic control established by Taylor's "Scientific Management"—but without the involvement of independent union representatives. It proposes that *every* employee be a manager, involved in decisions and contributing intelligently to the goals of the corporation.

The origins of this movement can be traced back to the early 1960s, when systematic efforts began with the aim of making jobs more interesting. These early experiments, under the name of "job enlargement," were aimed at combating the boredom felt by workers in highly fragmented, routinized jobs. They consisted in putting back together some of the pieces that had been cut apart by the analytic thrust of Scientific Management. In the ensuing twenty-five years this has been followed by a series of increasingly ambitious experiments in worker involvement: first "job enrichment," which added responsibility as well as variety to work; then problem-solving groups, which gave workers a forum for discussing significant changes in their work environment; and most recently, semiautonomous work teams, in which groups of workers have direct responsibility for implementing their own work schedules, distribution of tasks, and even hiring and discipline.[1]

All of these efforts involved sharp attacks on accepted premises of job design. The assumption of Scientific Management was that, given any freedom, workers would shirk; therefore that approach stressed above all the importance of control. The theorists of worker involvement, by contrast, argued that the *motivational* costs of Scientific Management in practice undercut the possibility of control. Workers who were bored and alienated, they said, simply could not be watched closely enough to make them perform at their capacity. By making the job more interesting, they hoped to *engage* the workers actively in the production process.

In order to reach such a state of engagement, these efforts stressed positive motivations—"achievement," "responsibility," and "advancement."[2] But these "motivational" factors are not merely ignored by Scientific Management; they contradict the basic paradigm. If employees are to be motivated by a desire for advancement, they cannot be treated as a class separate from management. If they have responsibility, they cannot be closely controlled and measured; they must be *trusted* to use their responsibility in the interests of the company. And the experimental programs proved that given the chance, most workers welcomed the opportunity to use their autonomy in the service of management goals, thus undercutting the foundation of suspicion on which Taylorism had been built.

At the same time, however, the efforts threatened many managers and stirred much resistance. Job enrichment cut deeply into supervisors' jobs, blurring the formerly sharp distinction between workers and management; autonomous teams now could all but eliminate supervisors. As the scope of the programs increased, other middle managers also began to worry about a loss of power and to create obstacles to the extension of participation. Finally, unions grew increasingly concerned about the potential for creating conflicting loyalties among their membership. A shopfloor problem-solving group clearly comes uncomfortably close to the functions of a union—especially when workers, in modifying Taylorist structures, begin to discuss work practices that have been enshrined in the contract. A few far-seeing labor leaders, as we shall see in the next chapter, tried to develop a positive union approach to the programs. The vast majority, however, showed their discomfort by either openly opposing or, at best, trying to ignore what was going on.

Given these strains, the experiments in employee involvement were on the whole only partially successful. Over time a clear and curious pattern emerged. Something would be tried—job enrichment, for example; a spate of success stories would emerge, showing that both satisfaction and productivity rose with the change.[3] Then, somehow, without any clear "failure" or dramatic problems, the effort would wither away. Analysts would suggest that the lack of fit between the experiment and the larger organization had blocked further development.

But the most peculiar aspect of the pattern is that the repeated demise of particular efforts never slowed the *general* enthusiasm for employee involvement. Indeed, in each instance the movement arose phoenixlike, in a stronger and more inclusive form. The succession from job enlargement to job enrichment to problem-solving groups to autonomous teams has steadily increased the responsibility of workers. The latest autonomous team plants come close to completing the trend: they may have a hundred workers with only two or three "managers" per shift, whose duties are primarily advisory. Again and again apparent failure has only spurred further experimentation. This paradoxical pattern of development indicates that the experiments reflect deep organizational needs.

As this evolution has continued, similar developments have been occurring within the ranks of management. As a rule, the highest levels of large companies have always operated in a relatively flexible manner, relying heavily on teamwork and persuasion. The degree of bureaucratization—the use of formal procedures and hierarchies—increases as one moves down most companies, until it reaches the extreme formality of Scientific Management on the shopfloor. But since the 1950s a growing industry of "organization development" consultants has been spreading the concept of teamwork gradually downward. One popular structural change, for example, has been the "matrix organization," which encourages dual lines of authority, decentralization of decision making, and flexible task forces.[4] The conceptual congruence with shopfloor teams and discussion groups is clear in retrospect; but throughout the 1960s and 1970s developments on the two levels proceeded almost entirely independently.

All these strands, however, have been brought together at last in the newest labeled movement: the "corporate culture" phenomenon. William Ouchi's *Theory Z* made the best-seller list in 1981 with the claim that the key to effective organization was the formulation and communication of clear values that draw on the commitment of all employees. Like many writers at the time, he was influenced by the experience of the Japanese, who were impressing American business with their penetration of many of our traditional markets. Ouchi found that Japanese organizations stress employee involvement and consensus to a degree that is rare in the United States and seem, in that way, to have generated tremendous internal creativity.[5]

As corporations have picked up the "culture" idea, they have often found that elements of a strong, involving culture are already in place in their organizations, in the form of various programs of job enrichment, group problem solving, teamwork, matrix structuring, and so on. Xerox, for example, having turned to Japan for a model of high-commitment organization, noticed belatedly that a worker participation program for years had been developing the same principles in its Rochester plant. The corporate culture movement pushes the scattered programs of the past two decades beyond the status of isolated experiments, clearly raising the problem of their relation to the whole organization. And it reveals that these disparate efforts have shared a common thrust: they have all aimed to decrease the emphasis on hierarchy and power and to increase variety and initiative at lower levels of organizations. Thus events that seemed to many at the time a succession of fads show an extraordinary coherence in retrospect.

What is behind this long-run change? The answer is more complicated than it might seem. In the early days of this story—through the 1960s and early 1970s—many writers argued that the work ethic of Americans was declining as education and wealth increased and that new techniques were necessary in order to revive it. The trouble was, however, that studies showed no such decline. Objective data on behavior—quit rates, absenteeism, unauthorized strikes—showed no upward trend during this period; and while job satisfaction showed a very mild decline in the late 1970s, it still remained high by historical standards, and it appears to have rebounded since. There is every indication, furthermore, that the importance of "hard work" as a primary value remains as high as ever throughout the work force.[6]

It has become clear only in the last few years that the real problem is not the decline of the old work ethic but the need for a new one. Companies have, in effect, *increased* the demands on employee motivation. Frederick Taylor sought mere obedience to rules. Managers today seek active involvement and creative input. The key issue is not satisfaction, but positive commitment. To use the common jargon, the aim is to have people work "not harder, but smarter."

The problem is sharpened by the growing importance of "knowledge work" and the need for frequent and rapid innovation to meet international competition. Both of these factors reduce the value of routine effort and put a premium on the ability to mobilize active cooperation at all levels. It is from this higher standard that Daniel Yankelovich's survey findings of a "widespread commitment gap" are cause for especially serious concern.[7]

Getting mere obedience was difficult during the early 1900s—when violent resistance to the assembly line was not uncommon—but the problem was solved by the gradual perfection of bureaucratic management. Getting the extra measure of commitment is just as difficult now, and the problem is still being worked through. What is clear is that techniques based on *power*—on clear order and strict hierarchy—do not work for the new task.

Managerialism: Participation Without Unions?

An internal document from a major telecommunications company expresses these issues clearly:

> As the issue of employee commitment in an organization is examined, there are two types of commitment perceived. First, the organization defines the minimum amount of effort (or commitment) which is required to avoid being fired or penalized. The feeling organizationally is that there is a benefit to be derived by establishing a corporate culture and climate which will initiate a second "above minimum" commitment. This commitment, known as discretionary effort, is the difference between the minimum expectation set by the organization, and the maximum amount of effort and care an individual *could bring* to the job. . . .
>
> We are looking for the key to the "hidden productivity" in [our] work force, both management and craft. We need to find a formula which, when applied, will result in a work force excited about, involved in, and committed to the strategies involved in our current corporate direction. We need a clue to the commitment phenomenon. . . .
>
> Organizational structure which supports an authority-driven environment tends to reflect the perception that job holders are less central to the success of the organization than their respective managers. This sense of "stratification" of the work force [is an] organizational inhibitor to employee commitment. . . .
>
> This proposal is a major move toward fundamentally changing the existing culture of this organization.[8]

Such concerns have not, of course, affected all companies equally. The vast majority of them, especially smaller and older ones, have hardly been touched by it. But by now it has deeply penetrated the leading sectors of the economy. A 1982 survey by the New York Stock Exchange found that more than 25 percent of the large corporations listed on the exchange had initiated programs that involved (by their own account) a "shift in their basic approach to management."[9] The language of "teamwork," "participation," and "commitment" is now thoroughly embedded in the culture of management. That language embraces many cases of mere rhetoric but also much real and significant change; by now it seems clear that it indicates a direction of movement.

No single company, as I have stressed, serves as a perfect example of a new model. All of them, to one degree or another, are struggling to develop new systems from old habits and traditions. Companies that are frequently taken as exemplars of the new direction include Procter and Gamble, Honeywell, Hewlett-Packard, Motorola, Intel, Digital Equipment, and Westinghouse—a veritable "Who's Who" of dynamic corporate organizations. Another group, including IBM, General Electric, Xerox, AT&T, and General Motors, is more mixed; these firms are developing many elements of a new structure within traditional frameworks. It is by piecing together these examples that we can construct a picture of the broad direction of change.[10]

Managerialism: Beyond Bureaucracy and Paternalism

Some critics deny that there is any real substance to these changes, viewing them as nothing more than management attempts to destroy independent worker representation. Such skepticism is not without foundation. This is not the first time that corporations have tried to develop their own forms of worker participation and to bypass organized labor. During the 1920s, in particular, a movement known as "Welfare Capitalism" promised to provide security and fair treatment through "company unions." By 1933, 45 percent of workers in mining and manufacturing were represented by such bodies.[11]

Company unions varied tremendously in their structures and their intentions. Some of them appear to have been serious and quite effective systems of representation. In a number of cases they sustained high levels of security and responsiveness deep into the depression, often taking deep cuts in profits to do so.[12] But it is also clear that they were vulnerable to manipulation. The drive for independent unionism gained considerable momentum from instances in which companies tried to provide a façade of representation without the substance.

Much the same can be said about current moves toward worker participation. They range widely, from shallow gimmicks to deep changes in policy and structure. In the midst of such a fluid situation, it is difficult to disentangle the essential nature of the changes. Specific instances can be cited to support almost any position, including the point that new forms of worker participation can be used as a warmed-over type of disguised management control.

But the developments in management organization in the past twenty years have been much too extensive to explain merely in terms of union busting. Team-based systems and new forms of employee involvement have been far from an easy way out of independent unionism—they have required a great deal of reorganization and experimentation, and they have faced major resistance from within management itself. At no time during that period have unions been a powerful enough threat to account for such radical behavior, nor has worker behavior (as measured in quit rates or absenteeism) changed so as to force this kind of reassessment.

The spread of worker participation can, in fact, only be understood as part of a wider process of change. I have already referred to the profound economic shifts that are forcing movement toward more flexible and "strategic" management systems. Those systems require fundamentally new principles and approaches. Though there have been many distortions and failures, the direction of movement has been consistent: from a system based on formal hierarchies of command—or bureaucracy—toward one based on coordinated networks of teams.

Bureaucracy was in its time a great social advance, an invention that unleashed unimagined economic power and made possible the coordination of resources on a scale never before achieved. It works by formalizing relations. An organization driven by personal whims cannot carry out very large projects, because it lacks the predictability needed to sustain a plan. The organizational revolution of the first part of this century—carried out by such men as Alfred Sloan and Pierre du Pont—therefore cut into the autonomous powers of supervisors, which previously had divided corporations into warring fiefdoms, subjecting everyone to the rule of the "organization chart." It built in stability of expectations through regular promotion systems, clear job descriptions, and single lines of responsibility.[13]

In an important sense, bureaucracy represented not only a new level of social power but also, from the point of view of workers, a liberation from the whim of capricious rulers. It marked the triumph of rationality over autocracy. Management's need for predictability, in large organizations, required limits on its own behavior: it had to submit to the law of formal rules and procedures. Thus workers received, in return for their loyalty, guarantees of impartial and fair treatment. Frederick Taylor, the apostle of Scientific Management, always stressed that everyone benefited from the application of objective, scientific standards. In an era when supervisors were often petty tyrants, that argument made sense even to workers and their unions.[14]

The Welfare Capitalism of the 1920s was part of this general move toward bureaucracy. It was centered in the new, large, mass-production corporations, and it went hand in hand with the spread of Scientific Management. It was "paternalist," however, in the sense that it only went part way: it tried to build loyalty and stability without *guarantees* and to achieve the benefits of bureaucracy without the reciprocal protections and rights that are needed to stabilize it.

From the point of view of those in charge, paternalism is always a tempting form of government; it enables them to command the changes they think best with very few restrictions. The only cost is the possibility of revolt—a danger they often attempt to fend off with direct benefits and shows of concern for their "subjects." Management's efforts in the 1920s did not, however, long forestall the "revolution" by industrial unions. As we saw, unionization was a key mechanism by which bureaucratic order was finally stabilized in corporate organizations.

It seems clear that a paternalist impulse is also a part of the movement going on today. Faced with increasing pressures from foreign competition, shaken by rapid changes in technologies and markets, many executives would like to consolidate their power in order to respond rapidly. They want to be able to command and to make things happen. Unions, government regulations, and employee rights are all so many obstacles in the way of swift action. The revival of company benefit plans and employee communications mechanisms, from this perspective, is once again a way of maintaining employees' willingness to carry out orders without protest. This aspect of corporate reform is an effort to return to something old, rather than the invention of something new.

But that description comes very far from encompassing the developments in many large corporations. Peter Drucker, the dean of corporate consultants, is also an eloquent spokesman against paternalism: "The important fact about 'enlightened despotism'—also the one fact that 'enlightened despots' always forget—is that while it appears as enlightenment to those in power, it is despotism pure and simple to those under it."[15] No representative of unions or workers could have put it more clearly.

What, then, are Drucker and other managerial reformers driving at? Far from advocating increased centralization of power, they stress the importance of "pushing decision making down" in the organization. Rather than tightening structures of control, they seek to increase individual autonomy. And most significantly, they return frequently to the metaphor of "entrepreneurship," seeking to increase creativity *within* the organization, not merely *by* the organization.

The implication of these theories is that paternalism and bureaucracy have reached their limits.[16] Those types of organization produced a quantum leap in social innovation by overcoming the restrictions of traditional values. But the innovations came from one place only—from the top, managerial corps. The rest of the organization existed to carry out the decisions made by these leaders, routinely carrying out standard operating procedures. This distinction between initiative and execution was, in fact, the foundation of Taylorism and was the basis of the "line" that delimited the body of union-represented employees. What is being suggested by the new reforms is precisely that this level of innovation is insufficient: "In most work environments," says Alden Raymond, a vice president of United Telecommunications, Inc., "standard operating procedures are . . . an obstacle placed in the path of workers who are trying to be productive. It seems that processes which are designed to protect the organization from stupidity also restrict the organization from intelligent responses from intelligent people."[17] The president of Intel Corporation adds: "I can't pretend to know the shape of the next generation of . . . technology anymore. That's why people like me need the knowledge from the people closest to the technology. That's why we can't have the hierarchical barriers to an exchange of ideas and information that you have at so many corporations."[18]

Managerialist Organization:
Toward Coordinated Independence

Managerialism is different from bureaucracy, whether in the paternalist or in the unionized version. The differences can be glimpsed in the extraordinary degree of social inventiveness that has characterized these developments. Take, for example, decision making by committee. It was not long ago that committees were the common butt of jokes—they were said to produce camels, and so on. It was thought that such joint decision making diluted responsibility and sowed organizational confusion. Yet today in large corporations committees and task forces are normal and vital in day-to-day decision making. The transformation has been brought about by a large amount of concentrated learning. More is known today than ever before about the techniques of running meetings and about the conditions that make them productive. Training programs have been devised to teach these skills rapidly to all levels of an organization. The effective task force has only recently become a reproducible, reliable element of successful organizations.

Or consider the issue of organizational structure. When corporations grew to unheard-of sizes in the early years of this century, it was thought that the only way to manage them was to establish very detailed and unambiguous lines of authority. The familiar organization chart, spreading down in an orderly network from the top, was the pictorial representation of this necessary clarity. That picture, while never completely representing reality, is by now completely inaccurate as a description of many large organizations. Their forms are continuously shifting.

The number of major reorganizations of very large systems is staggering; for example, the transformation of AT&T from a million-employee telecommunications company to eight or ten (depending on how you count) multi-product companies in less than two years would have been quite impossible in a purely bureaucratic format. That transition, along with several other major ones in the decade before it, was largely accomplished by using shifting, temporary task forces at many levels, which cut across established boundaries and constituted their authority "on the fly." The confidence of the corporation's leaders that the change could be pulled off shows how much has been learned about the use of these mechanisms.

Even in calmer times, when no overall transformation is under way, the structures of decision making in these companies are far more fluid than those of the bureaucratic model. T.J. Peters and R.H. Waterman summarize their research on highly successful American companies in this way:

> . . . we find the excellent companies quite flexible in responding to fast-changing conditions in the environment . . . [T]hey can make better use of small divisions or other small units. They can reorganize more flexibly, frequently, and fluidly. And they can make better use of temporary forms, such as task forces and project centers.[19]

These are the pieces that have been worked out through a slow process of trial and error over the last three decades or so. It has been convincingly shown that fluid, team-based decision making is an extremely effective way to generate innovative activity. The overall shape of the emerging structure of managerialism, however, is only beginning to emerge from the detailed experiments. In the past few years a new image has been brought into focus that breaks radically with the controlled hierarchy of Taylorism.

Judging by the best-seller status of their work, Peters and Waterman's metaphors have clearly struck a responsive chord in many managements. They begin with an unsparing attack on the "rational model," which they associate with Taylor—they call it "conservative," "heartless," "negative." To describe their alternative vision—which, they say, already characterizes many of our most effective companies—they use words like "informality," "management by wandering around," the "absence of a rigidly followed chain of command," "smallness," "value-driven," "entrepreneurial," "experimental." The simplest image I have seen, however, comes not from a social scientist or a consultant but from the Swedish Employers' Federation (SAF). The key to production under the new economic system, they say, is organization based on "coordinated independence of small groups."[20]

This is an extraordinary notion—independence with coordination. We usually assume, almost unconsciously, that independence means fragmentation, and that the only way to coordinate people is to subject them to a hierarchy of command. But the reality is that increasingly the job of management is to coordinate those whom they *cannot* command. Recent trends, as John Kotter of the Harvard Business School puts it,

> are making [managers] more and more dependent on government officials, technical experts, key subordinates, other departments in their firms, key customers, important suppliers, major unions, the business press, and so forth without automatically giving them additional ways to control these groups. As a result, they are turning . . . management jobs into leadership jobs—jobs in which there is a sizeable built-in gap between the power one needs to get the job done well and the power that automatically comes with the job.[21]

Coordinated independence is not only necessary for the structuring of such nonhierarchical relationships; it is also capable of producing enormous social energy. If it works, it will represent the most important social invention since the development of bureaucracy, making far more effective use of creativity and commitment at all levels of an organization. It promises to unlock a huge reservoir of potential that has lain dormant within large organizations until now. Those who are trying to manage complex organizations in today's climate are intensely aware of the need to mobilize that potential.

The pieces of this organizational change can be fitted into a logical pattern. Change itself, of course, is not logical—it happens in scattered and inconsistent ways. No company can be taken as a perfect exemplar of managerialism. Yet there is a value to bringing out the pattern underlying the confused surface of events by restating the change in more abstract terms, as an "ideal type" description of an emerging system.

In these ideal-type terms, bureaucracy is driven by the need for stability; managerialism, by the need for flexibility. From employees, bureaucracy requires obedience and, if possible, loyalty; managerialism requires creativity and commitment. Finally, the organizing principle of bureaucracy is *command;* of managerialism, *coordination* of diverse and autonomous units. If innovation can come from any part of the system, the problem is to get all the pieces working in the same general direction.

Though managerialism resembles paternalism in being, generally speaking, a nonunion structure, there are clear differences between the two. Paternalism retains the power hierarchy characteristic of bureaucracy, merely overlaying it with improved benefits and other indications of "concern." Managerialism fractures the power hierarchy in very clear ways, replacing it with shifting teams, matrices, and other decentralized forms. Paternalism seeks to improve the effectiveness of commands by ensuring that people will enthusiastically obey and put forth maximum effort. Managerialism tries to draw out the special knowledge of each member as a contribution to the collective direction.

One central element in managerialism is the development of a shared "culture," or corporate value system. In a command-driven system values are less important, since most actions below the top levels involve carrying out routine procedures. When innovation at the bottom is encouraged, however, it becomes essential to define the general *principles* needed to organize the diversity. Hence the sudden growth of corporate value statements.

This aspect is the source of some of the strongest emotions that have been aroused by managerialism. Our society retains a deep suspicion of social values from its historical struggles against religious oppression. The right to believe in whatever we please is one of our most cherished freedoms. We tend to emphasize impersonal and rational rules because they protect us from arbitrary uses of personal power. Thus any attempt to build shared values arouses suspicion. On the other hand, there seems to be an equally deep social longing for the sense of community that has been shattered by bureaucracy, a longing that creates an unresolved tension in many of our institutions.[22]

Both managerialism and paternalism tend to use notions of "family" and "community" in their attempts to build unity. There is a difference, however—at least in concept—between the managerialist's notion of community and the paternalist's. It is often a subtle distinction, but its implications are vast.

In paternalism, community is diffuse and encompassing, laying claims on an employee's whole life and soul—the company town is the symbol of this kind of tyranny. In managerialism, community is focused around the cooperation needed to accomplish the task. It depends, in other words, not on diffuse traditional solidarity, but on the kind of associational solidarity described in the last chapter—a relatively concrete and rational perception of common interests and shared goals.

In paternalism, shared values are an "add-on." The system is able to function without them, as long as the procedures are clear; a common sense of purpose merely adds an extra measure of effort. The managerialist system, on the other hand, does not work at all without such overarching unity. Peters and Waterman, as well as Ouchi before them, show that a clear set of principles provides an essential framework to steady a system that is otherwise shifting and flexible. Thomas Watson, Jr., former head of IBM, expressed this point clearly: "I firmly believe that any organization, in order to survive and achieve success, must have a sound set of beliefs on which it premises all its policies and actions. . . . And . . . I believe if an organization is to meet the challenge of a changing world, it must be prepared to change everything about itself except those beliefs."[23]

In short, managerialism proposes to unite social elements that so far have been at opposite poles: community and change, shared values, and individual freedom. No wonder it arouses such strong emotions, both enthusiasm and mistrust, among observers.

The role of power is another organizational element that is radically transformed in the emerging system. Bureaucracy is essentially an order built on commands, which paternalism tempers with soft words. Alfred Sloan's description of his style touches on these different versions of power: "I never minimized the administrative power of the chief executive officer when I occupied that position. I simply exercised that power with discretion; I got better results by selling my ideas than by telling them what to do."[24]

But within managerialism, the aim is not to impose ideas from the top, whether by "telling" or "selling." Organization leaders do not want mere obedience; from this perspective, even the most enthusiastic yea-sayer is a drag on performance. Leaders want and need *active contribution of knowledge* from those people who are "experts" about a given problem. That cannot be done with power—it requires the use of influence.

Managerialism: Participation Without Unions?

In chapter 2 I defined influence as the ability to persuade, as opposed to the ability to command. The use of influence, when effective, enables groups to remain independent while pooling their knowledge and skills in a common enterprise, each contributing knowledge rather than mere obedience. It is not an easy thing to achieve. Some people seem to have a gift for inspiring this kind of coordinated teamwork; we call them natural leaders. But an organization cannot rely on gifts. It has to create an order in which the conditions of effective influence can reliably be found and reproduced. All the innovations we have reviewed so far—the development of effective team-building methods, the techniques of value clarification, the changes in well-known hierarchical lines of authority—can be summarized as ways of increasing the amount of influence in an organization. They all run counter to the effective use of mere power (a fact that naturally creates a great deal of resistance among old-line managers), for it is clear that the use of power interferes with the free exchange of knowledge. Finally, these innovations all help people make effective use of their expertise, improve communication channels, and reward effective cooperation.

Managerialism and Unions

It should not be surprising that such a dramatic shift in the nature of organization should throw into question the system of worker representation that was developed in bureaucratic settings. In fact, the companies that come closest to the managerialist model generally are openly antiunion. In a few cases—General Motors and Ford being perhaps the most visible—managerialist reforms continue in a strongly unionized setting, but in those cases the reforms have generally begun outside the standard labor-management relationship and conflict with it to a large degree.[25] They cannot proceed far without significant changes in the union, in the whole structure of labor relations, and in management. Thus most companies that have taken the managerialist direction have systematically sought to avoid unionization.

The reason for this attitude does not appear to be a simple desire to cut costs; these companies almost always pay at or above the prevailing union rates. Nor does it seem to be the paternalist motive of clearing out obstacles to the use of management power; managerialist companies seem to use arbitrary force infrequently, perhaps less often than do unionized companies. Even most labor organizers will admit that these corporations are nearly impossible to crack, not primarily because they use coercive and illegal tactics, but because their employees have few reasons to rebel.[26]

Managerialist companies are antiunion because unions by their nature are organizations that oppose power with power, whereas the relationships in a managerialist company, in principle, are of a quite different sort. The logic of power requires that workers be *separated* from management. Taylor drew the line between the two groups by distinguishing those who conceive from those who execute. Management built up a wall based upon this distinction in which every aspect of work emphasized the difference. "Workers" were paid by the hour, "managers" by a set salary; workers wore blue collars, parked farthest away from the plant, used a separate entrance, and had their own cafeteria. Each of these elements reinforced the sense of solidarity that enabled unions to mobilize countervailing power effectively.

The increased use of influence in a managerialist company requires first and foremost the elimination of this "line." After all, what defines its structure is that every employee is seen as a manager. Thus the whole system of symbols is revised—in managerialist companies it is common for *all* employees to be paid a salary rather than an hourly wage, and to share the same set of benefits. The special management privileges of parking lots and cafeterias are often eliminated. Furthermore, these symbolic changes reflect a real transformation in relationships: workers are responsible for "managing" their jobs; they perform specific activities such as scheduling and planning, which had always been the prerogative of management; they may be brought onto task forces in which they function as equals with their bosses.

These changes back unions into a corner. The irony is that after World War I unions fought bitterly against the introduction of Taylorist deskilling, which threatened their craft-based autonomy; but now, as management finally begins a real move away from Taylorism, unions find themselves defending it. The elimination of narrow job definitions and close controls is seen through this distorted lens as a "giveback" to management—an abandonment of hard-won union gains.

There is, of course, good reason for these fears. Unions have succeeded in defending themselves against abuses of management power only by clarifying and by making explicit the rules of Scientific Management. Dismantling the rules increases the potential for abuse of power. However, there is also potential of a different sort, for a new system of worker representation that recognizes a broader spectrum of workers' needs.

That system, as it is emerging in the managerialist firms, has these basic characteristics:[27]

- *An enormous expansion of channels by which employees can voice their concerns, especially about job-related matters.* These channels include not only the aforementioned team structures and task forces, but also an array of suggestion systems, open doors, opinion surveys, and communications sessions. At BankAmerica, for example, there are three separate formal systems that give workers a chance to voice their concerns. First, "Employee Assistance Officers"—also called ombudspersons at some companies—can receive any individual's complaints on a confidential basis and attempt to work out solutions with the appropriate managers, with or without the open involvement of the complainant. Second, there is a standard grievance mechanism, with a serious attempt to bring in impartial third parties as final judges. Third, an "open line" system is available for issues related to company policies; again, protection of confidentiality is assured.

- *Considerable protection against arbitrary power.* There is an understanding that influence cannot function if people are afraid to speak out. Thus personnel departments in these companies tend to be quite strong and independent and to form a quasi union that actively represents employees in grievances against their bosses. There is ordinarily a clear code of due process, regular job posting and bidding, and a strong emphasis on avoiding discrimination.
- *Relatively high job security, to reduce the ultimate fear that always hangs over employees.* Many of these companies avoid layoffs quite successfully by maintaining effective transfer policies and using job-sharing in emergencies. IBM and Hewlett-Packard, among others, have had lifetime employment policies for years. Motorola is one of the more recent companies to adopt this approach. During the 1981–82 recession, the company decided that layoffs would be too costly in terms of retraining and the disruption of trust. At some plants, instead of laying people off, the company placed all employees on a four-day work week and helped them make up much of the loss in wages with unemployment insurance and other mechanisms.
- *Encouragement of career development and movement within the company,* to reduce the hardening of "lines" and habits. These companies are among the leaders in internal training efforts. A 1985 IBM advertisement reads:

    Over the years, we've retrained thousands of our employees by offering them the opportunity to learn new skills.

    People who worked in supplies manufacturing are now senior assemblers. Customer engineers have been retrained as education coordinators. Machine operators have become senior inspection specialists.

    Retraining has shown us how a company and its employees can change together in a changing world. Above all, it has shown us that jobs may come and go.

    But people shouldn't.[28]

Some of these mechanisms reproduce the role of unions by controlling abuses of power. Others, however, go beyond anything that unions have traditionally been able to do. The union-based system of representation, for instance, has never been able to expand the channels by means of which workers can have a voice— indeed, as we have seen, it has generally been hostile to direct participation. Nor has it encouraged career movement that might take people across the boundaries of the bargaining unit. At its best, then, the managerialist order offers genuine improvements in the situation of employees as well as in the effectiveness of the organization. Indeed, the two are indissolubly linked: the effective coordination of independent expertise depends on a much higher level of security and trust than is found in a bureaucracy.

The traditional assumptions of a unionized order are well expressed by a recent *Harvard Business Review* article, which makes "the case for adversarial unions":

> Management *always* seeks to . . . exert greater control of the work force. . . . To management, a rapidly increasing productivity rate means improving profits; to workers, it means the loss of jobs. To management, an increasingly tough standard of discipline means improving profits; to workers, it means that the workplace can become more like a prison than a shop or an office. To management, a declining cost from reduced wages and benefits means improving profits; to workers, it means a declining standard of living.[29]

Within a bureaucratic firm, those equations are accurate, and they form the framework for the growth of unionism. The experiments and innovations that have produced the vision of managerialism, however, dissolve these patterns. From this perspective, which has been put into practice by a large number of tough-minded managers, strict discipline does not mean improving profits—it kills the spirit of creativity and cooperation on which profits are based. Increased productivity calls not for layoffs but for opening new product lines and retraining existing workers to fill the new positions. And reducing wages produces only short-run gains while destroying the fabric of managerialism, which is more profitable in the long run. Therefore, managerialist companies such as IBM or Motorola, despite their nonunion status, do *not* use close supervision, do *not* often deprive people of work, and do *not* pay below-average wages and benefits. That is the problem unions must face: it is a challenge for them to create a better system.

The Limitations of Managerialism

Managerialism is a real change in corporate organization, but it is still incomplete. It is not widely understood and accepted; neither employees nor society know quite what to expect from these changes. The companies that are developing this form have to create their own systems of values and expectations, usually in the face of substantial resistance that is based on the habits of bureaucracy. Many of the specific techniques and pieces, moreover, such as the process of "cultural" change, are only now being defined and explored. In practice, therefore, managerialism remains vulnerable to many forms of distortion and confusion.

This is certainly true in terms of the system of employee representation.

Managerialism: Participation Without Unions?

Managerialism has essentially rejected the Wagner Act structure, with its emphasis on formal bilateral bargaining. Most managerialist companies, as I have said, prefer to do without unions altogether, and even those that are heavily unionized are struggling to transform the nature of unionism to fit the new system. However, they have not yet gone far enough to establish a new form of independent representation.

Standard industrial unionism, with its emphasis on the division between managers and workers and its focus on rules, is probably not the right form of independent voice for the managerialist system. But the failure so far to find a replacement constitutes a limitation of that system. It is true that much innovation can and has taken place on a unilateral basis. The development of autonomous teams, for instance, greatly expands the ability of employees to shape their own working conditions without the constant intervention of industrial engineers. It is also true that a few companies have set up strong internal systems to deal with conflicts and grievances. But without independence, these systems remain unusual and fragile, subject to many forms of distortion ranging from gross manipulation to subtle self-deception.

The practical problems fall into three general categories. First, there are many ways in which the language of managerialism—communication, participation, decentralization—can be used merely to strengthen the power of management rather than to produce real changes. Second, even genuine attempts to develop participation and influence can easily misfire by failing to understand the real needs of employees. Third, there are things no one company can do alone— boundary problems that involve support from "outside," and therefore require some form of representation that goes beyond the firm.

Disguised Uses of Power

First, a great deal of fakery passes under the banner of reform. Michael Maccoby, a well-known consultant and author, tells of a visit to a plant that presented itself as a model of teamwork and good relations. A few conversations with workers on the shopfloor, however, quickly convinced him that all was not as management had pictured it. When he returned to meet with the plant manager, the conversation went something like this:

MACCOBY: I think there's a problem of communication in this plant.
MANAGER: I know there's a problem of communication. I try communicating with them every way I know how, and nothing works.
MACCOBY: No, I mean two-way communication.
MANAGER: That's what I mean, two-way. I use memos, and I use speeches, but they still won't listen.

That just shows that the spirit of paternalism is still abroad in the land. Beneath the language of "communication," this manager clearly holds to the bureaucratic concept of issuing commands, rather than the managerialist system of coordinating varied expertise.

There are also slightly less obvious cases of manipulation. A colleague of mine recently interviewed the employees at a manufacturing plant that contained many of the elements of the most up-to-date systems. Teamwork was stressed everywhere; everyone was very aware of guiding principles and referred to them often (sometimes by initials!); status distinctions were minimized. Yet interviews with workers revealed very high levels of resentment. They did not subscribe to the hyped-up language of the plant, in which workers were, for instance, referred to as "associates." They felt the company was prying into their personal lives by encouraging them to participate in "wellness" programs. Most of all, they felt that the rhetoric of participation was not carried out in reality. When a large number of "associates" were abruptly and unilaterally laid off, it only confirmed their cynicism.

Such cases occur frequently. The bureaucratic system of management, perfected over fifty years and carrying with it particular attitudes and approaches toward everything from incentive systems to the physical layout of work areas, will not vanish overnight. Many managers do not really believe that "coordinated independence" is possible, and they feel a need to *control* the independence of their employees. They themselves confuse paternalism with managerialism. In many cases the result is a hidden anger that seethes below the surface among employees, as in the case just described. In others, the anger may burst out; General Motors, for instance, tried to run a plant in Oklahoma City as a nonunion team-based system but did it so badly that the union handily won a representation election.[30] There are also many cases in which companies have rolled back the reforms, returning to the safe ground of traditional structures.[31]

Even in companies that aim explicitly to reduce the reliance on commands and lines of authority, the goal is often subverted by the failure of the middle levels to understand or believe in the changes. Most managers have succeeded in the old framework by coming in and "turning things around" in a hurry with the strong use of authority. Only now are companies beginning to revise their reward systems to encourage teamwork and leadership rather than such hierarchical approaches. Meanwhile, those who have succeeded within another value system usually resist the sharp change in style required by managerialist reforms—often by disguising their uses of power with participative rhetoric.

The most "advanced" companies deal with this danger by establishing grievance systems that, although internal, are strongly independent of the main management hierarchy. In a few cases, these procedures end in outside arbitration. When high job security is already a norm, as it is in many managerialist companies, these systems produce something very close to a genuinely independent base for worker participation, but without traditional unions.[32]

However, these mechanisms, while far more common now than a decade ago, remain rare. Without independent pressure, it is difficult for management to set up protections strong enough to withstand crises and changes in leadership—and perhaps even more difficult to convince employees that they are indeed protected. It is far too easy, and too common, to fudge. The classic form of fudging is the "open door" system, by which employees are permitted to appeal over recalcitrant supervisors' heads by going directly to higher managers. Leaders in this system generally insist that they are truly fair-minded and open to complaints, and that they would never permit retaliation against someone using the system, but no matter how strongly they insist, the perception remains that it is a risky channel to try.

Abuse of power not only harms the interests of employees but also undercuts the foundations of managerialism itself. Fear, whether open or subtle, works directly against commitment and the free use of intelligence; intimidated workers will not act like "associates," even if that is what they are called. Furthermore, the continued reliance on power enables management to avoid the hard changes in organization and style that give the new system its effectiveness. In trying to fool workers, management may only fool itself.

These problems therefore point to a need for a system of representation that can stand up to misuse of power and that does not rely on an extraordinary level of managerial enlightenment. The Wagner Act system was designed to do just that and has been generally successful at it; it is much harder for managers in a unionized environment to deceive themselves or their employees in these particular ways. The failure to replace unions' function as a "security-base" against illegitimate coercion is one major weakness of the new system.

Failures of Influence and Leadership

Power problems are, in a sense, obvious; for that very reason they are not the most difficult to deal with. Another distortion of managerialism consists, not in sugarcoating power, but in failing to develop effective *influence*. When this happens, management believes that there is unity and commitment when there is not; they overestimate their ability to persuade, mistaking token agreement for active enthusiasm.

It is extremely easy for those at the top to assume that their ideals are fully understood by everyone in the organization—an assumption that is often unjustified. The mistake is especially common when there are no clear mechanisms for the collective definition of employee concerns. If large groups of people are run through training programs in which they are exposed to new value statements by their company president, they are likely to nod agreement; that does not mean that they will feel enthusiastic. They may even have trouble defining their concerns. In this case resistance goes underground, taking the form of lack of implementation or of complaints on the grapevine. It can be spotted in two closely related ways: in hidden disaffection, which slows reform in seemingly unexplainable ways; and in management's excessive reliance on personal or charismatic leadership.

The resistance to changes in values is a particularly important case of this hidden disaffection. Managerialist companies stress the crucial role of unified values, asking not only for obedience in return for pay—as in a bureaucracy—but also for employees to *believe* in them. But, one might ask, why should they? What makes people commit themselves to these values?

Managerialism has so far developed most frequently when a charismatic founder has established clear values from the beginning. This was the case, for example, of Hewlett and Packard, of Walt Disney, of Johnson at J&J. (It is, incidentally, notable how often these men have attached their names to the companies.) In the initial growth periods of these companies, values were relatively malleable. Functions, roles, and interests had not been hardened, enthusiasm was high, and the leader came to embody the collective process of creating the new order. All these companies, moreover, have continued to be large and prosperous, so that their values have not subsequently been put under serious strain.

But this is obviously not a sufficient mechanism for establishing values. Businesses cannot count on a supply of charismatic leaders. Furthermore, though organizational values are the most stable element in a managerialist order, a reference point during changes in structure and strategy, they are not eternal. As markets change, values themselves can become an uncompromising influence that prevents adaptation. Both Xerox and AT&T, for instance, found that the cultures that were effective while they held monopoly positions were very ill suited to a competitive environment. There is a growing recognition, therefore, that organizations need a method for generating orderly changes in values.

Every text on cultural change in organizations stresses one major theme: it must start at the top. "During all my work on corporate strategy and culture," says one consultant, "I have learned that guiding beliefs are invariably set at the top and transmitted down through the ranks."[33] The most common pattern appears to be that senior managers meet to clarify their own values about the business; the CEO then blesses the resulting statement before it is spread through the company.[34]

We really have no idea whether such a process of directed cultural change can work; there are few major efforts of this type, and most are still in their infancy. But the notion of deliberately transforming the fundamental principles guiding a large social system runs against all our knowledge about how values are formed. I can think of only one instance in history when this has been tried before—the Cultural Revolution in China. That example is not encouraging.

As Mao Tse-tung found out, it is easier to establish an effective bureaucracy than to change the values of an entire system from the top. Mao ran into trouble with his "middle management," as do many corporate leaders today. They are aware that their efforts to change values run into a great deal of resistance, but they do not clearly see the nature and extent of that resistance. And the top-down approach almost guarantees that they will not see it. Two anecdotes can serve to illustrate the difficulties:

- In one troubled company the CEO and a consultant decided that workers had lost their work ethic and that a major participative program—including employee owner-ship—was needed to restore motivation. From the point of view of the shopfloor, however, the problem lay not in their motivation but in strategic blunders made by top management. The workers saw the participation effort as a way of trying to get them to remedy the mistakes made by their superiors and resisted the whole enter-prise. One team actually proposed a very creative and effective reorganization of work and then dissolved itself, saying in effect, "We've shown you how to manage. Now manage." The incongruity between the CEO's definition of the situation and that of the workers was never confronted and, ultimately, that destroyed the attempt at cultural change.
- The CEO of a Fortune 500 company recently described his company's cultural change process to a class of Harvard Business School students. It was a sophisticated, state-of-the-art approach that was several years in development. Starting with top-level task forces, it was followed by educational sessions throughout the company. The students questioned him closely, sometimes sharply, about the justifications, the costs, and the techniques. At the end of the class, he asked the professor for a copy of the tape of the session. "I want to take it back and play it for my managers," he said. "I know they have a lot of these questions and problems, but I never hear them."

If these leaders, both of whom seemed genuinely open and eager to listen, did not hear the doubts and questions, then it is hard to imagine that the values they proposed could fully reflect the needs of their employees. Good consultants of cultural change have tried to bring resistance into the open where it can be freely discussed, but that is not easy to do when the top management has already blessed a particular approach.[35]

It is not likely, therefore, that the top-down approach to culture change will work widely, though it may have a few successes under particularly effective leaders. Those who advocate it, I think, have missed an important point in understanding values: that values are essentially a reflection of practice, nothing more than the conscious ordering of what we do every day. The proper role of the top leadership is not to create values, but to catalyze the process of reflection—to help an organization understand itself. And in an organization that is structured as a coordinated body of experts, as managerialism aims to be, the independent bases of expertise—from top to bottom—must all be involved in the process.

Mobilizing genuine enthusiasm from an entire organization can be done only through extraordinary leadership. That is another aspect of the present weakness of managerialism as a system. Leadership, along with the idea of cultural change, is one of the "hot" topics of management literature. There are two common themes to these works: first, that it is essential to develop a style of management that builds involvement and teamwork, that empowers subordinates rather than constraining them; the second is that this is extremely difficult to do.[36]

A major reason that leadership in a managerialist system is so difficult and rare is that it tries to *substitute* for an adequate form of representation. Somehow, in order for the system to work, the doubts and resistances of employees must be accounted for and dealt with in formulating principles and strategies. If there are no adequate mechanisms for employees to express their concerns, it falls to a leader to guess them—to be so sensitive, so aware, so dynamic, as to incorporate all the points of view in the organization and produce a synthesis. That is a very tall order, and those skills are not taught in business schools. It is no wonder that such attempts at leadership quite often produce hidden disaffection rather than real commitment.

The problems of leadership and commitment call for a system of representation that can effectively express the complex concerns of employees in a managerialist system. For this purpose, traditional unionism by itself is not sufficient. Collective bargaining is too blunt an instrument; it deals well with a few issues, such as pay and benefits, which are of general concern, but it is not very good at building consensus on an organizational strategy. Most industrial unions would in fact reject that function, saying that it is management's role to lead and theirs to react. Yet reliance on management's leadership and workers' enthusiasm is not an adequate substitute. What is needed in this new setting is a way of articulating employees' points of view.

Relations to the Outside

It is notable that the exemplars of managerialism are unusually *closed* companies. Their rejection of unions is only one manifestation of a general resistance to the outside. Companies like IBM and Procter and Gamble, for instance, are known for their emphasis on secrecy and their reluctance to share information. They also seek to minimize outside competition for the attention and commitment of their employees. They often avoid the cities that were the center of the old industrial economy and prefer small towns; almost all the new team-based

106

factories have been started in such places, frequently in the rural South. Another tactic with a similar effect is to move personnel (especially managers) so often that they never build up strong attachments that compete with their commitment to the company. William Ouchi notes that his *Theory Z* exemplars frequently use both these techniques to maintain the dominance of the corporate community over the outside community.

This is not, of course, a problem unique to managerialism. American corporations in general often take a pugnacious attitude toward outsiders—government, unions, interest groups, and any other body that tries to interfere with their autonomy. All these relations are more adversarial here than in other industrial countries, and there is relatively little willingness to negotiate with outside groups that are affected by corporate actions.

Managerialist companies share in this wider problem, but they also seem to have a tendency toward even greater "inwardness" than the norm, because of their effort to build a new culture within the boundaries of a single firm. They are creating something that consciously breaks with the traditions and expectations of most of the economy. This spirit of innovation can easily shade into a sense of "specialness" that cuts off communication with the outside. Thus, according to Maccoby—who has observed many of these corporations as a researcher and consultant—"They are highly ideological. They feel their way is best." One can often hear in their statements of values a defensive note: "An Intel corporate objective is to be and be recognized as the best, the leaders, #1, in both technology and business . . . Our ego is strongly tied into this aspect of our culture."[37] If one's ego is "strongly tied" to being "recognized as the best," there is little room for honest dialogue or constructive criticism from outsiders. At times these companies feel that they are so far ahead of, or different from, others that they do not need to exchange information. A Procter and Gamble manager explained the corporation's past reluctance to reveal details of its worker participation efforts in this way: "We felt we couldn't learn much from most other companies."

Whatever its degree, such inwardness has costs. No company, not even the largest or fastest growing, can truly "go it alone." Corporations require a great deal of support from the outside—from educational systems, labor markets, and political bodies. That means that some sort of system is needed to negotiate conflicts and claims. Industrial unions have not been entirely effective in this respect, but they have had an important role in connecting corporations and other interests. Organized labor has been both "inside" corporations, as the representative of employees, and "outside," through its position in wider coalitions; it is a *cross-cutting* institution. As these connections have broken down, however—and they are especially weak in the managerialist sector—corporations risk even greater isolation.

The problems of isolation can be seen on several fronts. The political dimension is a crucial one. During the 1970s business leaders began to complain loudly about how "misunderstood" they were. They read the poll results about their low standing in public opinion, and they felt the consequences in terms of increased regulation. At that time they began to do something about it. They launched ad campaigns to polish their image, and in some cases they appointed internal staff to set up ongoing relations with outside groups. In 1972 a group of corporate chief executives established the Business Roundtable to work toward a positive and "constructive" role in public policy.[38]

These initiatives have, of course, paid off in many ways, most notably in the warm relationship between the business community and the Reagan administration. Such successes have given corporate influence a visibility that it has not had for more than fifty years. But the underlying connection to the public is no better now than it was a decade ago. The polls still show very high mistrust of big corporations. More than three-quarters of the population see them as putting profits above the public interest, and less than 20 percent have confidence in corporate leadership. These sentiments have not only greatly slowed the administration's antiregulatory efforts, but they continue to fuel effective drives by interest groups in other forums—especially in state legislatures and the courts (see chapter 8).

There is the potential for major trouble in these trends. Sooner or later, increased political demands without increased public support produces a crisis in legitimacy. Like much of the rest of this story, the current pattern has a particular historical resonance. The 1920s—to return to our frequent reference point—was the last period when business became as politically visible as it is today. At that time, too, leading corporations fought to keep unions out and to constitute themselves as closed, unitary societies. The result was that when the economic tide turned, business stood alone in taking the blame, and unions benefited from the reaction. The depth of hostility that was focused on management at that time still colors public opinion.

Managerialist firms often lay particularly heavy demands on the political sphere because of their emphasis on strategic flexibility and change. It is now common for large companies openly to link their strategic decisions—where to invest, where to operate—with the political climate of states or nations, lobbying legislatures for the best terms on taxes, regulation, and infrastructural support. When General Motors was searching for a site for its innovative Saturn plant, which combines state-of-the-art technology with autonomous team systems and high worker participation, governors from twenty states competed to see which could promise the corporation the most benefits. When GM expressed concern about the poor educational system in Kentucky, the legislature met in a special session to pass a $360 million education aid bill. Despite these heroic measures, the nod finally went to Tennessee, which promised a "pro-business government."[39]

Such dealings risk further undermining public support for both business and government.[40] This issue calls for a structure by which the concerns of "outsiders" who are affected by corporate decisions can be represented in the decision-making process. Yet it is not obvious how to do this. Industrial unions have not performed this function very well in the past. To some degree they acted as proxies for the interests of other groups in the general "New Deal coalition," but it is not clear that that mechanism ever worked very well, and it certainly is failing now in view of the fragmentation of that coalition. Unions are widely seen as special interests rather than as representing the public interest. Nor is increased regulation a very good solution. Though this has been, in fact, the method by which outside interests have expressed their claims for the past twenty years, it has proved too clumsy and too costly to be used as a routine way of resolving conflicts at the corporate boundary. The current political backlash against it, I have argued, is more than a temporary phenomenon.

The most promising developments lie in another direction: in processes that bring corporations and public groups into direct relations with each other. There are instances where ad hoc representative bodies have developed to negotiate relations at the boundaries of corporations. A few utilities have sought to work out agreements on changes in rate structures directly with consumer groups before proceeding to the adversarial forum of regulatory boards. A number of corporations have managed to avoid lengthy legal wrangles or increased regulation by negotiating environmental concerns with affected groups.[41] When successful, these initiatives have reduced the tension and suspicion between corporations and public groups and have stabilized acrimonious political conflicts.

In the meantime, however, there is no established way to negotiate conflicts between corporations and outside groups. This is especially important because the future development of managerialism might easily be threatened by a public backlash against corporate power. Distrust of business and its motives has fueled a series of major restrictions during the past two decades, and despite a change in tone in the executive branch, the underlying state of public opinion on this matter has not changed. It would be a mistake to assume that the Reagan rhetoric has eliminated the pressure of outside claims on the power of corporations. On the contrary, the high political profile of the business community today only increases its visibility as a target.

A second "boundary" problem involves the relation of managerialist corporations to labor markets. These companies, as I have mentioned, stress high employment security. They have strong reasons for this policy. Cultural unity and wide participation are not compatible with the fear that comes from constant instability.[42] Furthermore, the extensive investment in training that is required for effectiveness in a participative setting is lost when employees are laid off. These are strong incentives to create a system in which employees can count on long careers.

On the other hand, this policy clearly creates significant problems for the business. The most obvious issue is that it restricts the ability to adapt to market fluctuations: downturns cause great strain. The only available responses are to absorb temporary losses by holding onto employees who are not needed or to institute some form of work sharing that spreads the pain of downturns. Both these responses have been used frequently in managerialist companies, but they are limited and temporary solutions to the problem. A policy of high security is, in this sense, a source of rigidity, closing many options for company strategy.

In addition, it puts very high demands on companies to meet all their employees' needs—in particular, to provide opportunities and challenges that will keep people going throughout their careers. It is difficult for a single firm to provide enough stimulation to sustain commitment and enthusiasm; a number of autonomous team efforts have broken down when the participants felt they had reached dead ends in their development.[43]

For these reasons many managerialist firms are moving toward what can only be described as a perversion of their basic concept. They have begun consciously to divide their work forces into a core, which has full rights and involvement in the managerialist system, and a secondary "buffer," which is used to absorb the effects of business cycles. These may be subcontractors or, increasingly, direct employees who are not seen as full members of the corporate community; they are therefore subject to layoffs and are generally excluded from expectations of advancement.[44]

This solution—also widely used among the large firms of Japan—is not very satisfactory from any point of view. From the public policy perspective, it simply sharpens the difference between "stable" and "transient" workers; the latter, who absorb the pain of economic shifts, necessarily increase claims on the public coffers. From the perspective of the business itself, it is difficult to maintain a unified culture in which significant numbers are second-class citizens.[45]

The policy of company-based employment security, moreover, further increases the difficulty of strategic change. Whenever a company makes a major strategic shift, the top managers say that about 20 to 30 percent of the old employees "won't make it" in the new system. The "rational" solution would be for those who prefer the old ways to be replaced by people who like the new. But a managerialist system cannot do this without seeming—in fact, without *being*— heartless and callous, undermining all the trust on which it depends. Thus it is forced to attempt the route of indoctrination, trying to get existing employees to change their values, which at best is difficult and at worst creates patterns of manipulation and hidden coercion.

Finally, only certain types of firms can even hope to provide the levels of security and opportunity demanded by this strategy; the self-contained, "closed" model of managerialism sharply limits its generalizability. Managerialist companies fall into two narrow classes: very large and successful companies, or smaller but rapidly growing ones. An IBM or a Procter and Gamble has the sheer size and diversity to offer a lifetime's worth of challenges to most employees. An Intel or a People Express can for a time grow so fast that everyone shares in the excitement. But this is no foundation for a *system* of management that can be stabilized on a wide scale.

Managerialism, in short, needs a larger stage; the attempt to confine it within single companies stifles and distorts it. The only way out would be to open the system—to provide institutions that cut across the boundaries of the firm. This would be useful in representing "political" issues in corporate decision making, and in enabling employees to move from company to company as their situation changes.

Such a system would be repugnant to managerialist companies, which seek to create a strong culture of loyalty. Yet in this they are once again confusing old concepts with new: what makes managerialism work is not *loyalty,* in the sense of blind enthusiasm for the corporation, but *commitment* to *particular* directions and approaches. By trying to build a loyal community, they are working against the very flexibility that is the greatest strength of the managerialist structure.

Mobility is not a function that can be filled merely by the revival of industrial unions. On the contrary, their tradition has been to tie their members closely to the fortunes of a particular employer by negotiating nonportable benefits, strong seniority provisions, and rules for advancement within the firm. Craft unions actually have more experience in this task of allocating skills across companies; professional associations are beginning to take up the same functions with quite a different group of employees. A few industrial unions are taking a hard look at their traditional policies and exploring ideas for retraining for jobs outside the collective bargaining unit or creating jobs through new ventures. However, these will involve significant reorientation of the standard labor relations framework. In this as in other respects, managerialism presents *new* challenges for a system of representation.

The Need for Worker Representatives

The long period of trial and error and the many experiments that have begun to coalesce in the managerialist system have produced some very important social innovations. They have shown that an organization that respects the knowledge of employees and focuses on coordination rather than command makes far better use of human potential than does a bureaucracy. For that reason, especially under conditions of rapid change and uncertainty, it is a far more effective form of organization.

One of the clear consequences of these developments—one that we will explore further in the next chapter—has been to make unions very uncomfortable. The traditional union role does not "match" the managerialist structure but tends always to pull back toward bureaucracy. Thus most unions prefer, or know better how to deal with, a bureaucratic organization of work rather than team-based work systems. Meanwhile, the companies themselves have tried to absorb the functions of unions into their internal structures by strengthening personnel departments and developing new mechanisms that enable workers to voice their concerns.

But they have not solved the problem of representation. The managerialist vision is subject to both open and subtle abuse. The rejection of "outside" groups, moreover, makes the structure more rigid than it needs to be. When managerialism collapses inward it cuts itself off from the needed support of the wider society.

The failure of representation is always reflected in a decline of the legitimacy of leadership. The erosion of public support for business, which goes back two decades, is a warning sign. It means that something needs to be done to bring corporations back in touch with the needs and expectations of their employees and of other groups whom they affect by their power.

Employee organizations, in short, are necessary even in the best managerialist firms. The functions of these organizations, however, must be somewhat different from those of existing unions. They include:

- *Articulating concerns.* In managerialist organizations, company personnel departments and sophisticated management consultants try to bring out objections and discontents in order to build genuine consensus, but they still miss such resistance with regularity. Very often the employees themselves do not clearly recognize the nature of their dissatisfactions, which therefore come out in distorted forms like infighting or alienation.

  The only reliable method for clarifying the positions of groups is for them to have their own institutions and representatives. Unions are not accustomed to articulating the kind of issues common to managerialist firms, but some type of representation is necessary for that purpose. Such representation must also extend to the expression of the interests of various groups in the strategic directions of the firm.
- *Defining standards.* Managerialism reduces the emphasis on formal rules but puts great weight on more general principles and standards of performance. These permit greater flexibility, at a price. Enforcing these standards and maintaining their legitimacy are more difficult than dealing with clear codes. Employees need representation in formulating standards, and unions, familiar with rule enforcement, need to learn the more complex techniques of interpreting standards.
- *Coordinating participation.* While managerialist firms encourage worker participa-

tion on the job, they rarely create mechanisms for linking different groups; each problem-solving team remains distinct, obscuring common issues and interests. Unions, meanwhile, are generally uncomfortable with the whole idea of direct worker participation, preferring to channel all problems through a single union structure. Institutions are needed to coordinate the independent groups without absorbing them.

· *Opening careers beyond the company.* If employees were not bound to a particular company, the result would be more flexibility on both sides. Such opening up of careers across corporate boundaries must be the job of an outside grouping: either through government retraining programs, as in Sweden, or through some association of workers, as is common among craft unions and professional groups.

· *Representing outside interests.* "Workers" are not the only group that needs representation. The power of management affects many groups and the growing emphasis on strategic planning makes this power more visible. Currently the only channel of expression for these "outsiders" is through government, and their sole tactic is regulation. Direct methods of articulating these multiple interests are needed to reduce demands on government without simply suppressing legitimate claims on corporate power.[46]

These representative functions are clearly more than simple variants of traditional unionism. Several of them involve rethinking the whole idea of representative bodies. Under the Wagner Act model, unions have never been conceived of as coordinators of influence or expanders of boundaries. At this point, there is some question about what kind of structures could fill the needs—whether *independent* bodies are essential, whether one institution is needed or many, or how representation should be organized. In the next chapters I will explore efforts to meet some of these requirements, and I will sketch a model of change that is based on a significant transformation of unionism.

However, no matter what model is developed, it is clear that some form of representation appropriate to managerialism is needed. This has implications for labor policy, since the developments analyzed in this chapter add some requirements to the government's role. Managerialism in its best form covers a very small fraction of the work force. The rest are still subject to the abuses of power, ranging from extreme exploitation to the more subtle distortions of paternalism. Any national policy must continue to help prevent such abuses, as the Wagner Act has done for the past fifty years.

On the other hand, managerialism in its full form, which is just beginning to be visible, carries enormous potential for improving both economic production and the conditions of workers. Policy should therefore seek ways to encourage the development of these best tendencies in management. Insofar as the NLRA framework blocks this kind of progress, by recognizing only a system in which sharp adversarial lines are drawn, it needs to be revised. The greatest difficulty is to find a framework that furthers the growth of managerialist systems while protecting workers against the abuse of power.

CHAPTER 6

Labor-Management Cooperation: Promise and Problems

FOR THE PAST DECADE both unions and corporations have been struggling to find new approaches to current challenges, including those posed by managerialism. In that time the greatest enthusiasm and creativity have been generated by the advocates of labor-management cooperation. Like the managerialists, they see the impact of foreign competition and maturing markets as shaking the foundations of the old system, requiring a much higher level of shared commitment than before. But rejecting managerialism as too unilateral, they stress the need for a relationship of mutual respect and active partnership between management and labor. This, they argue, is the only way to mobilize effectively for the economic battles ahead.

Within organized labor, this camp has included leaders of some of the largest American unions: Glenn Watts of the Communications Workers of America (CWA), Irving Bluestone and Don Ephlin of the Auto Workers, and Lynn Williams of the Steelworkers.[1] "It's time our adversary system was changed," says Ephlin succinctly. "It's a system that is causing us to run in second place."[2] These unions and many others have moved in concrete ways to encourage better relationships. They have established worker participation committees sponsored jointly by labor and management, and they have increasingly shared in the strategic decisions of their industries. Not surprisingly, they are encouraged by a chorus of scholars such as D. Quinn Mills of the Harvard Business School: "The unions . . . should be ready to work with management toward a broader conception of collective bargaining than has been common in recent decades. . . ."[3]

What is much more surprising, and confusing, is that the advocates of cooperation have also found themselves cheered on by some who are not usually seen as allies, including key players of the right wing and the Reagan administration. The former secretary of labor, Ray Donovan, was anathema to much of the labor movement; in fact, Glenn Watts made it almost a personal crusade to get him out of office. Yet Watts could hardly have taken exception to Donovan's position on this issue: "Clinging to a collective bargaining relationship that was forced a half century ago—regardless of how well it has served us—can only be a prescription for mutual disaster, not mutual survival. If economic and social progress is the name of the game, then labor-management cooperation should now be the preeminent rule under which it is played."[4] Meanwhile, President Reagan's Commission on Industrial Competitiveness laid great stress on the need for such cooperation as a way of "meeting the competitive challenges we face."[5]

This is an impressive lineup, with an argument that cannot easily be ignored. It seems plausible that the economic success of Japan and the northern European countries is linked to their record of labor peace. Jack Peel, director of industrial relations for the European Commission, believes flatly that "economic success depends on good industrial relations. It is no accident that the richer countries like Denmark, Austria, and Switzerland have progressive, harmonious industrial relations systems. This correlation rests on . . . professionalism and economic realism in management and trade unions."[6]

In addition, this approach taps an important vein of public opinion. Polls have clearly revealed a widespread desire for more harmonious relations and a disenchantment with the bitterness and narrowness that have been traditional in the labor-management realm. A solid majority of the population believes that the current lack of cooperation damages the economy. And the same polls show that the leaders of business and labor—often despite their actions—long even more overwhelmingly for a less adversarial order.[7] Apparently, each party blames the other for the failure to achieve lasting harmony.

Yet the very diversity of support for the concept is troublesome. Surely Ray Donovan and Glenn Watts do not mean exactly the same thing by "labor-management cooperation." The term can mean many things, or it may mean nothing at all. It can be seen as mere rhetoric, or as an attempt to undermine unions, or as a temporary swing of the historical pendulum with no lasting significance, or as the precursor of a profound change in the labor relations system. All these aspects, in fact, can be found within the general movement.

There are also many who oppose the whole idea of labor-management cooperation. Most of these base their suspicions on the centuries-long history of hostility and, to reinforce their claims, they cite the revival of open antiunionism among "respectable" managers. "If an employer . . . wants trade union members to cooperate with him on the shop floor," asks William Winpisinger of the Machinists, "why does he plot our demise in the secluded circles of his peers and in the body politic at large?"[8]

Suspicion also rests on a more fundamental tenet of American political theory: that justice and progress are best achieved by independent parties in fierce competition rather than by collaboration: "These objectives," argues a recent *Harvard Business Review* article, "are best achieved by having labor and management on opposite sides of the negotiating table, where both sides are conscious of their inherent differences and respectful of the other's interests and where the strength of each side serves to check the reach of the other."[9]

In order to make sense of the landscape of labor-management participation, it is useful to separate three major strands whose origins and courses of development have been quite different. The first, a distorted form similar to distorted forms of managerialism, involves manipulation of new language without real change. The second includes cases in which unions have taken on a new role at the highest levels of management, as "partners" in the formation of corporate strategy. These instances are dramatic but, I will argue, limited as models for a general *system*. The third includes worker participation programs at the shopfloor level, which have been called "Quality of Work Life," or QWL. In many ways QWL has posed a greater challenge to the existing order than either of the other two, but its potential for labor relations is still largely unexplored.

False Cooperation

As in every aspect of this study, a considerable proportion of the apparent innovations can be dismissed as opportunistic power plays. The tug-of-war between labor and capital has gone on for so long that there are always many players searching for new tactics in the old battle. In the present instance, the driving force behind the move toward cooperation is the economic distress caused by the deep shifts in markets. Unions and management can easily identify a common enemy—outside competitors, especially those from foreign countries—and draw together for mutual defense. Although some employers may be genuinely seeking creative solutions to the problem, others are using the developments as a club to exact concessions from their workers while the rhetoric of cooperation muffles the blow.

Labor-Management Cooperation: Promise and Problems

The extreme form of false cooperation is cynicism. One version involves a conglomerate (or multifirm) company using the genuine troubles of one of its pieces to milk cash from the workers, then taking the money out and investing it elsewhere. Usually the concession agreement involves promises to keep the plant open, which are then frequently violated. Something like this happened at both Goodyear and Firestone Tire & Rubber, which ignored concession understandings by cutting back their tire business and broadening into other fields; at Otis Elevator; and at (then) U.S. Steel, which, despite its moving pleas of poverty, managed to find $6.5 billion to buy Marathon Oil.

There are also many cases in which companies have pursued cooperative relations only as long as it suited them, returning to the use of force when that seemed opportune. Wilson Foods, for example, had a very harmonious relation with the Food and Commercial Workers—few grievances, joint committees, etc.—until 1984. In that year the courts ruled that companies could use bankruptcy proceedings to abrogate union contracts. Almost immediately the company, seeing its chance, destroyed its previous relations by taking this course and unilaterally cutting wages by 40 percent.

The clearest evidence of cynicism, however, lies in what businessmen say when they are asked directly. The data indicate that there is a minority group that is prepared to take advantage of fashionable rhetoric to pursue old-fashioned power objectives. Almost 20 percent agreed, for example, to the following item on a 1982 Business Week/Harris poll: "Although we don't need concessions, we are taking advantage of the bargaining climate to ask for them."[10]

In a slightly grayer area are a large number of companies that genuinely need concessions to deal with increased competition but who seek to achieve them without significant structural changes. At least two-thirds of concession agreements give no permanent improvements to their unions or workers in exchange.[11] In some of these cases informal understandings guarantee some job security to the existing work force, but these understandings are fragile and evanescent. Others include new joint committees to study the crisis in one way or another, but these have a very poor record of survival.[12]

These negative cases do not prove that the present movement has no value. It is extremely easy to match cynicism with cynicism—to assume, because there have been failures in the past and there are failures now, that the whole movement for cooperation is a fraud. That is as far as most criticisms have gone to date; they are hardly more sophisticated than their opposite, the "gee-whiz" enthusiasm of the proselytizers of participation.[13]

There are, in fact, many instances of a very different nature that have involved real transformations in the relations of labor and management. These are potential models for the regeneration of effective worker representation.

Cooperation at the Top: The Promise
of Partnership

In recent years there have been instances in which unions have gained an ongoing voice in the formulation of management strategy at the highest levels. This is a realm that has always been fiercely protected by managers, that the UAW tried and failed to penetrate after World War II, and that is increasingly vital to the survival of the labor movement. Furthermore, it is an area unprotected by the Wagner Act as interpreted by the courts, and it falls within the zone of "permissive subjects of bargaining" in which the employer has no legal obligations. In fact, the NLRB has had little to do with these instances. In most cases unions have made these gains not on the basis of law or of mass action, but on an imperative need for cooperation that has overridden the traditional objections of company managements.

At Chrysler, for example, Douglas Fraser, the head of the UAW, gained a seat on the company's board of directors during its near-bankruptcy in 1980. This was the first important American instance of union board representation, or "codetermination," since the 1920s. Fraser claimed that his influence helped sensitize the board to the effects of job loss and increased their willingness to look at alternative strategic options.[14]

The airline industry was the next to follow the lead, taking the concept a few steps further. Pan American, struggling with the effects of deregulation, appointed a pilot as the representative of unions on the board in 1982. Eastern and Western Airlines soon followed suit. At Eastern each union gained a seat, for a total of four. Furthermore, they attended not only board meetings (which can be rigged to avoid important issues), but all the major strategy meetings of management.

Other industries have followed with their own versions of codetermination. The Rubber Workers have won the right to appear before the board of Uniroyal at least once a year. At AT&T the Communications Workers do not sit on the board, but the company has met with the union after board sessions to brief them on the issues.

Implied in these developments is a union achievement of enormous significance, one that had been sought in vain since Walter Reuther's grand campaign at General Motors in 1946: the right to examine the company's books. A board representative has access to all the major financial data of the company. In many of these cases, such as Uniroyal and Eastern, the unions regularly review the figures. In addition, other companies that have stopped short of codetermination have nevertheless opened up their financial information. At United Airlines, for instance, two rank-and-file pilots were granted "insider status" and verified the accuracy of the company's data.

The events at Eastern and TWA are perhaps the most extraordinary; for here the unions—especially the Machinists and the Pilots—formed relationships directly with banks and financial groups in order to put pressure on management. At TWA the unions were the decisive force that gave a victory to Carl Icahn over Frank Lorenzo in a takeover battle.

But it is still General Motors that carries the greatest symbolic weight. Reuther's demand in the 1940s—seen as extremely radical at the time—was that wage concessions should go toward lowering prices. In order to protect its pricing "prerogative" from such interference, the company took—and won—a long and bitter strike. Yet in 1981 General Motors reached an "agreement in principle" with the UAW under which an independent auditor would verify that the company was using all future concessions to reduce car prices.[15]

Another aspect of the auto, airline, and other pacts could be of even greater significance in the long run: in exchange for wage concessions, employees gained large blocks of company stock. At Eastern workers received 25 percent of the firm's common stock (as well as three million preferred shares); at Chrysler the figure is 15 percent. More dramatically, at Weirton Steel and at the Hyatt-Clark ball-bearing plant, the employees bought the entire company. Though so far unions have expressed no clear idea of how this ownership stake might be used, it certainly offers enormous potential leverage in strategic battles to come.

These developments are quite different from rhetorical calls for cooperation. They draw managers and unions together to an unusual degree, thus bringing worker representatives into domains from which they previously have been excluded by interpretations of the Wagner Act and traditions of management resistance. Western Airlines, among others, used a dramatic term—"partnership"—to characterize the new relationship, and the word is a useful summary of all these efforts.

Western Airlines established an extremely important positive point: it is possible for worker representatives to be involved in strategic decision making without disrupting the process or destroying the company. This is a lesson that has long been accepted in Europe. The tradition of codetermination has a long history in Germany and has spread throughout the European Economic Community (EEC).[16] Nowhere have these developments had "radical" consequences; competitiveness and profitability have remained strong, and the free enterprise system has easily survived the shock.

On the other hand, it is not clear that partnership has had extraordinarily positive consequences. In many cases it has failed to bring companies back from the brink of insolvency; Eastern Airlines is a recent example. At Chrysler the parties talk enthusiastically about improved understanding, but no great change in direction has resulted from the union's seat on the board. There has been no stampede of unions to follow the examples cited. This, too, is in line with European experience. Most analysts of these top-level forms of involvement see modest benefits for workers, and probably for management as well; but most are also surprised by the relatively modest size of these effects.[17]

The idea of union involvement in strategic decision making sounds dramatic. It seems to be a step toward "socialism" or "workers' control." This is often the framework within which it has been posed in the European debates by advocates of both the management and trade union sides. The gap, however, between such rhetorical excitement and the relatively undramatic reality is very large. The real significance of codetermination is, I believe, far less than it appears at first.

The Limitations of Labor-Management Cooperation

The meaning of any change depends in large part on where it is located. All new initiatives are by definition unusual; but those that appear on the leading edge of economic and social development hold far more promise than those found in backward sectors. Thus, the fact that the major examples of "partnership" have appeared primarily in companies that are in severe trouble raises immediate questions about its value as a model for the future.

The circumstances favoring this development are both narrow and rare. The key factors have been the combination of a strong union with a weak company; only under these conditions has the balance of power tilted enough to allow the union to expand its scope beyond the normal range. What this means, in effect, is that it is a phenomenon of the *old* unionized sector— companies that had established an accommodation with labor under very different circumstances from those they face now. In particular, it is found in industries that were formerly quasi-monopolistic but that recently have been opened to major competitive inroads—and most often in the weakest companies in those industries.

An examination of airlines shows just how limited these circumstances have been. Eastern and Western Airlines—the two that went furthest in extending the partnership with their unions—were in serious economic trouble when they did so. Stronger companies, like United, reached concessions without structural change. At the same time Eastern and Western had very powerful unions, led by the aggressive and centralized Machinists. Other companies facing other unions were able to avoid giving up as much.[18] In the auto industry it was Chrysler, on the verge of bankruptcy, that put a union representative on the board; the stronger companies have been far more circumspect. In fact, every instance of "extended partnership" cited involves a company that is almost 100 percent organized and that has been damaged by a sudden increase in competition.

"Cooperation" of this sort is nothing mysterious. It involves a simple human tendency to pull together in the face of overwhelming outside threats. As such, it has a desperate and almost accidental character. It is clear in these circumstances that the old relationships are not working and that something needs to be tried, but the participants do not seem quite sure of what they have stumbled into. For instance, a Machinists' representative who has been heavily involved in that union's innovative moves in the airline industry is less than enthusiastic about the direction: "I'm almost like an investment banker now. That rubs me the wrong way. I like it the old way where you beat on the table, got all you could, and ran." And an adviser to the same union insists: "One does this not because one wants to. This isn't a social program. Employees are better off in a traditional adversarial relationship. This is just a means of problem solving during a transitional period."[19]

There is also nothing new about this phenomenon. There have been waves of this kind of top-level cooperation throughout the history of unionism. One of the most notable periods for it, once again, was the 1920s. At that time the garment and railroad industries—former "core" industries that were being pushed aside by the growth of mass-production firms—went through a wave of concession bargaining, accompanied by joint committees to study new production methods and, in some instances, by agreements to stabilize employment. Though these agreements were hailed by many as the wave of the future, they failed to penetrate beyond these industries—which were less and less important in the overall economy—nor did they survive the depression.[20]

The implication is that one should not look to these efforts for a general model for the future.[21] Unions are already too weak in the United States for the conditions of extended partnership to be widespread, and it is clear that the overall trend in recent years has been for the balance of power to shift further toward the employers. The result is that, far from expanding their activity, unions have generally been pushed back. The dramatic partnerships at Eastern and other companies are the outcome of the unusual circumstances in which labor has more power than usual and the company is weak. Thus it is not surprising that many examples of this development are swallowed up in the collapse of the whole.

The Dangers of Corporatism

It seems essential for a system of worker representation in the current economy to provide some form of ongoing involvement in strategic decision making. Technological change and industrial restructuring are moving too fast for the ponderous and reactive process of collective bargaining. The examples of partnership previously cited remain attractive to many labor advocates, despite their weaknesses, because they suggest one model for how that extension of representation can occur. But it is only *one* model. Both its attraction and its weakness flow from the same central fact: it is the approach that requires the least conceptual change from the familiar framework of the Wagner Act. It involves new relationships between unions and management, but no major change *within* either body.

Many accounts of these efforts focus on their cooperative nature, contrasting it with the usual adversarial bitterness of the labor relations system. That is, I believe, a fundamentally inaccurate portrayal. In the cases I have described, management and union pushed each other as far as possible; then, as in any normal bargaining process, they worked out arrangements they could both live with. The negotiations were noisy and often bitter, and the relationships since have not usually been models of harmony. Frank Borman, the head of Eastern, stirred up enormous resentment among workers by unilaterally extending concessions in early 1986; the unions at Western Airlines battled long and hard over the various contract concessions; Ford and General Motors have been forced by unions' outrage to rescind pay increases for their managements. There is a certain underlying cooperation, but only in the usual sense—both parties want the company to survive.

What is new, in the American context, is simply that the balance of power in these unusual instances has shifted more toward the labor side. Thus the range of union action has stretched further than usual. Ordinarily union officials work closely with management on personnel issues, and in many decisions about discipline and transfers they have effective codetermination. It is less common for them to work together on the company's strategic plan. The latter creates certain new opportunities and problems, but it does not challenge fundamental assumptions.

Partnership leaves intact the basic separation between worker and union involvement in decisions. It changes relations at the top but penetrates only indirectly to the workers themselves. Their views continue to be channeled through the organizational hierarchies of union and company, and they remain distant from the drama that is being played above them. That is one major reason why that drama is muted, why the effects of partnership are less visible than might be hoped: workers themselves seem rarely to gain any major new sense of involvement from these initiatives.

The pattern can be summarized as a *corporatist* variant on the basic Wagner Act framework. The reader will recall that corporatism is the reduction of participation to interactions between a very few "peak" organizations maintaining a balance of power. Throughout the industrialized world this has generally meant a tripartite system of large and powerful bureaucracies—labor, management, and government. The American version has had comparatively weak labor bodies; the cases of partnership move the system toward something that looks more like that of many European countries. That has advantages, but it fails to deal with the increasingly visible problems common to all forms of the balance-of-power approach, overseas as well as in the United States.

A number of European countries have in fact extended the concept of partnership far beyond anything we have seen in the U.S., or can even conceive of in our context. Germany, for instance, gave us the model of "codetermination"; by law that country has had worker representatives on company boards of directors since the end of World War II. In the iron industry, workers and union officials compose half the board—an impossibly radical notion for the United States, even though we had a major hand in imposing it on Germany. Then there is Sweden, where union membership approaches 80 percent of the work force. The labor movement there has long been involved in strategic planning at the company and national levels and has detailed rights to all company information that could affect workers.[22] These countries are often taken as models by those American unions that are pursuing this road.

At present, there is no question that these systems have accomplished a tremendous amount for the workers in those countries. The levels of employment security, protection from employer abuse, and workplace safety are significantly higher than our own. It should be added that although employers complain mightily about the burdens imposed on them by these protections, their economic performance has been no worse—and in many respects much better—than ours over the past decade.[23]

Yet for the past decade and a half these systems have been showing signs of increasing degeneration. The watershed was probably the widespread period of unrest after 1968, which touched nearly every country in Europe and involved workers much more heavily than in the U.S. The wildcat strikes that were a central feature of the uprisings—and directed almost equally against unions and management—profoundly shook established patterns, and unions in country after country were forced to reassess their policies.

The most visible point of criticism was that unions had become too *centralized;* that though they handled top-level strategic questions well, they had lost touch with their members. The wildcat strikes were, in a sense, a demand for more of a voice *within* the union structures. Thus the early 1970s saw an almost universal move to decentralize hierarchies and strengthen the power of shop-level representatives. A related theme was that the system was *exclusionary.* The cozy triumvirate of government, labor, and business was seen as dominating decision making to the detriment of other important interest groups that demanded to be heard. Thus, simultaneous with the internal protests against unions, there was a fracturing of the political coalition that had held the Social Democrats solidly in power for most of the postwar period. It was during this period that the concept of corporatism was widely redefined in Europe as a criticism of the labor relations system.[24]

Though open protest has declined since the uprisings of the 1960s, underlying discontent with the triumvirate has continued to sap its foundations. It is astonishing to find, for example, that despite the high level of unionization, confidence in unions is as low in most of Europe as it is in the United States.[25] Polls also reveal with great consistency that people everywhere—from England to Sweden to Mexico as well as the United States—strongly disapprove of heavy labor involvement in the political sphere.[26] In the polls that count, voters have substantially weakened the power of the Social Democrats in both Sweden and Germany. And most recently, the numerical strength of European unions has dropped sharply for the first time in decades.[27] It is, I think, fair to say that the corporatist system is everywhere in retreat.

One striking fact about these events is how slow the criticisms have been to penetrate the corporatist organizations. In 1977, for instance, Swedish unions achieved the passage of a law that could potentially decentralize the industrial relations system quite dramatically. But in the private sector they long failed to negotiate the implementation of the provision, with the result that local union bodies continued to feel as powerless as before, and perhaps more frustrated. Meanwhile, organized labor put tremendous energy into the passage of the Meidner Plan, an act that would have greatly increased the power of the central labor federation by channeling a share of corporate profits into a union-administered fund. The plan's initial form, which called for one central fund, was highly unpopular. The revised version, which was somewhat decentralized, managed to become law with intense union pressure, but even then at the apparent cost of much popularity for labor and its Social Democratic allies. In fact, the whole episode has severely strained relations between the party and the labor movement.[28]

Nevertheless, European labor movements are undergoing a painful reappraisal of their traditional approaches. Most have moved visibly in the direction of decentralization of bargaining, greater involvement of members and of nonunion bodies (such as works councils), and encouragement of direct worker participation. Because they start from a stronger position, these changes are in some respects easier than changes in the U.S.: there is less immediate danger of self-destruction in the event of a wrong step. Still, as the Meidner Plan episode shows, resistance is strong, and the vision of the new direction remains confused.

The point of this comparison is that the essential problems with the balance-of-power model are universal. The reasons are equally universal. Corporatism—a balance between *organizations*—tends to produce structures that are centralized and exclusive. They must be *centralized* so that the parties can be free to reach agreements without too much distraction from their constituents; they must be *exclusive* so that the parties in the discussion can be limited to a manageable number. The members of the organizations are viewed essentially as having to be held in line, while those outside the organizations are seen as interfering nuisances. In a mature political and economic system these features undermine public support both inside and outside the labor movement.

When we have seen such problems writ large on the European scene, we can observe them more easily in their restricted version in this country. Though we have had fewer and more limited experiences of partnership, they have been subject to similar difficulties. Back in 1959, in the steel industry, a top-level union-management "Human Relations Committee" was formed to work out mutual solutions to long-standing problems. Although both the company and the union considered it a success, someone forgot to tell the local leaders. They voted it out at the convention in 1966. This kind of failure of communication between top-level committees and the membership base has plagued other efforts as well, such as the Mechanization and Modernization Agreement among the West Coast longshoremen.[29] And it continues today: the UAW leadership has had to deal with a continuing series of challenges from militant members who do not trust their "cooperative" dealings with management. Thus the vulnerability of strategies that rely on central labor-management deals is visible here as in Europe.

We can also observe the ways in which such "partnerships" in this country, as in Europe, have tended to unite *against* members of the outside public. The simplest way for the two parties to get together is to stop trying to beat each other down and to start pushing extra costs onto others. The most notable example is that of the postwar wage pattern set by the auto industry; once managements and unions accepted that they had to live with each other, they made deals on wages that were passed on in consumer prices.

But there are many other examples of such "externalization" of costs by a labor-management partnership. Both the steel and auto unions have joined with their managements in seeking import duties, which puts the costs of sustaining the domestic industry on the consumer. In telecommunications, the CWA has historically supported the company's position in rate cases—generally in opposition to consumer groups—and it also joined in advocating access charges for long-distance service. To avoid paying the costs of pollution, joint committees in steel and other industries have worked against strong enforcement of environmental laws. The two parties have also worked together to put pressure on the government to improve relief for laid-off workers, instead of dealing with job security issues.[30] And unions have often struck deals with employers that, in effect, sacrifice the jobs of future workers for protection in the present.

Recent instances of "partnership" have invented a new and interesting variant of the externalization of costs. Within the small group of examples just described, almost every contract has established a two-tier structure of job security. At

General Motors' Saturn plant, for instance, the agreement establishes a category of "associate members"—in effect, second-class workers—who can comprise as much as 20 percent of the work force. Unlike full "members," they can be laid off.

This is nothing but a variant of the managerialist strategy, discussed in the last chapter, of establishing a "buffer"—only it draws the union into the same exclusionary game that some managerialist companies play alone. It means that the union and company protect their existing employees and members, but they pass off to the wider society the costs of absorbing business cycles; they draw a sharp line between those "inside," with full rights, and those who remain basically "outsiders." The similarity to the Japanese system, in which workers with lifetime security work alongside temporary contract employees in good times, is striking.

A growing number of unions have also been willing to accept two-tier pay systems, by which new employees will be paid on a lower scale than the old. This once again demonstrates the focus on protecting those current members at the expense of those still "outside" the boundaries of the organization.

We have seen that labor has become increasingly isolated from other public interest groups. That is not accidental; it is in the nature of corporatism to create such divisions. The chief negotiator for B. F. Goodrich summed up this aspect of corporatism very neatly, and apparently without self-consciousness: "Union leaders," he said, ". . . are realizing it's not 'us against them' but 'we against the world.' "[31]

The exclusionary consequences of labor-management cooperation are explicitly drawn in the "social contract" theories of labor relations that are the most sophisticated justification of the present order. John Dunlop, the former secretary of labor, is the chief spokesman of this school, though labor leaders such as Douglas Fraser use similar language. A consistent theme of Dunlop's work, since at least the 1960s, is that there are too many pressures on union and management to be "open." He is critical, for example, of provisions of the Landrum-Griffin Act that require minimal levels of union democracy; he sees this as interfering with attempts to strike effective deals with management. And he attacks the recent "sunshine" laws, which make it impossible for tripartite committees (those that include government) to meet in secret: "The mandate that such meetings . . . 'shall be open to the public' . . . seriously impedes or negates effective consultation and negotiations."[32]

Dunlop speaks from long and distinguished experience, and he is, of course, entirely right: corporatism cannot function in an atmosphere of open information and widespread participation. The problem, however, is that the pressures for openness are not ephemeral or imaginary. They have emerged strongly in every Western society during the past twenty years, and they show no signs of diminishing. A system that cannot cope with them inevitably suffers a loss of legitimacy— which is precisely what is happening everywhere to the labor relations system.

Labor-management cooperation at the top levels, in brief, presents a "Catch-22" for unions. The labor relations order is structured, by law and tradition, as a contest of power between organizations; cooperation comes from equilibrium in the struggle. Because unions have generally lost power in recent years, there are few opportunities for them to establish cooperation on favorable terms. And—here is the catch—attempts to recoup strength by establishing top-level partnerships only further undermine labor's long-run support, for they make unions appear distant from their members and cut off from outside groups. The more unions pursue *power*, which is the basis for cooperation in the present order, the more they lose legitimacy and *influence*.

It is, of course, a natural reaction to deal with trouble by simply redoubling effort. That is what unions are doing when they try to extend the Wagner Act framework to new levels of partnership with management. But the successful examples of extended partnership, both here and in Europe, have paradoxically revealed the underlying weakness of labor relations systems that are conceived as a balance of power. Such systems have gone beyond their base of legitimacy, and the farther unions go on that road the weaker they become. If there is a way out of the present crisis, it will have to involve something more different in substance from the strategies of the past.[33]

Cooperation on the Shopfloor

During the last ten years a different form of cooperation, with a different set of dynamics, has developed: joint programs that involve rank-and-file workers directly in decision making on the shopfloor. As noted earlier, this movement has generally taken the name of "Quality of Work Life," or QWL. The awkward name is a compromise shaped by the need to avoid offense; it reflects the fact that the idea does not fit easily into existing patterns. Yet during the past decade it has shown a surprising resilience and ability to survive adversity.

We have observed that unions have historically been uncomfortable with direct worker participation. Because they have far fewer resources than employers, the only way unions can control the situation is to concentrate those resources on reaching centralized agreements that are easily policed. The dispersion of representation can easily lead to confusion and ineffectiveness. That, essentially, is the reason why labor has been generally skeptical toward all forms of direct worker representation, and especially toward the QWL movement since its inception in the early 1970s.

Whereas labor-management "partnership" at the top levels is almost always pushed by unions on a reluctant employer, the opposite has been true of QWL. Its roots lie in the management-sponsored programs that evolved into managerialism, and it is often carried out in nonunion situations. Labor has been faced with the reality of these participative efforts and has groped for a response. It has been an excruciatingly slow and painful process. On the one hand, union leaders have been reluctant to say that worker participation is a bad thing and to oppose it openly. On the other, they fear that if they endorse it they will invite an alternative, management-dominated form of representation. The tension between these two poles has made it impossible for any unified position to develop. Many labor leaders have simply tried to ignore the whole phenomenon, hoping it would soon fade away; but it has not.

What exactly is this QWL that is so disturbing to unions? It was Irving Bluestone, then director of the General Motors Department of the UAW, who popularized the term in the early 1970s and did most to define its parameters. When General Motors began to try out worker participation at its Tarrytown, New York, plant in the late 1960s, Bluestone argued that it was important for the union to have a hand in shaping the program. He fought for a contract clause establishing a joint committee to oversee it; though the company rejected the union's involvement in 1970, it gave way three years later.

The Tarrytown QWL effort established the basic model that still shapes the movement today, not only in General Motors but also in many other companies and industries. It has taken many forms, and it would be fruitless to enter the debate about its exact definition. Most generally, however, it consists in the following: groups of ten to fifteen workers meet in problem-solving sessions, on company time, for about an hour a week. Their task is to identify concerns they feel on the job and to propose solutions for them. They have no direct power; their proposals go to the normal organizational decision makers for implementation. But because they are close to the problems and can bring group knowledge to bear, the worker participation groups have great *influence*. In most cases 90 percent or more of their proposals are accepted.

Most QWL processes begin by defining some basic guidelines. These have varied little, in essence, from those originally sketched by Bluestone. First, he insisted, the effort must be a joint one: the union must be fully involved at all phases, and either party can terminate it for any reason. Steering committees with equal numbers of union and management representatives oversee the development of the process. This is essential to guarantee sufficient mutual trust as a foundation for the effort. Second, it must be voluntary: employees are free to choose whether or not to be involved. Third, QWL is not to interfere with collective bargaining; contractual issues are not a proper subject of discussion in the new forum. Fourth, it cannot be used to lay off workers.

The specific accomplishments of QWL groups vary, of course, from industry to industry and even from work site to work site. Generally they begin by proposing small improvements in their physical environment—better lights or ventilation—as a way of testing the limits of their new influence. If they are successful at this level, they frequently move to reducing the burden of controlling work rules and improving their relations to supervisors. In the late 1970s, for example, operators at AT&T generally had to raise their hands to get permission to go to the bathroom; among the first actions of many QWL groups, when these were formed after the 1980 contract negotiations, was to propose methods of self-monitoring so that people could make their own decisions.

These are small successes, though from the workers' perspective far from trivial. As the QWL process matures, however, it increasingly encroaches on domains that have been defined as "management prerogatives," arousing sharper resistance. Groups often propose, for example, changes in measurement and evaluation systems or in training methods. In some instances they have suggested the elimination of supervision and the formation of autonomous teams. But the majority of efforts are blocked before they reach this point: after an initial round of successes they reach a "plateau," discouraged at every turn from proceeding to more ambitious projects.[34]

It is hard to estimate the penetration of QWL in the economy as a whole. The majority of General Motors and Ford plants have problem-solving teams of this sort; at AT&T, more than 1,200 teams were started between 1980 and 1984; in steel, several hundred Labor-Management Participation Teams have been established as a result of a provision in the 1980 contract. These are the only instances in which national unions have coordinated large-scale, multiplant programs. But it is also clear that there are thousands of QWL-like agreements at the local level which involve unions to a greater or lesser degree.[35] In the last few years the concept has been taken beyond problem-solving groups to far more extensive forms of participation, including autonomous work groups.

This spread has forced the debate to a new level. QWL has proved, if nothing else, that it will not quickly disappear, and that labor leaders can no longer sit on the fence. No longer is Irving Bluestone's a lonely voice; in this decade countless union officials, including two heads of major national unions—Glenn Watts of the CWA and Lynn Williams of the Steelworkers—have become active advocates of QWL and have pushed it within their organizations. Even more significant, the AFL-CIO, after years of cautious skepticism, changed its position quite markedly in its 1985 call to action:

> . . . the survey data suggest, and our experience indicates, that there is a particular insistence voiced by workers, union and nonunion alike, to have a say in the "how, why, and wherefore" of their work. These needs and desires are being met in some cases by union-management programs affording greater worker participation in decisionmaking

at the workplace. Several major unions have developed such programs and report a positive membership response. The labor movement should seek to accelerate this development.[36]

Consequences for Organized Labor

The debate over QWL has created more heat within the labor movement than almost any other recent issue. Whereas top-level initiatives like board representation produce reactions of caution, worker participation programs often generate intense and polarized feelings among union officials. For even in the restricted and quite inoffensive form defined by Bluestone, QWL challenges fundamental traditions of labor strategy. It means in essence that the union is no longer the sole representative forum for the workers; it has to deal with channels of expression that are independent of its structure. The implications of this change are profoundly troubling.

Enough experience has been gathered by now to permit the labor movement to draw some practical lessons. The first is that when QWL is instituted *without* a union, it can serve—at least in the short run—as an extremely effective antiunion device. There are many specific examples. We saw that managerialist firms like IBM, which have remained effectively unorganized, make heavy use of worker participation. General Electric and General Foods, among others, have explicitly credited work improvement programs with the aim of helping to defeat union organizing drives, while other companies have clearly instituted them for the same purpose without necessarily admitting it.[37]

There is also more generalized evidence of the danger of QWL for unions. Data from a 1977 national survey indicate that nonunion workers who enjoy autonomy and responsibility on the job are significantly less likely than the average worker to vote for union representation.[38] A recent study found that three-fourths of companies facing white-collar organizing drives established some sort of employee committee to help in their defense.[39] And there is this startling and crucial finding from an AFL-CIO survey of organizing campaigns: "The one major company 'benefit' that drastically affected union organizing drives was the quality of worklife plan, particularly in manufacturing establishments. Unions won but 8 percent of the campaigns in manufacturing industries with QWL plans [as opposed to 36 percent in these industries overall]."[40]

Many union officials react to this evidence by attacking QWL as an antiunion device that should therefore be opposed. But from another perspective, what it shows is that participation meets a real need and desire of the work force. This is confirmed by a second major finding: when QWL is done *with* the involvement of organized labor, it *strengthens,* rather than weakens, the union. The point is highly controversial, but the evidence is considerable:

- Members approve of their unions' involvement. National survey data indicate that organized workers who have a high level of responsibility and autonomy on the job are more satisfied than the average with their unions.[41] And a study by the CWA and AT&T showed that among workers who saw their officials as supportive of the QWL effort, 90 percent were favorable to the union, but among those who did *not* see the union as supportive, that figure dropped to 50 percent.[42]
- Local officers who have seen QWL in action like it. In a study of five companies with joint QWL efforts, roughly 55 percent of the local union officers felt that it was good for the union, while only 20 percent felt it was harmful.[43] In my own experience, the level of support is even higher than that among local officers who have been *directly* involved in the process. Even among those who begin with a skeptical attitude, most agree that it has made their job easier and their relations with their members smoother.
- While QWL is often effective in *preventing* unionization, I know of no case in which it has helped in the decertification of an existing union.
- There are many individual illustrations of benefits for unions. At the Harman auto mirror plant in Bolivar, Tennessee (a right-to-work state), for example, more people joined the union after the start of a QWL effort than before. And in a number of instances there have been documented increases in the number of people attending union meetings.[44]

At first glance it seems paradoxical that QWL should help unions among their members but hurt them among nonmembers. Yet the findings make sense on reflection: it is simply a matter of who gets the credit. In joint QWL efforts, both union and management are seen in a better light by employees. When management alone does it, it gets all the benefits. But the crucial underlying fact, which can be ignored by labor only at great peril, is that workers *like* direct participation in decisions that affect them.

An additional benefit of QWL, from the point of view of local officers, is that it gives them more avenues than ever before to communicate with their members. As we have seen, union officials ordinarily have very few opportunities to see their constituents on the job. The only reliable occasion is when someone files a grievance, but those who do are a very small percentage of the work force—at most 15 percent. Beyond that 15 percent the members rarely see their leaders in action on a day-to-day basis. This is one of the factors that make it difficult for unions to sustain decentralized actions. But QWL, as it is practiced in most settings, brings about an important change. Union officials are involved in training, facilitating, and participating in problem-solving groups with the rank and file. They have a chance as never before to be visible and to exert continuous leadership. It is for this reason that the activists in the survey previously cited claimed that QWL "improved the union's communications with its members."[45]

Thus while QWL is *bad* for unions in the sense that it can be used to prevent their spread, it is *good* because it strengthens their standing among their members. The third major lesson of experience is harder to evaluate: in time, QWL forces significant changes in union structures and policies.

Irving Bluestone, in his uphill struggle during the 1970s, used to deny that such changes were necessary. QWL, he argued, could be kept separate from collective bargaining and carried out by traditional union structures. That claim was needed to reduce resistance at that time, but it has become increasingly clear as the process has spread that QWL is not so easily absorbed. First, it certainly involves a shift away from legalism and contract enforcement, which have been the core of union activity to the present. In almost every case of QWL, the number of grievances declines dramatically—sometimes more than 90 percent—and many problems are solved in informal discussions rather than through formal procedures.[46] Thus union officials, who are generally highly skilled at legalistic argument, need to learn a new set of tools: techniques of persuasion, group dynamics—in short, *leadership*. The decline in the importance of grievances is seen with profound ambivalence by local officers. On the one hand, generally they are glad to reduce their grievance load, an unpleasant job that gets them little gratitude. On the other, they are uncomfortable without the clear-cut roles and procedures that it provides them.

Second, QWL involves a decentralization of responsibility within the union. Even if the original guidelines are adhered to and collective bargaining issues are decided in QWL sessions, someone on each team has to make sure the rules are being followed. QWL must be led by people very close to the rank and file—that is, by stewards—but this involves more discretion than stewards normally exert. Most of them are not expert on all the contractual provisions, and the "line" of permissible subjects is by no means clear-cut in practice. A fine sense of judgment and diplomacy is needed to steer groups away from forbidden areas. In order to carry out their role effectively, therefore, stewards need to gain both competence and trust from higher levels of union officials. Successful efforts have involved extensive new systems of communication and training for local union officers.[47]

Most important, it has proved in practice impossible to keep QWL forever out of the traditional collective bargaining arena. It is common for detailed job descriptions to be written into the contract as a check on management abuse and for job categories to become finely graded, with crossovers prohibited. Almost any real change in work methods that might be proposed by workers on QWL teams will run up against some of these contractual provisions. At that point the union is placed in an unpleasant bind: if it forbids discussion of such topics it is seen as preventing desired changes; if it permits discussion, it opens up the contract in ways that the union is not equipped to handle.

These troubles are minor in the early stages of QWL, but they become unavoidable when it moves on to the harder issues—especially when workers begin to propose increases in their autonomy on the job. The end of that route is the autonomous work group, which violates almost every principle of "classic" unionism. In that structure, workers share tasks, crossing lines of craft; they allocate work themselves, often violating seniority standards; and they perform many traditionally supervisory duties. All of these developments, which are natural outgrowths of worker participation, are anathema to union traditions—so much so that the opposition is often violent. Here is one reaction to the involvement of the Energy and Chemical Workers' Union's (ECWU) local 800 in an autonomous team plant in Sarnia, Canada:

> The . . . Canadian Labour Congress literally threw out the ECWU national representative . . . when he attempted to defend his union's behavior in the chemical plant. . . . At the ECWU founding conventions some delegates from other locals called the local 800 delegates "bastards" and "phony unionists". . . . The shop chairman of a large UAW local accused [the vice president of local 800] of being a traitor to the union movement.[48]

And Peter Kelly, head of UAW local 160, put the fears in a nutshell in opposing a similar effort between his union and General Motors. The plan, he said, "could lead to the demise of the UAW union movement as we know it."[49]

These people understand the transformation required by the growth of worker participation, and they see that transformation as bad. This sort of resistance has meant that the labor movement, for the most part, has played a restrictive role in QWL—preventing it from expanding the scope of worker autonomy as much as it might, policing it rather than developing it. There are, in fact, far fewer cases of autonomous team structures in unionized rather than nonunionized settings, despite the fact that teams are almost universally favored by workers who experience them.[50]

Resistance to QWL and worker participation comes from many sources, including reluctant managers (especially in the middle ranks) as well as unions. Both parties seek to hold on to their traditional forms of power. I believe this resistance accounts for the fact that in practice the potential of QWL has rarely been fulfilled. Perhaps three-quarters of joint QWL efforts, by my estimate, have fallen prey to the malady of "plateauing." The problem-solving groups generally begin with a great burst of enthusiasm, dealing successfully with minor issues in their immediate environment and improving relationships with their supervisors; but they soon run up against resistance that discourages them. At that point teams lose momentum and become stagnant, or slowly fade away.[51]

It has become apparent that QWL cannot long survive in a halfway, limited form. Either it must become part of a total organizational culture of participation or it becomes isolated and dies. Management certainly finds it difficult to make the commitment to such far-reaching change; the failure rate in nonunion settings is very high over time. But it is equally difficult for the union, and when the two sources of resistance are put together, lasting success is difficult indeed. General Motors' Tarrytown plant, which inaugurated the QWL movement fifteen years ago, has gradually lost its enthusiasm and today has few vestiges of the participative structures. It is a symbol for what happens when union and management believe they can create a QWL program without fundamentally changing their nature.

There is, however, another alternative. The thesis of this book is that the transformations required by QWL are essential to the survival and further growth of the labor movement. If unions are to survive, they must learn to adapt to a system in which workers share work flexibly and allocate their own tasks. It is among those relatively rare cases in which labor has successfully involved itself in a thoroughgoing participation effort that we can see the outlines of the future.

The Legal Context

Worker participation is not exactly encouraged by the Wagner Act's policy framework. It may even be illegal.

Technically, the problem lies in Section 8(a)(2) of the Wagner Act, which was designed to prevent employers from setting up their own "unions" to avoid independent representation. Such company bodies had been a favorite employer device to get around the prounion provisions of earlier New Deal legislation. Senator Wagner argued that "The greatest obstacles to collective bargaining are employer dominated unions"[52]; his act therefore made it illegal for employers to "dominate or interfere with the formation of any labor organization or contribute financial support to it."

Until quite recently the NLRB and the courts interpreted this provision strictly. On these grounds the Supreme Court's *Cabot Carbon* decision in 1959 outlawed employee committees established by a company to discuss problems of mutual interest to workers and management.[53] There is little question that this decision, if applied to QWL efforts, would rule them out as well. In QWL, employees deal directly with management on a wide range of working conditions; the committees meet on company time and receive direct financial support for training and research. A more clear-cut violation of the restriction on "company-dominated unions," as interpreted in *Cabot Carbon*, would be hard to imagine.

The legal problem goes even further: under a strict reading of Section 8(a)(2), even *joint* union-management QWL efforts could be prohibited; the company, in many cases, provides a substantial amount of financing for union facilitators and trainers outside the bounds of the contract. Disgruntled members—and there are always some—could object on the grounds that the company was thereby "dominating" their union.

The growth of worker participation, however, has put the courts in a bind—the same bind, really, that unions are in. Courts generally recognize that direct participation does not fit easily into the Wagner Act framework, but they also see it as a good thing. *Cabot Carbon,* therefore, has never rested secure. Many decisions since the 1950s have rejected charges of employer domination in similar circumstances. In 1982 the Sixth Circuit Court approved an employee participation plan using very broad language that would, if upheld, essentially give employers a free hand in establishing their own systems of worker representation.[54]

The logic behind this recent trend in the courts is that it promotes the free choice of employees. The 1982 case concluded that the employees, having defeated union organizing attempts, had freely chosen the committee concept over traditional collective bargaining. "We see no reason under the Act," said the court, "to disturb that choice." And the Ninth Circuit Court, in a related opinion, argued that "a myopic view of section 8(a)(2) would undermine its very purpose and the purpose of the Act as a whole—fostering free choice—because it might prevent the establishment of a system the employees desired."[55] That seems an eminently reasonable argument: if workers *choose* direct participation, and if they prefer it in many cases to union representation, then there would seem to be no policy reason to interfere.

But there is a snag: the definition of "free choice" is not as simple as the courts suggest. At least since the great theological debates about freedom of the will, this has been a difficult and controversial topic. The Wagner Act confronted this problem in the apparent success of company unions: did employees freely choose them, or not? The issue was resolved by saying, in effect, that there can be no free choice in situations of grossly unequal power. Employees cannot make a truly unhindered choice of representatives while their employer holds uncontested the power of the job and the paycheck. Equality is fundamental to liberty, and that is a condition not normally met in the workplace.

The Wagner Act thus treats company-dominated unions as *necessarily* impeding free choice, no matter how enthusiastically the workers might appear to support them. Only an independent base of power for workers can, in this view, offer sufficient protection to make a choice meaningful. The act therefore supports employee freedom *by supporting unions;* the strengthening of unions is its primary focus. The preamble quite unmistakably states a policy in favor, not of freedom of choice, but of collective bargaining and equality of bargaining power.

All this is ignored by the recent court rulings. By making a broad exception to Section 8(a)(2), they clearly weaken the collective bargaining framework. We saw earlier that QWL efforts in nonunion settings are highly effective in defeating organizing drives. The 1982 ruling explicitly recognized a choice between collective bargaining and the employee committees. In brief, the decisions validate an alternative form of representation, which is precisely what the Wagner

Act sought to prevent. In the laudable effort to promote new forms of participation, the courts are rather careless about throwing out the old.

There is one simple and immediate solution to this dilemma, which I have not heard proposed. That would be to permit QWL efforts in unionized settings only. Such an approach by the NLRB and the courts would encourage unions, instead of digging in their heels, to explore these new developments, and it would encourage employers to work with unions in promoting direct participation. It would be much closer to the spirit of the Wagner Act than that determined by the recent court rulings, since it would place the employees' choice of participation in QWL within the context of an equality of bargaining power.

But the simple nature of this proposal should not obscure the fact that it would profoundly test the current order. The fundamental perception underlying the debate on QWL, both for and against, is that it *competes* with traditional unionism. The evidence, as I have argued, supports the claim that it cannot be a mere "add-on." It is true, as Pete Kelly fears and as others hope, that QWL "could lead to the demise of the . . . union movement as we know it." To encourage unions to participate in joint QWL efforts is to encourage them to change many of their most cherished traditions. Thus the interpretation and use of Section 8(a)(2), however important, will solve nothing by itself; it must be part of a larger approach to change.

The courts' treatment of QWL so far has failed to deal directly with its significance for labor relations. By allowing participation, they offer workers an alternative to collective bargaining, but they have no general description, either in theory or in legislation, of what that alternative might be. Thus, while it may make sense to open doors to new approaches, they are opening them so wide that they risk letting in all kinds of situations they may not desire. The whole issue, in short, is another instance in which the protection provided by the Wagner Act has become a barrier to needed change. The problem is to distinguish effective new forms of representation from manipulations and mistakes; the law at present provides no help in making that distinction.

Toward a New System

We have examined two different kinds of cooperation. The first is between *organizations*. Here the focus is on a relationship between two bodies that have competing goals but are forced by circumstances to live together. A relationship of this kind represents one variant of the Wagner Act's balance of power framework. The second kind of cooperation is less easily defined. It involves individuals and groups who are essentially working for the same ends, though they may differ in their interests, their knowledge, and their approaches. It involves not two, but a multiplicity of groupings at many levels and in different combinations—in some cases a work team cooperating with company headquarters to change a procedure, in others, one work site cooperating with another. It is this form of cooperation that is envisaged by QWL as well as by managerialist systems. Yet unlike the organizational form, it appears to undermine the foundations of the traditional labor relations framework. Its attractions are clear, but it has not been worked out in a complete and enduring form.

Though the two forms have often coexisted, as in the automobile and airlines industries, they have rarely merged. The problem is that the two have fundamentally different dynamics and premises. Top-level cooperation is an extension of a power model, appealing to leaders who like to command; it works most effectively when those leaders can make commitments for their organizations with a free hand and expect obedience. QWL appeals to quite a different sort of person, one who likes teamwork and discussion and is uncomfortable with naked power. One centralizes and excludes; the other decentralizes and includes. They cannot simply be added together to make a complete system.

This disjunction, however, is *practical,* not absolute. In theory, one can imagine a system in which codetermination at the top levels is closely connected to participative bodies on the shopfloor—in which the structures of discussion that characterize QWL extend to the highest levels of the organization. This would, however, look quite different from the familiar corporatist forms of cooperation. It would mean, in effect, that both sides agree to develop a *managerialist system with an independent basis for worker representation.* It would require greater transformations in the roles of both parties than have been seen either in partnership or QWL initiatives.

When one looks at the scene from this point of view, there are a few examples that approach this higher level of integration. In this chapter, I have deliberately slighted certain cases of "partnership" that go beyond the typical limitations I have described and that begin to break the pattern defined by the concept of corporatism. I will turn now to these for further clues to the shape of a new system of representation.

The Next Step: Examples of Extensive Participation

WHEN Quality of Work Life (QWL) breaks out of the boundaries set by the Wagner Act framework, unexpected things begin to happen: changes in the patterns of union action and management authority undermine the basic assumptions of bureaucracy. When shopfloor mechanisms are linked up with participation at the highest levels of a firm, the whole framework needs to be reconstructed. The nature of these changes now can be glimpsed only in a few pioneering organizations. These cases are necessarily strange because they lie at the edge of the labor relations system or even outside of it entirely; but they show the possibility of organizing representation on a model different from that of a two-party balance of power, and of extending participation to people and to issues that are excluded by the current order.

Shell-Sarnia/Energy and Chemical Workers' Union (ECWU)

It is always risky to rely on foreign examples, because so many things change in unexpected ways when one crosses national borders. The company that has most stimulated my interest is, however, foreign—but barely. It is in Sarnia, Canada, just across the river from Michigan and scarcely an hour from Detroit. Crossing the river, one enters a country in which unions are somewhat stronger than those here, but where the overall labor relations system and the cultural background are quite similar to our own.[1]

Sarnia is a quiet town, bordered on one side by Lake Michigan, on another by farmland, and on the east by an astonishing sprawl of vast complexes spurting flame. It is one of the major petrochemical centers of North America, the New Jersey of the lakes, a home to the giants of the industry. It is also a center of innovation in the management of personnel. Work in these plants is on the leading edge of the apparent direction of industrial development. In a highly automated and capital-intensive environment, almost all semiskilled work has been eliminated. The bulk of the jobs involve sophisticated monitoring and adjustment of the automated process, and a considerable level of skill and responsibility is required to handle unexpected breakdowns. These are, in short, "semi-professional" jobs. Because of this, many companies in the area for years have been exploring the most advanced forms of managerialist organization of work.

The Shell chemical plant, one of the furthest from town, started operations in 1978. The planning process had begun two years before and had involved the Energy and Chemical Workers' Union (ECWU) almost from the beginning— long before the hiring of the work force. The union had agreed to participate in the planning process on two conditions: that it be an equal partner and that it maintain a high profile. It was an unusual beginning.

The result was an unusual structure, based on the principles of teamwork and interdependence. The plant is organized in six process teams, each composed of about twenty production workers. Each team can (and frequently does) run the entire plant by itself. Its members are responsible for such normally managerial tasks as assigning work, scheduling vacations and overtime, and providing technical training. A fourteen-member craft team handles specialized, nonroutine maintenance tasks.

Every worker in the plant is expected to master all the tasks performed by the team. They are encouraged in this by a pay system that bases advancement on the number of skills acquired ("pay for knowledge"). It is expected that within another year or two everyone will have learned the skills required for the top pay rate—a distinct difference from a traditional structure, where top pay is restricted to a few slots. In addition, everyone is expected to develop and practice a "second skill." Some are learning engineering, some a technical craft job, and others help in the relatively low-skilled warehousing operation. Thus traditional boundaries are continuously breached by the rotation of workers through the system.

The effectiveness of the teams is increased by two factors. First, they can meet relatively easily on an informal basis; since people are not tied down to fixed stations or routine movements, they can carve out time for discussions on the job.

Union officials can network far more effectively in such a setting than on an assembly line. Second, team members have access to *all* the information contained in the plant's computer system, including confidential chemical formulas and—more important—financial and operating data. Thus they are unusually aware of what is happening, and they know that they cannot easily be fooled.

Since the plant started to operate, this structure has helped maintain a strong commitment among a highly articulate and educated group of workers. It has also provided management with extraordinary flexibility, which is crucial in a system that runs twenty-four hours a day, 365 days a year, can run almost unattended much of the time, requires much problem-solving ingenuity when it breaks down, and depends on close cooperation among people with sophisticated skills. The Shell-Sarnia structure is so effective that the plant now runs well above its design capacity. Unlike comparable plants, moreover, its performance has continued to improve sharply long after start-up. Almost every operating measure, from energy efficiency to waste to quality of product, showed steady improvement during the 1980–85 period. These advantages have been carefully documented by an internal company study that compared the Sarnia plant's performance with that of similar plants around the world. As a result of the study's findings, a new Shell factory that opened in Alberta in 1985 was designed on the same principles.

The most important aspect of the Shell-Sarnia case, however, is that innovation has not stopped at the level of the teams. The entire structure of governance and of union-management relations has been revamped in order to achieve maximum participation and flexibility. Within this structure, decisions are made in ways that are quite different from the formal procedures of traditional organizations.

The collective bargaining agreement, for instance, consists of just ten short pages, a sharp contrast to the more usual sixty-five-page contract at a neighboring plant. Only wage levels and the irreducible skeleton of employee guarantees are negotiated in the traditional way. Among the things left out of the contract are management and union rights clauses. Also omitted are all the details of implementation such as the pay progression system, vacation and overtime scheduling, confidentiality, hours of work, the grievance procedure, and all the rest of the body of detailed rules that burden the traditional system.

This contract works because it is supplemented by other mechanisms of participation, as well as other documents that define working procedures in unusually flexible ways. Two documents are of particular importance: the *Good Works Practices Handbook* (GWPH) and the collection of team norms.

The team norms deal with the day-to-day interactions of workers with each other and with management; they constitute, as it were, the guidelines for cooperative activity. In a traditional setting, many of these issues are not open to negotiation or discussion. Some are considered "management prerogatives," while others simply have no mechanism for resolution. At Shell-Sarnia, the teams develop their own norms for interaction. A small sampling includes the following:

- Support team decisions even if not in total agreement.
- Clarify all team rumors immediately.
- Keep confidential personal problems as long as they do not affect other teams.
- The team will perform a checkout of persons in their weak areas.
- The opportunity for equalized overtime should be present.
- Overtime meals will be supplied if needed.
- Teams should be instrumental in choosing new team members.
- Personal records open to respective individuals.
- Company provides teams with up-to-date information.

One can sense behind the informal language of many of these norms the intense, emotional disputes that generated them—the kinds of conflicts that swirl constantly around every workplace and that usually have no place to go. In nonunion settings they are driven underground; when a union is present, they are usually diverted by the need to find a formal rule as a handle, and they end by swelling the load of grievances. The Shell-Sarnia approach provides a more appropriate mechanism for such issues: they are resolved by a process of informal *negotiation*. Depending on the nature of the problem, the discussions may occur within teams, or between teams and management, or between different groups that cut across the teams.

This negotiation process is supported and coordinated by the Team Norm Review Board (TNRB), composed of representatives from each of the work groups, from management, and from the union. The TNRB, operating on a consensus basis, adds a plantwide perspective to the norms. Its responsibilities include dealing with issues that apply to more than one area, maintaining needed consistency through the plant, and facilitating in cases of blockage. Since much of the disciplinary responsibility is held by the teams themselves, and since disciplines are based on the norms, the TNRB also functions as a review board for discipline and grievance issues. Though it lacks binding authority, its influence—based on its representative makeup and the requirement of consensus—makes it quite effective in this role.

The informal team norms, however, do not solve all the problems of governing the plant. They are insufficient to deal with certain complex and formal issues that are normally at the heart of the adversary relationship. These matters—including many that are normally part of the collective bargaining contract—are handled in another document: the *Good Works Practices Handbook*. The progression system (how workers can move through successive levels of skill and pay) is one example of an issue that normally is handled in highly detailed form in contracts, but at Shell-Sarnia, in the GWPH.

The advantage of this system is that the handbook is negotiated not periodically but continually. A union-management committee (separate from the Team Norm Review Board) reviews it monthly at the least, and can make revisions at any time. Changes can be proposed by any team or individual. Major alterations generally go through a lengthy plantwide process of discussion and often include the formation of ad hoc task forces of interested parties.

The decision-making process sounds confusing to one schooled in the procedures of bureaucratic organizations. It is, in fact, difficult to describe in general terms, because it is continuously modified or invented according to the nature of the problems. It can perhaps best be understood by using as illustrations a few major changes that have occurred during the life of the plant.

The shift schedule. In the original design, the process teams operated on the traditional rotating eight-hour shifts, which resulted in their spending one-third of their time on each of the three shifts. Soon, however, team members began to explore the possibility of reorganizing the schedule so as to take advantage of second skills. They developed a complex proposal that involved four and a half teams working a twelve-hour rotating shift, with the remaining one and a half teams working eight-hour day shifts in their second skill areas. This plan allowed team members to spend a startling two-thirds of their time on days, and also permitted more frequent breaks for long weekends or more extended periods.

The plan was initially rejected by management, and it was also opposed by the national union representative. Both felt that twelve-hour shifts would increase stress and reduce safety, and they feared the effects of the precedent on other plants. The proposal was nevertheless kept alive in team discussions and in the Team Norm Review Board until an effective consensus was built. The new shift schedule was incorporated into the *Good Work Practices Handbook* late in 1979 and into the contract the next year. Within a short time there was widespread agreement on the beneficial effects of the system.

Progression for process workers. The complexity of the plant's start-up phase meant that some skills could be developed much more rapidly than others. This led to inequities in the pay-for-knowledge progression system: some workers were stuck in areas that were still trying to stabilize the production process, while others were learning new skills and moving up the ladder. Management, moreover, felt that some people were moving too quickly and creating operating inefficiencies. These problems led to a move to redesign the progression system entirely.

The discussions began in team meetings, then moved to discussions among teams and among union stewards. When a consensus emerged that the problem required plantwide attention, the union insisted that it be handled by the Union/Management Committee rather than by the Team Norm Review Board. A task force was formed, consisting of top managers and union executives.

The Next Step: Examples of Extensive Participation

The union immediately held a general membership meeting to clarify the mandate of the task force. An unexpected outcome of this meeting was that a new task force member was chosen by the workers to represent those with prior experience in the industry—a group that, though not represented among the union leadership, had special concerns about the progression issue.

The task force took three months to develop its recommendations. The union membership then spent two days reviewing and clarifying the proposal with their elected leaders; this led to some modifications. Finally, the executive board decided to hold a membership vote to ratify the change. The turnout was 100 percent, with an approval vote of about 90 percent. Subsequently a specialized, streamlined grievance procedure—distinct from the usual system—was set up to handle the inevitable disputes and confusion that resulted from the change.

Progression for craft workers. The skilled craft workers, who formed a seventh team separate from the operating groups, often felt that they were left out of the design. In addition to their regular duties, they had to train process operators in second skills, and this role went far beyond craft jobs in other plants. Yet despite this increased responsibility they were paid at the industrywide level, which was significantly less than operators who had made the top rate. As more and more reached this top level, the craft workers became the lowest-paid group in the refinery. Management, while acknowledging the problem, did not think it demanded urgent attention.

During 1984 and 1985 the craft workers and the union used several tactics to draw attention to the issue. Craft members refused overtime call-ins, while process operators temporarily "forgot" their craft skills. The union also put forward new contract demands, which management was unwilling to meet. Finally, the company agreed to set up a joint task force. At that point all the pressure tactics, including the new contract demands, ceased.

In this case the union was less insistent on maintaining a direct role for its elected officials in the decision process than in the case of the operating groups. Although an executive board member was initially on the task force, he withdrew once its ground rules had been developed. After three months of work, the approval of the redesigned system was handled essentially by the craft team rather than by higher management, the union, or the membership as a whole. The final solution allowed craft workers to achieve higher grades by cross-training in other maintenance skills.

Many other important changes went through similar processes of discussion and participation in the plant's first seven years. For example, a plan to introduce a new computerized control system in the warehouse came under attack because it would interfere with the progression system of the process operators; a task force selected a different computer system and redesigned the control mechanisms to avoid these adverse effects. In the period after 1980 productivity increases made possible a reduction in team sizes from twenty to nineteen. Management and the union agreed to seek this goal by attrition, and the teams were continuously involved in evening out their memberships and in replanning the distribution of their work. As demand continued to increase, however, overtime requirements became so heavy that by 1986 discussions were beginning about increasing the team size again.

The normal process of collective bargaining would make such sustained and participative treatment of these issues impossible. When issues are bundled together in a package and settled in a single burst of bargaining, they cannot be opened to such lengthy and public scrutiny. By contrast, the flexibility of the GWPH and the team structure encourages increased involvement.

This effort is distinguished from most managerialist structures by its elaborate system of participation, backed with the power of a union. There is certainly a good deal of uneasiness among the managers in the plant, an uneasiness probably exacerbated by the fact that they must continue justifying themselves to an uncomprehending and often hostile environment. Some hold on to an ingrained sense, expressed almost wistfully, that without all these meetings and rotation and so on, they could design a system that would really hum. Yet they are continually confronted with the dramatic fact that the system *works*—and has kept on working so well that new Shell plants started in the past few years have all adopted its principles and basic mechanisms.

The changes required of the union are equally dramatic, though less familiar. As one ECWU local official, Judy McKibbon, puts it, "We are just one party in a galaxy of parties—the union, management, and seven teams." Coordinating this complex set of relationships is more difficult than the traditional role, in which the union is essentially the only channel for dealing with disputes. "A worker can speak to his manager," says McKibbon, "and if anything's going to undermine the union, that's it. You can't stop people from trying to make individual bargains. You almost want to go back to the old days, when the union cracked the whip and said, 'You will not,' in order to keep our strength."[2]

But McKibbon and the other union leaders see beyond the limitations of the old balance of power, and they have developed a number of ways of dealing with the new situation. Several people, both in the union and in management, speak of the ECWU at Sarnia as "the conscience of the company." There have been numerous instances when management has tried to override the participative process but has been brought up short by the union's reference to the mutually agreed-on values. "We make people conscious of principles," says local president Bob Huget. "We make people wake up." Indeed, workers in the plant talk frequently and with detailed understanding of "the concept" of the plant, using it as a measuring stick to evaluate management. "The company probably thinks they made a mistake, really, writing down so much at the beginning," suggests another officer. But it is precisely the existence of written principles and norms that enables the complex and flexible social system of the plant to function as smoothly as it does.

Internally, the local is unusually decentralized in its own decision making. Though the executive board retains full responsibility for collective bargaining and major issues that touch on the contract, it allows the teams to deal directly with a significant range of issues. Management, for instance, offered two options when supervisors went on vacation: either to take on the normal supervisory functions as a team, without extra pay, or to promote someone temporarily to the position. The union, after some debate, allowed each team to make the decision on its own. On other occasions the union leadership has recommended positions that have been rejected by some teams. "I know it's heresy," said one union official, "but sometimes the interests of the local don't coincide with the interests of the members."[3] Heresy or not, it is a fact—and this is one of the few locals to do something about it.

The role of the local officers, including the stewards, is demanding. National representatives have been very impressed by their knowledge and problem-solving ability. They spend very little time in the usual business of handling grievances; in the first seven years there were only eleven formal grievances in the plant. Instead, they play a major role in coordinating discussions of controversial issues, keeping the membership aware of the strategic concerns of the union, and maintaining communication with the executive board. They find themselves dealing with a far broader slice of the membership than is usual in other unions, because they are not just representing those who have grievances. As Bob Huget puts it, "The difficulty is that you have to look at both sides: you have to look at the person with the problem, and you have to look at the people who *don't* have the problem." Sometimes it turns out that the quiet ones, who are rarely heard in traditional settings, disagree with those who are prone to file grievances; then the union must chart a difficult course toward consensus among its members.

With all this interaction, claims McKibbon, the officers are *"really* accountable to the members. They actually impeached someone, even though we don't have an impeachment mechanism." Attendance at union meetings was very high during the first few years, and the general level of activity in the union remains strong.

Earlier I described management as being somewhat puzzled by the success of the process despite their lack of clear control. Something very similar can be said about the union leaders. At some level they feel this *cannot* work, with all these different groups involved in representation and cutting into the role of the union; yet they have to admit that somehow it *does* work. In terms of hard results: the rate of pay is above the norm because everyone has the chance to progress to the top; and in the life of the plant, no one has been laid off from the bargaining unit. Moreover, the leadership agrees that members' loyalty to the union remains high and that they remain willing to engage in militant action if necessary. Two strike votes have been taken during the life of the plant, and in both the union leadership was supported by more than 90 percent of the members. The process operators rallied behind the craft workers in their demand for changes in the progression system, and all the employees supported the union in refusing to handle output from a plant that was under strike by another local. There had been no major splits within the membership and no grievances over the handling of peer discipline.

Of course, as with any system, there remain problems. The major one at present appears to be the role of the "team coordinators." The early phase of the plant's operation, seven years ago, was difficult and slow, due primarily to the inadequacy of the operators' initial technical training. To fill in the gaps in knowledge, management appointed "temporary" coordinators for each team, who were formally in the position of first-line supervisors. That temporary position has now become frozen in place. The union refuses to allow the coordinators to return to the bargaining unit if it would mean laying off existing workers; management, uncertain of what to do with the people, argues that they perform necessary functions. Many team members apparently feel the coordinators do little and that they could carry on just fine without them—though there is controversy on this point—and they resent the implied lack of trust in their continued presence. Task forces so far have failed to come up with a solution.

To some of those immersed in the situation, this issue touches the basic principles of the plant and threatens their overall level of commitment. Yet from an outsider's perspective, this seems no thornier than a number of the issues that have been solved in the past. A certain level of tension and discontent appears to be almost a constant in the social order. The point is not that the Shell plant is fully harmonious but rather that disagreements have generally led to creative solutions that have reinforced the basic structure. The system could not otherwise have continued to be successful for nine years.[4]

Other Examples

The Shell-Sarnia case can hardly be taken as the key model. It is obviously unusual; neither the policy framework nor other social institutions and expectations support it as yet. What it does offer is a set of ideas and mechanisms that may be useful. More importantly, it indicates the *possibility* of a system of representation quite different from those that have become familiar.

Once one begins to search, there are many other such cases in which the process of representation has moved beyond the usual two-party interaction, and in which the forums for resolving disputes are multiple and continuous. Within the standard labor relations framework, there are several other examples of autonomous team structures that are actively involved with unions, including an Alcoa plant organized by the Steelworkers and several General Motors auto factories. Beyond that framework, the horizons broaden greatly. One can find many examples of systems of representation that are more flexible than that of traditional collective bargaining. I will discuss a few among many.

The Pontiac Fiero plant in Detroit. Not far up the river from Sarnia, the Pontiac Fiero plant also was designed with the union as a consensus partner from the start. The work structure resembles a traditional assembly line, but the governance system has some significantly different characteristics. One level of management has been completely eliminated and three others cut substantially, leaving the slimmest managerial structure in General Motors. Workers are organized in teams that have responsibility for inspecting their own work and catching quality problems at the source. The workers, I am told, did not believe at the start that they would not be punished in some way for noting defects, but over time the trust has grown, and the plant ranks consistently at the top of all General Motors plants for the quality of its production. The teams meet for one-half hour each week to discuss any concerns they identify.

Like many QWL efforts, this one has run through its initial burst of enthusiasm and is in danger of losing momentum. Unlike most, however, its plant management and union are committed to pushing forward: "We need to do something bold, something drastic," says operations manager Frank Slaughter. He agrees that the next phase must involve widespread participation in basic policy issues in the plant. Recently, twenty-four "slice" teams—representatives from all levels and parts of the organization—have been formed to look at fundamental processes "with a view to dramatic change."[5]

The union facilitator, Leo van Houten, has some interesting comments on the effects of this system on the union. "It used to be," he says, "that the 15 percent of troublemakers were the ones who really elected the officers, the ones who were really represented. Now the other 85 percent get a voice. Sometimes they don't want the union to defend the 15 percent. That puts us in a bind, but it means we are really doing a better job of representing all the people." Many union officers had trouble adjusting to the new demands, though most have made the transition. The whole electoral base has changed. "We used to represent just the wrongs of people," he continues. "I can see the next election being based not on the wrongs, but on people's *rights.*"

General Motors' "Saturn Project." The Saturn Project took off from the Fiero experiment and brought the use of slice groups to a new height. A team of ninety-nine people designed a new plant from scratch that is intended to be the answer to the Japanese challenge. The group included top managers, engineers, operations managers, union officials, and line workers, with a total of fifty-five nonmanagement representatives. According to those involved, the discussion process was extraordinarily open and freewheeling. During a two-year period they considered a wide variety of possible structures. Even more astonishing, they operated on the basis of consensus. This wide array of disparate perspectives was melded into a highly innovative design, including what UAW president Owen Bieber calls "a degree of codetermination never before achieved in U.S. collective bargaining"[6]—and all ninety-nine supported the recommendations. After that, as the UAW's chief negotiator with GM puts it, formal collective bargaining simply "rounded off the edges."[7]

The design itself stresses consensus decision making, team-based participation, and extensive information-sharing throughout the company—the key elements of a strong system of influence. Many remain skeptical that the plant will operate as planned, which is a natural response to such innovation. But at this point, the final design is not the most important thing about the Saturn agreement; it is the *planning process* itself that has already broken the standard mold of collective bargaining. The group of ninety-nine was given a considerable demonstration of the power of a more flexible form of negotiation to explore new territory and to expand the scope of possible agreements.

Professional unions. As we move beyond the narrow confines of traditional labor relations, interesting cases multiply. Studies of professional unions, for example, are all too few, but the results are suggestive. They find a tendency for the unions to focus on broad frameworks in collective bargaining—sets of standards, or principles, rather than detailed rules—allowing space for individual bargaining to account for variations among the membership. Thus, according to Richard Walton, engineering unions tend to support merit systems, rather than seeking formally equal treatment or stressing objective factors such as seniority. Their effort is directed primarily at making the standards of evaluation *public.* By opening principles to public scrutiny, they seek to make influence an effective lever in the evaluation process.[8]

Unionization has presented a particularly difficult problem in universities, which have had a strong tradition of collegiality. Though unions have made considerable inroads in public-sector universities, they have not settled into classic forms. In many cases they coexist with faculty senates and create a differentiation between two types of issues that are handled in different ways. The senates deal with "professional" issues of curriculum and academic standards, and their collegial mechanisms stress openness and cooperation. The unions, on the other hand, take over the concerns of professors as employees: the classic "working condition" concerns of pay, workload, and grievances. Though some unions have tried to move into the "professional" area, they have not been nearly as successful with this range of issues.[9]

Norway's experience. The European scene is much richer in experimentation than our own. To take a single example, in Norway a general agreement was reached in the late 1970s to involve unions in the implementation of new technological systems. In some companies this has been taken to mean a voice for labor from the very beginning of the design process. The general functions and outlines of the system are negotiated *before* it is developed. This involves, of course, an unusual amount of disclosure by management and the development of new skills and knowledge by the union representatives.

Among the important lessons of the Norwegian experience is that unions, even with such expanded powers, have not automatically been able to affect management policy. Those that have been effective have had to make two important changes in their usual strategies. The first was to thoroughly involve shopfloor workers in deliberations about implementation decisions—initially through a network of shop stewards trained in technology issues, and later through discussions with the wider membership. The second change was to reach out actively in all directions to mobilize support for their positions, forming alliances with groups outside the union, especially with systems analysts within management. Alliances have also involved personnel department officials, other professional groups, and union federations.[10] The normal tactics of adversarial mobilization are insufficient to work out the kinds of detailed agreements that are demanded by this process.

Negotiations with interest groups. Moving further beyond traditional labor relations, the multiplication of interest groups in the past decade has produced many efforts to broaden the concepts and techniques of negotiation. Environmental disputes, for example, may involve dozens of interests, all willing and eager to attack any attempt at regulation by experts and to take their cases to court. In some instances, it has proved to be possible to achieve stable agreements by bringing all the parties together in a multifaceted negotiation process, with the aim of achieving consensus on regulatory solutions. The fragmenting forces of factional squabbling have not proved insurmountable.

One early instance of this approach was the National Coal Policy Project (NCPP). The oil crisis of the late 1970s had created great pressure to increase the use of coal, which in turn sharpened disagreements over its environmental impact, setting up a classic situation of bitter conflict that focused on regulatory action by the government. In 1978 leading conservationists came together with labor and management representatives from coal and other resource-consuming industries to seek a solution that would avoid the costs of extended litigation. Initially, the level of skepticism was intense. Some environmental groups denounced the very idea of negotiating as a sellout to industry. Gradually, however, networks and coalitions were formed of the major interests affected by the problem. They succeeded in reaching agreement in principle on more than two hundred recommendations, establishing an important level of policy consensus in an area that had been highly fragmented.[11] This pioneering effort has been followed and greatly extended in more recent environmental disputes.[12]

Implications

What do these examples prove? From the perspective of labor relations, they are surprising; they do some things that, under the usual assumptions, cannot be done. They have explored many types of issues that are not dealt with effectively by collective bargaining, from work processes to strategic planning, and they show that it is possible to build agreement on matters that are too complex or too detailed to fit into the confines of periodic contract discussions. They have involved a wide range of employees, including professionals and other groups not covered by the Wagner Act, and have involved them more deeply and continuously than is normal. They have even brought management and workers together with groups who are not employees at all, but who are, nevertheless, affected by corporate decisions. They have managed a high level of diversity and a multiplicity of perspectives, demonstrating that conflict can be handled without narrowing it down to two opposing points of view.

These may be seen as models of cooperation; indeed, they manage to coordinate the efforts of many people more effectively than do most organizations. But "cooperation" in these cases does not mean harmony and sweetness. It is certainly not a simple matter of new attitudes among traditional adversaries, a magical triumph of reason. These systems are full of conflict that is sometimes quite sharp. They differ from a traditional system in the way these conflicts are resolved. The *structure* of roles and relationships no longer encourages polarization; it provides many options for working out disputes at different levels. Therefore, there is a greater chance that an appropriate forum can be found to deal with problems immediately, before seeking a more dramatic form of confrontation that is favored in the Wagner Act framework.

All this is possible because, as these cases indicate, influence can be a powerful form of pressure. The conflicts in these instances center, not on efforts to coerce other parties through strikes or lockouts, but rather on winning a critical mass of opinion. Management might be able to win a pitched battle, but in such a victory it would hurt itself as much as its adversaries; it needs to maintain its *reputation* for the long run. That is why the union at Shell-Sarnia, for example, has been able to exert pressure as the "conscience" of the company. Management in this case can be hurt as much by an attack on its honesty as by a strike.

A system of representation that downplays power thus need not rely on "niceness." It is simply a different way of dealing with conflict. But that way has major advantages. It need not involve pitched camps, with a winner and a loser; issues and alliances can grow and shift over time, and the outcome can be a clarification of *shared* principles and a strengthening of commitment to them.

There are, however, some important preconditions to the effective functioning of such a system. One is that there be no major inequality of power. In most of these cases, traditional unions have been there to provide the balance, though they have not focused on their traditional weapons and tactics of mobilization. Still, this is clearly an awkward, hybrid solution; these unions are constantly worried about undermining their organizational strength. The solution in some universities, as described earlier, is to split the functions of power and influence, giving the former to a union and the latter to a "senate." Quite a different solution is provided by the case of environmental disputes: the public interest associations are in no way a match for companies *as organizations*, but rely on their effectiveness in *political* appeals to establish a rough equality.

A related condition is that influence has to be important. A company that does not care what anyone thinks is not going to be swayed by any of these pressures. But such a go-it-alone stance is more and more a rarity. Even the most hard-nosed company is vulnerable to organized attacks on its reputation. This vulnerability has been increased by several developments in the past two decades. First, it grows with the sophistication of markets, as "image" becomes more vital to sales. It is interesting in this context to note that a number of companies, such as IBM, Ford, and Motorola, have made their enlightened personnel policies an important theme in their advertising. Second, the growing internal need for employee commitment makes companies more sensitive to the use of influence. A company like Shell-Sarnia, which has to rely on the intelligence and flexibility of its workers, cannot ignore their complaints. Finally, the ability of interest groups to mobilize the support of government is another powerful reason for business to pay attention to its reputation.

Obviously, this is not an easy road. The groups described earlier are traveling it because collective bargaining has reached a dead end in attempting to solve many of the important problems of employees and other groups. The classic balance-of-power framework in the Wagner Act, faced with a situation requiring strategic flexibility and major restructuring of the economy, has served only to increase mistrust and rigidity. At the same time, bureaucracy—the context for industrial unionism—appears more and more limited and vulnerable. The examples described in this chapter, and many more, are part of a widespread societal exploration of alternatives to the bureaucratic organization of power.

PART III

BUILDING A NEW SYSTEM

INTRODUCTION

Three Elements of
Representation

THE EFFORTS that were sketched in the last chapter expand the possibilities of what a system of representation can include. It is not enough, however, to cite particular models; social change does not happen by copying cases. Each of the examples described is necessarily atypical, born under highly favorable conditions. The parties have been unusually secure and willing to try new ideas. The employers have had a highly "enlightened" understanding of the value of commitment and participation, and the unions have been relatively strong and innovative. The experiments, moreover, remain quite vulnerable because they are surrounded by an environment that has different values. The Shell-Sarnia case, effective as it is, might be quickly wiped out by a major change in the market for polypropylene.

Thus the cases do not in themselves constitute a generalizable system. For that we have to look at larger social forces and movements. Trends at this broader level must fit with and support a new system in order for it to move beyond the stage of experimentation and exceptions.

Any system of representation must have ways of dealing with at least three problems. First and most fundamental is the issue of *power*. No mechanisms of expression can function effectively when the ability of one party to coerce another creates an underlying climate of fear. Second is a structure of *representation*. There must be legitimate bodies that can develop collective positions, avoiding both excessive centralization and its opposite, endless factional splintering. Third is a method of *dispute resolution*—mechanisms for reaching agreement among the parties.

The Wagner Act framework, by law and tradition, gives one set of answers to these issues. It supports the creation of powerful worker organizations to balance management; it groups individuals into homogeneous bodies on the basis of industry or occupation and offers exclusive rights of representation (within a bargaining unit) to organizations that win a majority vote; and it centers on collective bargaining to resolve competing claims. This structure creates the balance-of-power model, with the rigidities and limitations we have already explored.

There are, however, three recent developments or social trends that are moving toward another set of answers. First, a new form of employee power, independent of unions, has been entering the workplace since the 1960s, through the steady broadening of *employee rights*. Civil rights and other legislation has enabled employees to make direct claims that are recognized by the courts and do not depend on the massing of organizational strength. This development, incomplete as it is, creates a dynamic that is different from the Wagner Act's balance-of-power model, offering enforceable channels for claims that originate outside the union structure.

Similarly, the concept of representation has begun to shift. Faced with growing diversity in their environments, many unions have explored the idea that representation must embrace local variation and participation rather than striving for contractual unity. They have begun to develop capacities for flexible strategy, including representation of members who are not part of an exclusive bargaining unit, and forms of pressure besides the mass strike. As they move toward more decentralized structures, they resemble more the types of *association* that were at the origin of the labor movement than the powerful bureaucracies that were encouraged by the Wagner Act framework.

Finally, the simple two-party model of bargaining inherent in the Wagner Act is already being strained by a multiplicity of groups that want a part of the action. Conventional collective bargaining has proved inadequate in dealing with complex issues and claims. In recent years, improved techniques of *multilateral negotiation* have produced agreements by bringing together all interested parties in a single process for resolving disputes. This opens up the possibility of dealing with many types of issues that do not fit within the limits of collective bargaining, especially issues that require continuous and broad involvement.

These three elements—employee rights, associational unionism, and multilateral negotiation—have not grown in any coordinated way. They have been, so far, largely separate and disconnected responses to the general breakdown of the old forms. Separately, they are limited in how far they can move; but *together*, they meet the basic requirements of a system of representation.

A system based on these three elements would expand the scope of employee representation, but it would reduce the danger of destructive conflict and fragmentation. That is one lesson of the successful "advanced" models already described. A system of representation that is weak, restricted, and inappropriate to the concerns of employees actually increases the chance for trouble, because it dams up discontent and then releases it in the wrong directions. A more complete system, such as that of Shell-Sarnia, provides mechanisms that can tackle directly the real problems of organizations and employees. Projects already in progress can help define policy and organizational frameworks that will encourage new developments.

CHAPTER 8

Employee Rights

The Quiet Transformation

The starting point for our exploration of a possible new system is in a transformation that is already well under way. During the past twenty years, while the traditional labor relations system has declined, the foundations of a different one have been laid. The waning strength of unions since the 1960s has been matched by a growing support for employee rights in the workplace. Far from being freed by their victories over their traditional enemies, employers have found themselves hemmed in by new forces that are often harder to identify and to deal with.

The Wagner Act made the smallest possible cut in the "corporate veil," leaving intact the fiction of the corporation as a private person. It granted employees one right, and one only: the right to form unions. All further limits on management power were supposed to flow from the private battle between management and labor, with government turning its face away.

Of course, that single right had the potential for far-reaching effects. In interpreting the act the NLRB and the courts have had to decide how far to extend it. On the whole, they have extended it in a peculiar way: they have attached further rights—but *to unions*, rather than to union members. Unions, but not people, have the right to information needed for bargaining, the right to strike, the right to good-faith treatment by the employer. Employers can fire workers without reason, but they cannot refuse to give reasons in the collective bargaining process. Employees are protected from reprisals when they protest through their union but not when they protest against it. In brief, the rights of workers have been derived from the rights of a particular organization sanctioned by the government—rather than the reverse.

The reason for this strange inversion, as I showed in chapter 3, comes down to the fear of faction: it is easier to control dissension and to limit its fragmenting effects when it is guided into a single channel. Yet this approach also results in a steady undermining of the foundations of labor. Unions originate as *associations* of workers coming together in a common cause, but they are pushed toward becoming *organizations* that emphasize stability.

However, one of the most important developments of the past two decades has been a steady societal shift away from this pattern. There has been a crumbling of support for unions as formal organizations supported by the state and, at the same time, a clear increase in support for *employees'* rights directly enforceable against corporations.

The shift began with legislative actions during the early 1960s. In practice, Title VII of the Civil Rights Act of 1964 has been the most significant labor legislation since the Wagner Act. For a large category of employees it amounts to a guarantee of due process in the workplace. Minority employees can, in effect, legally be disciplined and discharged only for reasons of work performance. Limited as this step was, people flocked to claim its protection. In 1975 more than 66,000 formal charges were filed with the Equal Employment Opportunity Commission (EEOC)—which does not even count the charges filed with state civil rights agencies.[1]

The effect of Title VII on employers, especially large ones, has been considerable. A suit filed against AT&T in the early 1970s was so costly to the company and required such massive changes in corporate policies that the shock waves extended widely. Many corporations revamped their personnel policies to ensure that disciplines and dismissals of minority employees clearly could be justified on the basis of work performance. That has led to a widespread adoption of progressive discipline systems and verifiable documentation in place of managerial whim.[2] So extensive has been the change, in fact, that the Reagan administration's recent attempts to weaken discrimination standards have actually been resisted by most large corporations. A spokesman for the National Association of Manufacturers contends that affirmative action has benefited business as well as minorities, and that without government action "the rate of progress would have been infinitely slower."[3]

Title VII was one of the first breaches in the "veil" of management prerogatives since the Wagner Act. Unlike the latter, however, it started a trend. During the 1970s a rapid-fire series of federal statutes further encroached on corporate personnel policies. Due process protection was extended to people over the age of forty by the Age Discrimination in Employment Act. Among federal contractors, the Vocational Rehabilitation Act prohibited discharge or discrimination based on physical handicaps or mental limitations. The Occupational Safety and Health Act provided workers important rights to enforce standards of safety in the workplace. And a long series of regulatory statutes have included specific protections for workers. Before 1974, a company could fire employees to prevent them from vesting in pension funds, but the Employment Retirement Income Security Act of 1974 put a stop to that. Polluters, after the passage of the Clean Air Act Amendments of 1977, could no longer punish whistleblowers in their ranks. The list goes on: at least twenty-six major statutes now contain similar protections.[4]

But some of the most significant advances have been made not at the federal but at the state level. State statutes have expanded discrimination protections to include, among other things, sexual orientation, political activity, medical condition (including pregnancy), criminal record, and marital status. At least thirty-five states have their own civil rights enforcement agencies, and thirty-one have restricted employers' use of lie detectors. At least eight have passed general provisions protecting whistleblowers. California, which has been on the leading edge of most of these developments, has now reached the point of giving serious consideration to generalized "just-cause" protection to pull together all the specific statutes. And almost all of these developments have occurred, remarkably, within the past twenty years.

In short, it is fair to say that both the legal right and the political ability of government to limit managerial power are now beyond dispute. Furthermore, the forces driving these developments appear to run deep; the legislative arena is not the only one to be affected, and the United States is far from the only country. The pattern reappears widely.

It has been paralleled and extended by critical changes in legal interpretation. Since the mid-1970s, the courts have been flooded with claims to rights on the job. Those who felt they had been unfairly fired or disciplined formerly had no recourse aside from a union; now they are more likely to find themselves a lawyer. And what is even more significant, the courts have begun to respond positively— reversing a position they had held firmly for almost a century. Their willingness to recognize individual claims against companies has been a fundamental shift in the law of employment.

Until recently, courts had been guided by the doctrine of "employment at will," expressed in a seminal 1884 decision that held that employers "may dismiss their employees at will . . . for good cause, for no cause, or even for cause morally wrong, without thereby being guilty of legal wrong."[5] This position made the veil of employer prerogative impenetrable to individual claims. Decisions throughout the country frequently held that not even dismissal for refusal to commit an illegal act could justify governmental interference.

This doctrine remained almost untouched until the mid-1970s. Then, rather suddenly, a number of jurisdictions agreed that terminations that violated public policy should be subject to court scrutiny. In West Virginia, for instance, a bank officer fired for questioning an order that he illegally boost customer service charges ("Add $50 or $100 to the charge," his superior had told him, "whatever you think you can get away with") won a right to a hearing—and, eventually, substantial damages.[6] A torrent of subsequent decisions has confirmed and broadened this "public policy exception" and has sent shock waves through the ranks of management lawyers. It used to be that lawyers would advise management to give no reasons when firing an employee; now the lack of reasons can raise questions of motive that lead to judicial intervention.

Another line of rulings has taken the public policy exception much further: some courts have been willing to read an "implied covenant of good faith and fair dealing" into all employment contracts. Any termination that is "motivated by bad faith or malice or based on retaliation," in this view, contravenes the general public interest and is subject to judicial review. A crucial decision of 1974 argues: "The employer's interest in running his business as he sees fit must be balanced against the interest of the employee in maintaining his employment *and the public's interest in maintaining a proper balance between the two.*"[7]

That is a very broad reading of the public interest in the employment contract. A more recent (1983) decision, of particular interest for our purposes, takes this interpretation still further: the decision derives a "cognizable expression of public policy" from the free speech provision of the federal Constitution.[8] Until now, constitutional guarantees have been held inapplicable to the "private" realm of the corporation; the reasoning of this last decision, if carried forward as a precedent, would complete the movement toward treating employer power as a public matter.

The issue of employee rights affects other countries as well. In 1971 the International Labour Organisation issued a call for unjust-dismissal protection in all industrial democracies. It was only following a current that was already running swiftly through its member nations. Italy, France, England, Sweden, and almost every other developed country passed major new protections for workers during the next decade. As one observer summarized the events: "Although it takes somewhat different forms . . . the new industrial revolution is fundamentally a single phenomenon: the fact that job rights . . . are being elevated to political and legal parity with property rights."[9]

Given the depth and breadth of the phenomenon, one would not expect the spread of employee rights to be greatly affected by changes in Washington. Indeed, though the Reagan administration has fought most such initiatives and has slowed the progress of federal legislation, the general movement continues to grow. Many of the events I have described, including the development of new legal doctrines and initiatives at the state level, have occurred during the Reagan years. Women's groups are seeking not only to eliminate pay inequities on given jobs but to end the widespread pattern of segregating women in lower-paying positions; this "comparable worth" movement has been a focus of numerous EEOC complaints and has had some major recent boosts from the courts.

Even at the federal level, movement is continuing. The right to pregnancy leave, another new claim, has progressed to the Supreme Court, has been supported by a series of blue-ribbon panels, and is receiving substantial support in Congress. The right to privacy has been advanced by a bill, which has passed the House, to prohibit most private companies from giving polygraph tests to prospective or current employees. *Fortune* recently expressed the dismay of many in the business community at this continued attack on their formerly protected position:

> Quietly, so quietly that most executives aren't yet aware of what's happening, courts and state legislatures are rewriting the rules by which managers run U.S. corporations. Some of the changes severely curtail the freedom of managers to decide fundamental business matters. . . . The success of this new attack on management prerogatives comes at a surprising time. Serious efforts in Congress to expand corporate "accountability" waned in the late 1970s and have practically vanished under President Reagan. But corporate reformers didn't surrender. They simply shifted the locus of their attacks from Washington to the states and from legislatures to the courts. They have won remarkable victories that impinge much more on day-to-day management than the myriad regulations heaped on corporations over the last six decades.[10]

These developments, occurring in a relatively brief span of time, have cut deeply into the "private" preserve of corporations, exposing them increasingly to public standards of right.

Rights: Divisive or Constructive?

The development of employee rights, which has come in bits and pieces over many years, has not been widely noted, and its effects are generally underestimated. Yet it has already changed the dynamics of industrial relations, and it has the potential for turning them upside down. I have argued that many of the limitations of the Wagner Act framework stem from the need to maintain a balance of power—to keep up the strength of the union as an organization that can meet management head-on in confrontation.[11] It is for that reason that, until recently, rights have been granted primarily to unions, and to their members only indirectly through the unions. The trend of events since the passage of Title VII, however, shatters that framework by allowing employees to make direct claims to the government. It pierces the walls around both union and management organizations, revealing that they are both made up of people.

At the same time, it immediately lifts some of the key limitations of the

Wagner Act approach. There is no longer a need to draw a sharp line between workers and management; the rights described here are available to all employees. Reliance on the strike is reduced; indeed, unions have often made use of legal pressure to make advances where the strike is inadequate. The whole struggle over organizing becomes less crucial, because rights can be asserted whether or not a majority has joined a single organization. The new rights, in other words, extend where unions have been unable to go.

But that is only one part of the story. Not all rights are equal in their effects; they can be divisive as well as constructive. Depending on how they are defined and structured, they can provide the foundation for an effective and cooperative system of worker representation—or they can encourage litigious fragmentation. The current movement has progressed only part way, and for the moment, there is an uneasy coexistence between traditional labor relations and the set of new employee rights. But as the latter continue to develop, it becomes more imperative to ask where they are going.

So far, the development of workplace rights has been largely divisive, seriously flawed by the fact that it has proceeded in a scattered and particularistic way. The recognition of new claims has resulted, not from a changed consensus about the relation of employees to employers, but as a way of solving *specific* problems of individuals or classes of individuals. The rights of blacks, of women, or of the disabled are protected in different ways and under different circumstances, but the rights of *workers* remain undefined. That is a misuse of the concept of employee rights. Rights in the form of broad guarantees can provide a foundation for a vigorous system of representation; but as particular "fixes" they undermine such a system and lead to inequity, confusion, narrow litigiousness, administrative overload, and poor implementation.

Inequity and confusion result from the fact that while one problem is being solved, others are being ignored; the scattered approach does not produce coherent principles of fairness. In the case of employment-at-will doctrines, according to a prominent legal scholar of this field:

> There are serious problems with the way the case law has evolved. . . . The standards, as enunciated by the courts, are vague. Some decisions use the same term—such as just cause—in different senses in the very same opinion. Thus, it is difficult to provide adequate counsel and advice to both employers and employees.[12]

As a form of employee protection, the network of rights is still full of holes. It would be grossly inaccurate to suggest that the law in this country now effectively protects employees from management abuses. On the contrary, the present situation is characterized by serious irrationality. If you work in California, you have a good deal of protection, but if you cross the line into Nevada, it is a very different story. In most states employees can still be fired for the color of their socks; in many, a woman can still be dismissed for refusing to sleep with her supervisor. Even in California and other "advanced" states, the protections form a patchwork that leaves out many categories of employees and issues. Finally, the costly and cumbersome nature of the legal process restricts its use largely to the most educated and affluent employees.

Indeed, from a slight distance, the scene looks more like a lottery than a system of justice. As many as 10,000 wrongful-discharge suits are now filed per year; a few of them end in awards of over $1 million; yet no one—neither the lawyers, nor the employers or employees involved, nor apparently the courts themselves— can safely predict, on the basis of settled principles, which will be successful and which will not.

But the greatest problem in the long run is that rights used as specific fixes replace a system of representation rather than strengthen it. They are, in effect, an effort to solve problems by fiat rather than by negotiation. It is this which encourages litigiousness and overloads administrative systems.

Conceptually, the structure that results from this approach is one of many individuals and groups making claims to a central body. That body must then stand "above the fray" and make "impartial" judgments. The claimants need exercise no *responsibility;* they are expected to press their interests as hard as possible. The responsibility for maintaining a coherent system rests entirely with the arbitrating agency.

The spread of employee rights I have described has generally gone hand in hand with precisely this kind of conflict resolution, leading to the development of neutral arbitrating agencies rather than strong systems of representation. Title VII, for example, spawned the Equal Employment Opportunity Commission and many state level counterparts; the Occupational Safety and Health Administration relies heavily on government inspectors and administrative law judges. The due process proposals in California and elsewhere go much further. They recommend enormously expanded mechanisms of dispute arbitration—"labor courts" of one form or another—which would enable many claims to be resolved quickly. In this they follow the existing models of many European countries, such as West Germany and England, which already have such separate court systems to settle cases of disputed discharge.

Such an approach simply replaces collective bargaining with government supervision. Thus it is not surprising that unions have been, at best, ambivalent in many of the struggles over rights; they have failed, for instance, to support strongly the California due process bill, because they see it as encroaching on their own function.

The scattered, particularistic approach to rights actually discourages the formation of consensus. Since the parties represent only themselves, without connections to wider groups, they can hardly avoid "selfishness" and narrow adversarial tactics. If general principles do emerge over time, they exist only in the minds of the "expert" judges, not among those who have to live with the decisions.

Nor can this approach by itself successfully *implement* new definitions of rights. Without a framework of organized relations, enforcement is almost impossible; at best only the most visible targets are hit. The history of the Occupational Safety and Health Administration (OSHA), for instance, has shown that no army of government inspectors can ensure compliance with health and safety standards without the help of local organizations for monitoring and implementation. As for due process, studies in both Europe and the United States have noted that courts cannot enforce orders requiring the reinstatement of dismissed workers without an effective union on the spot. The courts and administrative agencies are too distant to oversee the carrying out of their edicts, and more important, they cannot work out the details and methods of implementation.

In the American context, this version of employee rights has particularly damaging consequences. It enormously increases the strain on a regulatory system that is already in crisis. It demands from government a greatly *increased* role in resolving day-to-day problems and conflicts in the workplace. Without some way of building agreement among the parties, there is no way a government agency can do anything but displease everyone by its judgments; the strain on the government's legitimacy, which is already great, can only grow.

That is the divisive side of rights—what happens when they are cut off from effective forms of representation. The whole process has happened not only largely outside unions, but outside any institution that can develop ongoing interpretations and agreements. Thus the entire burden falls on the government. The continuation of the current trend of piling up many separate guarantees is likely to lead toward an unpleasant state of universal contentiousness, in which administrators try to take on the thankless job of holding apart numerous parties, all aggressively asserting their claim. That is not, however, the only choice.

Employee Rights in a System of Representation

There is an alternative: rather than *replacing* negotiation, rights can provide the foundation for *extending* it to the full range of employee issues. But this would require simplification, not multiplication. Instead of continuing to add specific rights to deal with each claim on employer power, it would involve focusing on a few more general principles, which could provide a common ground on which effective negotiations and discussions might take place.

The Bill of Rights of our Constitution can serve as a model. The guarantees in that document are stated in extremely brief and general terms; some of the most important are subclauses within single sentences. They list no exceptions, detail no qualifications. They express only the most essential boundaries that define a free society. They do not attempt to invade the function of legislation by solving specific problems, leaving that to a representative body. As a result, they have been broad enough to support a changing society and to provide a common ground for some of our most critical national debates for more than two centuries.

Almost any of the recent developments in employment law contrasts with this model. The rights are detailed and highly qualified; they try to embed the complex compromises and balances needed for solving specific problems in the basic structure of the law. But there is a growing awareness of the need to broaden the approach. To take one example: it is becoming evident that the attempt to win a right to pregnancy leave builds on too narrow a base. In tackling a specific, though important, problem, it divides women from men, and it excludes other disabilities that are equally significant. Some advocates are therefore suggesting a different and broader approach, "gender-neutral," which would provide job protection for all forms of disability. Another case: though job security has been a central theme of labor struggles for a century or more, it is becoming clear even to many unions that no one can expect to hold on to a *specific* job as a matter of right. Such a view of job security in a rapidly changing environment is too rigid to be practical, and it also ends by setting different segments of the membership at each others' throats. In the light of these problems, unions like the UAW and the CWA have begun to work toward a more flexible concept of "employment security." That concept, in turn, opens up a whole new range of creative approaches, including various forms of retraining, employee ownership, and the creation of new ventures.[13]

These initiatives begin to move toward the enunciation of general principles rather than specific guarantees. They help separate the task of defining values from that of implementing them and begin, therefore, to provide a foundation for an autonomous system of employee representation, rather than attempting to replace it. But in order to transform the basic impulse for the extension of employee rights from a divisive form to a constructive one, the process of simplification needs to go much further.

The essential question is: What minimum of rights is needed as a foundation for an effective system of representation? That question focuses on the limits to management power that are necessary to permit the expression of employee concerns. Once the problem is put this way, I believe, it is possible to reduce the myriad of specific rights to four general ones: due process, information, speech, and association.

1. Due process. For most employees, the ultimate fear that compels obedience at the workplace is the ability of management to dismiss them at will. A small story told by David Ewing, of the Harvard Business School, captures some of the emotion involved:

> Judging from what people said, the event was carried out like an execution, only the . . . victims were marched out from offices instead of cells . . . Holger Hjortsvang and Max Blankenzee were the first ones to go. On March 2, the security chief and a guard appeared suddenly at Hjortsvang's office. The security chief ordered Hjortsvang out and left him momentarily in the custody of the guard. The security chief then went to Blankenzee's office with another guard and ordered him out. All this happened quickly, and apparently took the two men by surprise. The two were marched by the guards and the security chief to the office of their superior, where they were given a choice. "Do you want to resign or do you want me to fire you—now?" Neither man offered to resign, so the superior told them they were fired. They were marched back to their office under custody and ordered to remove their personal possessions and leave. The offices were locked behind them.[14]

The two men worked for the San Francisco Bay Area Rapid Transit District (BART), and their offense had been to raise concerns about the safety of the system they were designing—concerns that later proved to be quite justified. But quite apart from the cause, the method is inexcusable. Ewing's analogy to a prison is apt: this was a raw display of force. Yet even prisoners are judged and sentenced according to norms of due process. If Hjortsvang and Blankenzee had committed murder, they would have received more civilized treatment.

An organization that treats its employees in this way cannot expect high morale and commitment, nor should it be surprised if, like BART, it finds itself crippled by scandal and corruption. Elaborate arguments can be made and evidence compiled to show that abuse of power hurts productivity and profit in the long run. But we cannot all wait for the long run; it should be a clear matter of public policy that such actions will not be tolerated.

Most corporate executives would probably agree that some mechanism of redress is needed to prevent occurrences like the BART firings. In another article, Ewing reports a "steady broadening of support for methods of assuring 'due process' to employees who feel they have been wronged by management."[15] As we saw in chapter 5, managerialist companies generally have rather elaborate systems for internal expression of grievances and careful processes for discipline and dismissal.[16] Frequently they imitate procedures developed in unionized settings. Unionized employees have always put the achievement of reliable grievance mechanisms near the top of their priorities—usually even higher than wage increases—and the structures that have been worked out are often counted among labor's most important achievements.

But neither the enlightened self-interest of management nor the pressure of unions has been sufficient to extend due process to the vast majority of the work force. Though the BART firings were dramatic, they were not unusual: about two million employees are discharged each year without the right to an impartial hearing.[17] That is about one in fifty, *every year*—quite sufficient for nearly everyone to see close at hand the fear that results.

Due process is the bedrock of any system that goes beyond naked force. Without it, trust can never be developed. It makes possible the opening of discussion and the channeling of discontent in constructive directions. Those who advocate "cooperation" should examine first the state of due process.

The *form* of due process—the methods of review and enforcement—may vary rather widely. Many managerialist companies actually combine several structures, such as ombudspersons, anonymous complaint channels, grievance mechanisms, and "open door" policies. The essential elements, however, seem to be the following:

- Standards for discipline must be publicly stated and commonly understood.
- Those standards should concern actions that affect work performance—not extraneous matters.
- The reasons for any disciplinary action must be available to the person accused.
- An impartial body must be available to review the relation between the specific charge and the accepted standards.

These standards of due process can already be derived from existing laws and court decisions. For example, the law on discrimination (Title VII) entails all of the standards. Employers who are challenged by minority employees on disciplinary matters must, in effect, be able to prove to a court that their reasons were based on work-related standards of performance. So far, however, due process advances have merely nibbled away at the veil of employer prerogative with a result that satisfies no one. The fabric is now too full of holes to protect authoritarian managers effectively, but it is still strong enough to smother expressions of dissent.

In Europe during the past decade there has been substantial movement toward solidifying a structure of due process. Most industrial countries by now have passed legislation requiring just cause for dismissals and establishing some sort of tribunal for reviewing complaints. In 1982 the International Labour Organisation adopted a "convention" that dismissals should be for valid reasons; the only negative votes, incidentally, came from Iraq, Saudi Arabia, Lebanon, Brazil, Chile—and the United States.

168

Examples of due-process requirements are varied and extensive enough to provide many ideas for specific approaches in this country.[18] It is probably too early to propose specific language; the field is still in an experimental stage. But the general lessons are clear: there is widespread pressure for protection against arbitrary uses of employer power, and such guarantees are essential to the development of trust and cooperation.

2. Information. Due process provides *negative* protections but no *positive* basis for a system of representation. Alone, all it does is encourage people with individual grievances to seek solutions. It does not help people to establish collective ways of expressing common interests and needs. A system in which leadership and commitment replace command and obedience must have a more complete foundation.

It is widely accepted that a system of capital exchange, for example, is impossible without accurate information about the true health of companies. That is why the role of the Securities and Exchange Commission has been so pivotal and so uncontroversial; it is quite apparent that falsification or concealment of company financial data destroys the trust that stabilizes the whole order. What is less widely accepted is that the same thing is true within companies: partial or distorted information is a destroyer of trust. Management that refuses to share with its employees the grounds for its decisions invites, almost compels, rigid "adversarial" reactions—not to mention creating ideal conditions for destructive rumors. "We can't trust you, we know you have something up your sleeve"—that is almost the archetypal relation of unions (and most unorganized employees) to their managers in this country.

In this realm, too, the old management "prerogatives" have been steadily pushed back. Managerialist companies have stressed the importance of full and open communication; in almost all cases they now regularly share data on company performance with their employees to a degree that was extremely unusual a decade ago. At Shell-Sarnia, where workers have direct access through their computers to all company data, they are required to sign pledges not to reveal proprietary data outside the company, and they could in theory be prosecuted for violating the pledge. But there have been no such leaks, and this structure has effectively prevented the growth of the suspicion that is so common in organizations.

Nevertheless, there remains a great deal of fear among managers that disclosure of information could get out of hand. Thus much of the recent progress, strongly resisted by employers, has occurred through legislation rather than voluntary reforms. For example, one of the most egregious types of concealment involves plant closings. Companies that plan to shut down part of their operations often hide it from their employees because they fear that angry workers will sabotage their equipment. Thus there are numerous instances in which workers show up to work in the morning and are told to clear out their lockers and leave on the spot. If these companies had been sharing information all along, the risk of violent reaction would, of course, be much less. This is an extreme example of how secrecy breeds mistrust and, in turn, requires more secrecy.

A number of states and cities have therefore passed laws requiring advance notice of plant shutdowns, so that employees will at least have an opportunity to prepare for the event. Similar legislation at the Federal level was passed in 1987, after years of slowly growing support.

The area of health and safety is another one in which pressure has grown for legislated requirements of notice. Many states have passed "right-to-know" legislation. In 1985 these were gathered into, and preempted by, a regulation published by the Occupational Safety and Health Administration that requires manufacturers to ensure that their employees are fully informed about potential chemical hazards in their workplace, not only by disseminating information but also by active training programs. A court review of the proposed standard has essentially validated it but—interestingly—has required OSHA to broaden it in crucial respects.[19]

Meanwhile, this general topic has been at the center of a storm in Europe for a number of years. Various Common Market nations have required extensive disclosure of information for a long time, without apparent ill effects. A directive has now been proposed by the European Economic Community (EEC) that would require multinationals to provide the same sort of wide-ranging strategic information.[20] Bitter resistance from U.S. and Japanese companies has slowed the initially strong momentum of this proposal; yet it keeps being revived even in the current conservative climate and still has a good chance of passage in some form.

A. W. Clausen, president of BankAmerica, has expressed with exceptional clarity the importance of a free flow of information for building a system of trust. In his own company, he instituted a thorough procedure to ensure that all except the most sensitive information is available to anyone who asks. Such "opening," he argues, is vital to the health of the economic system:

[V]oluntary disclosure . . . can help business earn the favorable judgment of our society: 1) by building and maintaining public support; 2) by focusing closer attention on internal methods and controls; and 3) by allowing the market system . . . to function in a more efficient manner.

In the long run, no company can thrive unless it has the understanding and trust of all those whose interests it serves: customers, investors, employees, and the public. A business is unlikely to secure and retain that trust if it treats its various constituencies as captive audiences which are entitled to very limited and slanted disclosures of information. If these constituencies believe that they lack necessary information to judge the adequacy of the company's performance by their standards and values, they will withdraw their support. Such a response was quite evident during the 1960s and early 1970s. Public confidence in the integrity of business underwent a massive erosion. . . .

We also view voluntary disclosure as a reaffirmation of our belief that the best regulator of business is the marketplace. . . . The essence of the market system is its reliance on well-informed participants rather than centralized authority for allocative decisions. The best way to preserve that market system is to demonstrate that, given adequate distribution of information, the market system is generally preferable to any system of regulation, direct or indirect.[21]

3. Speech. In a system of representation by power, speech is not a crucial issue: a silent strike is as effective as a noisy one. But when the focus shifts to influence, speech has a special importance. It constitutes the fundamental form of "pressure" that each of the parties can apply to the other. Under the present system, if one group wants to assert its demands, it organizes its power base; in an influence system, it mobilizes publicity in an attempt to build support for its position. The key to the battle is reputation instead of economic strength.

It is hard to find good examples of this process within companies. The thought of open criticism and discussion seems to stir managers' deepest fears. Even the most developed managerialist companies tend to hedge on this one; in their emphasis on unity, they view any open expression of dissent as an attack on their fundamental identity. Few people take criticism well, but many are skilled in finding justifications for suppressing or ignoring it. When those people hold power in organizations, the temptation is seldom resisted.

Thus, expressions of dissent in managerialist companies tend to be confined to closed channels—involving only the grievant and the relevant managers. There are some partial exceptions. Irving Shapiro, when he was head of Du Pont, was an advocate of a "free press" within the company. Dow Chemical's company magazine has printed letters attacking raises in top executive salary and other touchy issues. Then there are the cases of underground employee journals that have cropped up with increasing frequency since the 1960s. These instances have not led to the downfall of the companies involved, but they have remained relatively rare and restricted.[22]

Unions have some opportunity to express critical opinions publicly through their newspapers, but they have seldom made effective use of that opportunity. That is in part because, as political organizations, they tend to be suspicious of a free press themselves; it is rare that they publish anything but the careful party line. Thus both management and union papers are so predictable and stilted that they are rarely read by employees.

It is outside the boundaries of companies that speech has begun to develop as a mechanism of pressure. A major tactical innovation of the labor movement has been the "corporate campaign," in which public pressure is mobilized against the target company, members of its board, and sometimes its capital sources. The bitter resistance of J. P. Stevens to union organizing campaigns, for example, was broken largely by such publicity-based tactics. These approaches may signal a recognition that, as the AFL-CIO's Robert Harbrant says, "the strike is no longer the ultimate weapon."[23]

At present, however, such uses of free speech are restricted for unions and totally unavailable for individuals. When pursuing campaigns outside the company, unions may run afoul of the ban on secondary boycotts in the Taft-Hartley Act; inside the company, they have little legal access to company property to make their case. Individuals, even when members of unions, are constrained by a series of court decisions that impose on employees a positive duty of "loyalty." When a group of radio technicians tried to move their employer by publicly attacking the quality of programming, their dismissal was found to be legitimate even though they were off duty and involved in a lawful strike at the time. Striking is one thing, said the court, but public criticism is quite another: "there is no more elemental cause for discharge of an employee than disloyalty to his employer."[24]

The rather rapid growth of "whistleblower" protection is the first major attempt to protect some forms of employee speech. The public concern in these cases is strong: an employer who fires people for upholding the law is asserting the primacy of private over public power to a clearly intolerable degree. Today almost every law that regulates corporations recognizes that effective administration depends on free channels of speech from inside businesses and therefore includes specific language protecting employees. Many courts and state legislatures are by now flirting with a generalized protection of whistleblowing.

The effect of restrictions on free speech, both within and outside the corporation, is to channel collective dissent into strikes—or to suppress it altogether. There are simply no other choices for dealing with conflict. A strong guarantee of this right, beginning with a reexamination of the court-imposed concept of "loyalty," is essential for building a more positive system of representation.

4. Association. The right of association was the foundation of the Wagner Act, the crucial limitation of employer "prerogatives." Its effects, however, have been sharply limited by subsequent interpretations. Instead of changing the fundamental relations between employer and employee, it has been treated as a very specific exception to the overall thrust of employment law. The Wagner Act's definition of a right of association flew directly in the face of legal tradition, and the acquiescence of the courts after 1935 was grudging and limited. They still do not treat association as a private right, available as a fundamental principle to all employees. Rather, they handle it as a matter of mere policy, granted by the Congress on a *contingent* basis for specific ends—namely, the promotion of collective bargaining and industrial peace.[25] The dominant interpretation of the

Wagner Act has therefore supported associations when they lead toward stable unionism, but not otherwise. The result has been a highly impoverished notion of collective action. Most spontaneous association, when unsupported by recognized unions, is unprotected and quickly crushed.

One small and inconsistent line of decisions, however, has gone in a different direction. It takes off from Section 7 of the Wagner Act, which protects "concerted activities for the purpose of collective bargaining *or other mutual aid or protection.* "[26] A simple reading of this clause would suggest that it covers almost any joint action of employees. Courts have occasionally interpreted it in this way, especially during the recent period in which they have been more open to restrictions on employment-at-will. Thus, for example, the Supreme Court has upheld an order to reinstate workers who left their work to protest abnormally cold temperatures on the job, and the NLRB has used this clause to defend whistleblowers.[27]

In practice, however, workers would be ill advised to rely on Section 7. The cases that have come down on the side of employees are exceptional, and they are overshadowed by a vast number that have not; as George Schatzki puts it, the legal system tends to deny protection "whenever there are any legitimate institutional considerations competing with the protection suggested by Section 7."[28] The Reagan NLRB, moreover, has been seeking to reverse the modest advances of recent years. As is the case with much of the rest of the law in this area, putting one's faith in legal protection is like trusting a roulette wheel, and one that is rather heavily tilted toward the corporate house.

The fault, however, does not lie entirely with the courts. One reason that the provision on concerted activity has not been effective in practice is that it conflicts with a central thrust of the Wagner Act itself: the mechanism of exclusive representation. The driving idea of the NLRA framework has been to balance the employer with a single powerful organization. That conception implies that competing associations are intolerable—they cut into the coherence of the established union, and they destabilize the balance on which peace depends. Ordinarily, then, unorganized groups are covered only when they are manifestly in the process of forming a union.

When the Wagner Act was passed, the structure that it established was only a slight formalization of the groups that had been created by workers themselves. But by trying to fix association in this form, the government, in effect, has encouraged the gradual separation of unions from their underlying communities. The NLRB, rather than the members, sets the boundaries of election districts; it then certifies the one body entitled to represent each district, though that body may not have the confidence of significant numbers of employees. Because associations may not be formed in competition with unions, minority caucuses, if they are to survive, must work within the union's political processes.[29] The consequence is that new communities of interest have a very hard time being heard.

Conversely, exclusive representation necessarily brings with it the requirement that unions represent everyone in the bargaining unit equally, whether or not they are members, whether or not they share interests with the rest. This burden, which has proved onerous and hard to interpret, makes it difficult for unions to develop clear identities or a sense of community; they become more like convenient administrative bodies impartially dealing with the complaints of their designated constituents. As privileged representatives, unions are further saddled with meeting policy goals that justify their status—most notably with preventing wildcat actions and otherwise holding members in line.

A true right of association would have to recognize that groups may shift and that their boundaries may not coincide with those drawn by the government. Protecting "living" communal groupings of workers, in other words, implies modifying the principle of exclusive representation, recognizing that groups may have legitimate claims that are not expressed through a certified union, and, indeed, supporting protests against unions themselves (which today are nearly as likely to get people fired as are complaints about management). These are inevitable consequences of taking seriously the idea of "concerted activity" in Section 7.

Any modification of exclusive representation is, to say the least, controversial. Exclusive representation is one of the fundamental pillars of the existing framework, and it is supported with intense emotion by those whose experience is bound up with that framework. To modify it by widening the right of association can be seen not only as an attack on unions but also as a threat to management: from management's perspective, the Wagner Act, by restricting dissent to a single channel, at least kept it from getting out of hand. If avenues of expression were allowed to take multiple, shifting forms, who knows what chaos—what "faction"—might result?

Yet there is considerable evidence that free association is not as dangerous as it would appear. It should be noted, first of all, that the system of exclusive representation is almost unique to this country: the industrial relations systems of Europe have gotten along quite well without it.[30] In addition, from the union point of view, it has one very harmful effect. It means that unless unions can win a *majority* of a bargaining unit (as defined by the government), they can have *no* presence. Thus they have to try to win a large number of supporters "before the fact," as it were—before they have actually demonstrated that they can do anything. When one thinks about it, this is a terrible way to try to start an association. If unions could gain a foothold on a minority basis in a workplace they would be far better able to build support on the basis of performance rather than on rhetoric.

174

Exclusive representation also has damaging effects once a union is recognized. It legitimates many forms of government intervention in unions' internal affairs. The duty of fair representation is one obvious instance; the Landrum-Griffin Act's requirements about unions' internal structures and the limits on their tactics is another. All of these consequences come from the fact that the union is designated by the government, rather than following structures established by its members.[31]

From management's perspective, too, exclusive representation has a bad side: it virtually forces all conflict into the form of adversarial confrontation. Setting up two opposing parties necessarily encourages polarization. In this framework, the best way for unions to pull its members together is almost always by stirring up resentment against the employer. A more differentiated network of associations would be less likely to seek a single enemy and therefore be more able to pose the "real" issues—the varied problems of work relations that are nearly always at the root of the resentment. These, in turn, could be dealt with effectively through problem-solving negotiations, instead of the damaging and massive confrontations of traditional bargaining.[32]

To put it another way, a full right of association would encourage a system of representation based on influence rather than power, reflecting more accurately the varied concerns of worker groups. It would therefore fit into, and strengthen the best qualities of, a managerialist form of organization, laying the foundations for the effective system of worker representation that such companies currently lack.

Rights and Resistance

These four rights—due process, information, speech, and association—would make no concrete promises to any person or group. They would not guarantee anyone secure employment or fair wages, and they would not in themselves end discrimination against any category of employees. Instead they would accomplish something quite different: they would support a system of voice for dealing with those difficult issues. Government would act as guarantor of fair negotiation rather than as problem solver of labor-management differences.

Such a system of employee rights remains, in one respect, firmly within the Wagner Act tradition. The act also sought to establish a flexible system of representation and to avoid governmental involvement in specific problems. But the foundation of that system—the right of association in unions—is too restricted for today's issues. The basic rights need to be broadened to support a more complex form of representation.

The development of these rights would, however, require a very different kind of political process than has existed so far. The extension of employee rights has been, as I have stressed, not a coordinated but a piecemeal process—sometimes, as in the case of Title VII, an offshoot of movements with quite a different focus. It has succeeded politically in large part because it has been piecemeal, and it has to some extent escaped notice. While each step has aroused opposition from the business community, the separate battles have not been seen as part of a larger process. As a result, the accumulation of new rights has not been perceived as fundamentally changing old definitions of the corporation, nor has it stirred employers to throw their united weight into the fray.

It is significant, however, that the battle lines seem to be growing clearer. This can best be seen in California, the state that more than any other has scattered new rights with abandon across the landscape of personnel management. The dozens of separate laws and the recent trend of large court judgments against companies have finally inspired an attempt to pull the field together in a single just-cause statute, drafted by a committee of the state Bar. That effort has raised the conflict to a new level. The business community to an unusual degree has been united in opposition to the proposal. The state Chamber of Commerce has countered with its own "just-cause" legislation; this, in turn, has been denounced by the architects of the original plan as "mak[ing] a mockery of any attempt to arrive at a balanced approach."[33] The legislation has so far been blocked by this polarization.

Such hardening of the lines is beginning in other places as well. Similar due-process proposals introduced in Michigan and Oregon have produced similarly united opposition from business. Attempts to develop international codes of due process or of disclosure of information have roused American business groups to passionate denunciation and threats to withdraw investments from Europe. They have won some important successes, notably in helping slow the movement toward disclosure legislation in Europe and in defeating several initiatives for plant-closing restrictions in this country. The rhetoric appears to be heating up, with the issues of "management freedom" and "prerogatives" introducing a sharper element of ideological confrontation.

These trends suggest that the pressure for employee rights is starting to coalesce, creating clearer "sides." If the movement is as well founded as I have argued, such polarization is probably inevitable; for the extension of rights challenges the basic definition of the private corporation in society. The outcome will depend on two related factors: on the breadth and attractiveness of the specific proposals for change, and on the strength of the coalition that can be mobilized in their support.

CHAPTER 9

Associational Unionism

THE EXTENSION of employee rights has provided an important source of leverage to employees who do not belong to unions or whose concerns cannot be encompassed by traditional collective bargaining. But the idea that every problem can be dealt with by the passage of legislation and the extension of judicial or administrative supervision is a kind of "short-circuit." It skips an essential element needed to make the structure hold together—a system of representation.

The problem is that the development of rights tends to fragment the *current* system of representation; in encouraging direct claims by individuals, rights reduce the power of unions as organizations. That trend joins many others that are weakening the Wagner Act's balance of power.

The challenge for employee organizations is to coordinate the growing diversity of claims and concerns. The traditional method of creating unity, by imposing contractual uniformity over an industry or a type of work, is now too limited and rigid for this purpose. Effective representation requires employee organizations that are, relative to current unions, more decentralized, have a greater ability to educate members about complex issues, and can build unity around a general vision rather than a fixed contract. The strength of employees must derive, not from the common needs of large masses in a single industry, but from awareness of the interrelations among the concerns of many local groups.

These are the main elements of what I call "associational unionism"; a kind of unionism that replaces organizational uniformity with coordinated diversity. There are many dangers along this path, including the risk that in reducing the focus on the collective contract unions may lose all leverage. Yet the current pressures from social and economic developments are pushing many unions and other employee bodies toward experiments that explore more associational structures.

The Breakdown of Uniformity

The traditional focus on uniformity in collective bargaining is under attack from at least two directions. Employers, on the one hand, have moved to reduce bureaucratic centralization and to increase strategic flexibility; companies increasingly span many industries and encourage local variations in management and in labor relations policies. Among the membership, meanwhile, the expansion of white-collar and semiprofessional employment and the developing self-consciousness of women and minorities has similarly challenged the Wagner Act framework.

Unions' efforts to deal with this diversity have been, for the most part, discouraging. In many industries companies have put great pressure on local unions to grant variations from the contract—"concessions"—to improve competitiveness. In most cases the national union is unable to handle the multiplying issues, and locals are not prepared to judge for themselves what variations make sense. Many unions have been deeply split by the resulting "whipsawing," with locals accusing each other and the national leadership of undermining the rules that had always stabilized the bargaining process.

As for the incorporation of new types of members, we have seen the problems labor has faced in appealing to white-collar workers. The same is largely true of women and minorities: despite the interest both groups have shown in unionization, their leaders have been highly critical of the conservative positions of the AFL-CIO on matters of vital interest to them, such as affirmative action.[1] The federation's executive council has only three minority members (blacks and women) out of a total of thirty-five. But that is not entirely the fault of the federation: because it is composed of presidents of the major unions, it reflects the almost pure white male composition of that leadership group.

Efforts to right the imbalance have, moreover, proved quite divisive. Glenn Watts, president of the Communications Workers until 1985, made it a personal priority to advance women to the union's board. This would seem reasonable in an organization that was more than half female. Yet his efforts met with sharp resistance. His nominee for executive vice-president in 1980, a woman who had led a large independent union that had recently affiliated with the CWA, was defeated by a male opposition candidate. Passions ran high in this struggle—creating just the kind of divisions that are seen as a threat when facing a powerful employer.[2] The continued spread of rights granted directly to employees is likely to further shake the uniform bureaucracies of most unions by giving new groups—long excluded from positions of power in labor—independent leverage.

Some unions have responded to the changes in the work force by abandoning their focus on a homogeneous industry and trying to organize anyone and every-one. The Communications Workers have made major forays into the public sector; the United Auto Workers have led organizing drives in banks and universi-ties; the Steelworkers have eyed insurance workers and engineers. But though the immediate reasons for these efforts are compelling, the long-term implications—even, or especially, when such organizing drives are successful—are often harder to digest. It soon becomes apparent that it is difficult to provide good service to the new members; the union staff is unfamiliar with their problems, and they are in such a minority on decision-making bodies that they cannot make a dent. The UAW has responded by giving the new members their own distinct structures within the union, with an unusual degree of autonomy from the central body. But this is a stopgap solution. The new members are not integrated but merely tacked on to an existing organization, and the interrelation remains an awkward one.

Industrial unions, in short, cannot adapt to diversity and change merely by stretching. Their structure and approach is built around maintaining a certain level of uniformity. When they go beyond that level, they run the risk of breaking apart.

Experiments in Structural Change

The problems faced by unions reflect those that have confronted many compa-nies: the differentiation of markets and the increased pace of change. We have seen the managerialist response, which consists essentially of developing under-standing, at every level and in every part, of the basic strategy of the organization. Given that shared understanding—which is not easy to accomplish—the parts can be organized in task-oriented groupings to work out variations on the basic theme, without the constraints of close bureaucratic supervision or adherence to uniform rules. As unions have wrestled with a changing environment, some have begun to move in the same direction.

The Communications Workers have been among the leaders in this process. Even before the antitrust agreement that led to the breakup of AT&T, it was clear that major change was in the wind. Instead of waiting for that change to happen before responding, the union took steps to anticipate it. In 1981 it established the Committee on the Future, with the mission of developing a scenario for the future and a strategy for meeting it.

The composition of this committee was extraordinary in itself. Usually any-thing of this type would be made up of the union's top officers; but this was composed of local presidents from each of the union's twelve districts. Glenn Watts, the union's president, was the only committee member from the executive board. It is hard to convey in a brief description how profoundly that choice of members violated the usual ways of doing business, threatening political jurisdictions and shaking up the hierarchy of power—but also opening major new channels of participation.

A second remarkable aspect of this initiative was that it involved extensive self-criticism and acceptance of open disagreement. The committee raised extremely controversial matters that are of concern in almost all unions but that rarely come to the surface: administrative inefficiencies, tensions between locals and the national headquarters, the divisive effects of political squabbling. Such public airing of "dirty laundry" is generally seen as threatening not only to the individual reputations of the officers but also to the fragile unity of the membership as a whole. The CWA felt, however, that the development of a coherent strategy required embracing disagreement rather than suppressing it.

After nearly two years of work, the committee came up with a far-reaching set of recommendations. At the start it recognized some of the important changes discussed earlier: that "CWA ought not to shape itself to conform to the structure of a single employer" and that "coordination and unification of CWA strategy around a master contract will be more difficult." Given the rapid transformation of the industry, it proposed as a basic principle that "our approach to the future must be strategic—not a piecemeal reaction to other people's moves—and the strategy must link together all CWA's activities."[3]

One of the major contributions of the committee was the formulation of the concept of employment security as a key long-term goal. This was explicitly contrasted with the usual pursuit of *job* security, which is much easier to define and focus on. The committee felt that seeking to hold on to specific jobs would keep the union in a defensive, reactive posture, trying to hold on to the past. Employment security is more abstract, but it can help guide a wide-ranging and flexible approach that may include retraining, creating new ventures, and other innovative tactics.

The key *structural* change in the CWA was the establishment of strategy centers. This union, like most others, had been built around particular contracts or geographic regions; union districts matched up with the largest operating companies, locals with company divisions. These lines were quite permanent, and they encouraged the solidification of political "fiefdoms." The Committee on the Future did not attack these elements directly ("It was . . . felt that CWA members face enough trauma in 1983 without the internal political consequences of a redistricting fight."[4]), but it coordinated them in a new way by focusing them on strategic goals such as employment security—with the expectation that these would shift with environmental demands. The strategy centers were given wide powers to coordinate funding and resources in order to make the best use of the union's energies. The report stressed: "One important thing to keep in mind is that it is the need to influence and respond to *outside* forces and events that should determine the boundaries of a union's strategy centers. If they are built for internal convenience, or based solely on internal politics, their cutting edge will be dulled."[5]

Another key aspect of the strategy-center approach was an emphasis on encouraging input and involvement from the local level. The first task of each center was to "develop a participatory process . . . to receive ideas and suggestions from Members and Locals as to what the strategy should be." This requirement was designed to give substance to a central theme of the report: "the necessity and opportunity to open up *new channels of initiative* and new roles at every level of the union."[6]

There was a peculiar tension running through the work of the committee. Many of its recommendations involved *centralizing* functions that had previously been the autonomous preserve of locals. Thus, for example, it sought to establish clearer performance standards for locals and to move the initiative for organizing activities from districts to central headquarters. But at the same time there were important *decentralizing* thrusts—in particular that of involving locals more heavily in decision making. The committee recommended, for example, that the selection of national staff representatives be redesigned to allow greater input from locals. Since the relation between staff and locals had always been a major area of friction, as it is in many unions, this shift could have an important long-term effect in building a greater sense of unity. At the same time, an internal Quality of Work Life (QWL) program was started for the union staff—an effort to establish a regular channel for their ideas and concerns, which had too often been ignored in the heat of political battles.

This tension between centralization and decentralization is similar to that faced by managerialist companies, and it has the same roots. There is a need to recognize diversity and local initiative, and simultaneously to unite a large organization in a strategy that can adapt quickly to environmental change. Strategy centers, more channels for local involvement in headquarters decisions, internal QWL efforts, and clearer performance standards are all approaches to that goal.[7]

The same kinds of developments have been occurring in other labor organizations as well. The Bricklayers followed the CWA's lead rather closely with their Project 2000 committee of 29 local officers, which made similar proposals in its 1985 report. Jack Joyce, the president of that union, was especially clear about the balance they were trying to strike: "We told the locals there was a tradeoff," he said. "We needed better coordination on some issues, like organizing, and we need to clarify standards for local performance. In return we offered the locals more representation in decision making at the national level and in the regions."[8]

The report also stresses the need for greater involvement of the members in their locals. The Bricklayers were careful to ensure that locals and members were thoroughly informed about the report and had a real chance to influence it directly; Joyce himself attended dozens of "focus groups" around the country to discuss the proposals.

The UAW has not initiated a formal planning process of this sort, but an important project with GM has had a similar thrust. Faced with major industry changes, the leadership tried, in the 1981 and 1984 contracts, to chart a complex new course that would maximize job security and flexibility. Resistance and divisions in the membership, however, began to threaten the long-term viability of this approach. The union turned to the joint training center that it had established with the company to prepare an educational program for some 900 local officers. These four-week sessions have included extensive discussion of the future of the auto industry, the role of the union, the significance of QWL and other forms of labor-management cooperation, and the importance of strategic planning. It was a revelation for many of the participants. They saw for the first time the full diversity of the experience of their fellow officers, as well as the overall problems in the industry, and they explored the question of how different local approaches could fit together into an overall strategy for the union.

Finally, in 1985, the AFL-CIO developed its own strategy document. "The Changing Situation of Workers and Their Unions" was an unprecedented attempt by the federation to sketch a direction for the labor movement as a whole. It contained some unusual self-criticism and some very important recommendations. It suggested, for example, the development of new categories of membership for workers who are not covered by a collective bargaining contract. It recommended the development of nonstrike tactics, such as "corporate campaigns" focusing negative publicity on antiunion employers. It stressed the need to increase members' involvement in union processes by developing opportunities "quite different from traditional attendance at meetings," such as expanding the use of committees. And it gave a qualified but clear endorsement to joint QWL efforts: "The labor movement should seek to accelerate this development."9 The federation's report has been taken up in a series of conferences for local leaders throughout the country in an effort to create a shared sense of direction.

These initiatives have been extremely costly for the organizations involved. The Bricklayers and CWA committees met for two years before developing their recommendations, and both unions contemplate years of educational programs and debates about the reports. The CWA, in fact, held a special convention to discuss and vote on the recommendations in detail, bringing together thousands of local delegates at a cost of many millions of dollars. The complexity of the educational process is a good indication of the profound nature of the changes. All these proposals, in attempting to respond to the current challenges facing unions and their members, have moved away from the central tenets of traditional forms of labor organization.

One dramatic symbol of the shift in focus is the AFL-CIO's recommendation that "associate memberships" be offered to those who are not part of organized units. This move explicitly severs the fundamental tie between unionism and collective bargaining. As Lane Kirkland, the federation's president, puts it, the proposal is designed to move beyond a key limitation of the current labor system: "Membership has become intimately linked to the contractual relationship with the employer. No contract, no membership." Associate membership, by contrast, "is addressed to the exploration of ways in which to establish and maintain and develop a relationship between workers who want access to collective action . . . but where the exigencies make it impossible to establish a contractual relationship with the employer."[10]

What Kirkland is advocating, behind his elaborate language, seems eminently sensible—but it is not unionism, or at least not the present form of unionism. It is more like an *association* of employees. While the exact nature of "associate membership" is left vague, the federation does have some suggestions that make even clearer the link to types of association that unions have rejected in the past. They suggest offering direct services to workers, such as job training and supplemental insurance coverage.[11] Such services create loose links of shared interest, not the tight solidarity of collective action.

Another startling part of this package is a backing off from the hitherto near-sacred principle of exclusive representation. That principle, which was key to the growth of industrial unionism, now appears as a limitation; it prevents unions from playing any role in places where they are not the sole bargaining agent. Tom Donahue, the federation's secretary-treasurer, makes the point cautiously but clearly:

> . . . how do public employee unions live in . . . places where we don't have exclusive representation? They live very well, or they live well in terms of the members they represent on a members-only basis. . . . In the Federal sector . . . from '61 to '73, recognition in the Federal service was at 3 different levels. We had an informal, formal, and exclusive representation level. . . . We all railed against that. We said that's terrible. It gives us a multiplicity of unions and we want to move on to exclusive representation. And we did. In 1973 the executive order was changed with the passage of the Civil Service Reform Act.
>
> I don't know if we're any better off. I can tell you that the American Federation of Government Employees is half its former size. . . . Wouldn't it be fascinating if when we lost an election, but got 35 or 40 percent of the votes, we could settle for something less than exclusive recognition and could maintain a representation of that 30 or 40 percent of workers for grievance rights or for whatever rights we had, until next year?[12]

Traditional patterns have also been shaken by a new emphasis on reaching out to public opinion. The labor movement has in the past done a poor job of building support among groups outside its boundaries, because it has centered its attention on building its autonomous power. It has said, in effect: we can pursue our interests on our own, by the use of the strike; what do we need with outside support? The AFL-CIO's 1985 report recognizes the urgent need for other sources of strength that can come only from public support. The huge Solidarity Day rally in 1982, an attempt by the federation to mobilize opposition to the Reagan administration, took a major practical step in that direction. Reversing the usual stand of the George Meany era, it embraced the participation of groups representing women, minorities, environmental, and other "liberal" interests. By this action labor symbolically placed itself among these more youthful associational movements.[13]

A growing number of unions are developing sophisticated ways of drawing support from outside groups. Cesar Chavez was a pioneer with his effective calls for consumer boycotts of nonunion farm products. The Communications Workers got great media mileage out of a "job pressures day" in 1979, when members dramatized their complaints about working conditions at AT&T. In recent years one of the most important innovations has been the "corporate campaign," in which unions bring the public spotlight to bear on companies that blatantly violate the law and the public interest in opposing organizing drives. All these initiatives blur the focus on the autonomous power bargaining that has characterized the labor movement.

The de-emphasis of collective bargaining is, finally, visible in the growing support for worker participation, which has been part of the reports and strategies of the CWA, Bricklayers, UAW, and AFL-CIO. An organization that permits members to "negotiate" directly with employers cannot maintain the discipline of an industrial union. That is the essential source of the bitter hostility toward QWL among many union militants. QWL clearly cuts across the "we-they" divisions that are so central to industrial unionism, undermining the base of mass solidarity that has been the source of union power. Nor can it be limited for long to a few places or a narrow scope. QWL has already "infected" the domain of collective bargaining, producing major changes in the rules that have been central to the contract. The General Motors Saturn contract is only the most far-reaching example of this, and Saturn itself has begun to influence the rest of the auto industry, serving as a model for other initiatives.

The question, though, is whether the demise of trade-unionism "as we know it" is a beginning rather than an end—the precursor of a new form of unionism. Many union leaders see QWL as potentially increasing the strength of labor, precisely because it allows for more diversity and member participation, for more "free association" within the union structure, and for more interaction between local officers and members. They believe that unions can turn this participation into a constructive force if they coordinate it around a shared vision. Glenn Watts has proposed a concrete image of how this might work. Unlike most, he accepts the intertwining of QWL and collective bargaining and sees them as supporting each other:

> I would certainly visualize QWL teams redesigning jobs; and this would . . . certainly lead teams into areas which are covered by the collective bargaining agreement. But I do not believe there need be any blurring of the *distinction* between collective bargaining and QWL. Our position is very simple: QWL groups cannot bargain or alter the contract. They can, however, make recommendations; if their recommendations involve contractual changes, they must then pass through the normal collective bargaining channels before being implemented. This approach, I believe, provides both security and flexibility in dealing with advanced developments of the QWL process.[14]

Watts's statement captures perfectly the tension faced by unions today. On the one hand, they are pressed to abandon the emphasis on the contract that has been central to their history; on the other, they need to preserve sufficient unity to press collective demands on employers.

This tension provides the energy for the experiments I have cited. The move away from a single industry focus, the development of generalized strategies, the de-emphasis of bureaucratic strength, the decreasing focus on collective bargaining, and the exploration of other forms of representation—these are all efforts or experiments that seek to manage diversity without surrendering to fragmentation. They lead unions away from bureaucratic uniformity toward an effort to build from the differences among groups of members. And they point toward an associational form of unionism, one that coordinates member interests rather than seeks contractual unity.

Employee Associations and Unions

Employee associations have generally been seen as the antithesis of unionism, and often as dangerous diverters of energy. In their traditional form, they have focused almost entirely on providing *individual* benefits to members and have shied away from the use of organized pressure. The idea of acting as interest groups has been profoundly repugnant to them.

But associations have some strengths that complement those of unions. The shape of associational unionism can be further clarified by looking at this other side of the coin. It is significant that while old-line labor organizations have been exploring ways of better meeting diversified needs, employee associations have been moving closer to unionism, in the sense that they have begun to reorganize themselves for more activist roles. Frustrated by their inability to affect employers, they have sought with increasing frequency to tighten their structures and exert pressure for their views. Unions and associations, in short, appear to be converging toward a similar combination of discipline and diversity.

There are many variations along the path from hard-line unions to pure associations. Those organizations that combine aspects of both present some of the most stimulating instances of innovative action. In the public sector, formerly genteel associations have been a prime seedbed for a rapid spread of unionism in the past two decades. The National Educational Association typifies this transformation, moving steadily toward more aggressive representation of its members. Yet it remains, like most public-sector bodies, far from a "typical" union. It is relatively decentralized, more like a federation of regional groupings than a disciplined organization. Although it has moved strongly to develop its collective bargaining capacities, that is far from its only focus of activity; lobbying and other public appeals are among its main avenues of collective action. It has become increasingly willing to use the strike but relies on it only as a last resort, preferring other forms of pressure. It is notable, in general, that public sector unions have used civil rights laws extremely effectively to advance their members' interests: American Federation of State, County, and Municipal Employees (AFSCME) has brought court actions based on new employee rights against the City of Los Angeles and the State of Washington, winning agreements that remedied the long-standing segregation of women into low-paying occupations. And these unions, which often lack the Wagner Act's privilege of exclusive representation, have had to develop a rich network of services for their members to supplement their bargaining activities.

In the private sector, too, similar "mixes" have been developing among groups that have not been fully represented under the Wagner Act. Engineers, for instance, have traditionally been among the most individualistic of occupations, highly resistant to any suggestion of pressure tactics. Their oldest and still dominant association, the Institute of Electrical and Electronics Engineers (IEEE), forbids engagement in collective bargaining. But in recent years new engineering associations have sprung up with far more aggressive stances. Under this pressure the IEEE has stepped up efforts to "advance the interests of the profession," and in vigorous lobbying campaigns has taken up such loaded issues as age discrimination and pension rights. These initiatives have been controversial, viewed by many members as undermining their professionalism; however, they have achieved growing legitimation and importance in the organization. In fact, organized pressure by professionals appears to be growing into a surprisingly widespread phenomenon. In a recent poll, almost 40 percent of professionals said they had protested work conditions as members of a group. Most of them, incidentally, were unsatisfied with the outcome.[15]

Finally, there is the extremely important case of women's associations. After beginning as associational "support networks" in the 1960s, groups of women formed pressure groups like Nine to Five, which agitated for changes in the workplace. That organization remains an effective force through its educational and political activity; it puts pressure on both unions and employers to take account of new issues that have special impact on women workers, like the health effects of video display terminals.

The women's movement, through Nine to Five and other organizations, has also strongly affected the unions that represent the heavily female sectors of clerical and service workers. These show considerable "associational" behavior, including a very decentralized structure. The Service Employees' International Union (SEIU) and District 1199, for example, have been unusually successful in organizing through local networks. "They succeed," according to the organizing director of the AFL-CIO, "by saying, 'The union is you—there is no outside organization. It's what you make it.' "[16] SEIU has developed some extremely innovative programs to encourage the development of career progressions, even when those lead outside the bargaining unit.

The Yale University strike of 1984–85 revealed many of the new aspects of this form of organization. A predominantly female, white-collar union overcame determined opposition from the university to win a first contract. The key issue was a rather new one for the labor movement: "comparable worth," or the discrepancy in pay between comparable male and female jobs. The tactics, too, were unusual. The workers struck, in traditional fashion, but the key move in resolving the conflict was a decision to return to work temporarily in the midst of the strike. This enabled them to develop other forms of pressure, including sympathy from students and faculty. Bargaining was largely open to the public— another violation of the usual approach. All this formed a strategy that was more complex, and in the end more effective, than a focus on collective bargaining alone.

A General Model of Associational Unionism

The need for complex strategy seems to require a form of representation that has elements of both associations and unions. It is more fluid and decentralized than the latter, and more aggressive than the former. It makes use of both collective bargaining and direct services and develops skills in mobilizing public opinion.

This form of organization can be characterized by the same term we used in reference to managerialism: as a form of *coordinated independence*. The classic political struggle within unions is between locals who seek autonomy and a national headquarters that seeks discipline and unity. Employee organizations today can accept neither pole. That is the basis of the tradeoff the Bricklayers' president, Jack Joyce, offered his locals: less autonomy in return for more representation in central decision making.

Associational unions do not yet exist. Their key elements can, however, be outlined by abstracting from some of the initiatives I have described:

1. A Focus on Principles. Unions that have gone beyond traditional contract bargaining have begun by formulating general goals and visions, far more complex than the rallying cry of "More!" dating from the days of Samuel Gompers. At Shell-Sarnia, for instance, the design process began with basic agreements about the responsibilities of employees and managers. These concepts, which have been important in regulating disputes ever since, included "advancement and growth to [an] individual's fullest potential and ability," "compensation on the basis of demonstrated knowledge and skill," and a "maximum amount of self-regulation and discretion."[17]

Associations, particularly professional ones, have always tended to have codes of ethics and elegant statements of intent, but only recently have they begun to use these to pressure employers in an organized way. The engineers so summarily fired by the Bay Area Rapid Transit Authority, for instance, were backed by the California Society of Professional Engineers in their resistance and in their later (successful) appeals to the courts, on the basis that they were conforming to standards of professional conduct that transcend any firm. This was seen as a radical move at the time because it involved the Society in an internal dispute between a company and its employees.[18] But since that time the IEEE, grandfather of engineering associations, has come to gradually accept the idea that a code of ethics should be supported by professional associations against employers, and they have sought to clarify the principles guiding their members.

It should be stressed that principles cannot simply be declared; inspirational wall posters do nothing. Principles must be worked out in discussion and negotiation among the parties concerned. It is this working-out process that has been established in the past decade. In the QWL process at AT&T, the union and management took months to hammer out their initial Statement of Principles— after which they found the going much easier. They also encouraged every group at all levels to go through the same struggle and to work out its own values.

2. Increased Internal Education and Participation. Organizations that have sought to develop such general strategies have also found that the existing mechanisms of internal communication are too "thin" to carry the difficult messages that emerge or to gather input from the membership. Union newspapers, and even the well-developed grapevines, are quite inadequate to the job. The UAW, the CWA, the Bricklayers, and the AFL-CIO have all put very substantial resources of their own into unprecedented meetings at all levels.[19]

These are not one-way communication sessions. In formulating an overall direction, each of these organizations has gone to extraordinary lengths to obtain active input at all levels, from wide-ranging small group discussion to membership polls. And the unions have set up new structures to ensure the continuation of this participation. Task forces, long a management "prerogative," have been taken over by unions; they are central to the strategy center concept of CWA, they produced the Saturn contract between the UAW and GM, and they are highly recommended by the AFL-CIO's report.

3. Multiple Forms of Representation and Service. Collective bargaining remains crucial, but has become only one element among many in employee representation. Participation in QWL meets important needs of the membership, largely because it deals with issues that are outside the standard labor relations framework. Direct services, long characteristic of associations, have been taken up by unions. The AFL-CIO has encouraged unions to provide extra insurance and other benefits not only for those in bargaining units but even for those outside.

Providing training for new jobs, even if those jobs lie outside the bargaining unit or the industry, is another new idea with wide repercussions. Both the UAW and the CWA have negotiated training funds for their members who lose jobs in industry shifts. This creates an alternative in situations in which fighting to retain a particular job makes no sense. And it means that workers who cannot be protected by a contract nevertheless can get help from their representative organization.

4. A Wider Choice of Tactics. As collective bargaining becomes one form of representation among many, so the strike becomes one tactic among many. While there are situations in which it is the most effective weapon, there are many in which it is not. All the groups to which I have referred are particularly skillful in the use of influence, or public pressure. They stress public image and communication; in many cases lobbying is a central tactic. This is as true of the unions I have described as of the white-collar societies and other nonunions. The public relations approach may be quite mild, as in the case of AFSCME's television ads showing the virtues of public sector workers, or it can be extremely aggressive, as in "corporate campaigns."

Public relations is not the only useful nonstrike tactic. The Bricklayers are trying to turn the usual logic of labor-management relations on its head by acting as the coordinating body for a fragmented industry. If they succeed—and they have already drawn large numbers of contractors into their effort to build the bricklaying industry—they will be vital to the health of the whole industry, serving as a positive rather than a negative force. In addition, this union, like the Machinists and some others, is experimenting with the encouragement of worker-owned businesses to combat nonunion employers.

5. Extended Alliances. For different reasons, both associations and unions tend to be quite closed to the outside. But as both sides seek to use nonstrike forms of pressure, the need for allies grows. Thus in the past decade there has been a steady movement among associations toward larger scale federations in order to increase their lobbying clout. An American Association of Engineering Societies, to take one important example, has recently been formed to "coordinate the common interests of engineers." The English language is now hard-pressed to handle the proliferation of federations of associations of societies.[20]

Unions have been extraordinarily slow to seek help from outside allies, but they are doing it, and they have found it in some strange places. During the dispute at Eastern Airlines in 1983, for example, it was bankers who linked up with the unions to force a settlement on management. Publicity campaigns against companies—the union-led "corporate campaigns" mentioned earlier—usually involve alliances of community groups and consumer activists along with labor.

All these moves require unions to broaden their appeal. They cannot press adversarial demands on bankers. For example, they have to argue that their interests in some ways coincide with those of others. This process of justifying demands in outsiders' terms is a difficult one, its techniques long forgotten. In the 1930s labor could effectively argue that its interest in increased wages reinforced the societal need for increased purchasing power. As that belief has unraveled, allies have drifted away; new arguments are now needed to bring them back.

Associational Unionism and Employee Rights

In practice the full development of associational unionism is tied closely to the spread of employee rights. The relationship works in two ways. First, the "opening" of unions requires a secure base of rights. Within the Wagner Act framework labor organizations must retain their unity and "tightness" in order to survive confrontations with management. For that reason, only a few old-line unions are now able to experiment—those, like the CWA and the UAW, whose bargaining power is so strong that they can afford to try new routes. But such cases are increasingly rare; the very weakness of most unions forces them back to more familiar tactics. The expansion of rights, on the other hand, offers *all* unions and employees a new and secure basis for strategic action. As that expansion continues, it will free more energy for change.

Second, the movements that fuel the spread of rights are also those that are driving change within unions, working against the resistances of tradition and jurisdiction. It is notable that unions that are heavily female have, to a disproportionate degree, led in the search for new tactics. More than half the CWA's membership, for example, is female; it was they who clearly led the push for QWL and increased worker involvement. SEIU, AFSCME, the Federation of University Employees, and others have all been inspired by the women's rights movement to create new approaches. The priorities of strategic unionism are affected in important ways by the demands of movements that have grown up outside organized labor.

What has been done so far, then, represents only the initial steps toward a more associational form of representation. These steps are sufficient to provide a glimpse of a coherent response to the crisis of unions. Completing the task will require work on many fronts.

CHAPTER 10

Multilateral Negotiation

ASSOCIATIONAL UNIONISM requires more than the internal transformation of employee groups; it also involves new types of negotiating relationships with employers. Collective bargaining has proved unable to deal with complex issues like the future effects of automation, the strategic direction of industries, or the diverse needs of workplace groups. As a result, unions are increasingly making use of new techniques of conflict resolution that can deal with more parties and issues than traditional collective bargaining.

One way of describing the limitations of the current system is that it assumes that disputes must involve only two parties. That is the core of the idea of "collective bargaining"; the Wagner Act, and its subsequent interpretations by the National Labor Relations Board and the courts, have pushed all problems into this general pattern. The act now draws a single line between management and workers, essentially allowing only conflicts that cross that line. By establishing exclusive representation in each bargaining unit, it insists that only one body can represent those on either side. By ruling out most forms of partial strikes or "wildcat" actions, the courts have further channeled conflict into simple confrontations between the twin colossi, management and unions.[1]

The scattered growth of employee rights in the past two decades, however, is essentially a symptom of the fact that disputes have grown too complex for this structure. In every social arena, many parties with distinct claims are clamoring to be heard. This differentiation of interests has produced a chaotic set of cross-pressures that cannot be handled by traditional means of conflict resolution.

The cases described in chapters 6 and 7 are essentially efforts to expand the conception of bargaining to include this full complexity. The Shell-Sarnia decision processes and the General Motors Saturn negotiations have gone far beyond the periodic clashes of contract settlement. They are explorations in *multilateral negotiation*—more open and continuous, and involving more groups and issues, than the familiar bilateral system. This—with employee rights and associational unionism—is the third essential pillar of a new system of representation.

The labor relations arena, however, has not generally led the way in exploring new forms of negotiation. The traditions, habits, and attitudes of bilateral collective bargaining have been built up over many years, and they are strongly supported by the legal framework. Opening up the process would trample established jurisdictions and demand new skills from people who have made successful careers on other bases. Thus in the area of labor relations, multilateral negotiation remains a very isolated phenomenon. Quality of Work Life is still widely resisted, and the more dramatic cases like Shell-Sarnia and Saturn have aroused howls of protest. It is mostly *outside* the traditional scope of labor relations that we can find the strongest examples of the potential power of multilateral approaches.

The Invention of Multilateral Techniques

The *general* problem—the growing complexity of disputes, the fragmented pressures for extended rights, the entry of new players on the scene—goes far beyond the arena of labor relations. It is more familiar, in fact, in such areas as civil rights, public health, environmental protection, and consumer advocacy. In each of these fields the courts and legislatures have encouraged individuals and groups to extend their assertions of rights. The initial results have not been encouraging. All of these areas have suffered from an explosion of litigation, huge pressures on administrative agencies, and a failure to achieve a workable consensus. They all share in the general crisis of the regulatory system, and together they have produced in the public mind the image of a polity paralyzed by interest group demands.[2]

As administrative solutions have broken down, however, a group of experiments has explored a different direction: negotiating the settlements of disputes about rights. These experiments have not begun with a predisposition to a two-party model, and so they have gone far beyond collective bargaining in the number of participants and the range of issues that could be tackled. They go under the generic title of "alternative dispute resolution"; and although they are very diverse in detail, they share some important qualities:

· They attempt to solve conflicts by extended negotiation rather than by rule making by experts.
· They bring together not two or a few, but as many as several hundred interested

parties—some of which may be formal organizations, but some of which are relatively unstructured associations.
· They take as a fundamental first step the clarification of principles or values shared by all the parties.
· They aim at the development of consensus.

The roots of this process of multilateral negotiation go far back. Similar processes can be traced in many other periods of ferment—including the 1930s in this country—when traditional structures had broken down. Until recently, however, the foundation for these efforts was tenuous. They were generally based on ideologies of harmony and goodwill that were sustainable only for brief periods of social enthusiasm, and they produced few reproducible, transferable techniques that could stabilize the process. In short, they depended on existing consensus rather than producing it in conditions of disagreement.

The current movement has had a somewhat different history. It has grown slowly and relatively quietly over at least the past twenty years, building a repertoire of techniques through trial and error. It has been pushed by an intensely practical need to overcome the paralysis that has so often resulted from the proliferation of interests and claims around any public action. Given this starting point, there has been little talk of harmony, and even the language of "cooperation" has been muted. Instead, the emphasis has been on focusing the conflicts—on achieving solutions that best meet the hard interests of all the parties.

This activity has produced evidence that there is indeed a middle road, somewhere in the vast area between the simple confrontations of two-party bargaining and the implausible state of universal harmony—a negotiation process that can build agreement out of complex disputes. It is not particularly quick or flashy, but it does seem to work—or at least it has worked in numerous instances. Since about 1980, its spread has accelerated rapidly, and its potential is still being explored.

Although multilateral negotiation has taken many forms, there has been a convergence toward a common outline that can be illustrated by one relatively recent and influential case. In 1984 the Environmental Protection Administration (EPA) began to revise its regulations for pesticide exemptions. The problem was typical of those that have so often created bitterness and misunderstanding between environmental and industry groups. Under a 1972 law, approval of new pesticides depends on satisfactory evidence about the risks to human health, but since the testing process often takes about two years, the requirement creates a long delay between development and commercial use of a product. Under certain conditions, the EPA is therefore empowered to grant exemptions from the normal registration requirements. When the number of exemption requests skyrocketed in the early 1980s, the stage was set for a familiar round of adversarial hearings, bitter denunciation of whatever action the agency might take, and lengthy court review.

Instead, however, the agency tried a new approach based on the concept of "negotiated rule making." Twenty-two influential groups were asked to form an advisory committee for the purpose of developing a rule by discussion among themselves. These included environmental associations, state organizations, agricultural user groups, manufacturers, and other interested federal agencies. A facilitator helped the groups to define an agenda and a decision process, and a one-day training session gave the participants a common set of problem-solving skills. The actual negotiation consisted of nine days of meetings during a four-month period. Subgroups were formed to work out detailed proposals on three key issues: defining emergencies, preserving health and safety, and implementation. In the end, all the participants signed a consensus agreement that included detailed regulatory language. The crucial test of the process came when the regulation was published; it drew no opposition. The agency and the courts could breathe a sigh of relief.[3]

This is far from an isolated instance, nor was it even the most dramatic. One could also point, for instance, to a 1985 pollution control dispute in New Jersey that presented a classic regulator's nightmare. For more than ten years implementation of the 1973 Clean Air Act standards had been paralyzed by conflicting interests. Poor towns lacked the money to pay for cleanup of their pollutants; richer towns resisted picking up any extra share of the tab; some key industries threatened to move if controls were increased; state officials claimed a lack of funds to help; developers were concerned about costs; and environmental groups had brought a series of suits against all these groups for violations of the law. This cacophony of claims had frustrated a series of judges, and development had been brought to a standstill. Finally an angry judge took action—but not by making a unilateral ruling. Instead he put a temporary ban on all new sewage hookups, appointed a "special master" to represent the court, and told the parties to work out their own agreement or risk his greater wrath. That moved things. With the help of the special master, a process was developed much like that of the EPA case just described; a few months of intense negotiation resulted in consensus among forty interest groups.[4]

The number of similar cases has burgeoned in the past few years. Multiparty community development groups, usually including labor along with many other interests, have become common. In Newark, New Jersey, more than 150 separate groups are working together in a consensus process to develop a long-range strategy for revitalization of the city. In Connecticut, the same process was used to determine the most contentious issue of all: the allocation of money. The distribution of federal block grants was successfully negotiated by a committee that included all the interests with a reasonable claim to the cash.

Such multilateral negotiations have not sprung up in a single flash of brilliance; rather, they have accumulated slowly through myriad small experiments, most of which began with failure but which, by a sort of natural selection process, have gradually evolved toward a new pattern. What has made them possible has been the trial and error invention of new social techniques. For example:

1. Selecting Credible Participants. This was a very troubling problem at first, because alternative dispute resolution does not rely on a few established and recognized organizations. Each problem has to be tackled afresh by defining who should be involved in its solution.

By now a variety of methods has been developed to identify associations with significant stakes in a given issue. These methods generally use the metaphor of the "snowball": they begin with a few groups who are clearly affected by the problem and ask them who else should be invited. This is usually supplemented by a "broadcast" request to see if anyone has been missed; in the EPA case, for example, a notice was placed in the Federal Register.

Following this phase there is usually an effort to group participants who have largely similar perspectives. This involves identifying the "breaks" at which the differences within a group become greater than the differences among groups. In the environmental dispute in New Jersey, 150 original parties were pared down to 40 for the final negotiations.[5]

In the labor relations field, Shell-Sarnia has assigned the selection of representatives to the overarching Labor-Management Committee, which functions as a kind of clearinghouse for issues that go beyond the scope of individual teams. The committee decides which issues should go to task forces, which to collective bargaining, which involve the *Good Works Practices Handbook;* and in the case of task forces, it determines their composition, usually by seeking expressions of interest.

Another variant was tried in public sector labor relations during the 1960s. An executive order by President Kennedy established different levels of standing: associations gaining the support of 50 percent of a unit gained exclusive recognition, but failing that any group of 10 percent gained formal rights of consultation.[6]

2. The Development of Training for Group Problem Solving. The dynamics of a task-oriented team are unfamiliar to most people; we are more used to having group functioning controlled by an "authority" who sets agendas and assigns tasks, and who may at most ask for input from the members. Lacking such an accepted leader, a multilateral setting must work out its own process. Simple techniques for identifying and prioritizing issues have proved effective in moving the process along. They have become part of the initial orientation of almost every group of this kind, from the regulatory negotiating committees to QWL teams.

3. The Role of the Facilitator. Like a traditional mediator, a facilitator is one who represents no interest in the issue at hand but focuses on group processes. Unlike most mediators (at least in labor relations), however, the facilitator must be quite active in leading the development of the group. This is because the process is by definition fluid. It is not a matter of coming into a fixed situation, like contract bargaining, and shuttling between the established parties. In multilateral negotiation the facilitator is needed to help select the parties, provide the training, and define the task.

Almost all QWL efforts have used such facilitators in the early phases. It is becoming apparent, however, that facilitators become even more vital as the process matures. The more QWL groups push past the confines of immediate "local" problems, the more they bump up against walls and boundaries in the traditional structure. Someone is needed who can make sure that middle managers, engineers, and others who may be involved in implementing group suggestions will be informed about what is going on and can be brought into direct discussions with the team when necessary. This "roving" function can be performed only by someone not anchored in the traditional hierarchy.

In the discussion of managerialism we saw the growing importance of coordination in organizations, as opposed to authoritative control. A multilateral negotiation is precisely a situation without authority, but needing a great deal of coordination. The facilitator is the new role for that new task.

4. Clarification of Basic Principles. Most successful multilateral processes focus first on principles on which everyone can agree rather than on the specific issues in dispute. Indeed, one of the most influential figures in the development of alternative dispute resolution, Roger Fisher, calls his approach "principled negotiation."[7] The movement back and forth between overarching agreements and detailed disputes is often crucial in "unfreezing" complex conflicts, enabling participants to pull back from the confusion of their many specific issues. By beginning with the formulation of a statement of principles, a multilateral negotiation process establishes guideposts that can be referred to in times of trouble.

5. Joint Fact-finding. Joint fact-finding has also proved effective in building confidence in the process. Disagreement about the facts can block movement from the start; but when participants in a multilateral process begin by defining what information they need and then go about collecting it together, they are establishing a solid foundation for agreement.

This step also helps deal with a major danger in multilateral processes, which is that the participants may be quite unequal in their ability to gather data and formulate positions. This can be just as problematic, of course, in a bilateral setting; during collective bargaining, management is often able to overwhelm unions with economic figures, and this only increases suspicion. But the problem of inequality becomes more critical when more groups are brought into the process. Joint fact-finding helps to equalize the information base of negotiation.

6. Handling Long and Complex Negotiations. Managing this process can become enormously complex. Great strides have been made in the past decade in developing techniques for keeping everything straight. One of the leading consultants in this area describes the process as one of "accordion" movement, back and forth between small task forces and larger sessions, slowly building the elements of agreement into an overall consensus.[8] This also requires careful tracking of goals and, as mentioned before, continuous interaction between the original principles and the specific decisions as they emerge.

The management of this process brings out more clearly the importance and the nature of the facilitator role. Without such a person, the details of coordinating the different elements would inevitably grow confused. With good facilitation, multilateral negotiations have been capable of bringing very large groups to agreement.

7. Consensus. This goal seems astonishing to those who have not seen it work. In our adversarial culture, it is usually difficult enough to get two people to agree, much less thirty or a hundred. One important advance has been a clarification of the notion of consensus. It does not, and cannot, mean that everyone is ecstatic with the outcome. I know of at least one instance in which a long and difficult negotiation came apart when the judge asked the participants, "Does anyone have any objections to this agreement?" Such a standard is, indeed, an impossible one to meet.

The problem is to develop workable standards of consensus that assure that everyone can live with the proposed agreement, at least pending further evidence of its effectiveness. Philip Harter, who has developed the most elaborated proposals in this field, suggests three possible standards: *structured decision,* in which an impartial and respected appeals body considers every dissent and then establishes the criteria for workable consensus; *concurrent majorities,* in which caucuses of major interests are formed and agreement is required only from the overall caucus rather than from each individual party; and *substantial majority,* which sets a standard for agreement that is high, but short of unanimity (three-fourths, for example, or all but one individual).[9]

All these lessons, and many more, have contributed to the growing scope and success of extended negotiation processes. Many of these techniques are essentially the same ones that underlie the "coordinated independence" of managerialist organizations. When, for example, more than twenty separate specialties and organizational domains in Ford Motors are brought together to design a car in concert—as is happening today—it is an event as surprising in its way as the EPA negotiation. For those groups, even though they are within a single company, have never worked together, and their relations have been characterized more by suspicion and infighting than by cooperation. It has taken much trial and error to learn how they can be coordinated. To do the same among fully independent organizations is perhaps harder but not different in kind.

The Dynamics of Multilateral Negotiation

The dynamics of multilateral negotiation are profoundly disturbing to those accustomed to the traditional labor relations system. A common concern of those used to collective bargaining is: what happens to power in this system? Collective bargaining, while it may be limited in some ways, has at least succeeded in balancing opposing forces. Multilateral negotiation appears to ignore the realities of power.

The answer is that multilateral negotiation neither ignores power nor finds a magical way to replace it. In most cases the primary force driving parties toward this approach has been the extension of rights—for example, of environmental or health regulations—and the consequent desire to avoid excessive litigation. Multilateral negotiation is, in short, a form of negotiation that makes rights work, just as collective bargaining was the form that made the balance of power work.

In multilateral negotiations power is held in trust, as it were, by some outside force—usually the government. It is used, however, only to prod the process. In the New Jersey environmental dispute described earlier, the judge got everyone's attention by placing a ban on new sewer hookups. But he notably did not try to solve the problem himself by a judgment. "What do I know about the design of regional sewage systems?" he asked, forcing the parties to come up with their own resolution. Similarly, everyone in the EPA negotiations knew the agency could step in and issue a unilateral regulation if they could not agree; they also knew the likely costs of that action in terms of long-term litigation. At Shell-Sarnia, finally, the strike—the power base of labor relations—remains available as a weapon, and it has been threatened in a serious way twice during the plant's history. For the most part, however, it is not a central element in negotiating strategies. The strike in this situation is not a standard weapon of battle but a security measure that can be used when the system breaks down.

The power in the background must also be used to prevent any one party from just digging in its heels and refusing to budge toward the consensus of the rest of the group. The EPA case again can be used to illustrate how this works. After, or even before, all the parties agreed on a regulation, it was in principle possible for one disgruntled group to go outside the process and pursue a court suit. But it is not likely that courts would look kindly on legal action in this context. They would tend to say: "Go back and work it out within the negotiation process." Thus an interest that refused to go along with the negotiation, unless it had very good reasons for refusing, would effectively lose its chance to push its position. This result comes, not from an active, directive use of power, but rather from power's staying *out* of the process except when negotiation fails repeatedly.

A second important point is that multilateral negotiation is not just a bigger form of bilateral collective bargaining, and it cannot be understood merely by imagining an extension of the latter. Bringing many different interests together in a single room fundamentally changes the dynamics. In particular, and paradoxically, it is often easier to reach consensus among thirty groups than it is between two, because two parties naturally polarize and lines tend to harden quite quickly—while with thirty, the "poles" are far less clear. Each party has to seek alliances with others to build a critical mass of influence, so that there is constant shifting and less rigidification of positions. This provides a great deal of room to maneuver for creative solutions.

The directness of communication is another very important change in dynamics. In bilateral bargaining, each party is representing a number of factions, and it has to ensure their ultimate support for the agreement. A lot can get lost in the translation. Union leaders face this all the time: it is often hard to convince the membership that they have gotten the best deal possible, because they have not experienced the play at the bargaining table. There has to be a very high level of trust between members and leaders to overcome this tension.[10] Lack of such internal trust frequently forces collective bargaining toward a more adversarial tone. On the other hand, when the factions are actually part of the process, this communication gap largely disappears, and the need to maintain a public stance of toughness is substantially reduced.

Finally, an important aspect of this approach is that it aims not only at the solution of particular problems but at the building of relationships among parties, which then becomes a foundation for handling further disputes. In this country, most examples are too recent to judge in the long term, but participants typically testify that the process increased their understanding of each other's concerns. Unlike power bargaining, this form of negotiation tends to increase rather than decrease trust, and to make subsequent negotiations more effective rather than less so.[11]

I do not want to give the impression that the techniques of multilateral negotiation are settled and widely accepted. On the contrary, the field is growing rapidly, almost explosively. It is only within the last few years that it has been viewed as a single subject and that theorists have tried to synthesize the lessons learned. Yet I think the potential of this approach is clear: it is possible to achieve consensus among large numbers of parties on difficult issues. The details of how the process might be stabilized, and the extent to which it can be generalized, are, however, still subjects of considerable debate.[12]

Multilateral Negotiation in Industrial Relations

What do such experiences imply for industrial relations? They certainly violate many of the rules of collective bargaining that have stabilized the Wagner Act framework. Yet collective bargaining is not an eternal truth; it is an invention, one that was developed to meet particular needs and that took many years to gain general understanding and acceptance. Multilateral negotiation is still being invented, but it already offers a more effective way of structuring relations in a diversified system.

We have already seen examples of both the promise and the problems of multilateral negotiation in union-management relations. Quality of Work Life efforts, for example, amount to practical systems of multilateral negotiation: each work group or problem-solving group engages other interested parties—management, the union, and other teams—in working out solutions to their concerns. The scope of negotiation is broadened beyond the scope of collective bargaining between union and management.

At the other end of the spectrum from the worksite problems of QWL groups are the broad strategic issues that have recently become such a conscious part of management's competitive techniques. When unions have gotten a voice in these matters, as we saw, it has usually been through corporatist mechanisms: closed, bi- or tripartite deal making. Some instances, however, have more closely resembled the multilateral negotiation approach. The GM-Saturn agreement described in Chapter 6 is the most notable, but there are many others. "Slice" groups composed of representatives from many layers and segments of the organization—similar to the Saturn structure though less ambitious—were involved in plant designs at Shell-Sarnia and GM-Fiero and have been used in several companies for the planning of new technologies.

At the national level, the building trades have been involved in some extremely interesting efforts to bring together contractors and unions—literally dozens of parties—to establish coordinated wage rates and work rules. The Construction Industry Stabilization Committee, set up by John Dunlop in the early 1970s, succeeded in evening out some major wage inequities across the country and reducing cutthroat wage competition in the industry. Opposition by the Reagan administration has made it more difficult to maintain a single federation of this type now, but more local initiatives continue to flower. The nuclear power industry has established a similar committee, and many regional labor-management groups have appeared—in Philadelphia, St. Louis, and other cities—to coordinate the fractured building industry. These often include community and local government representatives as well as many unions and contractor associations.

A final development of interest is the rapid growth of area labor-management committees, which have in recent years been increasingly active in charting the course of local economic development strategies. One recent study found forty-six of these bodies, all but five of which started after 1965. By bringing together diverse sets of interests, they have been able to coordinate resources effectively and, in many cases, to avoid the fragmentation and conflict that often impedes economic growth.[13]

These initiatives essentially comprise a new form of "industrial policy." While the political parties have loudly debated the value of planning, the growth of multilateral groupings in response to strategic challenges has gone almost unnoticed. Yet such groups have managed, in several industries and in many regions, to bring together so wide a spread of interests that their policies have had staying power. The dynamics of multilateral negotiation have had much to do with this success. According to John Dunlop, for instance, the Construction Industry Stabilization Committee achieved something that could never have been accomplished by separate negotiations: in order to promote equity throughout the industry, certain unions agreed to roll back increases that had already been won, and certain employers agreed to increase wages. The fact that everyone was present and accountable made it possible to broaden viewpoints beyond the usual focus of local self-interest.

These are just a few indicators of the potential power of a system based on multilateral negotiation rather than on the narrower structure of collective bargaining. The problem is to weave together these different and partial experiments into a continuous structure. This is where the Shell-Sarnia case is particularly fertile. It shows how one can, in practice, distinguish several levels and types of issues and develop mechanisms appropriate to each type—issues that need to be fixed in contracts for a specified term, those that can be continuously negotiated at higher levels, and those that are best dealt with by various "slice" combinations of directly interested parties.

In a sense, this approach is merely an extension of the basic concept behind the Wagner Act, which is that discussions among the parties concerned is the best way to achieve just solutions. But where bargaining under the Wagner Act has been sporadic in time and limited in scope, alternative dispute resolution techniques are *continuous* and *broad*. They indicate a way out of the limitations of collective bargaining, a way of involving more parties and more issues than the present framework. Adapted to the workplace, this form of negotiation would make it possible to recognize multiple groupings with a broad membership, and to have frequent meetings involving many levels of organization—rather than the limited bipartite system now in place.

CHAPTER 11

Completing the System

THE DEVELOPMENTS outlined in the last section anticipate, as it were, the three main pillars of a new system of employee representation. The central one is a set of public *rights* defining which uses of employer power are coercive and illegitimate. These rights can stabilize a form of *unionism* that is more flexible and strategic than current organizations, and a system of *negotiation* that involves more than periodic confrontations between two parties.

Together, these three developments make possible a system of multiple representative bodies negotiating continuously about a wide range of concerns. The structure is large enough to encompass far more territory than the Wagner Act framework. Because it assumes no sharp line between management and workers, the structure can include the large and rapidly growing number of those who fall on neither side of that traditional division; it thus fits the reality of what many have referred to as a "society of employees."[1] It can handle not only the relatively simple issues of wages and working conditions but also matters both above and below that level: the complex and massive effects of strategic decisions by management and the detailed concerns of workers in their day-to-day jobs. Finally, it is not limited to adversarial confrontations as the key method of resolving disputes. It can use, depending on the issue, more inclusive and thorough forms of problem solving.

When it comes to completing these changes, however, the architectural metaphor soon breaks down. The structure is not being built according to some unified plan; on the contrary, all three "pillars" are currently under construction in different places, according to different plans, and before the ground has even been thoroughly cleared. Thus, though each piece is taking shape, their interrelations have not yet been worked out.

In principle, as I have argued, they are closely interconnected; the structure cannot stand without all of them:

- By itself, the extension of employee rights creates the danger of explosive litigation and administrative chaos; therefore it needs an appropriate form of representation to organize the new claims. It also opens the door to many groups who have been excluded from the current system, making it essential to develop a way to resolve conflicts among many parties.
- By itself, the effort by unions to broaden their tactics and issues creates the danger of "overextension," weakening the tight organizational discipline needed within the Wagner Act framework. The growth of rights helps free them from this requirement so that, no longer forced to rely so exclusively on their independent muscle, they can explore other forms of action.
- Finally, multilateral negotiation is vital to resolving complex disputes among various competing points of view, but it requires both a background set of rights to bring everyone to the negotiating table and a skilled and flexible set of representative groups to carry out the process.

But these connections have not been made in practice. The transformation of these various social developments into a unified *system* of representation lies in the future. In this chapter I will try to fit the existing pieces together, projecting what a system would look like if current trends are continued and linked. The question here is: even if associational representation fits with broad social developments, as I have argued, could it actually work?

The Structure of Associational Unionism

From the standpoint of the existing system, the developments I have outlined raise two familiar worries: the problem of *power* and the problem of *faction*. The first concerns avoiding domination by any single group, especially employers, who are almost always the most organized. The second is the opposite: how to avoid disintegration into warring and ineffective fragments.

The Problem of Power: Limits on Domination

Any system of representation depends on the basic willingness of all parties to make it work. I have suggested that there are good reasons on all sides for developing the kind of structure I have described: employees would be able to voice a broader range of concerns and employers would be able to achieve the high level of commitment that is necessary in a rapidly changing economy. In the individual cases I have cited as models—Shell-Sarnia, Saturn, and the various QWL efforts—these reasons have effectively kept the parties working out their disputes rather than splitting off into intransigent positions. But when we pass from individual cases to a *system,* reason is not enough. It is crucial to establish solid security bases to protect both workers and management against abuses.

In a straight battle, as everyone since (and including) Adam Smith has known, employers are necessarily better organized and better provisioned than employees. The role of policy in the Wagner Act was to even out this disparity; the extension of employee rights does the same thing, though in a different way. But this evening-out process is delicate. There is always the danger that it may tip too far in the other direction, encouraging irresponsibility and intransigence among employees if they are too fully protected from the consequences of such attitudes.

There has to be, in short, a careful balancing of incentives. Employees need ways of pressuring unresponsive management, and vice versa. In the Wagner Act framework it comes down to a balance between the loss of production and the loss of pay during strikes. What are the equivalents under the evolving system?

The most basic form of *employee* pressure in associational unionism would surely remain the strike. I would not propose any essential change in policy in this regard. The effect of policy is probably exaggerated anyway; strikes are normally an act of desperation, and their incidence is not greatly affected by their legal status. The fact that they are illegal in the public sector has not stopped their use, nor have attempts to restrict them in various European countries. Regardless of the law, when workers are stirred to widespread anger by serious inequities, the strike is an almost inevitable response.

On the other hand, there is no reason to encourage the further use of this weapon. It is costly to all parties, including innocent bystanders; it is also an extremely blunt instrument, which is useful only for a narrow range of issues. The combination of policies I have outlined would reduce the emphasis on the strike—not by outlawing or further limiting it, but by providing employees with *other* weapons that are less costly and, in many circumstances, more effective in resolving disputes.

The most important of the new forms of pressure would be the expanded framework of rights: rather than striking, employees could sue. The ability to enforce rights has already proved especially valuable for "cross-cutting" groups that are united not by organizational position but by other interests. An issue of concern to aging workers, say, is hard to back up by a strike, since these employees are scattered throughout an organization; but it can be backed up by a discrimination suit.

Rights could also be effective against that segment of employers who are simply abusive. Such companies would often be far more vulnerable to unjust-discharge or discrimination suits than to traditional organizing campaigns. It only takes one person to file a legal charge, yet the consequences for management policy can be enormous. Equally important, a union does not have to be a recognized bargaining agent to support that person. Such action can be a far more effective opening wedge than the standard tactics of the Wagner Act framework.

The third form of pressure would be publicity. Even today, the required disclosure of financial information and more recent obligations to disclose potential health and safety hazards are important forces preventing corporate abuse. The expansion of rights, especially the right to information, would greatly increase the effectiveness of this weapon. Increased notice about plant closings, layoffs, or major restructuring of work would give employee bodies similar leverage in new domains. Information can, in other words, act as a check on power. It is not a weapon that can be used every day; but in an economy in which profitability depends ever more heavily on image, and in which reputations are bought and sold on the merger markets, its impact can be great.[2]

On the other side of the equation, it is important to avoid giving employees so many options that they have no incentive to negotiate. The appeal to the courts can, as I have stressed, be abused as a way of circumventing negotiations rather than encouraging them. There are, however, some natural limitations to such abuse: suits are not cheap, and there are ways to discourage frivolous court actions (I will have more to say on this later). More important, in the long run the new weapons—suits and publicity—are necessarily limited by their strong dependence on public opinion. Outrageous demands can sometimes carry a strike, but they will not win in the courts or the legislature. These forums, which are being used increasingly by unions, make labor more dependent on allies and reputation outside its boundaries, and thus reduce the risk of "go–it–alone" intransigence. That is a necessary foundation to an effective multilateral system.

Thus the leverage in the expanded system would be well balanced; neither management nor unions could ignore public definitions of justice. Irresponsibility on either side would be costly to the perpetrators. This system is also quite different from a simple balance of *power*. Today the deciding factors in union-management conflicts are matters quite extraneous to the issue at hand—things like how much inventory the employer can build up, the kind of technology in place, and the short-term state of the labor market. All this has nothing to do with whether the parties are right or wrong in terms of general norms of employer-employee relations. The weapons available to associational unions, by contrast, would depend essentially on their relation to these norms.

It is important to notice also that the newer tactics do not depend, as the strike often does, on the power of unions over their own members. Though in my experience the incidence of internal union abuse is low, there is no denying that it can happen—in large part because the Wagner Act grants rights to unions as organizations rather than to their members. The system I am envisioning returns rights to the members without reducing their capacity to exert effective pressure when necessary.

Power in Everyday Disputes

These "ultimate weapons" deal with only part of the problem of power—the extreme cases where the normal system breaks down. They have to be supplemented by forms of pressure that can be used every day in the vast "gray area" of disputes. Most employers are neither openly abusive nor highly enlightened. They fall in a middle ground: they are worried about the motivation and loyalty of their employees but would rather ignore discontent, keeping it underground, than encourage its expression. The true test of the day-to-day worth of a system of representation is in how it handles the problems that are not severe enough to produce open conflagration but that smolder at the heart of the corporation.

In the current system the grievance mechanism is essentially the only channel for the expression of "normal" discontent. Yet it often misses the mark: it is litigious and slow and, most important, *individualistic.* The only problems it considers are particular violations of contract language; it is not designed to handle collective concerns of the workplace.

In a system of associational unionism the use of publicity and public discussion, rather than formalistic procedures, would become a primary form of pressure inside as well as outside the corporation. QWL efforts have already taken the first step by providing a forum for discussing policies and relationships as well as particular grievances. But it has often been limited by management resistance because a single group may lack the skill and confidence to hold management to its stated commitment to participation. An associational union can broaden the range of QWL by making sure the goals of the process are widely understood and that violations of the process do not pass unnoticed. The Energy and Chemical Workers Union at Shell-Sarnia, in fact, does that regularly, and the Communications Workers and the Auto Workers have also learned a good deal about these tactics.

The rights of information, speech, and association would further strengthen the base for this kind of pressure. They would help bring the grapevine, that universal corporate plant, from its usual underground haunts into the open; there would be a basis for a kind of "free press" within companies, public channels for communication among employees, a vast extension of the normal union bulletin boards and newsletters. In many respects such an opening of internal communication would strengthen companies, by making it extremely difficult to cover up hidden discontent. It would certainly strengthen employees in their ability to express clearly their day-to-day concerns at work.

Representative Bodies and the Problem of Faction

The successful use of the basic weapons—strikes, suits, and publicity—in effect would establish the fact that no party can escape from the necessity to work things out together. It is likely that there will be a period of testing, in which various groups try to go outside the framework of negotiation to impose their will. If the system is well balanced, as I have argued it is, those attempts will fail. At that point it becomes possible, and desirable to everyone, to open up serious negotiations. The process of negotiation in a multilateral system, however, is not automatic or obvious; it presents some new problems of coordination.

The Wagner Act model has at least the virtues of simplicity and clarity: one management and one employee group per unit. The key feature of associational unionism, by contrast, is that it would not be structured to "match" employer organizations. It would not be "industrial," because it would not base representation on industries. Representation would be based instead in natural groupings of employees, many of which have developed their self-awareness during the past few decades.

- There are today very important associations of employees whose claims are based, not on their organizational positions, but on *social* concerns rooted outside the workplace. Women, for example, share certain issues regardless of whether they are white-collar, blue-collar, managerial, or professional. The same is true of, among others, aging workers, the disabled, parents with small children, and minorities. With the expansion of employee rights, all these groups have a new basis for pressing their demands.
- *Geographical* groupings are similarly assuming increased importance. As consciousness has grown of the ways in which corporate decisions can affect towns and regions, interest has grown in managing economic development and labor relations on a local basis; multilateral committees of labor, management, and community activists have taken a hand in shaping employment relations. Workers in the Midwest may in certain respects share more concerns than employees of a single company scattered in plants throughout the country.
- While craft solidarity seems to be continuing to decline, *professional* solidarity is on the rise. Even for many semiprofessional groups, such as nurses and teachers, identification with their occupation is an important basis for defining their relations to employers.
- Attachment to a *plant* often competes with attachment to an industry. The current trend toward decentralization of management structures increases the differences in interests among workers in different plants.

Associational unionism would not select any *one* of these bases of interest: it would not, for example, replace industrial unionism with company unionism or geographic unionism. Rather, it would provide mechanisms for representing multiple and cross-cutting associations of employees.

The danger in such proliferation is that it could make ordered decision making impossible. Already there are cases in which splintered associations bring action to a halt by clamoring for separate deals. But the growth of associational consciousness does not necessarily mean that all groupings must be independent and competing. On the contrary, there are important counterpressures that discourage fragmentation. These can be used by employers, associations, and government to reduce the risk of factionalism. With such effective use of policy, the current splintering of associations can result in a moderate increase in the number of organized groups instead of uncontrolled breaking-apart.

The greatest counterpressure against faction is the need for resources. A small group is generally ineffective: it cannot afford to press lengthy court cases; it has little lobbying clout; nor can it, except in particularly dramatic circumstances, attract public attention and sympathy. Above all, it lacks money and, therefore, all that money can bring—skilled staff, access to information, and time. Effective representation is tied in many ways to economies of scale. Thus specific interests need to seek out federations and alliances to advance their causes.

This natural force, which works against fragmentation and encourages strategic unionism, can be reinforced by government policy. The effect of the extension of employee rights is to make it easier for individuals or small groups to pursue claims outside the framework of organized representation. If it becomes too easy, however, such individual claims can completely undermine that framework and produce a free-for-all. That is one danger in proposals to set up efficient labor tribunals that could quickly settle large numbers of individual complaints: they would reduce the need for unifying organizations. Policy should rather be aimed at encouraging association and cooperation in handling disputes and discouraging individuals or groups that ignore negotiation processes.

Management actions can further structure the situation. In the current system it is often in companies' interest to encourage fragmentation, because that reduces the organizational discipline that is the basis of union strength. But with an extended base of rights, such a policy only makes things worse for management by multiplying claims. It becomes more in their interest to push for consolidation. They can find a model in the Tennessee Valley Authority, which by refusing to bargain separately with its many constituent unions and requiring them to develop a unified position, has developed a successful form of multilateral bargaining.[3]

But perhaps the most important development working against fragmentation is a more positive one: the gradual development by unions and employee groups of the capacity to accommodate diversity within a single organization. The answer to the problem of fragmentation lies primarily in the further strengthening of this movement toward associational unionism. For associational unions are precisely organizations that can *incorporate* many interest groups with different bases.

Unions that come closest to the associational model have already begun to use the need for resources as a powerful unifying force. When the United Auto Workers' union, for example, starts organizing in banks, universities, and insurance companies, it is no longer "united" in the traditional sense. What the UAW offers a university clerical worker is not mass unity and organizational power: the fact that the union can shut down the U.S. auto industry is not going to do its white-collar members any good. What it offers is money, expertise, and experience. It becomes, in a sense, a unifying resource bank for a diverse membership; it is this function that provides the "glue" to hold the organization together.

Starting with this kind of leverage, unions that have moved in an associational direction have begun to integrate new types of participation—QWL on the shopfloor, joint committees at the higher levels—into an overall approach. They have been unusually open to the claims of "movements," such as those of women and minorities, encouraging these groups to organize within the body of the union and often to exert pressure directly on the employer. Several unions now hold regular minority and women's conferences, and in some cases these caucuses formulate rather elaborate strategies and demands around their own issues. In this way they have been able to gain strength from the increasing diversity of their members.

The recent history of Sweden offers a plausible image of how employment systems can move away from a balance of power model without complete fragmentation. Sweden used to be a clear example of a simple two-party system, with a single employer federation confronting a single employee body. In the past decade that structure has been breaking apart under many of the same pressures that we face here in the U.S. White-collar unions in particular have shown an increased eagerness to go their own ways. But the fragmentation has not gone to extremes: new federations have formed to pool the efforts of the newly aggressive employee groups. It is probable, given our history, that we will end up with a more decentralized model than the Swedish one, but it is also probable that employees will continue to form themselves into large enough units to exert effective pressure.

Mechanisms for Handling Multilateral Interests

Even a modest increase in the number of representative groups, however, might lead to confusion. The existing system, by narrowing the channels of representation down to a single one—the union—at least puts clear boundaries on the discussion process. If, on the other hand, the system of representation were thrown open to more groups and more issues, it is reasonable to fear that people might spend all their time in meetings instead of in productive work.

But some of the cases already discussed have demonstrated effective mechanisms for *coordinating* multiple channels of expression. It has proved possible to link a rich variety of decision-making systems—labor-management committees, teams, task forces, and informal discussion groups—into a unified whole. The fears commonly aroused by the concept of extended participation are not illusory, but there are manageable solutions.[4]

Shell-Sarnia shows that it is possible to manage a shifting constellation of decision-making bodies without chaos. The Labor-Management Committee and the Team Norm Review Board bring together the main interests in the organization. They make some decisions themselves; but, more importantly, they are capable of inventing or structuring new decision-making processes for particular issues. Not every party needs to be involved in every decision; the coordinating bodies can select the important representatives for each case. This model of a "council" of representative groups can be widely adapted to structure negotiations in a flexible system.

QWL experiences in general demonstrate that when the lid is taken off, people will not spend all their time in meetings discussing petty gripes. It is true that QWL in all its forms requires a fair amount of meeting time to work through problems adequately. Yet it is widely agreed, from the top management to the shopfloor workers, that the meetings do work through problems well and that they yield better agreements and stronger commitment than methods that appear more speedy in the short run.

My experience, moreover, is that in participative firms considerable peer pressure develops against those who are seen as time wasters. When QWL groups feel they have run out of important issues, they generally stop meeting; and at Shell-Sarnia, there is a stronger tendency among the workers to closely question the usefulness of task forces than to multiply them. Judging from European experiences, the same thing is true at other levels as well. The incidence of irresponsible use of the new forms is low. When England, for instance, passed a law providing redress for unjust discharge, there were dire warnings that the system would be swamped with complaints. That did not happen, and most experts were taken aback by how smoothly it worked. The same is true in many other European countries.[5]

The question of resources—who will pay for the meeting time and other needs of representative groups—has also proved to be manageable. In practice they have been paid for by the company, and the union has been able to exert sufficient pressure to make sure that they are not cut back arbitrarily. This is nothing more than an extension of the current practice for union representation. The amount and conditions of time off for meetings, grievance handling, and other duties are always bargained between management and the union. When ongoing participation is required, minimum levels of resources are usually set in the contract, and these are supplemented by more informal and continuous negotiations as the process develops. The time allocations have ranged from a common norm of one hour a week for QWL meetings to a great deal more in certain instances.

These experiences have already shown the feasibility of most of the *mechanisms* needed to complete a multilateral system.

Handling Key Issues: Pay and Job Security

Wages and Industrial Policy

Collective bargaining was essentially invented to raise wages. No other issue has so defined the current system, and no other is so revealing of its limitations.

The determination of wages involves at least two levels. The "private" sphere of collective bargaining—the battle between workers and corporations—operates to keep a reasonable ratio between profits and wages.[6] The "public" sphere involves allocations among many groups in the society in an attempt to strengthen the economy as a whole; it affects not only workers and managers but also those on welfare, the aged, farmers—indeed, everyone. The second level, which has the greatest effects on the overall standard of living, currently lies outside the boundaries of the system of employee representation.

The first, "private" level of wage negotiations has not proved to be dramatically different under the existing precursors of associational unionism. Collective bargaining works very well *in this range,* and it generally remains intact even in the most innovative systems. Those companies that have pushed joint problem solving or QWL the furthest (such as certain Shell and GM plants) and that have moved many issues out of contract negotiations nevertheless treat wages in a relatively conventional manner. They continue to hold periodic bargaining sessions, backed by the threat of job action, with the aim of reaching a stable contractual wage figure. The various subgroups involved in the representation system—teams, task forces, caucuses, and so on—pull together quite effectively at such periods.

The major difference seems to be that they are more open to establishing wage *formulas,* which may yield varying amounts depending on the performance of individuals or the company as a whole. The GM-Saturn agreement, for example, sets a "floor" wage rate of 80 percent of the GM standard; the remaining 20 percent, and more, can be made up in extra payments based on the company's productivity and profits. Shell-Sarnia is just one of many companies that has adopted "pay-for-knowledge" systems, in which employees' pay is tied to the number of skills they acquire. At Eastern Airlines, among other companies, unions have accepted company stock as a form of "deferred compensation" for wage concessions.

These forms of flexible compensation have been anathema to most industrial unions because they threaten contractual uniformity. Yet the combination of stable *minimums* with flexible formulas for setting wages is a sign of the ability of associational unions to build unity around more abstract principles. And it is significant that such approaches have been quite normal for many years in fringe areas of the labor movement: among unions of engineers, artists, athletes, and other nonproduction workers. In those contexts the ability of individuals and groups to negotiate increases above the contractual minimum has not undercut the unions but, rather, has reflected the nature of the solidarity of the members.[7]

The question of what specific compensation systems are best is still unsettled. What can be said is that it seems essential that a system of employee representation be capable of adopting such plans when they are appropriate. The dynamics of industrial unionism have long restricted consideration of flexible pay formulas; associational unionism, based in a broadened system of rights, is able to be more open to them.

It is at the second, "public" level—the level of economic policy—that the current system of representation really reveals its limitations. As the complex interdependence of a modern economy has become more widely apparent, the importance of an active government role in shaping the direction of economic activity has grown. The core functions of unions—representing employees' interests in the setting of wage levels and maintaining of security—now require systematic involvement at this level "above" collective bargaining.[8]

At present the mechanisms of decision making on economic policy, like other issues that are connected to the economy, are in a state of transition. During the New Deal, the government made a major leap in the level of its activity in this realm, taking on the role of macroeconomic regulator. Now, however, there seems to be a need for something else. The challenges of change—international competition, technological development, and industrial restructuring—require more coordination of economic effort. The visible threat to national prosperity gives a sharp edge to the public sense that business and labor are selfish institutions, ignoring the general good. Hence the common call for "cooperation" and the need for improved methods for building consensus around a unified direction.

So far there has been little success in reaching such consensus, here or elsewhere. During the 1970s most European nations tried to establish political mechanisms for the coordination of wage setting. So did Presidents Nixon and Carter, in their different ways. In essentially every case, the efforts broke down in wrangling and contention. In Germany and Sweden, most notably, the attempts to reach tripartite accords among labor, management, and government produced rank-and-file rebellions that undermined the legitimacy of the process.

In the years to come, the problems are likely to grow far more acute. The increase in automation and the growing ease of capital movement to foreign countries—to note only two major developments—carry the potential for large-scale disruption and possible massive unemployment. The economic choices will, moreover, involve multiple conflicts among employees and among various sectors of management. A policy that seeks to retain the industrial manufacturing capacity of the United States will probably be more costly than an "open" policy and will benefit some sectors of workers at the expense of others. Policy encouraging investment in capital equipment or research in high technology is likely to produce major dislocation among the traditional sectors. Nor will a lack of policy reduce the differential consequences of the enormous changes we are experiencing.

These challenges put great strain on the government's legitimacy; it becomes increasingly difficult to gain support for overall policy. The Reagan administration is not an exception: President Reagan's own Commission on Industrial Competitiveness stressed, in its 1985 report, the imperative need for improved coordination in meeting the challenge of foreign competition:

> *Consensus is vital.* The need for finding consensus on a national level is acute. The competitiveness issues facing America today . . . remain unresolved. The ability of the political decisionmaking process to deal with them is impeded by conflict among the very sectors needed to solve the problems we face. Policymakers must deal with widely disparate points of view presented by a diversity of interested parties. . . . Government decisionmaking can be strengthened significantly by providing a forum in which consensus can be reached on an issue and in which the implicit tradeoffs among policy options can be made explicit. . . . This recommendation . . . could have a far-reaching impact on America's ability to solve a wide range of competitiveness problems.[9]

This problem is reflected in the current idea of "industrial policy." The term is vague; even its advocates have a hard time defining it. It refers not to a solution but to a problem, in the sense that the present mechanisms for developing support for government's economic role are inadequate to the job.

It is beyond my scope to enter the debate on types of industrial policy. From the perspective of employee representation what can be said, however, is that to be effective, coordination of the economy needs stronger mechanisms of employee representation; and conversely, employee concerns cannot be addressed without participation at this level. In short, industrial policy and associational unionism need each other.

Past efforts at industrial policy have failed primarily because they have been based on the old institutions—in particular, on the concept of tripartite consultation among representatives of labor, management, and government. Today these three parties do not effectively represent many of the most important concerns. "Management" has many separate interests, and "labor" is not adequately summed up by central labor federations. To add to the problem, purchasing power is far more than a labor-management matter: it involves farm policy, trade policy, taxes, and many other political issues that touch on important interests outside the employment arena. The tripartite process is viewed everywhere with deep suspicion, as major elements of the population feel excluded from decisions that profoundly affect them.[10]

In the United States it is particularly absurd to think that the current body of organized labor, which includes less than 20 percent of the work force, will be seen as a legitimate spokesman by most employees, or that all the other interested groups will passively accept the government as their representative. The labor movement today does not represent most white-collar workers, does not represent middle managers at all, does not cover even 40 percent of its base in mass-production industries, and does not reflect in its leadership the importance of women employees. How can it, in its current form, speak for employees as a whole? Any policy whose legitimacy is built on such a fragile base is in trouble from the start.

What is needed for a solid and *legitimate* industrial policy is a system of representation that can include the major affected groups—a form of multilateral negotiation at the national level. This is essentially the direction recommended in the end by the presidential commission whose diagnosis of the problem was just cited: "[Current] advisory committees . . . are ineffective because both their membership and their charters are too narrow. As currently constituted, [they] are ill suited to the task of bringing together the disparate segments of business, labor, academia, and the public sector to discuss and resolve their policy differences."[11]

The development of associational unionism is therefore an essential condition for strengthening industrial policy. Only with such a system can managers, white-collar workers, women, and all the other categories of employees who are left out of the present framework develop institutions that voice their concerns. And only in this way, in turn, can wide consensus and cooperation be built.

The converse is also important: workers cannot be effectively represented—that is, they cannot begin to gain a voice in the factors that determine their standard of living—without being involved in some such consensus-building mechanisms on economic policy. Collective bargaining simply does not have a large enough reach to cover the crucial issues that continue to affect the wage levels and security of employees.

Security: Protection of Careers Rather Than Jobs

Industrial unions represent people in their occupations or companies. Most employees have traditionally defined themselves as holders of a particular type of job at a particular company and expect to remain relatively stable throughout their working lives. Thus it makes sense for their benefits and services to be provided by the employer, through negotiation with a union.

That premise of unionism, like most others, is changing. The idea of *job* security is becoming untenable; fewer employees can expect to stay with one job, or one company, or even one type of work, until they retire. The rapid pace of change has forced a higher level of flexibility. Increasingly, therefore, people are attached not to jobs but to *careers:* they seek to build a succession of opportunities for advancement as their skills grow and as the demands of the economy shift. The problem, however, is that there are few mechanisms, aside from individual luck and aggressiveness, to help an individual sustain a career.

In much of Europe governments have come to play a very active role in this area, offering support for retraining and adult education and making it possible for pension and other benefits to be carried along as one moves through a varied career. In the United States most of these protections are largely unavailable. The current pension system, for example, virtually forces people to stay with a single company, whatever other opportunities there may be. Moreover, there is little likelihood of strong government intervention on the European model.

Associational unions, however, would be natural mechanisms for coordinating career development. Many people in middle management and professional jobs today, and an increasing number at all levels in the future, would be attracted to a group that represented them on this basis rather than as members of a particular company. Unions, cutting across the boundaries of single firms, could help open opportunities for their members—and would increase their own leverage and strength in the process.

Craft unions, through their control of apprenticeship, have always been important in developing the careers of their members. Among industrial unions, however, there are only a few foreshadowings of this sort of function. The Service Employees' International Union has developed a very interesting program called LEAD (Lifelong Education and Development), which aims to create career ladders in currently dead-end jobs; but this does not open possibilities outward beyond the firm. The UAW and, more recently, the CWA have gone further: in their contracts with major employers, they have established joint funds for retraining laid-off workers for jobs either within the industry or, if necessary, outside. There are even provisions for encouraging new entrepreneurial ventures to create needed jobs.[12] The limitation here is that this has been a crisis mechanism, a response to layoffs, and not a promotion of the general idea of regularized career growth.[13]

Still, these examples point in a fruitful direction. Employers have much to gain by developing the full capacities of employees. Most managers know that opportunity for advancement is one of the most important aspects of a good company climate.[14] Many companies already pay a considerable amount for retraining, and I would expect that good negotiation would broaden that, as it has in the auto and telecommunications industries. However, the problem of funding could not be solved entirely by company contributions; it is essential to the idea of extended negotiation that it go beyond the limits of single employers. At least two other mechanisms could bear parts of the burden. First, the government's interest in an effective labor market—reducing costs of unemployment compensation and other support for those who are victims of the present system—could legitimize contributions from its coffers; I am envisioning a modest extension of the Job Training and Partnership mechanisms that currently aid in retraining. Second, employees themselves, who are certainly concerned with the issue, could pay into a kind of insurance fund. It seems likely that the best way to fund the effort would be through a combination of these three sources.

Associational unions, as groupings of employees, would be in the best position to coordinate these efforts and to develop effective counseling and retraining programs. Employers are too narrow; the system would have to go beyond the bounds of any company. Government is, in a sense, too broad, too far from the problem. There is also considerable resistance to such direct government involvement in labor allocation. Associational unions, by definition representing the perceived needs of employees and having the flexibility to change with those needs, would be the right institutions to take the lead with this issue.

Career flexibility also requires the "freeing" of other benefits from attachment to a particular employer. Pensions, health insurance, and many other essential services currently function to tie workers to their current jobs; in this system moving around or risking unemployment incurs huge costs. There have been some experiments in recent years with negotiating "portable" benefits, in which the employer essentially pays into some form of centralized insurance fund. In some instances—craft unions have always tended to do this more than industrial unions—the union itself has administered the services for its members, regardless of where the jobs were. The logic here is exactly the same as for training services: unions can provide a framework for benefits that is far more flexible than one tied to the employer.

The point has wide ramifications. A key source of employer power over employees is the fact that labor markets are not really free, that most workers cannot easily move around. To the extent that this changes, management's coercive ability is reduced. It is obvious, for example, that skilled technicians in high-tech companies cannot be squeezed for production; the fact that they are highly mobile and have many opportunities means that their employers must manage them through influence rather than power. Associational unions could help organize this mobility and extend it to new groups, giving them a further means of pressure on management: a bad employer would find workers leaving at untenable rates. That would provide an additional base for an influence-based system.

Most important, the development of these capacities would give unions a new weapon in the vital fight for security. In the past decade they have tried through collective bargaining to prevent job loss. But that has proved to be a losing battle. In many cases there is nothing that unions can do to enable their members to count on holding existing jobs. There are, however, things they can do to help members develop skills and move smoothly through employment careers. That is obviously not sufficient to guarantee security; it must be supplemented, for instance, by economic policies that prevent massive unemployment. Yet it is an effective approach in many instances where collective bargaining does not work.

Management and Associational Unionism

The Development of Managerialism

Associational unionism should be able to "work" across a wide range of management styles. In an abusive or authoritarian system it can take a form that is similar to industrial unionism, though with greater use of the leverage provided by employee rights. The real strength of the new form of representation, however, is that it would encourage and develop the managerialist direction of change.

The lack of balancing mechanisms in managerialism leaves it vulnerable to various failures and distortions that undermine its goal of mobilizing employee commitment. These weaknesses of managerialism today, like those of bureaucratic management fifty years ago, call for a new system of representation. It is needed, first of all, to give employees a sense of security; fear of coercion is absolutely destructive to commitment and flexibility in a managerialist system. Second, it must enable employees to organize the expression of their own concerns and viewpoints, so that constructive ideas will develop and hidden resistance will be prevented. Third, it must allow the expression of concerns from outside the firm, such as environmental issues, to penetrate the company's decision making; otherwise such forces are pushed into the legislative arena and tend to take hostile forms.

Above all, it must be able to organize the interpretation and enforcement of rights. For rights are among the most powerful of motivators: they always generate intense feelings and connect with people's deepest personal beliefs and self-definitions. An organization that violates employee rights, wittingly or unwittingly, immediately destroys the commitment that sustains a managerialist system. An organization that respects them and turns them to constructive forms, on the other hand, strengthens the self-respect of its employees and taps into resources of creativity and energy that are unavailable to a command-driven system.

Many managerialist companies without unions appear to be quite successful in meeting these needs, at least for the present, while most of those that are moving in the same direction *with* unions are undergoing severe turbulence. These contrary currents are not surprising in the short term. The former group consists largely of firms that have always had a relatively open and participative culture; the latter are trying to transform not one but two organizations—management and union—both of which have been locked in a symbiotic adversarial relationship. The question is whether in the long run managerialism and associational unionism will come together in a stable structure.

I believe that they will, because the combination of the two provides a reliable system of worker representation that is lacking in managerialism alone. Associational unionism, even in its current preliminary state, both increases employees' sense of security and forces an "opening" of the corporation that helps overcome the key limitations of managerialism. In places like Shell-Sarnia, it helps to surface hidden issues and develop broader consensus about solutions. At the same time, it makes it easier for employees to move out of the firm. Innovations like the retraining programs negotiated by the UAW with the major auto companies make it less crucial for any single company to guarantee security as a condition of motivation, and they protect employees from the vicissitudes of rapid changes in strategy and in the economic environment.

Such an opening is essential to prevent managerialism from turning into a caricature of paternalism. As long as an individual's identity and future are tied exclusively to one company and one social system, the opportunities for manipulation are simply too great. The only way to sustain individuality and creativity in the long run is to encourage sources of support that reach beyond the firm.

Associational Unions and Small Companies

Managerialism is generally restricted to the "primary sector" of the economy—to firms that are relatively stable and large. It works where the key factors in profitability are not wage levels but strategic planning, innovation, and flexibility. These are also the companies that are most obviously vulnerable to influence pressures, in the form either of withdrawal of employee commitment or of attacks on the company's image.

It is easy to forget, however, that more than a third of the labor force works in companies of fewer than twenty-five employees. Many of these workers are low skilled and poorly paid, and the competitive advantage of their companies derives primarily from cost cutting. The largest single employing industry in this country, for instance, remains the garment industry; one will not find many new participative systems there.

Certainly associational unionism would look different in this "secondary" sector, but it has the structures to adapt to the different environment. Industrial unionism, on the whole, has not worked well here; most of these firms are too small to make an organizing drive worthwhile and too unstable to build a collective bargaining relationship. Associational unions, by contrast, would have a way of getting a foot in the door without the expense and effort involved in a full organizing drive, by offering support to individuals and groups asserting their rights, through court action if necessary. Even with only a small number of members they could make a visible dent on an abusive company, thus demonstrating their effectiveness *before* winning an election, rather than afterward as is now required. If they also had the capacity to offer services, such as education and placement, their value would be even more widely evident.

Once associational organizations were established in small companies, they would be able to operate more effectively than industrial bodies. Unlike existing unions that concentrate their energies at the organizational center and allow small units outside the center to drift, unions that are moving in an associational direction are developing increased capacities to educate and support their local officers. The union officials at Shell-Sarnia, for instance, have received important support from the national organization, but they are also unusually skilled at operating independently.

The relations between union and management might be more adversarial and "militant" in these firms than in managerialist companies. The strike would perhaps be used more frequently. But because associational unionism would also offer other forms of pressure, there would be a better chance, over time, of developing a different kind of consciousness among the membership—one directed toward positive proposals rather than on hostile relations with the management enemy. The problem of industrial unions in this context has been that because their strategies and weapons are so limited, they have difficulty maintaining continuous involvement and solidarity among their members; associational unionism would be a better *educational* vehicle, because it would deal with problems more continuously and broadly. This would weaken the simple adversarial cycle, to everyone's benefit.

The example of the masonry industry suggests another potential role for associational unions in the secondary sector: they can help coordinate industry-wide labor markets and even business policies. The Bricklayers' Union, for instance, is the only effective institution uniting the fragmented contractors. As a result of its strategic planning process, it has gone well beyond the common craft union function of allocating labor; it has recently been central in putting together a research institute to maintain the competitiveness of masonry, and it is coordinating an industry marketing campaign. In the long run, marketing may not be a good role for an employee body, but the development of skills and the movement of personnel do seem to be important ways in which associational unions can help the functioning of small companies.

The Role of Government

Substantive Rights and Representative Mechanisms

Government policy has been central in the changes I have described, especially in defining new employee rights, and it will surely have a major hand in shaping any system of representation. But its role is particularly confused now. Government as a whole is suffering from a lack of public confidence, with discontent focusing particularly on the regulatory function. A policy framework for worker representation needs to take account of these long-term strains by avoiding a government "takeover" of industrial relations.[15]

The labor relations system seems to be in the midst of a transition that is only partly conscious. The Wagner Act, as I have noted, aimed to keep the state out of the *substance* of negotiations, but to involve it in regulating the *procedures*. The more recent growth of employee rights, by contrast, brings government directly into substance. It no longer matters whether unions can or want to negotiate antidiscrimination provisions; employees have that right available to them through legislation. It no longer matters whether the contract has health and safety language; the Occupational Safety and Health Act frames that issue. In these areas, and increasingly in the field of unjust discharge in general, courts and legislatures have decided that it is not enough to support collective bargaining; they have begun to define universal standards for working conditions.

These two pieces—the procedural rules of the Wagner Act and the substantive base of employee rights—have grown up at different times and on different bases. Yet in theory they must support each other. Rights are the foundation that defines the public terrain of legitimate relations, and representation is the mechanism for building detailed structures and private relationships upon that foundation. Each needs the other.

In fact, as well as in theory, both developments have been distorted by their separation. Increasingly, the Wagner Act system of labor relations has lost touch with the public sense of right. It has produced gains for only a small portion of the work force, has left many workers uncovered, and has been largely ineffective in representing the major movements for women's and minorities' rights. Even the gains it has made have been widely seen as harmful by the public because of effects on prices and international competition. Thus much of the energy for workplace reform has been channeled into legislative activity rather than into unionism; the Wagner Act system has been cut off from the nourishment of public support.

The spread of employee rights, meanwhile, has suffered by its overdependence on governmental enforcement. There is no way that a government by itself can interpret principles so as to fit the infinite variety of specific situations. Moreover, no matter how well it is done, such regulation takes disputes out of the hands of those directly involved, furthers the dominion of neutral experts, setting up those experts as the targets of everyone's resentment, and ends by increasing litigiousness and undermining the legitimacy of government.

Another version of the pattern can be seen in public sector unionism. There a strong set of employee protections has been provided by the Civil Service system; meanwhile, unions have developed rapidly to handle concerns that have not been met by these rules. But in most cases, the two mechanisms—unions and Civil Service boards—have nothing to do with each other. Thus the Civil Service system has developed just the kind of administrative rigidity that gives regulation such a bad name, while the unions have been greatly weakened by their separation from the administrative machinery.

The proper role of government is not to supplant mechanisms of representation. It is to define basic societal standards of fairness. A strong and independent system of representation is needed to turn those standards into reality. In order to achieve the interrelationship of societal standards and representative systems, the present directions of both need to be modified.

In the area of employee rights, the need is for generalization. Pulling together scattered legislative and judicial advances into a coherent "employee bill of rights" is a necessary next step to move beyond the current confused and contradictory state. I have suggested that guarantees of due process, speech, information, and association are the essential pieces needed to support a strong system of representation.

The other term of the equation is equally important: the need to revise the Wagner Act's definition of representation. The act was established to encourage collective bargaining. Policy today needs to be aimed at supporting the more inclusive and flexible structure of multilateral negotiation.

Reshaping Labor Law: Legislative Support for Multilateral Negotiation

I have noted throughout this study how the Wagner Act framework limits the definition of collective bargaining. A first step in encouraging associational unionism would be to remove some of the boundaries inscribed in the law. There is no valid reason for drawing a sharp line between managers and workers, or "exempt" and "nonexempt"—the differences within these groups are often as great as those between them, and all of them have concerns that require representation. The attempt to find a line between decisions that affect employees ("wages and working conditions") and those that are purely management's domain is equally arbitrary: the growth of strategic planning is fundamentally an attempt to pull all these elements into a single coherent whole. Nor is it necessary to grant exclusive rights of representation to a single organization in each bargaining unit. Such governmental boundaries have come to freeze in place a system that no longer reflects the true shape of the issues that concern employees or of their natural association. In the framework I have sketched, moreover, these distinctions are unnecessary.

That is the negative side—the need for the removal of constraints. But there remains also a *positive* role for government in encouraging multilateral negotiation. This involves a substantial revision of the legislative framework.

The task of legislation is to establish the essential boundaries of the new system, as the Wagner Act established the boundaries of collective bargaining. Multilateral negotiation is more informal and continuous than collective bargaining, but it is not wide open; to function effectively, it has to meet certain standards. These, which need clear and consistent expression, include definitions of *standing*—the identification of "valid" employee groups—and rules of *procedure*.

The problem of standing has already been wrestled with in many contexts: agencies and courts now regularly make judgments about which interests and groups are entitled to involvement in regulatory decisions. They have evolved complex approaches that boil down to a simple principle: "any interest that would be substantially or materially affected by the regulation should be represented."[16]

My suggestion for applying this principle to the labor relations field would involve combining an idea from Shell-Sarnia with the "10 percent rule" used in the federal sector during the 1970s. Any association with at least 10 percent of a unit would have rights of representation. Within each unit a committee would be established composed of representatives of all employee groups that met this criterion—a kind of multilateral "labor-management committee." This committee would then have the authority to constitute task forces to negotiate specific issues, choosing their membership according to the nature of the problem. This is similar to the function of the labor-management committee at Shell-Sarnia, which has successfully permitted the creation of flexible and ongoing types of dispute settlement and problem solving.

As for rules of procedure, the essential ones are, once again, simple enough. It is vital that all the interested groups with standing, however that is defined, be involved in the negotiation process and accept the outcome, and that sufficient time and resources be put into it for the parties to make informed judgments. The first of these is (once the definition of standing is established) relatively easy to determine. The second involves more complex judgment, but it is not fundamentally different from the current NLRB requirements concerning the basic resources (time, information, and so on) needed for "good faith" collective bargaining.

These basic concepts—the general definition of standing, the requirements of inclusion and consensus, and the need for resources—need to be embodied in legislation. It is *not* critical, however—in fact, it would be quite impossible—to work these standards out in detail in legislation. The Wagner Act did not presume to create elaborated regulations about collective bargaining, and there is no need to do so in establishing multilateral negotiation. The important thing for policy is to set up a mechanism, analogous to the NLRB, by which the standards can be developed with experience.

The Regulatory Role:
Toward a National Employment Relations Board

The NLRB has interpreted labor law by making rules. It has never attempted in any systematic way to consult with either unions or management in formulating rules for bargaining, but it has codified very complex standards through the accumulation of administrative rulings. It both interprets the principles of collective bargaining and enforces them. That method has some obvious problems. It means that the interested parties themselves bear no responsibility for the regulations; they stand in an adversarial relation not only to each other but also to the agency that defines the system within which they are supposed to be working. Their compliance is therefore unlikely to go beyond the gross behavioral level, and not even that far without continual monitoring. The NLRB has, in fact, always been ineffective in developing criteria for "good faith" bargaining that are not easily circumvented, and its rulings in general are openly flouted with disturbing frequency. This is just one instance of the legitimacy crisis of regulatory bodies, a problem with wide ramifications throughout our society.

The alternative to expert rule making is regulatory negotiation. I have already described examples of this approach in the EPA, and it has been used successfully in other agencies as well. It consists in bringing together interested parties to draft regulations themselves, rather than taking potshots at the bureaucrats after the fact. The experience with it so far indicates that, as one might expect, resistance to the final rules is much lower with this approach, litigation is reduced, and compliance is apparently improved.[17]

What is needed to implement a multilateral system is a new labor board that would focus on negotiated rule making. This agency might be called the "National Employment Relations Board," or NERB. That name reflects the overlap of function between this agency and the old NLRB; but the substitution of "employment" for "labor" underlines the broadened scope of the new system. The NERB would be responsible not for governing the relations of two parties— business and labor—but for structuring discussion among many groups of employees and managers.

The new board would function primarily as a coordinator of negotiations among concerned parties by arranging the following steps:[18]

- *Defining issues* that need regulation. By gathering complaints from employees or companies, the agency would identify those areas where the negotiation process is subject to distortion, or where the intent of the legislation is unclear—including details of standing and procedure briefly discussed earlier.
- *Issuing a public "offer to negotiate,"* which can be seen by all parties with an interest in the problem.
- *Certifying participants* to the negotiation. This would involve working out coalitions among groups with similar interests, as well as weeding out any who have no identifiable interest in the matter.
- *Appointing a facilitator* to help establish the process of the group—setting agendas, coordinating task forces, clarifying objectives, and so on.
- *Publicizing the completed standard* and gathering comments.
- *Monitoring the working of the agreement* and renegotiating it as necessary.

This process of regulatory negotiation would create a shared "buy-in" by all affected parties, reducing the need for litigation and administrative enforcement.

The NERB would have two further functions in supporting the system of multilateral negotiation. One would be the provision of technical support for workplace negotiations. I have mentioned that the multilateral approach seems to require a rather strong facilitator to search out the relevant parties in disputes and to establish ground rules for the discussions. It also depends on the skills of the participants in group problem solving and it breaks down when there are severe inequalities of skill and confidence. These foundations are not easily built on a local and scattered basis; they need some central coordination. A government agency is in the best position to provide training for participants and facilitators who need it, and perhaps also to maintain a register of certified facilitators from which the parties could choose.

Finally, the coordination of information, a classic role of government, would become even more important. In a system of extended worker participation, it is essential that knowledge be easily and equally accessible. With many parties both inside and outside the firm involved in crucial decisions, employers could not carry the full weight of keeping all of them informed. The danger of leaving people out would be reduced if notice of major issues—strategic shifts by management, plant closings, health hazards, and so on—were provided to a central agency. Again, the definition of *what* information should be supplied should be a matter for legislation and negotiated rule making; it would be the coordinating task that would properly fall to the NERB.

In certain respects, I should add, government is already moving in these directions. In the Department of Labor, a new Bureau of Labor-Management Cooperation is working to develop wider awareness and skill in QWL, area labor-management committees, and other new types of negotiation. The Federal Mediation and Conciliation Service is starting to explore "preventive mediation"—helping develop solid relations *between* contract negotiations, rather than just when a crisis hits. Certain states have also developed agencies aimed to support rather than regulate.[19] These initiatives, which have all occurred outside the NLRB, have begun to strengthen the capacity for multilateral negotiation.

Judgment and Enforcement

The approach I have advocated amounts to pulling the NLRB, or rather the NERB, out of the role of *judging* disputes. Judgment, as a function of government, should be a last resort, not a routine matter. Every time it is used, it takes initiative out of the hands of the parties themselves and undermines the system of representation.[20]

This argument implies the need for a careful separation of functions. Many of the problems of the labor relations system so far can be viewed as the result of merging roles that should be kept distinct. The NLRB tries to define standards as well as to apply them, thus usurping a proper role of labor-management negotiation. The legislature has defined many rights so specifically that it undercuts negotiation. The judiciary has increasingly second-guessed the NLRB, further invading the domain of interpretation that is best handled by those directly involved in disputes.

The court system, in particular, has increasingly become an almost routine part of the system of representation. More than half of the unfair-labor-practice decisions of the NLRB end up going to the judiciary—not to mention the burgeoning number of unjust-discharge and discrimination cases. As *regular* mechanisms of dispute resolution, the courts have some very bad features. They are slow and expensive, restricting access to large groups or to individuals with a lot of money. And they are irrational: they tend to grant very large awards in a few cases, while the vast majority of problems slip through the cracks. In part because of the slowness of judicial review, it now takes an average of three years from the filing of unfair labor practice charges to the enforcement of a remedy.

If, on the other hand, the judgment role is truly an *exceptional* one, aiming to support a system of representation rather than to take it over, these very weaknesses of the courts become strengths. With strong representative mechanisms, government judgment would be only a last resort for exceptionally difficult impasses. It should therefore have two key characteristics: access should be fairly difficult and judgment should be very hard hitting when it is called into play.

These are precisely the qualities of the current court system. The "irrationality" of court awards is destructive when they constitute the main avenue of recourse but constructive when they are coupled with strong representation. For it means that when the parties abandon their negotiations to appeal to the courts, they are taking a large risk. They will have difficulty predicting how the results will turn out, and the costs of adverse judgment can be major. There are, therefore, powerful reasons to try to work things out directly rather than appealing to the outside. A union that goes to court too quickly is spending significant resources on a very uncertain quest; but an employer who stonewalls, forcing a dispute into the judicial forum, is also taking a risk of a large judgment if it loses.

Thus a small number of decisions can have wide ramifications. Already, in fact, a very few awards of more than $1 million for wrongful discharge have forced a great many companies to rethink their personnel policies. Furthermore, courts do effectively encourage negotiated solutions; relatively few disputes go all the way to a decision, and a great many are settled along the way by the parties. These incentives are in the right direction.

The slowness and expense of court action, furthermore, tends to discourage frivolous or casual action. In an expanded framework of rights, it would reduce the tendency for individuals to try to bypass the representative system; it would also increase the incentive for people to group into large enough associations to support rights suits when necessary, thereby encouraging the growth of association unionism as a way of coordinating resources. The difficulty of access would also lessen the danger that the courts would undermine negotiations by too frequently meddling in the outcomes: those who rejected the outcome of multilateral negotiations would have difficulty seeking a remedy in court, *unless* they had the support of some association to help spread the risk.[21]

In order to work out a smooth interrelation of functions, however, the courts must back out of the increasingly active and direct role they have taken in labor relations. They have generally adopted a "hard look" standard in reviewing the results of regulatory decisions, such as NLRB rulings; that standard has permitted frequent judicial overturning of agency decisions, undercutting administrative autonomy. If the same standard were applied to regulations produced in negotiations, it would remove all incentive for the parties to participate seriously.

What is needed instead is for the courts to encourage multilateral negotiation by showing deference to the outcomes of such a process. This is similar to the kind of support that the judiciary today provides for arbitration. It is rare for courts to overturn arbitration awards; very good and very exceptional reasons are needed for them even to consider the possibility. As long as an arbitration has been carried out properly, according to a process agreed to by both union and management, it is generally assumed to be valid. During the past thirty years that approach of the courts has been crucial in encouraging the rapid spread of arbitration as a mechanism of dispute resolution.

Similarly, in order to encourage multilateral negotiations, the judiciary should be reluctant to intervene as long as the basic principles of a fair process have been observed. They should refuse, for example, to consider complaints by parties who turned down an opportunity to be involved in negotiation. They should intervene only when the party who brought the complaint has standing but was excluded from the dispute-resolution process, or when gross violations of procedure prevented the parties from reaching a valid consensus.[22]

Where consensus has not been reached, they should do everything they can to push the parties toward negotiations. But when that is impossible, courts should continue, as at present, to be hard-hitting in the last resort, imposing such costs on parties blocking negotiation that intransigence becomes a dangerous tactic.

This approach would not only strengthen the system of representation but also solidify the role of the judiciary and reduce the strain on its legitimacy. It would mean that judicial rulings would be founded on public norms rather than from standards that are obscure to the public. Employers or employee groups who violated agreements and resisted opinion pressures would be quite clearly "in the wrong"—much more so than in most cases today, when the principles on which the courts decide are unclear and conflicting. Companies that tried to repress representation, if they violated standards that had been publicly negotiated, would be isolated even from the rest of the business community. The judicial task, in this case, would be relatively simple and transparent.

Summary: Administrative vs. Coordinating Agencies

The implementation of the Wagner Act framework has centered on the concept of the administrative agency; the NLRB was part of the flowering of this structure during the New Deal. A background theme throughout this book, however, has been that the day of the administrative agency—tied as it is to the concept of direct regulation by the executive—is past.[23] In the labor relations field, at least, it is clear that the NLRB's rule-making powers simply do not address the crucial issues. As the board struggles to get a handle on the broad changes it faces—the multiplication of interests, the growth of mechanisms other than collective bargaining—it finds itself less and less able to cope and increasingly confined to a narrow and peripheral role in the arena of employer-employee relations.

The current burden on administrative functions is part of a vicious cycle. Administrative regulation removes initiative and responsibility from private actors on the grounds that they cannot resolve their own disputes. It thereby weakens local systems of representation, which in turn throws more responsibility on the agency. Hence the paradoxical nature of the current crisis in labor relations. As the Wagner Act system of collective bargaining has declined, the pressure on the NLRB has increased; unfair labor practice charges have shot up in the past twenty years, and proposals have been made for dramatic increases in the board's reach—from the relatively mild version of labor law reform to more far-reaching concepts of "labor courts." Yet these proposals, which are indications of the breakdown of the system of representation, would only hasten its decline by further encroaching on its function. Meanwhile, the board lacks the legitimacy to implement its rulings even within its currently restricted domain.

The situation requires a "rebalancing" of the system. There are three governmental functions that need to be defined. The job of setting the basic principles and parameters of employer-employee relations should be the legislature's. The final enforcement of these principles is the role of the courts, which are properly designed as "last resorts" for disputes. But the intermediate level, the interpretation of the standards for particular situations, should be carried out by those who are concerned with and affected by them, that is, employees and employers themselves; the government's role in this area is to coordinate and support their negotiations. That is the task for an agency like the National Employment Relations Board.

Coordination and support are needed because employers and unions are too scattered, too decentralized to produce overall consistency of principles spontaneously. Yet it is they who bear the responsibility of implementation, and it is they who must therefore work out the particulars of broad legislative standards. Government agencies—at the national, state, and local levels—are properly placed to bring together representatives of the parties beyond the boundaries of any one firm.

The form of this new invention—the coordinating agency—can be seen only in outline. Current efforts at regulatory negotiation provide the best concrete evidence of its effectiveness. But it is becoming steadily more necessary. The decline in public support for direct government regulation is clear and deeply rooted, but so is the apparently contradictory movement for increased protection of rights against the power of large organizations. Those forces cannot be reconciled within the current framework.

CHAPTER 12

The Process of Change: Strategy and Resistance

THE PROCESSES OF CHANGE that I have sketched challenge all the interests—in management, unions, and government—that have leaned on the Wagner Act framework. More than that, they involve redefinitions of central political concepts: of the relation of private enterprise to the public interest; of the interests of "workers"; and of the regulatory role of government. Together, these form a formidable mountain of resistances.

On the other hand, changes *have* been happening. Employee rights have grown to a surprising degree; unions have begun painfully redefining their strategies; managers have been restructuring their organizations. Clearly forces for change exist that are strong enough to roll the rock part way up the mountain. That leaves two questions: first, whether they can push it over the top, overcoming the opposing pressures; and second, what short-term tactics will help in this effort.

Forms of Resistance

Divisions Within Management

The focus of management's resistance to change is the extension of employee rights. It is clear that such rights conflict with the idea of the corporation as private property: from that perspective the public has no basis for "interfering" in the internal workings of a firm. The right of property forms a veil around the corporation, behind which management can run things as it sees fit. It is to be expected that the further extension of employee claims would be strongly opposed by the business community. In practice, too—as I mentioned earlier—the business community has opposed most of the rights I have described. The opposition has intensified when they have been proposed at a more general level: the California proposal for a general employee right of due process, for example, has drawn unusually heavy fire. Business objections have been instrumental in blocking this effort, at least for the moment.

Yet the picture is not quite so unified and simple; there have been some unexpected variations on the pattern of polarization. There is, for example, the surprising fact that a heavy majority of large firms have resisted the Reagan administration's attempts to roll back affirmative action quotas; these firms have maintained their support for strong antidiscrimination goals. There is also evidence of strong and growing support among managers for the general concept of employee rights. A pair of *Harvard Business Review* surveys during the 1970s showed substantial majorities favoring protection for privacy, off-the-job freedom of expression, and on-the-job whistleblowing. The data also indicated a significant increase in real mechanisms of due process—independent grievance processes and ombudspersons—in the respondents' workplaces.[1] The Business Roundtable, a major forum for discussion among corporate leaders, has seriously debated a proposal very much like my suggestion in the last chapter: the need for the extension to employees of constitutionally guaranteed protections of personal privacy, freedom of expression, and due process.

There are several reasons for these indications of openness. The most important, I think, is the growing managerialist conviction that increased employee commitment, rather than greater management control, is essential for competitiveness. There is little question that commitment cannot be obtained except in exchange for rights: that is, for guarantees to employees of fair and nonarbitrary treatment. The rights do not have to be guaranteed by the government, but they must be secure within the walls of the corporation.

A second reason involves a more traditional calculation: there is a fear that intransigence might create a reaction with even worse consequences. Managements are deeply concerned about the public's low opinion of business and what it might lead to in the long run. Many of their discussions of employee rights are framed in these terms: "If we don't do something ourselves, something worse will be forced on us."

These worries have abated somewhat with the tide of support from the Reagan administration, but they have not been pushed far below the surface. Surveys show no significant decrease in the public's suspicion of large corporations. During this period, the growth of government-defined employee rights has not slowed at all; court decisions and state legislation continue to expand their scope.

At the most fundamental level, there are strong signs of uncertainty about the core ideology that justifies management's traditional protection of its prerogatives; the idea that private property justifies control is no longer fully convincing. More than fifty years ago A. A. Berle and G. C. Means pointed out that *control*—the exercise of power over people and resources—had already been effectively separated from ownership in most large corporations by the diffusion of stock shares. More recently Peter Drucker, a widely respected theorist in the business community, has gone a step further by pointing out that most stock, and most capital in this country, is not even owned by individuals any more; it is held in pension funds for the benefit of workers. This strange twist, which Drucker calls "pension-fund socialism," makes it hard to sustain the idea that management has a right based on property to absolute power over workers.[2]

These facts, plus the increasingly visible public role of large corporations, has led many influential business writers to argue that attempts to hold on to the "Lockean ideology" of private control are doomed to failure. Drucker and Irving Shapiro, the former CEO of Du Pont, are among those who believe that management legitimacy today is fragile, and that more openness to employee claims as well as outside interests is imperative. The most elaborated views on this line are those of George Lodge of the Harvard Business School. He argues that a "communitarian" ideology, involving greatly expanded roles for workers and the public in management decision making, is the only way to restabilize business legitimacy in the new economy. His research among managers, moreover, produced this extremely suggestive result: of a sample of 1,800 executives polled in 1975, 70 percent preferred Lockean values to communitarian ones; but 73 percent thought the latter would soon become dominant.[3]

Thus two major factors—a positive desire to generate employee commitment and a negative effort to avoid a public backlash—serve to reduce the unity of management's opposition to employee rights. In California and the other states that have proposed due-process legislation, these factors have not prevented the business community from rallying against the proposals. But it has meant that management has been slow to establish a clear position in the face of the quite major encroachments on their prerogatives outlined earlier, and also that they have at times appeared eager to support at least the idea that employees deserve rights. Such irresolution has led some business leaders to argue that it is better to join the extension of rights than to fight it.

Union Resistance

The resistance of unions is quite different in form. It is not, for the most part, explicit and ideological, like the management opposition to employee rights. It is instead buried deep in the structure of unions as organizations and is hard even to locate.

Some labor leaders, it is true, are opposed to these developments on principle. They are the ones who maintain a strong commitment to the idea of adversarial, militant, disciplined unionism as the only "real" form of worker representation; they see experiments like the Saturn contract as attacks on the labor movement. On the whole, however, these ideological resisters are now very much in the minority. Among leaders of major unions, there are almost none who would take such an intransigent position. The willingness of the AFL-CIO to explore dramatic new ideas in its 1985 strategy report is sufficient proof that a consensus for change is building. That consensus, though far from detailed or coherent, certainly involves a willingness to consider almost all the ideas I have outlined.

The dominant form of resistance among unions consists not in open opposition but in failure to follow through. Its subtlety does not make it any less effective. The fact is that while few labor leaders would now openly oppose extensions of employee rights or strategic reorganization—and many would strongly support them—the movement for change remains slow and tentative.

Almost all the new initiatives within the traditional labor movement have been slowed by counterforces:

- In 1982 the AFL-CIO sponsored an enormous "Solidarity Day" demonstration that brought together a coalition of liberal groups to protest the policies of the Reagan administration. Yet despite the drama of the event, it built little momentum or lasting alliances with outside groups. The isolated position of labor was reaffirmed in the 1984 presidential election.
- Corporate campaigns—the tactic of bringing public pressure to bear on corporations that mistreat their workers—have been troubled, despite a major initial success at J. P. Stevens and the endorsement of the AFL-CIO in its strategy report. In a widely publicized strike at a Hormel plant in Austin, Minnesota, a corporate campaign by a local union was opposed by the national union leadership, who viewed the tactic as a form of agitation that threatened the unity of the national contract.
- A trumpeted initiative by the AFL-CIO to reenergize organizing efforts by bringing together many unions in a model coordinated campaign has bogged down.
- Unions have generally failed to work together to solve their problems. It is discouraging, as the airlines and railroads pass through periods of damaging upheaval, to watch the unions representing their employees all working separately to make their own deals. Even where the unions sit together on the board of directors, as at Eastern or Western Airlines, they have not gone beyond token cooperation in developing united positions.
- Despite continuous rhetoric about the need to bring women and minorities more centrally into the labor movement, the leadership remains dominated by white males.
- Efforts at internal change to increase the focus on strategy have had only partial success. The report of the Communications Workers' Committee on the Future was

embraced in principle by the union's convention delegates; but several recommendations that would have involved intrusions into the autonomy of locals, such as
tightening performance standards or creating pressure on locals to increase organizing expenditures, were voted down. The penetration of the AFL-CIO's own strategy
report has likewise been slow. Two years after its publication most state federations
had not discussed it in any organized way. Some states had held conferences to
discuss its recommendations, arousing considerable debate and enthusiasm; but in
most instances the conferences did not produce sustained momentum for a reexamination of priorities.
  · Where comprehensive employee rights legislation has been proposed, as in California, labor has generally backed the bills but has not made their passage a high priority.

In part, these disappointments are functions of the magnitude of the proposed
changes. It would probably be unreasonable to expect the full weight of the
AFL-CIO report or the recommendations of the CWA's Committee on the
Future to be felt in anything less than five years, and much time must certainly
be spent in quiet and slow processes of education. There may be surprises in store.
Nevertheless, many observers close to the labor movement believe something
more fundamental is involved—that the thrust of the new proposals is being
blunted by unorganized but widespread resistance.

There are a number of important reasons for this frequent dissipation of the
energy for change. First, the labor movement is poor in resources and stretched
for time. With only a handful of staff, state federations and local unions can rarely
spare anyone to organize seriously around the long-term implications of change.
They cannot afford to put together, as companies can and have, systematic series
of seminars spreading throughout their organizations to develop a shared understanding of strategic shifts. If local leaders go to a conference about the AFL-CIO
report, their desks pile so high while they are gone with urgent problems—
grievances, strikes, decertification campaigns, and so on—that they quickly forget
what they have heard. There are so many old things to do that they cannot
concentrate on the new.

Second, almost all these initiatives require new skills, and the labor movement
is short of training opportunities. Everyone in the movement agrees, for example,
that it is imperative to develop better relations with the media in order to improve
the image of unions, but it will be a very long time before layers other than the
very top leadership receive any training in public relations techniques. Most
unions cannot even provide their officers with the skills needed for collective
bargaining. Labor leaders learn from experience, a conservative school that
teaches people to respond pragmatically to pressures rather than to plan ahead
for a changing environment.

The key problem, however, involves the protection of political turf. Unions as
organizations are caught in a contradiction that is continually frustrating. Though

they need unity and discipline to mobilize for mass action, unions are composed of officers who draw their power not from above but from below—from their members' votes. Therefore they have a basis of independence that no manager has: they cannot be fired by their superiors. They are very concerned, moreover, to protect their base of power, their relation to their voting constituents, from any outside interference, including pressures from other parts of their own unions. The result is a universal tendency for political fiefdoms to appear within the bureaucratic organization of unions. In addition, unions are independent fiefdoms within the labor movement as a whole, and the AFL-CIO has no effective power over them. This structure can be pulled together in a centralized way when conflicts produce an identifiable threat to all, such as during strikes. But attempts to produce unified movement toward long-term goals can rarely overcome the defensiveness of officers protecting their jurisdictions.

Jurisdiction was, of course, the central problem that prevented the AFL from adapting to changes in its environment during the 1920s. At the time, no craft union would cede its territory to permit the building of industrial groupings of workers. This form of resistance clearly retains its ability to slow strategic shifts.

Given these conflicting forces, it is difficult to build a simple picture of the outcome. On the one hand, there are real changes under way: many unions are breaking with long-held assumptions and patterns. The *need* for a new form of unionism is by now clear to most leaders of the labor movement. On the other hand, the forces of resistance are also great, though subtle, and they seem to be effectively preventing the sort of thorough reassessment that is called for by the AFL-CIO strategy report.

The conclusion, I think, is this: the labor movement is exploring important new avenues for worker representation, but it is unlikely to put its undivided energy into leading a movement for change. While major unions are engaged in the slow and painful process of transforming their own structures, it seems likely that much of the driving force for new forms of representation will come in the end from outside the formal boundaries of the labor movement—from "new unions" with relatively little historical baggage and from other associations and pressure groups.

Support for Workplace Rights

The evidence so far suggests that in terms of the extensions of representation that I have proposed, management will be opposed (though with some ambivalence) and unions will be uncertain. The process of change, therefore, must involve forces other than these two traditional adversaries.

From a historical perspective this conclusion is not surprising nor necessarily pessimistic. It is neither reasonable nor necessary to assume that change will come in sudden, spontaneous transformations of existing organizations; at the moment of creation, the energy must be provided by less structured *movements*. Unions developed as they did because they gave structure and coherence to deep, unarticulated needs of unorganized groups. It is these groups and needs that energize and define the basic shape of labor unions—and it is they, not the organizations, that produce structural changes.

This was certainly true of the period that has been a reference point throughout this study—the 1920s and 1930s. The regeneration of the labor movement at that time of crisis was led, not by the existing AFL unions, but by a movement that grew up outside and, to a large extent, in opposition to them. As the existing labor movement struggled to redefine its role, industrial movements swept ahead of it. Even when the Wagner Act was proposed, the AFL's support was late and equivocal. In no sense was the new type of unionism created *by* the old.

The problem of worker representation today is usually posed in terms of whether labor or management will prevail in their struggle. But the historical lessons suggest that this view misses major possibilities. The driving force for change is more likely to come from outside the existing framework or from its borders than from its center. Thus the real question is whether there are any movements today with the power to create a new system of representation.

There is no easy answer. Movements cannot be pinned down for examination: unlike organizations, they have no hard structure, no formal relations. They are more like ocean currents, always shifting, never directly visible, and able to drift deep out of sight for long periods without losing force. They can be seen only in the waves they create when they surface, which may be for brief periods in their long courses. So, for instance, the industrial movements that erupted into widespread conflict during 1933 and 1934 had been building for at least thirty years, coming to the surface before and after World War I but receding again from view during the 1920s. In retrospect they show an obvious coherence; they seem inevitable responses to a profound change in management and in the economy. But at the time it was easy to be misled by the temporary shifts in course, and it is equally easy to be misled today.

Nevertheless, I believe there is now strong evidence for the existence of a movement—a deep response to major social change—that centers on the need for employee rights. This does not mean the movement is *organized*. It is still in the form of a shifting current, one that has already shown its force for brief moments but is now running below the surface. That current contains, however, the potential to energize a coalition for political action.

One way to try to grasp this movement is by its effects. The last twenty years, as we have seen, have been far from a simple period of increased employer power, despite the steady weakening of labor unions. Major things have happened in different arenas and at different times that have limited employers in a novel way. The Civil Rights Act of 1964, the Occupational Safety and Health Act of 1970, the Age Discrimination in Employment Act, the dozens of federal whistleblowing provisions, the hundreds of state prohibitions of various forms of discrimination in the workplace, many other state laws protecting employee privacy, the growing body of court rulings limiting employers' ability to fire at will—to recap just a few of the highlights of this history—have all brought public criteria of fairness to bear on the employment relationship. They have acted not indirectly, by trying to strengthen the private capacity of unions, but directly, by defining specific management actions as violations of public standards. The cumulative effect has been to greatly weaken the fabric of the legal veil of managerial prerogative.

Although these acts and decisions have developed in a scattered way, they clearly have a kind of mysterious unity. It is mysterious because there has been no single leading organizer or organization—no Nader of labor (although Nader, the consumer activist, has been involved himself at times), no Congress of Employees. Many different groups, from judges to middle managers to women's associations, have found themselves acting on similar principles. This pattern, traceable over at least two decades and throughout the industrial world, can only be explained by the presence of a consistent force—a movement—in the background.

Strains, Changing Beliefs, and New Coalitions

To further explore this underlying force we need to borrow a few concepts from analysts of political change. The first condition for the creation of movements is *strain* in social institutions, a failure to meet the needs and expectations of groups. The second is a change in *beliefs:* the beliefs that supported the old order lose their effectiveness, and a new set redefines the situation. The final crucial element is the crystallization of *new coalitions* and groups that transform institutions.[4]

The strains among many categories of employees today are very clear. The trials of blue-collar workers in the declining mass-production industries, faced by unemployment and technological change on a massive scale, are familiar. What is less familiar and less public is the growing discontent among semiprofessional employees: middle managers, technicians, sales representatives, engineers, investigators, and others who constitute the core of an economy based increasingly on the production of knowledge. The expectations of this group are defined largely by the traditional concept of "management." In the past their positions have brought job security and privileged working conditions: in bad times workers get laid off, not managers. They have been part of the "family" of management, trusted to do their jobs and, in return, offering loyalty and commitment to the company.

But semiprofessional workers of all sorts are currently experiencing new levels of uncertainty. At the same time that the baby-boom generation is entering mid-career, corporations have embarked on an unprecedented and often ruthless restructuring of their white-collar and management staffs. Competitive pressures have moved up from the factory floor. This has produced an abrupt end of innocence among many managerial employees—a closing of opportunities and a new sense of insecurity. "As the rules of the game change," says *Business Week*, "the faithful feel betrayed."[5]

The tension is increased by the fact that many semiprofessionals are at the center of the most dynamic and productive parts of the economy. These are "knowledge workers," who are frequently portrayed as the saviors of American competitiveness. Their insecurity comes, not from a decline in their basic industries, but from rapid change and restructuring in which their interests are not sufficiently represented. This is an excellent formula for unrest.

There are only a few surveys that enable us to document the effects of these changes on the attitudes of managerial employees, but they tell a dramatic story. The Opinion Research Corporation (ORC), for instance, has conducted periodic surveys in about 200 companies for the past thirty years. During that time period, they have found that the attitudes of managers toward their companies have worsened drastically:

- The percentage who rate their companies favorably in terms of fairness in the application of policies and rules has dropped from almost 80 percent to less than 40 percent.
- The percentage who viewed their companies as responsive to employee problems has dropped from almost 75 percent to barely 30 percent.
- Those who feel their company provides them job security have declined from close to 100 percent in the 1950s to about 65 percent now.
- Asked whether their company was a better place to work now than when they started, 52 percent said yes in the early 1960s; by the end of the 1970s, that had dropped to a little over 25 percent.

These are extraordinary numbers. The change they record is not only enormous, as surveys go, but it has continued for a very long period. It is also widespread; the ORC data for professionals show almost identical patterns of decline on most of these questions, though starting from a lower base. Other sources, though less complete than the ORC figures, confirm the general picture. A *Business Week*/Harris poll in 1985, for instance, "revealed a startling undercurrent of dissatisfaction with management, even among professional employees and executives." "The lack of satisfaction," said Harris of these results, "is ample evidence that the seeds of discontent are very deep."[6]

That does not complete the inventory of employees under strain. In addition to blue-collar workers and semiprofessionals, many others feel a growing gap between expectations and reality. Another important group is the lower-level white-collar employees—the "white-collar semiskilled"—who, while never being seen as a full part of management, used to be considered somewhat privileged. Many of these, especially in clerical categories, have seen their prestige and security significantly reduced as well. The ORC figures show the results: from the 1950s to 1979, clerical workers' approval of company fairness dropped from 70 percent to 20 percent.

A final category that cuts across all of these, and adds a new dimension as well, is that of "contingent" employees. In recent years a large and well-defined segment of workers has developed that absorbs a great deal of the insecurity in the economy. Audrey Freedman, of the Conference Board, estimates that today 28 percent of U.S. workers are not on regular payrolls: these include temporary workers, freelancers, contractors, and part-timers, and their proportion is expanding rapidly.[7] Their presence allows companies to offer the regular employees a higher degree of job security, using the others as a buffer. We have already observed this phenomenon as a deliberate strategy of managerialist firms for maintaining loyalty among their core workers. It is hard to predict the consequences of such an "externalization" of a large sector of the work force, many of whom are quite well educated: but these employees clearly form a massive group with no loyalties to any corporate organization. They are a "wild card" in the current deck.

These groups include the bulk of the labor force. The traditional blue-collar occupations, those most dramatically threatened by the changing economy, form roughly 20 percent of employees; semiprofessionals (including middle managers) another third or more; the declining white-collar semiskilled close to 20 percent; and contingent employees add an undetermined amount.[8] It is, I believe, fair to estimate that more than three-quarters of the work force is undergoing significant disruption of expectations.

That is not as surprising as it might seem at first: it simply reflects the enormous economic restructuring process underway in the move from national to worldwide competition, and from an emphasis on mass production toward some still-undetermined mix of services and flexible specialization. Almost all industries and most individual firms have felt these pressures directly over the past decade, and they are struggling to find new strategic and organizational ways to cope. As we have seen, the changes in many companies have been profound. It is only natural that those who make up these organizations should be feeling the disruption.

Strain generally shows up on attitude surveys, but by itself it does not produce collective actions; it can remain underground for a long time. It begins to be volatile only when it leads to a change in *beliefs*. This includes both a negative aspect—the lessening of support for old institutions—and a positive one—the rise of new belief systems.

That we are deeply in a negative phase is quite clear from survey data. The decline in support for labor is absolutely unmistakable, but business is not very far behind. It is important to stress that while there has been an increase in general optimism and support for the presidency under Reagan, that did *not* extend to any real revival of faith in the major organizations of the economy.[9]

The next step in the generation of collective action is the spread of a *positive* set of beliefs that redefine the situation. In this country, no one has yet unfurled the banner of general "employee rights"; no major political figure has made the claim that has transformed the European scene—that "job rights [have] political and legal parity with property rights."[10] But that is not to say that this belief does not, in an important sense, exist, and on a wide scale.

Positive assertion can be seen, though sketchily, in opinion polls. Almost no one asks employees what they think their rights are, perhaps because it still seems like a taboo concept. But one study did ask the question quite directly: "Which, if any of these things, do workers have a *right* to?" (Emphasis is in the original.) Some 69 percent checked job security, and 60 percent checked "a voice in decisions that affect them." And a 1979 Harris poll showed that about two-thirds of employees want Congress to pass legislation regulating the information private employers can collect about individuals; even higher percentages favor laws giving employees access to their personnel files, banning lie detectors in hiring, and forbidding monitoring of employees.[11]

The trend is more clearly visible in the reasoning for the myriad specific extensions of employee rights. In pushing these claims, many different groups have accepted and acted on a single basic premise: that corporations, while they may have property rights, have no right to abuse their employees. This is quite different from the premise that fueled industrial unionism; indeed, it has clearly gone hand in hand with the weakening of support for the latter. The generalized belief behind the 1930s movements was unionist, but this is more directly political. The first said, "Give us half a chance and we can stop the bastards"; the second says, "There ought to be a law." The first puts its faith in the private conflict of workers against managers, the second in a public definition of principles of fair treatment. It is well summarized by John Dunlop: ". . . the notion that an employer can get out of bed and fire anybody for any old reason is repugnant to a society of employees, whether they are organized into unions or not."[12]

The new belief has existed so far largely in particularistic versions, but it is moving gradually toward a more inclusive form. Groups are seeing that they can achieve more with broad claims, which encourage extensive support, than with narrow ones. General "just-cause" legislation, at least at the state level, is becoming a serious possibility for the first time.

That brings up the final element in the transformation from a latent movement to an open force: the mobilization of a coalition for action. Though the other elements are already present, this one obviously lies in the future. It is to a large degree a matter of the specific course of events—far too specific to predict. A major recession would probably accelerate the crystallization of new demands; a Democratic administration in Washington would reduce the resisting forces. On the other hand, continued prosperity, an extension of Republican control, or major foreign conflicts, while they would not affect the underlying movement, would all tend to slow down its emergence.

But the process of mobilization is also largely a matter of political will and imagination. Those who remain fixed on old images—of large unions balancing large employers, of formal collective bargaining, of exclusive representation—are being left behind by the movement of most employees. The support for that narrow form of representation is now extremely low. It is difficult, however, for politicians to shift their attention. They are accustomed to dealing with organizations rather than with movements, and labor, despite its weakness as a movement, is still a very large organization. There is a considerable danger, therefore, that the Democratic party may continue, as it did in 1984, to tie itself to the classic image of unionism, missing the chance for wider mobilization.

For a coalition of a much greater scope is building around the concept of employee rights. It includes the groups that have traditionally carried the union banner, blue-collar workers who have been forcefully confronted in the past decade with the limitations of collective bargaining. It also includes a great deal more: white-collar workers and semiprofessionals, middle managers and engineers, women and minorities at all levels—all those who resist the classic calls to mass solidarity but whose concerns are growing sharper. And many low-level service workers whose jobs are too scattered to support the usual institutions of bargaining would be better served by direct rights than by traditional approaches.

All of these groups have already been engaged in developing effective forms of political action. They have formed increasing numbers of pressure groups, which are outside the standard labor relations framework and which rely primarily on tactics of publicity and lobbying. In many respects, these "quasi-unions" are more attracted to the sort of system I have described than is the traditional union sector, because they have less attachment to the Wagner Act alternative. They have been the primary driving force so far in the extension of employee rights. They are currently making significant advances in pushing for state legislative protections—for pregnancy issues, whistleblowing, due process, and many other areas—and in forcing courts to reconsider old doctrines of employer prerogative.

An image of representation that encompassed their needs and their preferred forms of action, as the Wagner Act framework does not, would provide a focus to these currently scattered forces.

Social movements are enigmatic phenomena, difficult to predict or to channel. It is for that very reason that they are the major engines of change. Organizations, by comparison with movements, are predictable but conservative. If we look only at the key organizations of the existing system—business, labor, and government—we find ambivalence at best, or resistance at worst. But *something* has been causing a profound though quiet upheaval in the structure of the employment relationship over the past two decades—something from outside these organizations has produced new tactics and foci for action. That "something," the force behind the growth of employee rights, provides the potential for rolling the rock over the barriers of resistance.

Short-term Tactics

Though I have proposed a rather wholesale change in the Wagner Act framework, I would not argue that the time is ripe now for making the break. There is still much need for model building and experimentation and for the construction of new coalitions. These two developments will help in preparing the groundwork for the new system—the groundwork of skills, of understanding, and of relationships. The more work is done now, the more likely it is that changes can happen without major conflict.

Developing Rights

The current state of employee rights includes, as I have emphasized, scattered guarantees backed by fragmented interest groups. The major task for the immediate future is to pull together the forces that have produced this agglomeration of rights. Networks are already growing naturally from the continuing ferment. Pregnant women have begun to define a common interest with the disabled in working toward generalized protection for both groups. Due-process legislation has drawn support from professionals and white-collar groupings. Plant closing laws are pushed not only by blue-collar workers and their unions but also by communities that can be devastated by shutdowns of key employers. These connections build a sense of unity among disparate groups, which is the way new coalitions are formed.

It is especially important to connect the movement for rights to unions.

The Process of Change: Strategy and Resistance

Organized labor has often been uncertain about these initiatives for fear that they will supplant its bargaining functions. Continued demonstrations of the ways in which rights can *strengthen* union representation—by providing them a handle on discrimination issues, for instance, or opening doors into workplaces that are not yet ready to give a vote for exclusive representation—are needed to bring labor more enthusiastically into this area.

Courts, as well as legislatures, can have an important effect in consolidating the framework of rights. For the past decade they have been tearing holes in the fabric of the old doctrine of employment-at-will without producing a consistent alternative. The new rulings are still viewed as "exceptions," justified on narrow and ad hoc grounds, though they now add up to a point where the doctrinal cloth is in danger of disintegrating. This produces a tense state of affairs and slows progress; judges fear that further exceptions will push them into a void with no accepted boundaries. There is a need for a theory that can embrace the newer developments as central rather than exceptional—for a general law of *governance* that defines the nature and limits of power.[13]

Union Strategies

All the major elements of what I have called "associational unionism" are currently being explored by unions and employee groups; if they were not, there would be little sense in proposing the model. Unions have been rapidly developing new capacities to understand and to respond to complex changes in technology and corporate structure; to communicate these responses to a diverse membership; to integrate shopfloor participation, or problem-solving groups, into the overall system of voice; and to reach out effectively to allies outside the organization through publicity and coalition building.

These initiatives, of course, present difficult tactical choices, particularly for unions in their current state of weakness. When the UAW, for example, supports the Saturn concept, it runs considerable risks. Its local officers are sharply divided over the merits of the course, which is creating internal turmoil; furthermore, the new contract increases the danger that the company will "whipsaw" the union by using the Saturn exception as a wedge against the solidity of the central agreement. It appears to be the judgment of the leadership, as it is mine, that the risks are outweighed in this particular instance by the absolute necessity of exploring new initiatives. That does not imply, however, that every experiment is good for every union. Such judgments can only be made within the context of a vision of the future toward which movement is directed.

Thus the crucial step for unions is not to think up new ideas but to bring current experiments together in a unified vision and to make a clear commitment to change. For that, in turn, two kinds of action are needed. There needs to be a strong *leadership* role by the AFL-CIO, both at the national and at local levels. The report on "The Changing Situation of Workers and Their Unions" has already been a catalyst for unions that are casting about for ways of dealing with their growing problems. Many state federations have organized seminars for their member unions to study the report and to work out their own ways of planning for the future. The task, however, is so difficult that one-shot education sessions are clearly insufficient; there is need for repeated follow-ups, exchange of experiences among unions, and resources for training and skill development. It is to be hoped that the current reductions in the AFL-CIO's resources caused by declining membership will not be taken out in these areas.

Second, *strategic planning* within unions is vital. Without it, there is a real and present danger that experiments, necessary as they are, will lead to confusion and fragmentation among members and staff. It is not enough to place a priority on organizing, without a clear idea of who are the proper constituency and how the union can serve them. It is not enough to spend money on publicity, without a common sense of priorities and direction on which to base the publicity. Strategic planning, though a long and costly process, is vital to build a shared understanding within unions of what is required to meet the current challenges.

The Role of Government

The executive branch of the government can also help, during this interim period, in clarifying the direction of change. Even in the Reagan-dominated political climate there is significant support for action on some of these issues. The Labor Department has established a Bureau of Labor-Management Cooperation that has sponsored conferences to spread information on labor-management cooperation and has published research reports on innovative efforts. The Federal Mediation and Conciliation Service now administers a fund for the encouragement of joint labor-management committees; and, as mentioned earlier, it is interested in the development of "preventive mediation" as opposed to crisis response. These similar developments in different parts of the government show that the need for consensus building is pushing even a conservative administration to explore some interesting avenues.

There are further functions that these agencies could naturally undertake. One is the encouragement of joint training, as discussed in the last chapter: government agencies can fill the necessary role of neutral facilitator or convenor, bringing together various unions and employee groups to develop techniques of multilateral negotiation. They could act directly to provide training, or maintain a pool of people who, like arbitrators, could do it on a private basis. Again, the scope of innovation should not be restricted to organized labor. Professional associations and other employee groups can use support for new negotiation techniques at least as much as unions and may offer important lessons for the future of representation.

Then there is the NLRB. In its role as regulatory agency, it is in trouble: the weaknesses of expert rule making have deeply eroded its legitimacy. Employers often ignore its rulings, and the bulk of its decisions are appealed to the courts. The Reagan appointments have further undermined it by polarizing its members.[14] As an "expert" body, it seems to be generating nothing but animosity.

I suggested in the last chapter a shift toward regulatory negotiation among the affected parties. This is not an idea that has to wait for other changes: it can be explored now. Take the issue of plant closings. A lot of doomsday rhetoric has been exchanged on this issue—employers saying that any restriction on their prerogatives will undermine the private enterprise system, unions insisting that plant closings destroy collective bargaining and worker rights. The pressure is heating up now as an increasing number of state legislatures consider laws to regulate this field. The NLRB's rulings have been extraordinarily inconsistent and contentious. Given these tensions and the threat of legislative "interference," this issue is a good candidate for regulatory negotiation: the alternatives to consensus are bad enough all around to motivate the parties to serious discussions.

This method would take a great deal of pressure off the board. It would no longer be in the middle between warring parties, but would only help the parties to fight things out themselves. At the same time, regulatory negotiation would lead in the direction of a more flexible system of representation built on agreed-on principles that are less dependent on a detailed web of rules to hold everything in place.

The courts could torpedo this effort if they subject regulatory negotiations to the same "hard look" as other rule-making processes. They can encourage it, on the other hand, by using a less strict standard of examination for rules that are developed by negotiation among the parties. That would solidify the motivation to take those negotiations seriously.

Management

Employers, finally, can also play a role in developing strategic unionism. I will mention this only briefly, because it has not happened much. On their own, employers have usually moved in the direction of managerialism, which is weakened by the absence of solid representative bodies. But cases like Shell-Sarnia, Saturn, or the advanced QWL efforts at Ford and other companies should be studied by employers who want to develop the maximum creativity and commitment within their organizations. Management, it is said, gets the union it deserves; to deserve employees who can contribute constructively to a flexible system, it needs to encourage a form of representation that meets their needs.

All of these are, it should be emphasized, preparatory steps. Though there is a great deal of ferment now in the field of employee relations, the current initiatives remain too specific to solve the deep problems underlying that ferment. There needs to be a shift from fission to fusion. The building of theory and of wider networks of action can help in uniting the movement. In the end, however, it will surely take some sort of "break"—a new administration or other political events—to focus the energy for change. At that point the work that has gone into the development of models and relationships will pay off by providing the building blocks of a new order.

CHAPTER 13

Conclusion

I HAVE USED the term "crisis" in this study frequently, but not lightly. Organized labor is in serious trouble. It is not merely that its membership has dropped dramatically, though that is certainly a concern. Nor is it merely that its leadership is widely viewed as selfish and unworthy of confidence. What is most alarming is that the labor movement is isolated from the growing and dynamic parts of the society. It is confined to economic sectors that are struggling for survival, largely failing to penetrate the growing ranks of service and white-collar employees. It is on uneasy terms with the movements—women, minorities, environmentalists, and the disabled—that have had the most significant impact on corporations during the past two decades. Unions are struggling with diminishing success to hold on to what they have, and they have ceased to reach outward into new areas.

The vast majority of employees, meanwhile, are poorly represented. The central issue is no longer, as it was a century ago, the pervasiveness of blatant abuse: child labor, physical mistreatment, company stores, and obviously unsafe conditions have certainly grown less common. But employees at all levels have concerns and ideas that are not being dealt with. Since protections of basic rights are weak, insecurity is almost universal; few people are willing to run the risk of discharge by challenging authority. In the past two decades, especially among white-collar employees, there has been a sharp decline in the perception of company fairness. Even in the most prestigious firms, employees believe that not enough effort is being made to incorporate their opinions and knowledge into decision making.[1]

Rather than responding to the challenge, organized labor has, in effect, collapsed inward. The context that once supported industrial unionism has changed. Its essential shape was set in the mass-production industries that grew from the great economic transformation early in this century. It was built around the needs of semiskilled workers in large production units, workers who were clearly set off from management by an almost unbridgeable gulf. It accepted the bureaucratic nature of the corporations it faced, taking the tack of clarifying the rules of "Scientific Management" and making sure they were equitably enforced. It drew essential support from the New Deal's philosophy of government's responsibility for social welfare. Today the mass-production sector is in decline, semiskilled workers are being replaced by white-collar workers and semiprofessionals, the line between worker and management is blurred by the burgeoning of middle layers, and the New Deal definition of the role of government has been deeply shaken. The labor movement used to stand near the center of activity and political concern of the society; but as other groups have followed the social transformations of the past thirty years, labor has remained behind. It now finds itself almost alone in an echoing chamber.

These changes are all pieces in a broad transition that is often characterized as a move toward a "postindustrial" society. The term, despite its vagueness, captures something real. Just as the mass-production revolution of the turn of the century was disorienting to craft unions, so the current shift throws industrial unions into disarray; they seem constantly mismatched to the situation. Their key weapon, the strike, is increasingly ineffective as economic activity grows more mobile and automated. Not only does the strike not work, but it further alienates vital public support. Collective bargaining has not stretched to deal effectively with corporate strategic planning, a force that has enormous consequences for the security and quality of life at work. The tactical focus on uniform rules and contracts, which has been essential to the solidarity of the labor movement, is impossible to maintain as industries fragment and diversify; and such uniformity is increasingly rejected even by many union members as rigid and bureaucratic. Labor's very successes, rare though they have become, often boomerang. Increases in wages of unionized workers are widely seen as contributing to a loss of national competitiveness and as reflecting narrow self-interest. There seems to be no place to turn.

That, however, is only one part of the crisis. The decline of organized labor affects not only union leaders and members; it has far wider implications. For unions have long provided a practical answer to issues that are central to every industrial democracy, today as in the past, and that ultimately affect every citizen.

Work is not a minor and peripheral sort of private institution. It is central to the public welfare, the source of wealth for every member of the society. Few individuals can survive without working, and every individual depends for survival on the work of others. The control of work, therefore—the way it is organized, its efficiency, the distribution of its product—is an issue whose consequences are vital for all.

The labor union is a particular mechanism for the expression of the needs of employees in the work process. Its importance has been proven by the fact that the union has appeared as a major force, and in fundamentally the same form, in every industrialized nation. Social change may undercut the effectiveness and relevance of this specific structure, but it does not in any way diminish the original problem: work is just as important in a postindustrial state as in every other period. Though unions today are so isolated that their further decline may seem like a minor matter to those outside their boundaries, the failure to create a functional equivalent is a matter of serious public concern.

Much discussion has already centered on the *economic* consequences of the lack of voice for employees. In a competitive world economy, one of the United States's greatest advantages is its highly skilled and educated work force. The evidence is clear that the potential of that work force is not being fully used. The research of Yankelovich and Immerwahr, among others, has demonstrated the existence of a widespread "commitment gap."[2] There is a substantial consensus, extending from the President's Commission on Industrial Competitiveness to the heads of many of our major corporations, that increased involvement of employees is important for economic progress. The disagreement comes in trying to work out a form for that involvement.

Though we talk most about the economic issue, the problem of labor representation has other crucial aspects. It is closely entwined with a central *political* issue of the modern state: the relation of private to public power. Corporations are theoretically forms of private property and association, but they have such power to affect social welfare that they can easily come to compete with and to challenge the state. As they have grown in size and strength during the past century, the dangers in such centralized private control have become more evident. Corporate decisions—especially those that involve plant closings, layoffs, international investment and trade, and new directions for technology—entail enormous consequences and costs that go far beyond their private boundaries.

The main political response to this need for a public check on corporate decision making has been the Wagner Act, which aimed to give workers the leverage to negotiate standards with their employers. As that framework has crumbled, increasing public pressure has been placed on the government to intervene *directly* in corporate behavior through regulatory rule making. Regulatory bodies have grown up around workplace civil rights and health and safety issues because those were not adequately handled by the forms of employee representation that were established within the Wagner Act framework. But the regulatory solution has strained the legitimacy of the state close to the breaking point, leaving a growing incapacity of government to deal with corporate power.

Finally, least acknowledged but most fundamental, the breakdown of representation has profound consequences for the *moral* contracts that are the foundation of a democratic society. The labor movement, whatever its faults, has increased workers' sense of dignity and self-esteem by providing an avenue for the expression of their concerns. It has enabled employees to stand up to abuses of authority and to avoid complete dependence on the will of their corporate superiors. The decline of unions leaves the vast majority of the labor force with no independent base, so that most employees have to rely for fair treatment entirely on the goodwill of management.

Unilateral power is despotism. It may be benevolent or abusive, but it is still despotism. And despotism necessarily undermines the moral strength of a society, producing cynicism and narrow self-interest. It is just this cynicism that is reflected in Yankelovich and Immerwahr's data on work attitudes and in the public's low opinion of corporate responsibility and leadership.

The crisis of employee representation, then, has repercussions throughout the social order. The need to reconstruct an effective system has given rise to four general proposals: labor law reform, direct regulation, managerialism, and associational unionism.

Labor Law Reform

The simplest idea is to strengthen the Wagner Act. The enforcement powers of the National Labor Relations Board are so weak that it is quite easy for employers to delay their recognition of union rights or even to flout the law openly. Labor law reform would restore something more nearly like a balance of power between unions and management.

This approach, however, ignores the changes that have reduced the effectiveness of the old model. Even if it "worked," by reviving unions, it would leave critical problems; for it would do nothing to deal with the necessary weaknesses of the balance-of-power framework itself, which have come to the fore during the current social transition:

- A balance of power is *rigid,* and therefore fragile. Balances reached through painful trials of strength last only so long as the situations of both parties remain quite stable. As soon as either side goes through significant changes, one or the other is likely to see the possibility of gaining a new advantage and will therefore initiate a new round of conflict.
- It is *exclusive.* A balance can be sustained only among a few parties; as the number increases, the instability of the system multiplies. Thus, open discussion and participation is discouraged, even within the competing organizations, because such openness weakens their unified stance toward the opponent—and new groups are systematically cut out of the action.
- While it encourages stability and order, it discourages active employee *commitment.* This is perhaps the central problem of bureaucracy in general: what is rewarded by the structure is the consistent carrying out of rules rather than the exercise of more flexible initiative and creativity. The balance-of-power approach encourages the development of explicit rules and procedures, locking both parties into bureaucratic patterns.

Conclusion

Each of these weaknesses has been harshly exposed by events of the last two decades—by the increased pace of economic change, by the persistent claims of new groups, and by the need to mobilize employee commitment. The current economic restructuring requires that unions be able to represent members through complex periods of change. That calls for establishing flexible standards and principles rather than strict contractual rules, being involved in planning rather than merely reacting as an opposition to management, and dealing with concerns of people who are not clearly on either side of the traditional "line." None of those weaknesses would be corrected by better enforcement of the existing legal framework.

Direct Regulation

Most of the effective expressions of new employee concerns during the past two decades have taken place, not through collective bargaining, but through regulatory laws. This is also the thrust of some influential proposals for the future: the due-process bill suggested by the California bar, for example, would establish a vast new administrative system to judge disputes about unjust discharges.

This approach has certain advantages over collective bargaining. It is more inclusive: it offers rights to all employees, not just those who have organized themselves into powerful unions. It is in principle fairer, since the standards established by government are applied uniformly, rather than varying with accidents of bargaining power. And it is potentially somewhat more flexible, since it can be changed by rational decision rather than waiting for the outcome of power conflicts.

The crucial disadvantage, however—in addition to the strain it puts on political legitimacy—is that regulation takes decision-making responsibility out of the hands of those directly concerned in disputes. The strength of the Wagner Act framework is that the people who are interested in issues are those who fight them out. Thus they can shape agreements to their particular needs, and they must accept responsibility for the results. Imposition of standards by expert administrators, by contrast, encourages everyone to take a narrow and litigious stance, freed from any need to confront the other side directly. It also usually results in universal dissatisfaction, because everyone can blame the outside decisionmaker. These are among the reasons for its lack of popularity today.

Managerialism

Both the regulatory and the labor law reform routes rely on a representation through formal rule making; the difference is in who makes the rules. The more innovative and promising approaches to employee voice, however, lead toward a system of continuous discussion and negotiation at many levels, involving employees directly as well as through representatives, and guided by general *principles*.

Most reforms along these lines have been undertaken by companies without unions, in an effort to mobilize the commitment of their employees. These "managerialist" firms, as I have called them, offer quite strong guarantees of employment security and fair treatment; on that foundation they build mechanisms of participation that include autonomous teams, flexible task forces, and various problem-solving forums. These companies include many of the largest and most successful in meeting the challenges of economic change. For in return for providing channels for employee concerns, they receive an unusual measure of *intelligence* and creativity from all levels of the organization.

But managerialism has its limits. The systems of representation are dependent on management, rather than independent. It is rare, therefore, that they are truly protected against deception and self-deception. They are vulnerable to abuse; and even in instances of goodwill it is quite common for management to miss hidden resistance, to believe that consensus is greater than it actually is, and to have too much faith in the power of charismatic leadership to sweep everyone along. It takes extraordinary, and therefore very unusual, efforts to guard against these problems that undermine the culture of managerialism. Most companies who embark on this route are satisfied with half measures—open-door policies and limited employee participation groups—rather than real structural reform; and there is none to challenge them.

From the societal point of view, moreover, managerialist firms are self-enclosed islands. They provide no ways of coordinating needs of employees across companies, including labor market movement, or of setting general standards. They offer *models*, in certain respects, for what a broader form of voice might look like, but they do not offer a *policy* that can be extended throughout the economy.

Associational Unionism

The final alternative, the one I have advocated, is the evolution of unionism toward a form that can effectively represent employees more flexibly than the present system—able to embrace diverse types of members, including managerial and professional ranks; able to deal comfortably with both long-term strategic concerns and shopfloor participation bodies; able to engage in multilateral negotiations among several parties around complex issues; and able to use a range of tactics according to the situation.

This associational unionism is foreshadowed in certain unionized companies that have pursued managerialist reforms—General Motors and the United Auto Workers, AT&T and the Communications Workers, and, most suggestively,

Conclusion

Shell and the Energy and Chemical Workers of Canada. These are often described as examples of labor-management cooperation. But "cooperation" is an inadequate and largely inaccurate word for these changes. They involve far more than a change of relationship between existing organizations, a simple pulling together in the face of adversity. Rather, they involve profound changes within both parties as well as between them, and a restructuring of the whole system of representation. These unions have had to learn to move beyond collective bargaining, to maneuver in situations where they cannot hold to contractual uniformity or rely on mass action; they have developed their own capacities for strategic planning. Conflict is not noticeably reduced, but it does change form. Rather than expressing itself primarily in strikes and grievances, it takes many shapes depending on the type of issue and degree of disagreement.

This is a painful and difficult evolution, made more difficult because it is unsupported by public policy. The Wagner Act framework—with its many layers of amendments and interpretations—offers a kind of security base on which parties can fall back when they cannot reach agreement. But it focuses on collective bargaining and the mechanisms of mass strikes, offering no help for breakdowns in the newer forms of dispute resolution. Thus in times of stress there is a natural tendency to drift back toward the familiar approaches.

The current transformation, like the earlier move toward industrial unionism, demands a new policy foundation. That foundation can be built with the energy of a movement that has already produced major changes in employment law: the demand for employee rights. While public support for unionism has declined, pressures for protection against abuses of employer power have increased. The challenge to the concept of the private nature of the employment relationship has produced laws against discrimination, health and safety abuses, and many forms of arbitrary discharge. The movement for rights has been the center of organized activities by many groups outside the formal labor movement: associations of women, minorities, and professionals. In the past two decades, the new rights have had a far greater effect on employers than anything achieved through collective bargaining.

The movement for rights has been scattered so far, seeking very specific protections for particular groups. In that form it divides rather than unites, and it leads more toward intrusive regulation than toward stronger representation. But it is beginning to coalesce into a more general conception of the rights of employees. That development probably defines the terrain for a major political battle with corporate interests; it also carries the potential for grounding and expanding the promising models of flexible representation.

A base of rights loosens the requirement that unions be unified and disciplined organizations: it permits a more *associational* structure, matching the type of solidarity characteristic of the semiprofessional work force. It provides forms of pressure to supplement and reduce reliance on the strike, including court action and the expanded use of publicity. It enables employees who are not part of a recognized majority to resist abuses and to express their concerns. If the government's role is kept in the background—as a reserve of power in exceptional cases, rather than as a regular channel of complaints—it can serve to increase the flexibility of unions, encouraging the "strategic" direction.

This is, in a sense, a matter of turning the Wagner Act upside down. Currently the government, through the NLRB and the courts, is drawn deeply into the details of labor-management relations, formulating shelves full of rules, but without a foundation of public consensus on principles. The movement for rights brings to the forefront once again the key issues: What are the proper functions and limits of corporate power? What constitutes fair treatment of employees? By facing these issues squarely, government can take back its proper role of defining basic principles, rather than functioning, as it too often does now, as a kind of interfering meddler in details.

Though the energy for change is centered outside the traditional labor relations system, its course will be greatly affected by the organizations at its center—management and unions. If they insist on maintaining traditional prerogatives and relations, they can act as effective blockers. In that case the likely outcome is a continuation of the developments that have led to the current crisis—the decline of unions and the complementary rise in demands for employee rights—until the pressure grows too great to withstand. That is essentially what happened during the last major transition: resistance dogged the development of the Wagner Act system from the beginning, resulting in extraordinary levels of conflict and the weakening of the resulting system of representation.

On the other hand, there are many opportunities for these organizations to turn the current forces to constructive ends. For unions, the embracing of rights and of flexible negotiation can lead to a great increase in their effectiveness as employee representatives. For management, they can help to build new levels of commitment and creativity in the work force. These choices are growing steadily more crucial as the crisis of traditional unionism deepens.

NOTES

CHAPTER 1

1. These figures are from the Bureau of Labor Statistics. Private sector unionization hit about 38 percent in 1954, declined steadily to 20.1 percent in 1980, then plummeted more sharply to 15.3 percent in 1984. The membership of the AFL-CIO dropped by more than 10 percent between 1981 and 1984 alone.

2. As R. B. Freeman and J. L. Medoff (1984) point out, unions have never had a success on general labor legislation since the Wagner Act, and they have had two major defeats: the Taft-Hartley Act of 1947 and the Landrum-Griffin Act of 1959. On other types of legislation their record is much better.

3. *Business Week,* 19 November 1984, p. 42.

4. In a 1976 Harris survey, 63 percent agreed that "unions have become too powerful and should be restricted in the use of their power by law." A poll by the Center for Political Studies in the same year showed an almost identical percentage—64 percent—agreeing that unions have "too much influence." A 1982 ABC News/*Washington Post* poll showed 55 percent agreeing that unions should have less influence than they do now (study number 0048, 5 February 1982).

5. S. M. Lipset and W. Schneider (1983), p. 52; S. M. Lipset and W. Schneider (1983), pp. 204–5. Among other things, these figures show that support for the union shop dropped from 44 percent in 1965 to 31 percent in 1977.

6. Employer unfair labor practices quadrupled between 1960 and 1980 (with an almost constant number of elections); a sharp takeoff began around 1970.

7. Quoted in S. Barkin (1985), p. 858.

8. S. Lipset and W. Schneider (1983), table 7-4.

9. The workers poisoned by cyanide worked at Film Recovery in Elk Grove Village, Illinois. They did get representation of a sort, though not through unions: their employers were convicted of murder for knowingly tolerating the fatal conditions. (The verdict was handed down by Cook County Circuit Judge Ronald J. P. Banks in June 1985.) The growing role of the courts in extending worker rights will be an important theme later in this essay.

10. Dr. Harvey Brenner has estimated that every 1 percent rise in unemployment results in an increase in mental hospital admissions of 4.3 percent for men and 2.3 percent for women; an increase in suicides of 4.1 percent; an increase in the murder rate of 5.7 percent; and over a six-year period, an increase in the death rate from heart disease, cirrhosis of the liver, and other stress ailments of 1.9 percent (testimony before the Congressional Joint Economic Committee, 1976).

11. See S. Lipset and W. Schneider (1983), pp. 311, 313. The first shows that union support declines sharply among those with a college education; the second shows the same for professionals and technical workers.

12. D. Yankelovich and J. Immerwahr (1983), pp. 2–3.

13. R. B. Freeman and J. L. Medoff (1984), chap. 11.

14. *Spiegel* no. 12, 1985, p. 96.

15. For an excellent discussion of unions' difficulties in dealing with strategic issues, see T. A. Kochan, R. B. McKersie, and P. Cappelli (1984).

16. The Wagner Act itself did not exclude managers from coverage, but this line was rarely crossed until World War II. Exclusion was written into the law by the Taft-Hartley amendments, and its scope has been steadily extended by the courts.

17. I. Bernstein (1950), p. 129.

CHAPTER 2

1. J. T. Dunlop (1967), p. 172.
2. E. Shorter (1973), p. 9. On this general topic, see also T. R. Brooks (1971), esp. chaps. 2–3; and E. P. Thompson (1963).
3. I do not intend here to romanticize guild and craft organizations or the movements of unskilled workers. The former were in many respects highly oppressive, and the latter were erratic and unstable. The point is merely that they expressed autonomous values based on communal experiences, rather than reacting to an "outside" managerial group.
4. See A. Chandler (1977).
5. See, for example, K. Stone (1974).
6. H. H. Gerth and C. W. Mills (1946), p. 228.
7. The concepts of power and influence used here are taken from T. Parsons (1969a, 1969b). The description of organization and communal action also owes much to Parsons (for example, 1960), and to a long tradition stretching back from him to Max Weber (for example, M. Weber [1947], pp. 329–41).
8. See T. R. Brooks (1964), pp. 78–79.
9. M. Mann (1973), chap. 6.
10. Additional examples of how factionalism undercuts mass movements can be found in S. J. Surace (1966), esp. p. 155; for Italy in the late nineteenth century, M. Clark (1977), chaps. 8–10; for the factory council movement in Turin, J. Brecher (1972); and for the United States, E. T. Hiller (1928), chaps. 19 and 20 on general strikes.
11. Report of the Industrial Commission on the Relations and Conditions of Capital and Labor, Hearings on 18 April 1899, 7 (Washington, D.C.: Government Printing Office), p. 645.
12. S. Gompers (1920), p. 102.
13. For data on industrial growth in the early part of the century, see A. Chandler (1977), esp. part V.
14. For histories of the very active working-class movements in this period, see (among many others) D. Montgomery (1979) and J. Brecher (1972). On conditions of workers, J. R. Commons and J. B. Andrews (1936) cite several studies showing that a large proportion of workers received wages falling well below standards of "simple decency."
15. See S. Perlman (1928), pp. 275–76.
16. The success of the Rockefeller plan was not an isolated one. As D. Brody (1980), chap. 2, has shown, the company unions of the 1920s were not doomed to failure, as has been the conventional wisdom in labor circles; on the contrary, many of them were highly successful and held out well into the depression. (For a contemporary account, see also Twentieth Century Fund [1975] chaps. 4–5.)
  For good general analyses of the weaknesses of mass (as opposed to communal) consciousness, see M. Mann (1973), esp. chap. 6, and E. T. Hiller (1928).
17. In a rapid survey such as this, I am naturally drawing only the broadest outlines. There are exceptions to these generalizations about craft and industrial unions, but on the whole there seems little doubt that the latter make greater use of the mechanisms of bureaucracy—formal hierarchy, centralization, coordination by rules—than do the former. I want to guard, however, against one possible misconception: I do not mean to imply that craft unions are more *democratic*. Many of them are characterized by strong "boss" control, and they are in fact more vulnerable to autocracy and corruption than are industrial unions.
18. On the development of union bureaucracy during the post–World War II period, see R. Herding (1972)—a dense but thorough examination of how the union bureaucracy separated from its communal base. Herding's evaluation is that this was a betrayal of the membership; I see it as a necessary evolution in dealing with bureaucratic corporations.
19. On the episodic nature of member loyalty to unions, see R. Herding (1972), R. W. Miller et al. (1965), L. S. Sayles and G. Strauss (1953); J. Bergmann and W. Mueller-Jentsch (1975) for Germany; D. Gallie (1978) for France and Britain; S. Verba and N. H. Nie (1972), esp. p. 42.
  On public confidence in unions, recent polls show about a 33 percent rate in the United States. This is higher than Britain (26 percent) and Italy (32 percent), and scarcely worse than Germany and France (both 36 percent). From the 1981 Surveys of the European Values Systems Study Group, reported in *Public Opinion*, February–March 1984, p. 11.
20. Quoted in National Commission on Productivity and Work Quality (1975), p. 7.
21. For an excellent analysis of the real workings of union locals, especially the importance of

Notes

"hidden" cooperation and the tensions caused by its relation to publicly adversarial relations, see L. R. Sayles and G. Strauss (1953).

22. J. L. Lewis (1960).

23. The most vocal "insider" concerning this point has been John Dunlop, the former secretary of labor, whose scorn for liberal reformists is scathing. Dunlop is an excellent deal maker himself, and he knows how the system works. That does not, of course, mean that the deals make sense to the membership and the public at large.

24. See, for instance, John Dunlop's comments on the Landrum-Griffin requirements in Independent Study Group (1961).

25. L. R. Sayles and G. Strauss (1953).

26. M. Stein (1960), p. 68. Stein is here actually summarizing studies of worker attitudes during the 1930s, but the statement continues to apply today, as shown by the studies on "dual loyalty" (see n. 28).

27. T. Connors (1975), p. 20. The tension between members and representatives is confirmed in many studies of local unions (e.g., L. R. Sayles and G. Strauss [1953], R. W. Miller et al. [1965], as well as by my own interviews of members and stewards within the Communications Workers Union).

28. The "dual loyalty" phenomenon—the fact that loyalty to the company and to the union vary together in normal times rather than inversely—is quite well established. Among other studies that have established this relation, see T. W. Purcell (1960), who seems to be the first to have documented it; B. Jacob (1978), who found it in a number of European countries as well as in the United States; and K. Odaka (1965), who duplicated it in Japan. I have also verified that the same relationship holds in the national Quality of Employment Survey of 1977 (R. P. Quinn and G. L. Staines [1979]).

Naturally these findings refer to the periods of "peace" between contract negotiations or strikes. At these latter periods, there is certainly a polarization of groups. The point is, however, that there is no *continuing* polarization or opposite pull between workers' loyalty to their unions and to their companies.

29. T. Connors (1975), pp. 61, 151–52, 154.

30. Craft unions also get legalistic in their contracts, but for a different reason from that of industrial unions. For the latter, as discussed in the text, the problem is to hold together a membership that has little ongoing sense of community. Craft unions have much stronger shopfloor institutions and therefore need less legalistic regulation within their own domains. They use work rules to protect their jurisdictions—to define the domains within which their communal norms operate and within which they maintain autonomy.

31. See S. M. Lipset and W. Schneider (1983), table 7-4.

32. See S. M. Lipset and W. Schneider (1983), table 3-1.

33. The Supreme Court recently ruled, for example, that unions may not penalize members who resign during a strike (*Pattern Makers* v. *NLRB*, 83 U.S. 1984). On the duty of fair representation, which compels unions to represent nonmembers in their bargaining unit, see B. W. Justice (1983), pp. 174ff. and C. W. Summers et al. (1982), pp. 1132ff.

34. Opinion Research Corporation poll, 18 February 1986.

35. S. M. Lipset, M. A. Trow, and J. S. Coleman's classic study (1956) found only one example of true "democracy" in unions: that was the highly craft-oriented typographers' union. L. S. Sayles (1953) found the most "strategic"—coherent, organized—action to come from craft workers.

36. Works that emphasize the *differences* between white-collar and blue-collar unions include R. E. Walton (1961), and J. W. Kuhn (1971). Those that emphasize the *similarities*—especially over time—include C. Jenkins and B. Sherman (1979); G. S. Bain, D. Coates, and V. Ellis (1973); and A. Sturmthal (1966b). The most interesting studies—including N. Nicholson, G. Ursell, and P. Blyton (1981); and D. Lockwood (1958)—show the ways in which the requirements of organized resistance to employers and the desires of white-collar workers remain in tension; both studies show a tendency toward decentralized and participative structures, partially overwhelmed by the pressures of the bureaucratic environment.

CHAPTER 3

1. See R. B. Freeman and J. L. Medoff (1984), pp. 242–43. The same is true of unionization of hospital workers and university faculty: on the latter, see E. C. Ladd and S. M. Lipset (1973); and K. P. Mortimer (1982).

2. A. Smith (1937 edition), p. 66.

3. Gallatin's remarks were made while introducing a profit-sharing plan in his glassworks; quoted in M. Derber (1970), p. 6.

4. T. Hobbes (1651), part II, chap. 29.

5. H. Arendt (1963) has a very interesting discussion of how the importance of freely compacted groups in the new world shaped the political consciousness of the nation.

6. See especially "The Federalist," nos. 10 and 51, in *The Federalist Papers*.

7. Justice Marshall's opinion in the Dartmouth College case of 1819—*Dartmouth College* v. *Woodward*, 4 Wheaton 518—was the first step: it stated that the corporate charter was a contract rather than a grant of authority, and therefore that it benefited from the protections given private contracts. Later decisions during the century identified the employment relation itself as contractual.

8. Another indication of the weakness of the contract theory of employment is the fact that the courts also relied heavily on master-servant law, which is roughly the opposite of contract, to define the employment relation. Thus they have frequently found an implied obligation of "deference" and "loyalty" on the part of workers; but the whole point of contract was to eliminate these aspects of relationships by establishing limited, focused relations among equals. See P. Selznick (1969), pp. 122ff.; J. B. Atleson (1983), chap. 5.

9. *Clara County* v. *Southern Pacific Railway*, 118 U.S. 394 (1886).

10. The 1890 case solidly establishing corporations' property right was *Chicago, Milwaukee, and St. Paul Ry. Co.* v. *Minn.*, 134 U.S. 418, ruling that a railroad could not be subjected to rate regulation without judicial investigation. It essentially reversed the 1876 decision in *Munn* v. *Illinois*, 94 U.S. 125, 113. For a discussion of this legal history, see R. J. Lustig (1982), pp. 52–53, 91–93.

11. *Liggett Co.* v. *Lee*, 288 U.S. 517, 565 (1933).

12. See M. Derber (1970), pp. 166–72.

13. The phrase is John Dewey's (1927). He was one of the most articulate promoters of the idea of a communal state.

14. S. Gompers (1920), p. 102.

15. Charles Wyzanski, then solicitor of the Department of Labor, recounts that at the beginning of 1934 Senator Wagner met with William Green (then President of the AFL) and John L. Lewis to discuss ideas for his act. The major concern of the labor representatives, according to Wyzanski, was to prevent any regulation of unions—"that they would not support, and indeed would try to defeat, any bill which included a provision making any practice of any labor union unlawful . . . [I]n particular they were opposed to any legal requirement that they should not discriminate in union membership on the basis of race." (Letter, Charles Wyzanski to Edward Weinfeld, 14 February 1984; Charles E. Wyzanski, Jr. papers, Harvard Law School Library.)

16. I. Bernstein (1950, pp. 125–26) reports that the president of the Garment Workers wrote the head of the Teamsters that the bill would "injure organizations like your own and possibly mine." The AFL continued to support the bill publicly, but with a sense that it was at best a necessary evil.

17. Cited in Brooks (1964), p. 164.

18. I. Bernstein (1969), p. 787.

19. Preamble of the National Labor Relations Act, 49 Stat 499 (1935).

20. *Congressional Record* 79, Rec. 7660 (1935).

21. One major provision did violate the simple "balance" approach: it requires management to bargain with the union (to which the NLRB later added the requirement of "good faith"). In this respect it did not rely purely on the unions' power to achieve a proper bargaining relation, providing instead direct governmental intervention to evaluate and support it. The NLRB could not, of course, determine whether negotiation had been "in good faith" without asking what had happened "behind the doors" of the bargaining room. This was one of the most controversial provisions, even among supporters of the final act, and it has been a source of confusion ever since.

22. The papers of the late judge Charles Wyzanski provide a fascinating glimpse at the strong internal disagreements among the drafters of the act; these differences were kept from exploding by the narrowly procedural focus of the bill. Charles E. Wyzanski, Jr. papers, Harvard Law School Library.

23. *Fortune*, October 1939, p. 52.

24. *American Ship Building* v. *NLRB*, 380 U.S. 300, 317 (1965).

25. Undated memo from Thomas H. Eliot to Charles Wyzanski, 1934, in Charles E. Wyzanski, Jr. papers, Harvard Law School Library.

26. The Madisonian argument is made explicitly by J. M. Sullivan (1984). The "feudal" metaphor is used by Roscoe Pound (1958).

27. I have glossed over some complications. The government does not, strictly speaking, compel anyone to join a union; union-shop provisions are agreed to in contract negotiations, so it is really the employer who forces people to join. But the informal reality is that the government does indeed have a strong role in the union shop, because it is the government's support of exclusive representation that makes it an effective bargaining demand. See T. R. Brooks (1964), chap. 15; D. Brody (1980), pp. 113–16.

28. *Steele* v. *Louisville & Nashville Railroad Co.*, 323 U.S. 192, 208–9 (1944). Karl Klare (1982) has written a very effective critique of the courts' inconsistencies in treating unions as private or public institutions. Just as in the case of the "private property" rights of management, I believe, these inconsistencies are manifestations of contradictions that the Wagner Act failed to resolve.

29. Wagner Act, section 1. This is echoed by the Supreme Court in its decision validating the act—*NLRB* v. *Jones & Laughlin Steel Corp.*, 301 U.S. 1 (1937): "Experience has abundantly demonstrated that the recognition of the right of employees to self-organization . . . is often an essential condition of industrial peace."

30. It is probably also true that real equality of power leads to peace; this has been the theory behind weapons races for centuries. But in labor relations, as in the international sphere, this kind of peace often comes only after long and costly trials of strength, and remains highly vulnerable to changes in the strength of either party. In the steel industry, for example, a no-strike agreement was reached between the parties after a long succession of extremely painful strikes. Now, in view of the decline of the Steelworkers' Union, the pact is in jeopardy, and many expect strikes to erupt again in the next round of negotiations.

31. Commentary by Keyserling on draft labor bill by D. Richberg (not dated, but clearly 1934), in Charles E. Wyzanski, Jr. papers, Harvard Law School Library.

32. Major steps in the narrowing of the right to strike have included the following:

- the Taft–Hartley Act made it illegal to strike in support of workers at other companies.
- most slowdowns and other "partial" job actions have been ruled out. (See B. Justice [1983], pp. 152ff. for a summary of cases.)
- in another example of creative interpretation, the Supreme Court has read an implied no–strike obligation into arbitration provisions of contracts, so that it has in effect become illegal to strike during the term of most contracts. (*Steelworkers* v. *Warrior & Gulf Navigation Co.*, 363 U. S. 574 [1960]; *Teamsters, Local 174* v. *Lucas Flour Co.*, 369 US 95 [1962]; *Gateway Coal* v. *Mine Workers*, 414 U. S. 368, [1974].)

33. Ibid.

34. See, for example, P. C. Schmitter and G. Lehmbruch (1979).
I am using the term "corporatism," generally following Schmitter and Lehmbruch, to mean a system based on the balancing and interrelation of a few large organizational actors. This usually means, for our purposes, the triad of business, labor, and government. For further discussions of the concept of corporatism, see, among others: P. C. Schmitter (1983); K. von Beyme (1980); and R. H. Salisbury (1979).
The opposite of corporatism would be a system in which *many* groups, formal and informal, bureaucratic and associational, could play a part in decision making without filtering their concerns through the tripartite structure. It is this alternative that I elaborate in part IV.

35. Charles Wyzanski to this day accuses Leon Keyserling, with whom he was involved in drafting the 1934 version of the Wagner Act, of seeking something "close to a corporate state"; and he believes the bill moved much further in that direction than was originally apparent.

36. R. H. Salisbury (1979).

CHAPTER 4

1. These figures are taken from the Bureau of Labor Statistics' data on union membership. They show that in 1980, 20.1 percent of all private workers were union members; in 1984, the figure was 15.3 percent. For all private and public wage and salary workers, the decline was from 23 percent to 18.8 percent; for private goods-producing workers, from 30.5 percent to 24 percent; for private

service-producing, from 13.5 percent to 10.5 percent; for government workers, from 35.9 percent to 35.7 percent.

2. Data drawn from S. M. Lipset and W. Schneider (1981), pp. 52, 55; S. M. Lipset and W. E. Schneider (1983), pp. 201, 311, 313; and polls by the National Opinion Research Center (April 1987) and the Gallup Organization (14 July 1986).

3. M. J. Piore and C. F. Sabel (1984).

4. The term "postindustrial society" was, I believe, coined by Alain Touraine (1971); see also Daniel Bell (1973). It is often taken to mean a postmanufacturing economy—an economy based primarily on services. That is not my prediction for the future, which is why I largely avoid using this term myself. I agree with Sabel and Piore in their emphasis on the continuing need for manufacturing, though within a new economic structure.

5. M. J. Piore and C. F. Sabel (1984), p. 17.

6. On the decline of U.S. competitiveness, see B. R. Scott and G. C. Lodge (1985); and R. B. Reich and I. B. Magaziner (1983).

7. See M. J. Piore and C. F. Sabel, esp. chap. 7.

8. On the devastating effects of plant closings, see B. Bluestone and B. Harrison (1982).

9. On the uncertain relation between technological change and overall employment levels, see H. Brooks (1985); W. W. Leontieff (1986); and National Academy of Engineering (1983).

10. R. B. Freeman and J. L. Medoff (1984), chap. 12. In general, there has been a long debate among econometricians about whether unions actually raise wage rates. R. B. Freeman and J. L. Medoff (1984, p. 46) estimate the union wage effect during the 1970s as 20–30 percent, which is substantial. Much of this, however, reflects increased productivity in the unionized sector. They also note that the effect seemed historically to have been higher in inflationary periods than during recessions. That pattern, at least, seems to have been broken during the 1980s, which confuses the picture still further.

In recent years, the nonunion sector has actually done better than the unionized sector: between 1982 and 1984 the former led the latter in wage increases by 1.5 percent (*Business Week*, 24 December 1984, p. 20). D. Q. Mills (1983, p. 104) also notes that worker concessions were confined almost entirely to the unionized sector.

11. On the reality of the plant-closing threat, see B. Bluestone and B. Harrison (1982).

12. There is some dispute over just how big the wage disparity between foreign countries and the United States really is, but there is no question that the difference is huge: in South Korea in 1983, by one calculation, average labor costs were $1.53 per hour, compared to $7.53 in the United States (*Business Week*, 3 May 1983, p. 63).

13. Census Bureau data.

14. S. H. Slichter, J. J. Healey, and E. R. Livernash (1960).

15. The development of a nonunion sector that pays union wage rates and provides greater employee participation than most unionized companies will be examined further in chapter 5.

16. G. Meany (1955), quoted in M. Derber (1970), p. 92.

17. T. A. Kochan, R. B. McKersie, and P. Cappelli (1984).

18. Thomas Balanoff, quoted in *The Boston Globe*, 15 September 1985, p. A7.

19. "They're Going Down with Their Heads Held High," *The Boston Globe*, 6 May 1985, p. 44.

20. Using figures for nonsupervisory production workers in manufacturing, as a percentage of total nonsupervisory production employees, for the years 1955 and 1983: U.S. Department of Labor, *Handbook of Labor Statistics*, June 1985, table 64.

21. Personal conversation, 13 November 1984.

22. There is considerable debate about the extent to which automated equipment, such as numerically controlled machine tools and automated testing systems, can replace human workers. Early systems have shown a tendency to break down more often than expected and to require considerable human intervention, though reliability is increasing with experience. The point I am making here, however, is not that machines will replace people; it is that they will totally transform the nature of craft work, destroying its base in traditional skills. The only questions concern what kind of transformation it will be. See, for example, L. Hirschorn (1984) and H. Shaiken (1984) as good starting points.

23. See S. M. Lipset and W. Schneider (1983), p. 313.

24. G. W. Latta (1981) documents the difficulties of organizing campaigns among engineers and the high number of decertifications. His conclusions about the possibilities of organizing this group are pessimistic.

25. Mark Reader, organizing director for the Office and Professional Employees' International

Notes

Union, quoted in *Business Week*, 25 January 1982, p. 92. The first sentence is a paraphrase of his words.

26. *Harper's Monthly Magazine* 164 (1932), p. 168.

27. The thesis that worker movements were often fueled by second-generation immigrants is made by C. Sabel (1979a).

28. W. A. Schiemann and B. S. Morgan (1982), pp. 28ff.

29. D. Yankelovich and J. Immerwahr (1983); and D. Yankelovich et al. (1985).

30. P. Selznick (1969), p. 189.

31. There has been astonishingly little research on the attitudes of white-collar workers. There is a long literature, primarily in a Marxist vein, that examines their class position, focusing on objective changes in their work structures (see H. Braverman [1974]; R. Hyman and R. Price, eds. [1983]); it rarely uses evidence from surveys or interviews. Another, related set of studies has looked at their organizations—white-collar or professional unions and associations (see n. 33). Finally, there was during the 1960s intensive research stimulated by Serge Mallet's (1975) thesis of a "new working class" (see also D. Gallie [1978]), centering on one small segment of the white-collar world: technicians. But the overall question of whether and how white-collar workers' consciousness differs from blue-collar has not, to my knowledge, been the subject of good empirical research. In particular, we do not have anything comparable to the rich studies of blue-collar workers by such authors as E. Chinoy (1955); R. Sennett and J. Cobb (1973); or J. H. Goldthorpe et al. (1968).

32. For a discussion of the literature on white-collar unionism, see n. 33.

33. The evidence to support the connection between managerial bureaucracy and unionization among white-collar workers is extremely varied and wide ranging. J. W. Kuhn (1971) establishes this relation quite explicitly for engineers. D. S. Bain, D. Coates, and V. Ellis (1973) show evidence that many white-collar seniority provisions are quite standard, and E. C. Ladd and S. M. Lipset (1973) show the same for professors. On the other hand, both books contain much evidence of the anguish involved in abandoning principles of merit; for example, R. E. Walton (1961) and J. W. Kuhn both show how professional unions attempt to allow leeway for individual "bargaining" and merit provisions. See A. Sturmthal (1966), esp. chap. 9, D. Lockwood (1958), R. M. Blackburn (1967), K. P. Mortimer (1982), N. Nicholson, G. Ursell, and P. Blyton (1981), G. W. Latta (1981), W. A. Wildman (1971), F. Bairstow (1977), and C. Jenkins and B. Sherman (1979).

34. P. F. Drucker (1969) and (1970).

35. H. Braverman (1974), part IV.

36. H. Braverman (1974), chap. 15. Joan Greenbaum (1976) is one who extends Braverman's argument to the computer field.

37. For the basis of this calculation, see n. 40.

38. For a good description of the growing role of such semiprofessionals, see G. Harries-Jenkins (1970). Peter Drucker's frequent descriptions of "knowledge workers" are similar. A fascinating historical note is added by E. T. Layton (1971): he shows how engineers, in the early years of this century, fought to achieve true "professional" status but were defeated over time by the employers, who managed to prevent the formation of effective independent organizations of engineers.

There are some occupations that are near the borderline between professional and semiprofessional status. Teachers, nurses, and engineers, for instance, do have specialized education and their own associations, yet they are not generally accorded the status of "professionals." This is because they are fundamentally dependent on their employers, rather than on their independent skills and associations, for their careers. Doctors can set up their own practices; nurses cannot. That difference marks off semiprofessionals from true professionals.

For further details on the way I have broken down these categories, see n. 41.

39. Managers and supervisors, as listed in the Bureau of Labor Statistics figures for 1982, constituted about 17 percent of the work force. Some proportion of these are "upper" managers who are truly involved in policy making and are part of the core circle who direct the company. The proportion is indeterminable from the BLS figures but is certainly small; my estimate that middle managers are 10 percent of the work force is quite conservative.

On the growth of the managerial cadres since World War II, see S. Bowles et al. (1983), pp. 254–55.

There is a substantial literature debating whether technical workers and managers form one class or two. Barbara and John Ehrenreich (1979) are among those who have argued that their similarities are greater than their differences. The debate is nicely summarized by R. Hyman and R. Price (1983). I have grouped them into one, though it makes little essential difference to my argument. They may divide at certain points, but they share many sources of discontent.

40. The figure of 20 percent covers clerical and related workers. I have omitted service workers, many of whom would normally be considered "blue-collar"—janitors, for instance—and whose conditions of work are for the most part quite different from the "white-collar semiskilled"; they constitute about another 10 percent. See n. 41 for details.

41. These figures are reached by sorting the Bureau of Labor Statistics (BLS) occupations into categories on the basis of my knowledge of their characteristics; it is a somewhat rough approach but probably as accurate as any more technical process. For the comparison over time, showing the relatively rapid growth of semiprofessionals compared to white-collar semiskilled and others, I compared 1982 data to 1975. After 1982 the categories were changed so that comparability is lost. (An analysis of the 1983 and 1984 categories, despite this lack of exact match, does, however, yield data on almost exactly the same curve as the 1975 and 1982 results.) For absolute percentages, I used the 1983 data:

- The "professionals," who increased from 3.1 percent to 3.7 percent in these seven years, include groups that have specialized education and ongoing societies with considerable occupational influence. These include BLS categories such as architects, math and computer analysts, lawyers and judges, life and physical scientists, physicians, dentists, social scientists, and college and university teachers.
- The "semiprofessionals" include "middle managers" and the rest of the BLS "white-collar workers," except for clerical workers and retail sales clerks: engineers, nurses, secondary and primary school teachers, writers, technicians, sales representatives, investigators, and the like. The BLS's managerial categories add up to 16.7 percent from which I subtract a rough 4 percent that represents *top* management. The remaining 12.7 percent for middle management, plus the other semiprofessional categories, adds up to 31.1 percent of the 1983 work force.
- The "white-collar semiskilled" include sales clerks, secretaries, stenographers, typists, bookkeepers, bank tellers, data entry keyers, and the like; they constitute 19.8 percent of the 1983 work force.
- I have separated most of the *service workers* into another category, since their conditions of work are quite different from white-collar workers in large organizations. A few of them, such as McDonald's servers, are barely distinguishable; but the bulk of bartenders, kitchen workers, nursing aides, barbers, public transport attendants, child-care workers, and the like must work in direct contact with customers and largely on their own. Their work is low-skilled, but relatively autonomous compared to the classic "semiskilled" model. This group constitutes 9.8 percent of the 1983 work force.
- Craft workers constitute 10.3 percent of the 1983 work force; machine operators and transportation workers (truckers and rail) add another 11.9 percent, for a total "blue-collar" figure of 22.2 percent.

D. Yankelovich et al. (1983, p. 18) asked people directly how much discretion they have on the job. Forty-three percent say they have "a great deal of freedom to decide how to do my work." Though the methodology is totally different, these results are certainly in line with those I derived from the BLS occupational data. The total of semiprofessionals, top-level managers, and professionals comes to about 40 percent; one would only have to add a few service workers and craft workers to reach the 43 percent figure.

42. The centrality of these particular occupations at successive phases of the labor movement is consistent in nearly every industrialized country, which further strengthens the association I am making. The major exception to the cross-national stability is the importance of trucking unions in the United States after World War II; and this is truly an exception that proves the rule, since trucking was far more central to the economic growth of the United States in that period, and had more prestige, than in any other industrialized country.

43. See, for example, R. E. Walton (1961); K. P. Mortimer (1982).

44. In particular, the *Fibreboard Paper Products Corp. v. NLRB* decision (379 U.S. 203 [1964]), which required all management decisions that would significantly influence employment security or work opportunities to be negotiated with the union.

45. In S. M. Lipset and W. Schneider (1983), table 7-4, p. 219. David Brody (1980, p. 241) has a very interesting characterization of labor's stance before the 1960s as an "aggregating political role." He points out—and Freeman and Medoff (1984, pp. 198–200) have developed further supportive

evidence—that unions have never been effective as a "mere" interest group, but they were crucial as a center of liberal political leadership. Michael Piore has made a similar argument in unpublished work.

46. Respectively: *NLRB* v. *International Van Lines* (1972); *Central Hardware Co.* v. *NLRB* (1976); *Boys Market, Inc.* v. *Retail Clerks* (1970); *Gateway Coal Co.* v. *Mine Workers* (1974); *Chemical Workers* v. *Pittsburgh Plate Glass Co.* (1971); and *NLRB* v. *Bell Aerospace Co.* (1974).

47. P. S. McGrath (1976), pp. iv, 2. The last sentence is attributed to Daniel Yankelovich.

48. Some evidence of the connection can be found in S. R. Lichter and S. Rothman (1983). P. L. Berger (1981) also describes this relation, though he does not develop hard evidence.

49. By "the present," I mean the latest analyses I have seen, which come up to late 1987 (see S. M. Lipset and W. Schneider [1983a], table 2-1, figure 2-1; B. J. Wattenberg [1984], p. 3; S. M. Lipset and W. Schneider [1983b]). The latter piece indicates that the Reagan administration has had no effect on the major trends but has slightly increased faith in the executive branch. Even this, however, seems to have been for a paradoxical reason: people like the fact that the executive branch is (under Reagan) cutting back its own power. They do not seem to be giving, through increased confidence, support for increases in executive power.

50. An exceedingly interesting demonstration of the problems of the Democrats in dealing with regulation can be found in a published transcript of a conference held by the American Enterprise Institute (1977).

51. S. M. Lipset and W. Schneider (1983a), p. 251.

52. For example, see ibid., pp. 253–54.

53. Ibid., table 7-4, pp. 219, 171, 173.

54. In a 1981 Roper poll, 76 percent said that businesses "tend[ed] to act more in their own self-interest [than] in the public interest"—higher than the figure for labor (62 percent), and up from 1976 (71 percent). Yankelovich, Skelley, and White's polls between 1968 and 1981 showed a very sharp decline in the public's faith in business: in 1968, 70 percent agreed that "business tries to strike a fair balance between profits and the interests of the public; by 1974 that dropped to 19 percent. The Opinion Research Corporation's polls show an increase in antibusiness sentiment (mean of six items) from 38 percent in 1965 to 58 percent in 1981. The percentage expressing "a great deal of confidence" in business leaders dropped from 48 percent in 1966 to 16 percent in 1982. (S. M. Lipset and W. Schneider [1983a], respectively, pp. 171, 173, 183, 33, and 50.) Polls through 1985 show no significant change in public confidence in business.

55. In a 1981 Roper poll, business and labor scored worst of the institutions listed on the question of whether they "tend to act more in their own self-interest or more in the public interest": 76 percent put business, and 62 percent put labor, on the "self-interest" side. In general, according to S. M. Lipset and W. Schneider, "The principal difference between the positively regarded professions and the negatively evaluated ones would appear to be the varying importance of self-interest" (1983, p. 80).

By the use of the term "power clique" I do not mean to suggest a "power elite" in C. Wright Mills's sense: there is no evidence of a revulsion against a group of people who are seen as holding excessive power. The reaction is, rather, directed against a small group of *organizations*.

56. P. Harter (1983), p. 475. Harter describes the regulatory process in practice not as a pure case of expert decision making, but as a "hybrid" that attempts to mix in some popular participation with the expertise—through notification requirements, public hearings, judicial reviews, etc. He judges the hybrid to be a failure.

The characteristic problem of expertise is that it cannot resolve differences of values. It can operate within a political consensus, working out the details of implementation, but it cannot create consensus.

For an excellent theoretical discussion of the problem of generating shared values, see M. Walzer (1983), p. 289. In general, expertise is currently under attack in much the same way as political power. An increasingly large area of decisions is handled by the "expert model of administration." The more these expert systems touch fundamental values, the more they strain their foundation of legitimacy—which is another aspect of the political crisis that lies in the background of the labor relations problem.

57. On the loosening of ties between unions and political parties in Europe in the 1970s, see: for the Netherlands, B. Peper (1975); for Sweden, E. Asard (1979); for Italy, P. M. Brandini (1975) and M. J. Piore (1978); for Germany, A. S. Markovits and C. S. Allen (1979).

There is a great deal of data from many countries that indicate that union members do not want their unions to be heavily involved in politics and, in general, resent the existing level of union political involvement. See, for example, W. H. Form (1973); B. M. Jacob (1978); L. Levin (1977); and J. Burton (1982).

58. This is a slight exaggeration. The NLRB had generally excluded these groups from protection through its administrative rulings, but the courts had not taken such a position. It was when the NLRB tried to relax the line—bowing to the obvious changes in the work force—that the Supreme Court made its restrictive ruling.

59. *NLRB* v. *Bell Aerospace Co.*, 416 U.S. 267 (1974).

60. *NLRB* v. *Yeshiva University*, 444 U.S. 672 (1980).

61. For an excellent discussion of the Yeshiva decision, see K. E. Klare (1983). A. Levenstein (1980) is less alarmed than Klare, taking the pragmatic position that the decision will probably not be pushed to its logical limits. He may well be right; but it is little comfort to say that the logic of the decision is so flawed that it cannot be fully put into practice. That still leaves the legal order without a coherent way of interpreting reality.

62. See, for example, M. B. Lehmann (1982), who argues that faculty unions should reject all forms of collegiality and remain strictly adversarial in order to avoid *Yeshiva* challenges.

63. Respectively: *Jefferson Standard* case; *NLRB* v. *Local 1299 IBEW*, 346 U.S. 464 (1953); *Teamsters* v. *Lucas Flour Co.*, 369 U.S. 95 (1962); and *NLRB* v. *Elk Lumber Co.*, 91 NLRB 333 (1950). See, in general, J. B. Atleson (1983), esp. chaps. 3 and 5.

64. *Fibreboard Paper Products Corp.* v. *NLRB*, 379 U.S. 203 (1964).

65. *First National Maintenance Corp.* v. *NLRB*, 101 S.Ct. 2573 (1981).

CHAPTER 5

1. Many "autonomous team" efforts trace their history back to the Tavistock Institute in England during and after World War II. See, among other writings, L. E. Davis and E. L. Trist (1974); E. L. Trist (1961).

2. F. Herzberg (1968).

3. See, for example, S. Srivastva et al. (1975): of twenty-seven good studies of job enrichment between 1959 and 1974, they found that 100 percent reported improved quality and 90 percent reduced costs.

4. A good brief description of matrix organization, together with references, can be found in J. R. Galbraith (1971). "Management by objectives," another popular middle management technique, also runs against basic bureaucratic principles: it involves the heavy involvement of lower levels in setting their own goals and a general stress on decentralization.

The literature on organization development in management ranks is huge, though I believe much smaller than that on workers. Good introductions and classic works include F. Friedlander and L. D. Brown (1974); C. Argyris (1970); R. Likert (1961). One treatment that explicity links the sociotechnical team-based efforts with changes at the managerial level is C. H. Pava (1983).

5. W. G. Ouchi (1981).

6. Two careful reviews of the evidence concerning a "blue-collar revolt," during the period when that was a fashionable assumption, are P. Henle (1974) and G. Strauss (1974). They reach the same conclusion about the "hard" evidence: that quit rates follow economic cycles, and that there has been no overall increase in absenteeism or turnover over time.

On job satisfaction, a flurry of studies raised an alarm in the late 1970s—for example, R. P. Quinn and G. L. Staines (1979), p. 305; P. J. Andrisani (1978), esp. chap. 3. These studies seemed to show a substantial movement among respondents from being "very satisfied" with their jobs to being only "somewhat satisfied." That seems a weak reason for alarm, especially if one takes a longer view. In 1957 Frederick Herzberg et al. looked over surveys from the previous decade that asked approximately, "If you had it to do over again, would you take the same job?"; they found about 45 percent saying yes (p. 3). The 1977 Quality of Employment survey, by contrast, found between 65 and 70 percent saying yes to the same question during the 1970s (R. P. Quinn and G. L. Staines [1979], p. 210), which would indicate that satisfaction has risen.

On changes in the general work ethic, see M. Maccoby and K. A. Terzi (1979).

7. D. Yankelovich and J. Immerwahr (1983), pp. 2–3.

8. General Telephone of the Southwest, corporate task force on employee commitment, unpublished report, 1984.

9. New York Stock Exchange (1982). I created this figure by combining two findings: first, that

Notes

53 percent of the NYSE-listed companies had personnel "programs"; and second, that one-half of these "credited a shift in their basic approach to management as a factor in their decision to initiate new programs" (p. 24). From the way this latter finding is written, it implies that one-half of all NYSE-listed companies have made such a shift; but from the context I can only deduce that what is meant is one-half of those with programs, which means one-quarter of the total.

10. Judgments about the extent of the spread of participative reforms must be based largely on impressions. The published data on participative reforms lag very far behind the actual events; and furthermore, they are rarely detailed enough to indicate the real character of the changes. I have been involved myself with a number of Quality of Work Life efforts and have talked to many consultants and managers in the field; they are the best source of information on what is happening now. I think it is clear that the more limited efforts, in particular Quality Circles, are on the downslide, while the more ambitious efforts at cultural change are increasing.

What "hard" evidence exists generally supports this view:

- A survey of 49,000 companies with more than 100 employees found that 14 percent of them had "human resource programs"; but the vast majority of these were in the largest companies, so that well over 50 percent of the employees were covered by these programs. Of this group, about one-third—and over one-half of the larger companies—claim they are engaged in a major shift in management philosophy. About half the programs involved job redesign and worker participation in setting objectives (New York Stock Exchange, 1982).
- Another survey of generally large companies found that over 70 percent encourage managers to set up "employee participation programs" for nonunion employees; 19 percent encourage autonomous work teams. (Private study in 1983 of 409 members of the Conference Board, a business research organization, conducted by the Board and the Sloan School of Management at M.I.T.)
- A *Harvard Business Review* survey in 1977 found that about 10 percent of the responding companies had strong internal grievance systems, such as formal hearing procedures or independent ombudsmen. Moreover, this proportion had grown sharply since 1971. The percentage of companies reporting "soft" procedures, such as open door policies—which may be more characteristic of a "paternalistic" approach—dropped somewhat during the same period (D. W. Ewing [1977]).

11. While 45 percent of workers in mining and manufacturing were represented by company unions in 1933, only 10 percent were in independent labor organizations. These figures are cited in W. Lippmann (1936), p. 143.

12. A major study during the 1930s found great variation in the effectiveness of company unions: A. L. Bernheim and D. Van Doren, eds. (1935). A more recent historical review by D. Brody (1980), chap. 2, reaches the conclusion that at least some of the company unions were a quite successful alternative to independent unionism.

13. The classic analysis of bureaucracy, of course, is that of Max Weber (1947).

Bureaucracy takes a somewhat different form in corporations from governments: for example, the former do not provide the level of job security that is seen as necessary to prevent corruption in the public sphere. Nevertheless, the basic principles sketched by Weber have been reproduced in economic organizations. Bureaucracy continues to stress formal and procedural rationality as opposed to personal authority, and for the same reason—to permit coordination of resources on a large scale.

14. The AFL-CIO, after initial opposition, officially supported Scientific Management during the 1920s.

15. P. F. Drucker (1946), p. 69. See also the critique of military metaphors for organization structure, in T. J. Peters and R. H. Waterman (1982), chap. 2.

16. Among the key theorists of this movement I would include: P. F. Drucker (esp. 1974), who discusses the breakdown of the "GM Model" in nonmanufacturing, multiplant, international, knowledge-based, entrepreneurial businesses. See also P.F. Drucker (esp. 1974); W. G. Ouchi (1981); T. J. Peters and R. H. Waterman (1982); A. Toffler (1970); R. A. Walton (1979, 1985); and T. Burns and G. M. Stalker (1961).

17. Speech to the Economic Policy Council of the United Nations Association of the USA, 4 February 1982.

18. Quoted in S. Lohr (1981), p. 308.

19. T. J. Peters and R. H. Waterman (1982), p. 308.

20. A. P. Sloan (1964), p. 54.

21. J. Kotter (1984), p. 26.

22. The classic statement of the tension between community and impersonal, rule-bound structures is F. Toennies (1887), who formulated the famous distinction between *Gemeinschaft* and *Gesellschaft.* In this country one of the most profound treatments was written by J. Dewey (1927). D. Riesman (1961) effectively popularized the sense of lost community. An excellent summary of the literature, including research studies on work and community, is M. R. Stein (1960), especially chaps. 2–3; somewhat more recent is E. Shorter, ed. (1973). Within management literature, the Human Relations school has long sought to maintain community within corporations; the more recent "culture change" movement does the same, but with a focus on the organization rather than on individual interactions. See, for example, W. G. Ouchi (1981); T. J. Peters and R. H. Waterman (1982). G. C. Lodge (1975) argues that business is shifting ideologically toward a more "communitarian," less impersonal, form.

23. T. J. Watson, Jr. (1963), p. 5.

24. A. Sloan (1964), p. 54.

25. The General Motors experiments with autonomous teams began during the mid-1970s in Southern plants that had not been organized by the UAW. The union was resistant to the concept; indeed, the whole idea of worker participation is still highly controversial. The extension of team structures to unionized settings has been a painful process for the union as well as for management, occasioning many political battles and policy shifts.

26. IBM, it seems, has never faced a union election. Motorola has had one—which it won handily.

Of course, many managerialist companies have some union representation, and a few are heavily unionized; among the latter I would include General Motors, Ford, and AT&T. They tend to try to live with their unions rather than entering into a potentially bitter struggle. That does not, however, make them any less fundamentally antiunion. I have avoided discussing these companies in this chapter because they raise issues more appropriate to the next.

27. The elements in the following list are drawn, in addition to my own experiences and the works previously cited, from F. K. Foulkes (1981) and C. L. Hughes (1976).

28. *The New Yorker,* 27 May 1985, p. 65.

29. B. Reisman and L. Compa (1985), p. 30.

30. This election was in July 1979. See "Sun Belt Showdown: Organized Labor vs. GM 'Teams,' " *Washington Post,* 19 July 1979.

31. See, for example, R. M. Kaus (1973) and J. Elden (1976). They discuss a number of cases of reversal in team-based programs, and Kaus develops a Marxist theory to account for them. I can add several more, though I would argue that these failures are less profound than Kaus claims (see C. Heckscher [1981], pp. 119ff.).

32. According to at least one study, there was a gradual increase during the 1970s in the number of "hard" channels for employee voice, as opposed to the "soft" mechanism of open doors, etc. (see D.W. Ewing [1977]). A 1983 survey of 409 firms by the Conference Board found that 73 percent "encourage managers to set up formal complaint or grievance systems for nonunion groups." For a general treatment of nonunion complaint systems, see F. K. Foulkes (1980).

33. S. M. Davis (1984), p. 7. The same theme is stressed in Ouchi, Peters and Waterman, and almost every other writer in the field.

34. This was essentially the process followed at Xerox and Honeywell, to name two. In each instance there was some minimal effort to "check" lower levels of the organization by polling or random interviews; but in no case that I know of was the organization as a whole involved actively in the formulation of the core values.

35. I am, however, basing my criticism on more than the two anecdotes in the text. I have been involved with a number of companies that have been trying to change values, usually in a participative direction; in five cases I or my colleagues have conducted systematic interviews at many levels of the organization. The one lesson that stands out from all these instances is how poorly the top management (and, in many cases, the consultants) understood the culture of those lower in the organization, and how much resistance remained hidden.

Published accounts of resistance and failure are rare: few organizations will let outsiders in to study failures, and few insiders are eager to write about them. Some interesting examples can, however, be found in J. Elden (1976), esp. chap. 5; L. A. Schlesinger (1979); and P. H. Mirvis and D. Berg (1977).

36. The leadership literature is growing rapidly. Two books that I have found valuable are J. Kotter (1985) and M. Maccoby (1981).

37. W. G. Ouchi (1981), p. 250.

38. This development is described at length by I. Shapiro (1984), esp. chap. 2, the ex-CEO of the Du Pont Corporation. Another aspect of the growing closeness between business and government is the growing move to "privatize" services that have previously been public, such as education and sanitation. Businesses taking over these functions had better be highly responsive to the public if they want to avoid major strains.

39. "GM Picks the Winner," *Newsweek*, 5 August 1985, pp. 42–43.

40. G. Lodge (1984) develops this point at length: the "inevitable drift" toward increased business-management cooperation, and the consequent strains on the legitimacy of both bodies. He uses as a major example of this strain the experience of utility regulators. See pp. 140–41, 150–51, 165.

41. See, for example, J. R. Emshoff and R. E. Freeman (1979); W. R. Dill (1975); L. Susskind (1987). For more on negotiation processes, see chapter 10.

42. I do not mean to argue that participation cannot survive layoffs. Some people made that claim during the early days of QWL, but experience has shown that it is not valid: participation programs and group loyalty have often been strengthened by company adversity. But I would argue that this is only true for crises—insecurity cannot be a constant state of mind in a managerialist firm.

43. See, for example, the case study reported in R. M. Kaus (1973), in which autonomous teams blew up as the workers sought to gain more and more autonomy. I was later told by an officer of the company that the situation was resolved by promoting all the team members into management. That is obviously not a viable approach on a continuing basis.

44. Motorola, for example, maintains a "buffer" of 10 to 15 percent of the work force. The GM-Saturn contract provides security to the most senior 80 percent of the work force but allows layoffs of the rest. A number of other collective bargaining contracts in these companies have also established similar "two-tier" security arrangements.

45. Writers on Japan often remark on the strains caused by the fact that workers with full rights work side by side with those who are considered "temporary." See, for example, R. Clark (1979), pp. 200ff.

46. S. H. Slichter, J. J. Healey, and E. R. Livernash (1960). Some of the most sophisticated management theorists have developed initial approaches to these problems under the rubric of "stakeholder theory." Their premise is that management itself "represents" a number of different groups—stockholders, workers, consumers, and the community; and that its strategic deliberations must balance all those interests. This theory has two possible consequences for action. One is that management should act like a "philosopher king" in considering all interests during its deliberations. The other is that it should negotiate directly with these other interests in making plans. This latter view has led to a number of very interesting efforts in which multiple groups are brought together to express their "stakes" in management decisions. (See chapter 10.)

CHAPTER 6

1. Watts retired in the summer of 1985, having developed an extensive network of cooperative committees with AT&T and the other phone companies. He was replaced by Morton Bahr, who is less openly fervent about cooperation but has shown in his actions no less commitment. Don Ephlin is currently the director of the General Motors Department of the UAW; the head of the union, Owen Bieber, is more cautious in his views, while the former head, Douglas Fraser, has become more openly enthusiastic since he left office.

2. Quoted in *Business Week*, 13 September 1985.

3. D. Q. Mills (1983), p. 22.

4. Speech to regional White House Productivity Conference, St. Louis, June 1985. Donovan put some action behind these words by establishing the Division of Labor-Management Cooperation in the Labor Department and later promoting it to the status of a bureau.

5. *Daily Labor Report,* 3 May 1984, p. A-12.

6. J. Peel (1978), p. 268.

7. Sentry Insurance Co. (1981), chap. 4. A Harris poll found that 52 percent of the public, 61 percent of business leaders, and 75 percent of union leaders felt there was "too little cooperation in

this country between business and labor unions . . . to improve the country's economic performance." A poll by Opinion Research Corporation for LTV Corporation found even higher proportions of business and union leaders (86 percent and 76 percent, respectively) strongly favored cooperative industrial relations; another by Harris for *Business Week* (6 June 1982, p. 66) found that 57 percent of executives in highly unionized companies would rather give unions "more of a voice in how the company is run" than to return to adversarial relations.

8. Quoted in the *St. Louis Labor Tribune*, 9 December 1982, p. 8.

9. B. Reisman and L. Compa (1985), p. 32.

10. *Business Week*, 14 June 1982, p. 8; the exact figure was 19 percent, from a sample of 400 "high-level executives."

11. This is Peter Cappelli's finding (1984, p. 298) from a sample of concession cases compiled by the Bureau of National Affairs.

12. There are a tremendous number of joint committees in such areas as health and safety; many of these have been in operation for decades. Few of them, however, have any real effectiveness. The more innovative joint committees tend to arise in times of crisis and die when the crisis recedes; see J. T. Dunlop (1977); J. J. Healy, ed. (1965).

13. For example, see B. Reisman and L. Compa (1985); S. A. Levitan and C. M. Johnson (1983); or many statements by William Winpisinger of the Machinists. These arguments boil down to saying: managers are bad, we haven't been able to cooperate with them in the past; therefore, cooperation is bad.

14. D. A. Fraser (1981).

15. *Business Week*, 1 February 1982.

16. A great deal has been written about codetermination. Among the more useful works are R. Mazzolini (1978); F. Furstenberg (1980); A. S. Markovits and C. S. Allen (1979b); E. M. Kassalow (1983); A. M. Thimm (1980); R. Blainpain et al. (1984); and H. Mintzberg (1983). See also n. 22.

17. See n. 16 for evidence on the impact of codetermination.

18. See P. Cappelli (1985).

19. Personal interviews, November 1985.

20. I am basically following Sanford Jacoby's (1983) analysis of these efforts, and Daniel J. B. Mitchell's (1982) analysis of more recent waves. For a contemporary critique of the 1920s experiments, see W. J. Lauck (1926).

21. It is interesting to note that the Saturn agreement between General Motors and the United Auto Workers—one of the most dramatic manifestations of extended partnership—has been downplayed by the union as a model for the future. Owen Bieber, the UAW president, sees it as a "special case" that does not set precedents for other agreements.

22. See n. 16 for a sample of literature on codetermination. In addition to those works cited, the following are informative about Sweden: N. Eiger (1983); S. Gustafson (1979); and J. Burton (1980).

23. See, for instance, R. B. Reich (1981).

24. Two good treatments of "corporatism" in the European context include C. Crouch (1977); P. C. Schmitter and G. Lehmbruch (1979); and P. C. Schmitter (1983). See also the discussion of the "quasi-corporatist compromise" in chapter 3.

25. See chapter 4, n. 57, for evidence on the low public regard for unions in Europe. I would add that a major cross-national survey in the late 1970s found the general level of satisfaction with unions about the same in Sweden and Germany as in the United States (B. Jacob [1978], p. 4).

26. For evidence that workers in a wide range of countries disapprove of heavy union involvement in politics, see chapter 4, n. 57.

27. For data, see "Europe's Unions are Losing Their Grip," *Business Week*, 26 November 1984, pp. 80–88. For further evidence on the decline of corporatism in Europe, see A. S. Markovits and C. S. Allen (1979); S. Gustafson (1979); S. Barkin, ed. (1975); C. Crouch and A. Pizzorno, eds. (1978); and R. Edwards, P. Garonna, and F. Todtling, eds. (1986).

28. The Danes had similar problems with their Meidner-type plan during the early 1980s; union leaders to whom I spoke were puzzled by the lack of public and worker support for such an obviously beneficial plan.

29. See J. J. Healy, ed. (1965), chaps. 6–7. In general, this work shows the difficulty of maintaining adequate communication with the membership in high-level joint committees.

30. Examples of the last two forms of externalization can be found in A. L. Ahmuty (1980). This interesting article sums up the experiences of several joint labor-management committees, including those in retail foods, men's clothing, construction, and steel. Many of the cases also reveal the problem unions have in effectively communicating with their members concerning these activities.

Notes

31. Jack W. Johnson, quoted in *Business Week,* 14 June 1982, p. 68.

32. The quote is from J. T. Dunlop (1984), p. 268. His position on Landrum-Griffin is found, among other places, in J. T. Dunlop (1967).

33. Some influential writers have suggested that unions could use their pension funds as a new weapon in the battle against management—fighting capital with capital, as it were. (See, for an enthusiastic advocacy of this strategy, J. Rifkin and R. Barber [1978]); for a more management-oriented, concerned perspective, see P. Drucker (1976).

There is an enormous attraction to the idea. Pension funds are, after all, workers' money—merely deferred until they retire. Perhaps more to the point, they currently form over a quarter of the total investment capital in the United States. That sort of money could effectively shape corporate strategies, encouraging companies, for example, to sustain employment in this country and to accept unionization.

The legal question of how much control unions might exert over pensions is complex. The Taft-Hartley Act gave management control of most pension funds, and the Employee Retirement Income Security Act more recently put restrictions on the "social" uses of the money. Though there is probably room to maneuver, it would require favorable legislation and court rulings. In the United States, where most of the population already thinks unions have "too much power," it is difficult to imagine political support being available for such an increase in labor power.

34. These conclusions are based in part on a study of the QWL effort at AT&T from 1981 to 1983. The study, which was conducted by outside researchers under the coordination of the union and the company, was based on in-depth studies of ten QWL teams in various regions and working conditions. The research included surveys, interviews, and observation of the QWL process. The report was published by the U.S. Department of Labor (1985).

35. Ed Cohen-Rosenthal (1980) summarized the situation in 1980, finding QWL efforts in a very wide range of industries, from mining to government to construction. The total has without doubt rapidly increased since then. One thing that makes it hard to estimate the exact number is that few sources distinguish between union-management committees and direct worker participation.

36. AFL-CIO Committee on the Evolution of Work (1985), p. 19.

37. I am aware of instances where QWL has unmistakably been started to defeat organizing campaigns at AT&T, General Motors, and Johnson & Johnson. I also know of dozens of similar allegations in other companies.

38. This finding is from my own analysis of the 1977 Quality of Employment Survey (QES) data (see Quinn and Staines [1979]). The survey asked nonunion workers if they would vote for a union if given the chance. I compared the means on a number of variables indicating freedom and interest on the job for those who would vote *for* the union versus those who would vote *against.* Those who would vote against the union had consistently and strongly higher levels of autonomy and "say" on the job than their prounion coworkers, even when occupational level is controlled.

39. F. K. Foulkes (1981).

40. *AFL-CIO Statistical and Tactical Information Report* no. 18, April 1984, p. 6.

41. Again (see n. 38), this is my own analysis of the QES data. In this case I ran correlations between variables indicating autonomy, interest, etc., and a variable on satisfaction with one's union. These correlations were consistently positive, mostly in the range of .20—which is well above the cutoff for the .001 level of significance.

42. U.S. Department of Labor (1985).

43. T. A. Kochan, H. C. Katz, and N. R. Mower (1984), p. 139. The basic figures—about 55 percent supportive, 20 percent opposed—remain quite consistent across a number of different questions about QWL.

44. Increases in membership participation in the union in participative workplaces have been documented by Gardell and Svensson (1979) at the Almex plant in Sweden; and by T. Rankin (1986) for the early phases of the Shell-Sarnia plant, to be described in the next chapter.

45. T. A. Kochan, H. C. Katz, and N. R. Mower (1984), p. 139.

46. There are a great many instances of sharp drops in grievance loads after the institutionalization of QWL. One of the first QWL experiments, for example, was started during the early 1970s in General Motors' Tarrytown plant, which had a long history of bitter labor relations and a backlog of several thousand grievances; by 1976 the number of grievances in process had been reduced to twenty-four. Among telephone operators at Illinois Bell, to take a case that I documented myself, the load dropped by 40 percent after one year of QWL, and by an additional 16 percent the next year. These instances could be multiplied many times; exceptions, in fact, are relatively uncommon.

47. The Communications Workers of America helped develop training for local facilitators, who

were usually stewards, which was far more intensive than anything they had received before from the union. The UAW has recently developed a five-week training package for its local officers that focuses on explaining the Saturn agreement and its implications.

48. T. Rankin (1986), chap. 1.

49. *Newsweek*, 5 August 1985, p. 42. Kelly is referring to the proposed contract for the Saturn Project; he was particularly incensed by the violations of seniority it entails.

50. For an analysis of union experiences with autonomous teams and their resistance to the idea, see M. Brossard (1981).

51. U.S. Department of Labor (1985).

Paul Goodman (1980), in one of the few studies of QWL efforts beyond the first phase, found that only 25 percent of his sample were still functioning after five years—and *none* of these were in unionized settings, despite the fact that most of these programs had experienced considerable initial success.

52. *Congressional Record* 78, p. 3443.

53. *Cabot Carbon* v. *NLRB*, 360 U.S. 203.

54. *NLRB* v. *Streamway Division*, 691 F2d 288 (CA-6, 1982). Other discussions of QWL and Section 8(a)(2) include R. Hogler (1984); W. E. Fulmer and J. J. Coleman (1984); T. J. Schneider (1981); A *Harvard Law Review* note 96 (1983), p. 1662; M. S. Beaver (1985); and J. Schmidman and K. Keller (1984).

55. *Hertzka and Knowles* v. *NLRB*, 503 F2d 625 (CA-9, 1974).

CHAPTER 7

1. I am heavily indebted for my understanding of the Shell-Sarnia plant to Tom Rankin of the Ontario Quality of Work Life Center: his doctoral research analyzes the plant as a model for a new, postbureaucratic form of union-management relationship. He has been extremely generous in sharing his ideas and data with me and in facilitating my access to those at the site.

Rankin's dissertation (1986) is the best source for those who seek further information about the case. Two published articles are also helpful: L. E. Davis and C. E. Sullivan (1980) and N. Halpern (1982).

2. This and subsequent quotes from employees at the Shell-Sarnia plant are drawn from interviews in March and October, 1985.

3. Quoted in T. Rankin (1986).

4. It should be added that the ECWU is pursuing a participative strategy beyond the Shell plant. Internally, it is the only industrial union governed by a board of rank-and-file members, rather than full-time elected officials. It has adopted with many of its employers a "continuing dialogue" approach to bargaining. This means that only wages are established at the contract expiration; all other issues are merely identified and farmed out to task forces that continue work during the contract. Their recommendations can be adopted whenever they finish. The union has also been involved, with Atomic Energy of Canada, in an effort to identify new products and ventures for the company.

5. Quotes from Frank Slaughter and Leo van Houten are drawn from my interviews at the Fiero plant in October, 1985.

6. Quoted in *Daily Labor Report*, 29 July 1985, p. AA-1.

7. Speech at Harvard University, 29 January 1986.

8. R. E. Walton (1961). Another study that largely confirms Walton's analysis is J.W. Kuhn (1971). In addition, I am incorporating here my own experience as the steward and member of the bargaining committee for a group of researchers within the Communications Workers' Union.

9. See T. A. Shipka (1982).

10. These comments are based on L. Schneider and C. Ciborra (1982), and on conversations with others who have had firsthand experience with the Norwegian case, especially Kirsten Nygaard of the Norwegian Computing Center.

11. See National Coal Policy Project (1981). For an assessment of the National Coal Policy Project's effects on policy, see the statement of Harrison Loesch in *U. S. Congress, Joint Hearings on Regulatory Negotiation Before the Select Committee on Small Business and the Subcommittee on Government Management of the Senate Committee on Governmental Affairs*, 96th Cong., 2d sess. 7, 1980.

12. For a discussion of environmental negotiations, see chapter 10.

Notes

CHAPTER 8

1. The original framers of the Constitution actually rejected a Bill of Rights, though they did so largely on the grounds that rights were adequately protected at the state level, and the federal government could not override them. In any case, the demand for a set of federally guaranteed rights was immediate and powerful, so that the passage of the first ten amendments to the Constitution was essentially a condition of its adoption.

2. On progressive discipline systems in nonunion settings, see F. K. Foulkes (1980).

3. William S. McEwen, quoted in *Daily Labor Report*, 11 July 1985, p. A-7. Similarly, a survey of Fortune 500 companies showed that better than 95 percent planned to continue the use of numerical objectives in tracking the progress of women and minorities no matter what the Reagan administration did.

4. For a list of federal statutes with antireprisal provisions, see W. N. Dutten and N. A. Kinigstein (1983), pp. 303–4.

5. *Payne* v. *Western & ARR*, 81 Tenn. 507 (1884).

6. *Harless* v. *First National Bank in Fairmont*, 246 SE 2d 270 (1978). There had been a few decisions in this vein before: *Petermann* v. *International Brotherhood of Teamsters, Local 396*, 174 Cal. app. 2d 184 (1959), for instance, granted a cause of action for an allegation of dismissal for refusal to commit perjury. But none of the previous cases had started or been part of a major trend; this was not true in the *Harless* decision. Since about that time courts in at least thirty states have cut into the traditional employment-at-will doctrine.

For more complete discussions of recent trends in the doctrine of "employment at will," see J. B. Kauff and M. E. McClain (1984), esp. chaps. 1–4; D. W. Ewing (1983); T. J. St. Antoine (1985); J. Stieber (1985); and B. Heshizer (1985). The first of these is extremely detailed, listing and describing all the relevant cases; the last is perhaps the best lay introduction to the subject.

7. This quote, as well as the previous one in this paragraph, are from *Monge* v. *Beebe Rubber Co.*, 114 N.H. 130 (1974); italics added. See J. B. Kauff and M. E. McClain (1984), pp. 28ff. for further cases in this vein.

Another line of rulings has held that promises made during employment interviews or in employee handbooks constitute contracts (*Toussaint* v. *Blue Cross of Michigan*, 408 Michigan 579, 292 N.W. 2d 880 (1980)) and are enforceable in court. This, like much of employment law, has a perverse effect: those companies that have tried to generate high employee commitment—the managerialist companies—become most vulnerable to suits, because they frequently stress the importance of employment security and due process.

8. *Novosel* v. *Nationwide Insurance Co.*, 721 F2d 894 (1983).

9. G. S. McIsaac (1977), pp. 22–23.

10. *Fortune*, 2 January 1984, p. 92.

11. For an elaboration of the argument that the balance-of-power framework limits the scope of union representation, see chapter 3.

12. W. B. Gould (1984), p. 3.

13. All of these have been tried by the UAW and other unions. Retraining is a centerpiece of the 1984 auto contracts; they also provide money for exploring new business start-ups for job creation. Employee ownership was tried, among other places, at the Hyatt-Clark ballbearing plant, which was about to be shut down by GM. With the (somewhat reluctant) help of their former owners, the employees managed to keep the plant operational and to save their jobs. This success, like many other such "rescues," proved to be short-lived: by 1987 the plant went into bankruptcy.

14. D. W. Ewing (1983), p. 118.

15. D. W. Ewing (1977)—the statement is based on results of a survey of subscribers to the *Harvard Business Review*.

16. A report on "nonunion complaint systems" by the Conference Board, a business research group, finds that systems involving appeals to third parties within the company are quite common and effective; those that have a final step of outside arbitration are much less frequent but are apparently even more effective in handling discontent in a way that satisfies all parties (R. Berenbeim, [1980]).

17. J. Stieber (1985), p. 558.

18. The European experience with unjust-discharge legislation has been generally positive, but not entirely. Some of the approaches have run afoul of the problems I referred to earlier: guarantees that are too specific, and excessive reliance on expert judgments. These result in relatively unwieldy and

rigid systems and have sparked something of a countermovement among employers in several nations (see S. Estreicher [1985]). In the model that I am proposing, guarantees of rights are only the first element: they would be developed and enforced through extensive negotiation among associational groups. This would make for much more cooperation and flexibility.

19. See L. E. Dube (1985).

20. See R. Blainpain et al. (1983).

21. A. W. Clausen (1981), p. 65.

22. On underground employee newspapers, see D. W. Ewing (1983), pp. 273–5.

23. Quoted in "The Picket Line Gives Way to Sophisticated New Tactics," *Business Week*, 16 April 1984, p. 116. Harbrant is president of the AFL's Food and Allied Service Trades Department.

24. *NLRB* v. *Local 1299, IBEW*, 346 U.S. 464 (1953), known as the *Jefferson Standard* case. For a general discussion of this topic, see J. B. Atleson (1983), chap. 5.

25. See K. E. Klare (1982).

26. Italics added.

27. Respectively: *NLRB* v. *Washington Aluminum*, 370 U.S. 9 (1962); and *Alleluia Cushion*, NLRB No. 162 (1975).

28. G. Schatzki (1975), pp. 915–16.

29. A key decision in this vein is *Emporium Capwell* v. *Waco*, 420 U.S. 50 (1975), ruling that activity conducted by individual union members that detracts from the union's status as exclusive representative is unprotected.

30. In many cases European countries have developed de facto forms of exclusive representation: C. Summers (1985), for example, points out that in Sweden the employers, rather than the government, gave exclusive recognition to one employee association. Nevertheless, the absence of a legal backing for such restrictions makes spontaneous movements more possible. The Swedes found this out in the late 1960s, when wildcats erupted that were directed as much against the unions as against employers; these forced a fundamental reevaluation of the whole system, which is still being worked out. In the United States, incipient movements of this kind—by black groups, for example—were by contrast effectively suppressed by the dominant unions and employers.

31. For a discussion of how exclusive representation justifies government intervention in internal union affairs, see chapter 3, pp. 47–48.

32. For another treatment advocating abandonment of exclusive representation, see G. Schatzki (1975).

33. Letter from Professor William Gould to members of the Labor and Employment Committee, California Assembly, 2 May 1984.

CHAPTER 9

1. The 1977 Quality of Employment Survey contained evidence of a strong desire for union representation among blacks and women. It asked: "If an election were held with secret ballots, would you vote for or against having a union or employees' association represent you?" The percentages answering "For" were: whites, 29 percent; nonwhites, 69 percent; men, 27 percent; women, 41 percent.

2. The Communication Workers finally did elect a woman executive vice-president in 1985.

Prof. Herbert Hill, a leading black scholar of labor relations, is sharply critical of the AFL-CIO for its relation to minorities. "The basic commitment of the AFL-CIO," he says, "remains to the diminishing number of white male workers in a collective bargaining unit." (*Daily Labor Report*, 28 April 1983, p. A-16).

3. Communications Workers of America (1983), p. 16.

4. Ibid., p. 54.

5. Ibid., p. 26.

6. Ibid., pp. 22, 26.

7. Many unions, including the Machinists, Steelworkers, and Food and Commercial Workers (UFCW), have been involved in instances of enforcing pattern contracts over the objections of a local membership. This can be vital in the short run to prevent "whipsawing" by employers, but it is not holding up in the long run. The UFCW was almost torn apart in 1986 by bitter controversy over such an action at the Hormel plant in Austin, Minnesota. The Machinists, after starting with

an unqualified policy of "no concessions" from master agreements, has been compelled to back down to a more flexible policy.

8. Personal conversation, November 1985.

9. AFL-CIO (1985), pp. 23, 19.

10. Lane Kirkland interview, reported in John Herling's *Labor Letter*, 2 March 1985.

11. AFL-CIO (1985), pp. 19–20.

12. Speech by Tom Donahue to New York AFL-CIO conference on the Future of Work, February 1986 (unpublished transcript).

13. Again, I cite this as an indicator of the need for change, not necessarily as a proof that a solution is at hand.

14. Comments by Glenn Watts, president, Communications Workers of America; in T. A. Kochan, H. C. Katz, and N. R. Mower (1984), p. 198.

15. *Business Week*, 8 July 1985, p. 75.

16. Personal conversation with Charles McDonald, 19 June 1985.

17. Shell Philosophy Statement (unpublished document).

18. For an account of this case, see D. W. Ewing (1982), pp. 118–28.

19. Swedish unions, by contrast, long ago negotiated extensive paid time for union educational programs.

20. The American Society of Association Executives has as members about seventy subassociations of associations, or "allied associations."

CHAPTER 10

1. See chapter 3 for further discussion of these points. It is extremely rare for more than one union to meet with the employer at a time, even when there is an obvious need for it. When Eastern or Western Airlines were in crisis, for example, it would have greatly benefited the various unions to work out a coordinated strategy. Though they made attempts in both instances to form multiunion committees, there was in fact little or no cooperation; each labor organization struck its own deal with management.

2. For a discussion of the crisis of the regulatory system, see chapter 4, pp. 71–77. My understanding of the European experience with unjust-dismissal statutes indicates it follows the same pattern: administrative agencies are frequently embattled, and there is now a strong move to roll back the new rights in order to reduce resulting rigidities. Relations are becoming, on the whole, more adversarial rather than more consensual.

3. The EPA case is described in L. E. Susskind and G. McMahon (1985). The EPA had a similar success with another regulation, on noncompliance penalties; it was sufficiently pleased with these efforts to commit itself, as of 1985, to several further attempts at negotiated rule making.

4. For a more complete description of this environmental negotiation, see L. E. Susskind and J. Cruikshank (1987).

5. There is disagreement among practitioners about how much grouping is required. Some advocate letting in anyone who wants to be a separate participant; the larger negotiations, involving several hundreds of groupings, have been the product of this school. Others believe that reduction in the number of participants is necessary. A few years ago it was generally thought that fifteen was the outside number, but that frontier clearly has been breached.

6. Organized labor largely opposed the provisions for multiple levels of representation in Kennedy's executive order; the AFL-CIO favored sticking by the traditional principle of exclusive representation. But Tom Donahue, the secretary-treasurer of the AFL-CIO, has recently expressed his opinion that that opposition may have been a mistake (see chapter 9, p. 183).

7. Roger Fisher, a professor at Harvard Law School, is the main exponent of "principled negotiation"; see R. Fisher and W. Ury (1983).

8. This phrase is used by David Straus, cofounder of Interaction Associates, which has conducted "collaborative problem-solving" in a wide variety of public and private settings.

9. P. J. Harter (1982), pp. 96–97.

10. If there is not a high level of trust between union leaders and members, the alternative is to reduce the effective control of members over contract settlements. That is why there is always a tendency to reduce the power of the membership contract vote.

11. R. M. Axelrod (1984) reports on an interesting computer simulation of influence bargaining

which shows why, in this structure, "niceness" pays—at least over time. A set of negotiating strategies, devised for the computer by some very sophisticated bargainers, were pitted against each other over a long succession of trials. It turned out that the most successful strategies in the long run were all "nice," in that they never initiated a noncooperative strategy—though they would respond in kind if their opponent initiated it. They established, as it were, a "reputation" that stood them in good stead as their relationships with opponents continued.

That is not to say that there are not many distortions of the process that can make "not-nice" approaches pay off. Inequalities of power are the most obvious danger; the foundation of rights is designed to counter that. Manipulations of influence itself—"unfair" uses of persuasion, without coercion, through demagoguery or (at the extreme) brainwashing—are more subtle but equally dangerous. Such risks can be minimized through joint fact-finding and other forms of information sharing, though probably never eliminated. I have taken up these problems at more length in chapter 11.

12. For discussion of the achievements and techniques of multilateral negotiation, see, for example, T. Colosi (1983); L. E. Susskind and C. Ozawa (1983); T. G. Cummings (1984); and L. E. Susskind and J. Cruikshank (1987). These, in turn, have further references.

Advanced processes of multilateral negotiation, called the "Negotiated Investment Strategy," have been used to develop community revitalization plans in Columbus, Ohio; Gary, Indiana; and St. Paul, Minnesota.

For summaries of empirical studies of the effectiveness of mediated negotiation, see J. A. Roehl and R. F. Cook (1985); K. Kressel and D. G. Pruitt (1985). Most of these studies focus, however, on "classic" mediation, which simply involves trying to get two parties to adopt a different attitude toward their dispute; they do not distinguish cases where the basic structure of dispute settlement is changed by the introduction of multiple parties instead of the original two. This latter field, which is of greatest interest for labor relations, has not to my knowledge been well evaluated.

13. The figures on the number of labor-management committees are from J. Cutcher-Gershenfeld (1984), p. 78. For more information on this topic, see also J. Cutcher-Gershenfeld (1985); and T. G. Cummings et al. (1983).

CHAPTER 11

1. This term was first used, to my knowledge, by Sumner Slichter in the 1940s. It is only more recently, however, that the concept has become real. The growth of the "semiprofessional" class (as described in chapter 4, pp. 62–71) has been enormous in the past thirty years, and it now constitutes nearly one-third of the work force. These are jobs that require discretion and initiative and therefore are generally classed as "management"; but they are also highly vulnerable to organizational power, increasingly insecure, and under pressure for wage reductions—which makes them more like "labor."

2. For a discussion of the effectiveness of publicity as a union weapon, see chapter 9, pp. 184 and 189.

3. See M. L. Brookshire and M. D. Rogers (1977). In Sweden the employer confederation likewise played a major role in the consolidation of the central union federation by refusing to bargain with the many smaller unions that grew up in the early period of industrialization.

4. See chapters 6 and 7 for other examples of extended participation and representation.

5. European experiences with unjust dismissal legislation are usefully summarized by S. Estreicher (1985).

6. See chapter 4, n. 10.

7. Even in production industries there are precedents for flexible compensation systems. The "Scanlon plan" developed by the Steelworkers in the 1940s involved a formula for sharing cost savings between management and workers; it has been applied in several hundred plants.

8. The concept of a zone "above" collective bargaining is developed by T. A. Kochan, R. B. McKersie, and P. Cappelli (1984).

9. President's Commission on Industrial Competitiveness, vol. 1 (1985), pp. 30, 34.

10. For comparative evidence of the near-universal criticism of unions, and especially, their political activity, see chapter 4, n. 57.

11. President's Commission on Industrial Competitiveness, vol. 1 (1985), pp. 30–31.

12. The idea of a new venture creation is in the 1984 UAW-GM contract, not in the CWA-AT&T

Notes

one; but there has been an agreement for new venture creation between the CWA and Mountain Bell in Phoenix. It has also been tried in some cases by the Energy and Chemical Workers in Canada—the parent union for the Shell-Sarnia plant.

13. Larry Snyder of Boston College has pointed out to me a very interesting college program run by District Council 37 in New York—a campus of the College of New Rochelle—which helps largely black and poor students develop career skills. This seems closer to the model I am suggesting for career retraining programs.

14. Analysis of the 1977 Quality of Employment survey data [see R. P. Quinn and G. L. Staines (1979)] shows that those who feel their opportunity for advancement is limited are far more likely than others to want a strong union voice and increased participation. Many polls of employees, including this one, show that better promotion opportunities is one of the strongest expressed desires.

15. For more detailed discussion of public confidence in government, and of the political environment in general, see chapter 4.

16. P. J. Harter (1982), p. 52. This article is an extremely detailed and learned proposal for the development of multilateral negotiation as a "cure for the malaise" of regulation. It carries much further than I have been able to the practical issues of implementing such a system: the necessary role of courts, the criteria of standing, the definition of consensus, and so on; and it is full of concrete examples and experiences. Anyone looking for specific ideas about how to establish standards for a multilateral system in labor relations would be well advised to start here.

17. See chapter 10, pp. 194–201, and Chapter 10, n. 12 for further details on the experience of regulatory negotiation.

18. Julian Gresser (1984) has incorporated the elements of multilateral negotiation into model legislation for negotiated industrial policy, which is being considered by some states, as well as at the federal level. Its details can readily be adapted to the labor relations scene.

19. L. Bierman and S. A. Youngblood (1985) describe a successful state-level experiment in developing an agency that mediates and supports negotiation, rather than regulating: in South Carolina, a low-key agency takes unfair dismissal complaints, pursues about half of them by supporting purely voluntary mediation, and has achieved a relatively high success rate.

20. Experiences with compulsory arbitration of contracts, for example, have regularly shown that the parties tend to give up on serious bargaining and to throw their problems in the lap of the outside enforcer. This enervation of the negotiation process is what I am seeking to avoid. See, for example, Independent Study Group (1961), p. 105; and P. Weiler (1984), p. 380.

21. In practice most employee suits are supported by some such association. In the BART case, as mentioned earlier, professional engineering associations were crucial in helping the discharged employees to press their cases. In the area of sexual discrimination and harassment, women's groups have often played a similar role.

22. My proposal that courts give deference to consensus processes echoes P. J. Harter (1983). See also P. J. Harter (1982), pp. 102–107, for more detailed proposals on standards of review; also P. G. Stewart (1975) offers a detailed analysis of recent court interventions in administrative regulation.

23. For a detailed discussion of the problems of interest representation in administrative law, see R. B. Stewart (1975).

CHAPTER 12

1. D. W. Ewing (1977). See also chapter 5, n. 10.

2. A. A. Berle and G. C. Means (1933); P. F. Drucker (1976). We appear to be coming close to the point where the last links between ownership and control are severed. Many managers of pension funds are reluctant to use their power to vote the stocks held by their funds, feeling that this creates conflicts of interest. For this reason a serious proposal has been advanced to strip voting rights from shares, allowing the former to be sold in an open market. See *Investment Dealers' Digest*, 19 August 1985, pp. 10–12.

3. G. C. Lodge (1977). On the need for new bases for management legitimacy, see also G. C. Lodge (1984), P. F. Drucker (1976), and J. Diebold (1977). Diebold—who, like the others in this group, is a well-regarded management consultant—argues explicitly the need for an employee bill of rights.

4. The three concepts I have chosen for analyzing the developing movement for change—strains,

generalized beliefs, and new coalitions—are drawn loosely from functionalist treatments of social movements such as that of N. Smelser (1962). But I would not class my treatment as "functionalist" in the classic sense. My focus is on the creation of new *meanings* among social groups. The difficult and important thing to understand is how people come to redefine their sense of how they are related to others. That long, slow, subtle process is what I mean by a "movement"; it defines the general shape of social change.

Overt collective action is only one manifestation of this shift in meaning, and not necessarily the most important. Thus I find the usual focus on trying to predict and define collective action to miss most of the point about social change. Collective action, as Smelser and others have been forced to conclude, depends a great deal on "precipitating factors" that are essentially random with respect to the change in question. The French Revolution could have been quite different in nature without changing its essential meaning and social thrust. Focusing on collective behavior is like focusing on the tip of the iceberg, trying to assess its nature and importance without looking at the underlying mass.

The focus on meaning actually brings me closer to the theories of A. Touraine (for example, 1985). I have been substantively influenced by his argument that modern associational movements are different in quality from past collective actions. There is still the difference, however, that Touraine tries to understand the nature of the collective action itself more than the underlying process of realignment.

Of course, I do not claim to be able to predict when or how a collective action in support of employee rights will occur. I aim to establish only that there has been a substantial redefinition of the meaning of employee rights vis-à-vis employers and a realignment of groupings based on that redefinition, which has been creating steady pressure for change for twenty years and which will continue to create such pressure.

5. *Business Week*, 25 April 1983, p. 60.

6. The ORC data on the growing dissatisfaction of managers and other white-collar groups are combined from two sources: Cooper et al. (1979), p. 122, which traces a decline from the 1950s to 1979; and W. A. Schiemann and B. S. Morgan (1982), p. 32, which brings the figures up to the early 1980s. The Harris survey is reported in *Business Week* (8 July 1985), p. 75.

For further evidence of the decline of satisfaction among white-collar and professional workers, see P. J. Andrisani (1978).

7. Reported in *Daily Labor Report*, 18 July 1985. There is a fair amount of discrepancy in different measures of the incidence of part-time and temporary employment. All agree, however, that these have increased since the 1960s. Yankelovich et al. (1985), for instance, estimate the percentage of part-time workers at 22 percent in 1977, up by 7 percent since 1954. The Department of Labor estimates *regular* part-timers at 17 percent of the work force in 1985, up 3 percent from 1968.

8. For an explanation of how I define the proportions of "blue-collar," "declining white-collar" (or white-collar semiskilled), and "semiprofessional," see chapter 4, n. 41.

9. According to Harris polls, those expressing "a great deal of confidence" in leaders of business have risen only slightly, from a low of 16 percent in 1981 to 19 percent in 1984—still below the general levels of the late 1970s. More extraordinary, a *New York Times*/CBS News poll in 1985 found that 55 percent of the population thinks that *most* corporate executives are not honest (*New York Times*, 9 June 1985, sec. 3, p. 1).

10. A labor relations director at McKinsey & Co., quoted in G. S. McIsaac (1977), pp. 22–23.

11. The poll on perceived workplace rights is reported in D. Yankelovich et al. (1985), p. 340. T. Ferguson and J. Rogers (1986) also report a series of Harris polls that show a dramatic recent increase in public support for affirmative action in jobs and education, from about 45 percent favorable in 1978 to over 70 percent in 1985.

12. Quoted in *Business Week*, 8 July 1985, p. 73.

13. Philip Selznick (1969), esp. chap. 7, made some very interesting suggestions on these lines over fifteen years ago. Their relevance has only increased with time.

14. The courts have several times attacked the Reagan NLRB for attempts to abruptly change policy without a reasoned explanation about how the new rule affects the statute better than the old. See, for example, *Ewing v. NLRB*, 83 Cal. 2d 4183 (1985). The new appointees have, in effect, made the political nature of the board's decisions more obvious, almost giving up on the claim to mere expert administration of the statute.

CHAPTER 13

1. For data on growing white-collar dissatisfaction, see chapter 12, p. 240. Data from detailed surveys over seven years at AT&T show that "a minority of employees think that sufficient effort is being made to get their opinions before decisions are made." (*Oculus*, April 1986, p. 8.)

2. See D. Yankelovich and J. Immerwahr (1983).

BIBLIOGRAPHY

AFL-CIO. *AFL-CIO Statistical and Tactical Information Report,* no. 18, Washington, D. C.:AFL-CIO, April 1984.

AFL-CIO. "The Changing Situation of Workers and Their Unions," Washington, D. C.: AFL-CIO, February 1985.

Ahmuty, Alice L. "Tripartite Cooperative Endeavors in Labor Relations in the United States," Washington, D. C.: Congressional Research Service Report, No. 80-209 E: 8 December 1980, F168-9.

Alexander, Jeffrey C. *Neofunctionalism.* Beverly Hills: Sage, 1985.

American Assembly (The), Columbia University. *The Worker and the Job: Coping With Change.* Englewood Cliffs, NJ: Prentice-Hall, 1974.

American Enterprise Institute. *Government Regulation: Where Do We Go From Here?* Washington, D. C.: American Enterprise Institute, 1977.

Andrisani, Paul J. *Work Attitudes and Labor Market Experience: Evidence from the National Longitudinal Surveys.* NY: Praeger Publishers, 1978.

Arendt, Hannah. *On Revolution.* NY: Viking Press, 1963.

Argyris, Chris. *Intervention Theory and Method: A Behavioral Science View.* Reading, MA: Addison-Wesley Publishing Co., 1970.

Asard, Erik. "Employee Participation in Sweden, 1971–1978: The Issue of Economic Democracy," mimeo, April 1979.

Atleson, James B. *Values and Assumptions in American Labor Law.* Amherst, MA: University of Massachusetts Press, 1983.

Axelrod, Robert M. *The Evolution of Cooperation.* NY: Basic Books, 1984.

Bain, George Sayers; Coates, David; and Ellis, Valerie. *Social Stratification and Trade Unionism: A Critique.* London: Heinemann, 1973.

Bairstow, Frances. "Professional Workers and Collective Bargaining in Canada: Reflections of the Last Ten Years," in Hinman, F. (ed.), *Professional Workers and Collective Bargaining: Selected Papers.* Los Angeles: Institute of Industrial Relations, University of California, 1977, pp. 13–23.

Barber, Bernard. *The Logic and Limits of Trust.* New Brunswick, NJ: Rutgers University Press, 1983.

Barkin, Solomon. "An Agenda for the Revision of the American Industrial Relations System," *Labor Law Journal,* 36, 11 (1985): 857–60.

Barkin, Solomon, ed. *Worker Militancy and Its Consequences, 1965–75: New Directions in Western Industrial Relations.* NY: Praeger Publishers, 1975.

Barnard, Chester I. *The Functions of the Executive.* Cambridge, MA: Harvard University Press, 1968. Orig. ed. 1938.

Beaver, Michael Stuart. "Are Worker Participation Plans 'Labor Organizations' Within the Meaning of Section 2(5)? A Proposed Framework of Analysis," *Labor Law Journal* 36, 4 (1985): 226.

Bell, Daniel. *The Coming of Post-Industrial Society: A Venture In Social Forecasting.* NY: Basic Books, 1973 (new foreword, 1976).

Bennis, Warren G.; Benne, Kenneth D.; and Chin, Robert. *The Planning of Change.* NY: Holt, Rinehart, & Winston, 1961.

Berenbeim, Ronald. *Nonunion Complaint Systems: A Corporate Reappraisal.* NY: The Conference Board, 1980.

Berger, Peter L. "New Attack on the Legitimacy of Business," *Harvard Business Review,* September-October 1981: 82–89.

Bergmann, Joachim, and Muller-Jentsch, Walther. "The Federal Republic of Germany: Cooperative

Unionism and Dual Bargaining System Challenged," in S. Barkin, ed., *Worker Militancy*, 1975, ch. 7.

Bernheim, Alfred L., and Van Doren, Dorothy. *Labor and the Government: An Investigation of the Role of Government in Labor Relations*. NY: McGraw-Hill, for The Twentieth Century Fund, 1935.

Bernstein, Irving. *The New Deal Collective Bargaining Policy*. Berkeley: University of California Press, 1950.

Bernstein, Irving. *Turbulent Years: A History of the American Worker, 1933–1941*. Boston: Houghton Mifflin, 1969.

Bierman, Leonard, and Youngblood, Stuart A. "Employment-at-will and the South Carolina Experiment," *Industrial Relations Law Journal* 7, 1 (1985): 28–59.

Blackburn, R.M. *Union Character and Social Class: A Study of White Collar Unionism*. London: B.T. Batsford, Ltd., 1967.

Blainpain, R. et al., *The Vredeling Proposal*. Deventer, Netherlands: Kluwer, 1983.

Bluestone, Barry, and Harrison, Bennett. *The Deindustrialization of America*. NY: Basic Books, 1982.

Blum, Albert A.; Estey, Martin; Kuhn, James W.; Wildman, Wesley A.; and Troy, Leo. *White-Collar Workers*. NY: Random House, 1971.

Bowles, Samuel; Gordon, David M.; and Weisskopf, Thomas E. *Beyond the Waste Land: A Democratic Alternative to Economic Decline*. Garden City, NY: Anchor Press, 1983.

Bradshaw, Thornton, and Vogel, David. *Corporations and Their Critics: Issues and Answers to the Problem of Corporate Responsibility*. NY: McGraw-Hill, 1981.

Brandini, Pietro Merli. "Italy: Creating a New Industrial Relations System From the Bottom," in S. Barkin, ed., *Worker Militancy*, 1975, ch. 3.

Braverman, Harry. *Labor and Monopoly Capitalism: The Degradation of Work in the Twentieth Century*. NY: Monthly Review Press, 1974.

Brecher, Jeremy. *Strike!* Boston: South End Press, 1972.

Brody, David. *Workers in Industrial America: Essays on the 20th Century Struggle*. NY: Oxford University Press, 1980.

Brooks, Harvey. "The Impact of New Manufacturing Technology on Employment and Work in Developed and Developing Countries." unpublished manuscript: Harvard University, 1985.

Brooks, Thomas R. *Toil and Trouble: A History of American Labor*. NY: Delacorte Press, 1964.

Brookshire, Michael L., and Rogers, Michael D. *Collective Bargaining in Public Employment: The TVA Experience*. Lexington, MA: D.C. Heath, 1977.

Brossard, Michael. "North American Unions and Semi-autonomous Production Groups," *Quality of Working Life: The Canadian Scene* 4, 1 (1981): 1–5.

Burns, Tom, and Stalker, G.M. *The Management of Innovation*. London: Tavistock Publications, 1961.

Burton, Jeffrey. "The Swedish Steel Merger: Government and Worker Participation," *Working Life in Sweden* 21: November 1980.

Burton, John. *The Political Future of American Trade Unions*. Washington, D.C.: The Heritage Foundation, 1982.

Cappelli, Peter A. "Union Gains Under Concession Bargaining," IRRA 36th Annual Proceedings (1984): 297–305.

Cappelli, Peter A. "Competitive Pressures and Labor Relations in the Airline Industry," mimeo, Massachusetts Institute of Technology, February 1985.

Chandler, Alfred D., Jr. *The Visible Hand: The Managerial Revolution in American Business*. Cambridge, MA: Harvard University Press, 1977.

Chinoy, Ely. *Automobile Workers and the American Dream*. Boston: Beacon Press, 1955.

Clark, Martin. *Antonio Gramsci and the Revolution that Failed*. New Haven, CT: Yale University Press, 1977.

Clark, Rodney. *The Japanese Company*. New Haven, CT: Yale University Press, 1979.

Clausen, A.W. "Voluntary Disclosure: An Idea Whose Time Has Come," in Bradshaw, T., and Vogel, D. *Corporations and Their Critics* (1981): pp. 61–70.

Cohen-Rosenthal, Edward. "The Involvement of U.S. Unions in Quality of Working Life Programs," *Quality of Working Life: The Canadian Scene* 3, 3 (1980a): 5–9.

Cohen-Rosenthal, Edward. "Should Unions Participate in Quality of Working Life Activities?" *Quality of Working Life: The Canadian Scene* 3, 4 (1980b): 7–12.

Cole, G. D. H. *Self-government in Industry*. London: Hutchinson Educational, 1972.

Colosi, Thomas. "Negotiation in the Public and Private Sectors: A Core Model," *American Behavioral Scientist* 27, 2 (November-December 1983): 229–53.

Commons, John Rogers, and Andrews, John B. *Principles of Labor Legislation.* NY: Harper Brothers, 1920.

Communications Workers of America. *Committee of the Future—Special Convention,* March 28–29, 1983. Convention transcript, 1983.

Connors, Terrence F. *Problems in Local Union Collective Bargaining.* Detroit, MI: United Auto Workers, 1975.

Cooper, M.R.; Morgan, B.S.; Foley, P.M.; and Kaplan, L.B. "Changing Employee Values: Deepening Discontent?" *Harvard Business Review* 57, 1 (January-February 1979): 117–25.

Couture, Dennis; Friedman, Donald; and Taylor, Thomas. "HOBIS: New Frontiers for the Quality-of-Work-Life Process," mimeo draft, 1983.

Crouch, Colin. *Class Conflict and the Industrial Relations Crisis: Compromise and Corporatism in the Policies of the British State.* NY: Humanities Press, 1977.

Crouch, Colin, and Pizzorno, Alessandro, eds. *The Resurgence of Class Conflict in Western Europe Since 1968,* vol. 1 (National Studies) London: Macmillan Press, 1978.

Cummings, Thomas G. "Transorganizational Development," *Research in Organizational Behavior* 6 (1984): 367–422.

Cummings, Thomas G.; Blumenthal, Judith F.; and Greiner, Larry E. "Managing Organizational Decline: The Case for Transorganizational Systems," *Human Resource Management* 22, 4 (Winter 1983): 377–90.

Cutcher-Gershenfeld, Joel. "Policy Strategies for Labor-Management Cooperation," in Woodworth, Warner et al., eds., *Industrial Democracy,* 1985: ch. 13.

Cutcher-Gershenfeld, Joel. "Labor-Management Cooperation in American Communities: What's in it for the Unions?" *Annals of the American Academy of Political Science* 473 (May 1984): 76–87.

Davis, Louis E., and Trist, Eric L. "Improving the Quality of Work Life: Sociotechnical Case Studies," in O'Toole, James (ed.) *Work and the Quality of Life,* 1974: ch. 11.

Davis, Louis E., and Sullivan, Charles S. "A Labor-Management Contract and Quality of Working Life," *Journal of Occupational Behavior* 1 (1980): 29–41.

Davis, Stanley M. *Managing Corporate Culture.* Cambridge, MA: Ballinger Publishing, 1984.

Derber, Milton. *The American Idea of Industrial Democracy, 1865–1965.* Urbana, IL: University of Illinois Press, 1970.

Dewey, John. *The Public and Its Problems.* NY: Henry Holt & Company, 1927.

Diebold, John. *The Role of Business in Society.* NY: Amacom, 1982.

Dill, William R. "Public Participation in Corporate Planning: Strategic Management in a Kibitzer's World," *Long Range Planning* 8, 1 (February 1975): 57–63.

Douglas, Joel M. *Campus Bargaining at the Crossroads.* NY: National Center for the Study of Collective Bargaining in Higher Education, April 1982.

Drucker, Peter F. *The Unseen Revolution: How Pension-Fund Socialism Came to America.* NY: Harper & Row, 1976.

Drucker, Peter F. *Concept of the Corporation.* NY: New American Library, 1972.

Drucker, Peter F. *The Age of Discontinuity: Guidelines to Our Changing Society.* NY: Harper Colophon, 1969.

Drucker, Peter F. *Technology, Management, & Society.* NY: Harper & Row, copyrights 1958–70.

Drucker, Peter F. "New Templates for Today's Organizations," *Harvard Business Review,* January-February 1974: 45–53.

Dube, Lawrence E., Jr. "OSHA's Hazard Communication Standard: 'Right to Know' Comes to the Workplace," *Labor Law Journal,* September 1985: 696–701.

Dunlop, John T. *Industrial Relations Systems.* NY: Henry Holt and Co., 1958.

Dunlop, John T. "The Social Utility of Collective Bargaining," in Ulman, L. (ed.) *Challenges to Collective Bargaining,* 1967, pp. 168–80.

Dunlop, John T. "Statement to the U.S. Senate Committee on Human Resources, Subcommittee on Employment, Poverty, and Migratory Labor," Washington, D. C., 27 September 1977.

Dunlop, John T. *Dispute Resolution: Negotiation and Consensus-Building.* Dover, MA: Auburn House, 1984.

Edwards, Richard; Garonna, P.; and Todtling, F., eds. *Unions in Crisis and Beyond: Perspectives From Six Countries.* Dover, MA: Auburn House, 1986.

Ehrenreich, Barbara and John. "The Professional-Managerial Class," in Walker, Pat (ed.) *Between Labor and Capital,* 1979, pp. 5–45.

Eiger, Norman. "The Education of Employee Representatives on Company Boards in Sweden," *Working Life in Sweden* 27, May 1983.

Elazar, Daniel J. "Constitutionalism, Federalism, and the Post-Industrial American Polity," in Lipset, Seymour Martin (ed.) *The Third Century*, 1979, ch. 4.

Elden, J. "Democracy at Work for a More Participatory Politics." Ph.D. dissertation, University of California, Los Angeles, 1976.

Emshoff, James R., and Freeman, R. Edward. "Who's Butting Into Your Business?" *The Wharton Magazine* 4, 1 (Fall 1979): 44–59.

Estreicher, Samuel. "Law Commentary: Unjust Dismissal Laws in Other Countries: Some Cautionary Notes," *Industrial Relations Law Journal*, Spring 1985: 84–92.

Ewing, David W. "What Business Thinks About Employee Rights," *Harvard Business Review*, September-October 1977: 4–17.

Ewing, David W. *'Do It My Way or You're Fired!'* NY: John Wiley, 1983.

Ferguson, Thomas, and Rogers, Joel. "The Myth of America's Turn to the Right," *The Atlantic Monthly*, May 1986: 43–53.

Fisher, Roger, and Ury, William. *Getting to Yes: Negotiating Agreement Without Giving In.* NY: Penguin Books, 1983.

Ford, Robert N. *Motivation Through the Work Itself.* NY: American Management Association, 1969.

Form, William H. "Job vs. Political Unionism: A Cross-National Comparison," *Industrial Relations* 12, 2 (May 1973): 224–238.

Foulkes, Fred K. *Personnel Policies in Large Non-union Companies.* Englewood Cliffs, NJ: Prentice-Hall, 1980.

Foulkes, Fred K. "How Top Non-Union Companies Manage Employees," *Harvard Business Review*, September-October 1981: 90–96.

Frank, Linda L., and Hackman, J. Richard. "A Failure of Job Enrichment: The Case of the Change That Wasn't," mimeo: Technical Report no. 8, Dept. of Administrative Sciences, Yale University, March 1975.

Fraser, Douglas A. "Labor on Corporate Boards: An Interview With Douglas A. Fraser," *Challenge*, July-August 1981: 30–33.

Freeman, Richard B., and Medoff, James L. *What Do Unions Do?* NY: Basic Books, 1984.

Friedlander, F., and Brown, L. Dave. "Organization Development," *Annual Review of Psychology* 25 (1974): 313–341.

Furstenberg, Friedrich. "Codetermination and its Contribution to Industrial Democracy: A Critical Evaluation," Industrial Relations Research Association, Proceedings of the 33rd Annual Meeting, September 1980.

Galbraith, Jay R. "Matrix Organization Designs: How to Combine Functional and Project Forms," *Business Horizons* 14 (February 1971): 29–40.

Gallie, Duncan. *In Search of the New Working Class: Automation and Social Integration Within the Capitalist Enterprise.* Cambridge: Cambridge University Press, 1978.

Gardell, Bertil, and Svensson, Lennart. "Co-determinism and Autonomy: A Trade Union Strategy for Democracy at the Workplace," mimeo: Ann Arbor, MI: Institute for Social Research, 1980.

Gerth, H. H., and Mills, C. Wright, eds. *From Max Weber: Essays in Sociology.* NY: Oxford University Press, 1946.

Goldthorpe, John H.; Lockwood, David; Bechofer, Frank; and Platt, Jennifer. *The Affluent Worker: Industrial Attitudes and Behavior.* Cambridge: Cambridge University Press, 1968.

Gompers, Samuel. *Labor and the Employer.* NY: E.P. Dutton & Co., 1920.

Goodfellow, Matthew. "Quality Control Circle Programs: What Works and What Doesn't," mimeo: University Research Center, Chicago, IL: 1981.

Goodman, Paul S. "Realities of Improving the Quality of Work Life: Quality of Work Life Projects in the 1980's," *Labor Law Journal* 31, 8 (August 1980): 487–94.

Gould, Mark. "The Devaluation of the Value of Labor-Power," mimeo: Haverford College, Dept. of Sociology-Anthropology, 3 September 1980.

Gould, William B. "The Rights of Individual Workers," *The Center Magazine*, July-August 1984: 2–14.

Greenbaum, Joan. "The Division of Labor in the Computer Field," *Monthly Review* 28, 3 (July-August 1976): 40–55.

Gresser, Julian. *Partners in Prosperity: Strategic Industries for the U.S. and Japan.* NY: McGraw-Hill, 1984.

283

Gustafson, Stig. "A Critical Review of the Swedish Codetermination Act," mimeo: Work in America Institute, 6 December 1979.

Hackman, J. Richard. "Is Job Enrichment Just a Fad?" *Harvard Business Review* 53, 5 (September-October 1975): 129–38.

Halpern, Norm. "Sustaining Change in the Shell Sarnia Chemical Plant," *QWL Focus* 2, 1 (May 1982): 5–11.

Harries-Jenkins, G. "Professionals in Organizations," in Jackson, J.A. (ed.) *Professions and Professionalization,* 1970, ch. 3.

Harter, Philip J. "Negotiating Regulations: A Cure for Malaise," *Georgetown Law Review* 71 (1982): 1–118.

Harter, Philip J. "The Political Legitimacy and Judicial Review of Consensual Rules," *American University Law Review* 32 (1983): 471–96.

Healy, James J., ed. *Creative Collective Bargaining: Meeting Today's Challenges to Labor-Management Relations.* Englewood Cliffs, NJ: Prentice-Hall, 1965.

Heckscher, Charles C. *Democracy At Work: In Whose Interests?* Ph.D. dissertation, Harvard University, 1981.

Henle, Peter. "Economic Effects: Reviewing the Evidence," in The American Assembly, *The Worker and the Job,* 1974, ch. 5.

Herding, Richard. *Job Control and Union Structure: A Study on Plant-Level Industrial Conflict in the United States With a Comparative Perspective on West Germany.* Rotterdam University Press, 1972.

Herzberg, Frederick. "One More Time: How Do You Motivate Employees?" *Harvard Business Review* 46, 1 (January-February 1968): pp. 53–62.

Heshizer, Brian. "The New Common Law of Employment: Changes in the Concept of Employment at Will," *Labor Law Journal,* February 1985: 95–107.

Hiller, E.T. *The Strike: A Study in Collective Action.* Chicago, IL: University of Chicago Press, 1928.

Hirschorn, Larry. *Beyond Mechanization: Work and Technology in a Postindustrial Age.* Cambridge, MA: Massachusetts Institute of Technology Press, 1984.

Hobbes, Thomas. *Leviathan.* London: 1651.

Hogler, Raymond L. "Employee Involvement Programs and *NLRB* v. *Scott & Fetzer Co.:* The Developing Interpretation of Section 8(a)(2)," *Labor Law Journal,* January 1984: 21–27.

Hughes, Charles L. *Making Unions Unnecessary.* NY: Executive Enterprises Publications, 1976.

Hyman, Richard, and Price, Robert, eds. *The New Working Class? White Collar Workers and Their Organizations.* London: The MacMillan Press, 1983.

Independent Study Group. *The Public Interest in National Labor Policy.* NY: Committee for Economic Development, 1961.

International Labour Organisation. "Workers' Participation in Decisions Within Undertakings," Geneva, ILO, 1976.

Jackson, J.A., ed. *Professions and Professionalization.* Cambridge: Cambridge University Press, 1970.

Jacob, Betty, and Williams, Gary L. "The Effective Trade Union," mimeo, 4th revised draft, July 1978, in J. Forslin, A. Sarapata, and A.M. Whitehill, eds., *Automation and Industrial Workers: A Fifteen Nation Study.* Elmsford, NY: Pergamon Press, 1979.

Jacoby, Sanford M. "Union-Management Cooperation in the United States: Lessons From the 1920's," *Industrial and Labor Relations Review* 37, 1 (October 1983): 18–33.

Jenkins, Clive, and Sherman, Barrie. *White-Collar Unionism: The Rebellious Salariat.* London: Routledge and Kegan Paul, 1979.

Justice, Betty W. *Unions, Workers, and the Law.* Washington, D.C.: Bureau of National Affairs, 1983.

Kassalow, Everett M. "Workers' Participation in OECD Countries: Varieties of Experience," mimeo: University of Wisconsin, May 1983.

Kauff, Jerome B., and McClain, Maureen E. *Unjust Dismissal 1984: Evaluating, Litigating, Settling, and Avowing Claims.* Atlantic Highlands, NJ: Practising Law Institute, 1984.

Kaus, Robert Michael. "Job Enrichment and Capitalist Hierarchy." B.A. thesis, Harvard University, April 1973.

Klare, Karl E. "The Public/Private Distinction in Labor Law," *University of Pennsylvania Law Review* 130, 6 (June 1982): 1358–422.

Kochan, Thomas; Katz, Harry; and McKersie, Robert. *The Transformation of American Industrial Relations.* NY: Basic Books, 1986.

Kochan, Thomas A.; McKersie, Robert B.; and Cappelli, Peter. "Strategic Choice and Industrial Relations Theory," *Industrial Relations* 23, 1 (Winter 1984): 16–39.

Kochan, Thomas A.; Katz, Harry C.; and Mower, Nancy R. *Worker Participation and American Unions: Threat or Opportunity?* Kalamazoo, MI: W.E. Upjohn Institute, 1984.

Kotter, John. *Power and Influence.* NY: Free Press, 1985.

Kressel, K., and Pruitt, Dean G. "Themes in the Mediation of Social Conflict," *Journal of Social Issues* 41, 2 (1985): 179–98.

Kuhn, James W. "Engineers and Their Unions," in Blum et al., *White-Collar Workers*, 1971, ch. 3.

Ladd, Everett C., Jr., and Lipset, Seymour Martin. *Professors, Unions, and American Higher Education.* Carnegie Foundation for the Advancement of Teaching, 1973.

Latta, Geoffrey W. "Union Organization Among Engineers: A Current Assessment," *Industrial and Labor Relations Review* 35, 1 (October 1981): 29–42.

Lauck, W. Jett. *Political and Industrial Democracy, 1776–1926.* NY: Funk & Wagnalls Co., 1926.

Layton, Edwin T., Jr. *The Revolt of the Engineers: Social Responsibility and the American Engineering Profession.* Cleveland: Press of Case Western Reserve University, 1971.

Lehman, Michael B. "The Industrial Model of Academic Collective Bargaining," in Douglas, J.M. (ed.) *Campus Bargaining at the Crossroads*, 1982, pp. 48–55.

Leontief, Wasily W. *The Impacts of Automation on Employment, 1963–2000.* NY: Institute for Economic Analysis, 1984.

Levenstein, Aaron. "The Legal Environment: The Yeshiva Decision," in Levenstein, A., and Douglas, J.M. (eds.) *Campus Bargaining in the Eighties*, 1980, pp. 24–38.

Levenstein, Aaron, and Douglas, Joel M. (eds.) *Campus Bargaining in the Eighties: A Retrospective and a Prospective Look.* NY: National Center for the Study of Collective Bargaining in Higher Education, April 1980.

Levitan, Sar A., and Johnson, Clifford M. "Labor and Management: The Illusion of Cooperation," *Harvard Business Review*, September–October 1983: 8–16.

Lewin, Leif. "Union Democracy," *Working Life in Sweden* 3, December 1977.

Lewis, John L. Address before the 43rd (1960) Consecutive Constitutional Convention of the United Mine Workers of America. *United Mine Workers Journal*, 1 November 1960: 12–15.

Lichter, S. Robert, and Rothman, S. "What Interests the Public and What Interests the Public Interests," *Public Opinion*, April–May 1983: 44–48.

Likert, Rensis. *New Patterns of Management.* NY: McGraw-Hill, 1961.

Lippmann, Walter. *Interpretations, 1933–1935.* NY: Macmillan, 1936.

Lipset, Seymour Martin, ed. *The Third Century: America as a Post-industrial Society.* Stanford, CA: Hoover Institution Press, 1979.

Lipset, Seymour Martin, and Schneider, William. "Organized Labor and the Public: A Troubled Union," *Public Opinion*, August–September 1981: 52–56.

Lipset, Seymour Martin; Trow, Martin A.; and Coleman, James S. *Union Democracy: The Internal Politics of the International Typographical Union.* Glencoe, IL: The Free Press, 1956.

Lipset, Seymour Martin, and Schneider, William. *The Confidence Gap: Business, Labor, and Government in the Public Mind.* NY: The Free Press, 1983.

Lipset, Seymour Martin, and Schneider, William. "Confidence in Confidence Measures," *Public Opinion*, August–September 1983: 42–44.

Lockwood, David. *The Blackcoated Worker: A Study in Class Consciousness.* London: George Allen & Unwin, 1958.

Lodge, George C. "Managerial Implications of Ideological Change," *New York State Bar Journal*, April 1977.

Lohr, Steve. "Overhauling America's Business Management," *New York Times Magazine*, 4 January 1981: 15–62.

Lustig, R. Jeffrey. *Corporate Liberalism: The Origins of Modern American Political Theory, 1890–1920.* Berkeley: University of California Press, 1982.

Maccoby, Michael, and Terzi, Katherine A. "What Happened to the Work Ethic?" mimeo, July 1979.

Mallet, Serge. *Essays on the New Working Class.* St. Louis: Telos Press, 1975.

Mann, Michael. *Consciousness and Action Among the Western Working Class.* London: Macmillan, 1973.

Markovits, Andrei S., and Allen, Christopher S. "The West German Trade Unions' Role in Democratization and Participation: Social Partnership or Class Conflict?" prepared for XIth World Congress, International Political Science Association, mimeo, August 1979.

Markovits, Andrei S., and Allen, Christopher S. "Trade Union Responses to the Contemporary Economic Problems in Western Europe: West Germany," mimeo: American Political Science Association, 1979.

Mazzolini, Renato. "The Influence of European Workers Over Corporate Strategy," Sloan Management Review 19, 3 (Spring 1978): 59–81.

McGrath, Phyllis S., ed. *Business Credibility: The Critical Factors.* NY: The Conference Board, 1976.

McIsaac, George S. "Thinking Ahead: What's Coming in Labor Relations?" *Harvard Business Review,* September–October 1977: 22–36, 190.

Meany, George. "What Labor Means by 'More,' " *Fortune* 5, 3 (March 1955): 92–176.

Miller, Robert W.; Zeller, Frederick A.; and Miller, Glenn W. *The Practice of Local Union Leadership: A Study of Five Local Unions. Columbus, Ohio: Ohio State University Press, 1965.*

Mills, D. Quinn. "When Employees Make Concessions," *Harvard Business Review,* May–June 1983: 103–13.

Mintzberg, H. "Why America Needs, But Cannot Have, Corporate Democracy," *Organizational Dynamics,* Spring 1983: 5–20.

Mirvis, Philip H., and Berg, David N. *Failures in Organization Development and Change: Cases and Essays for Learning.* NY: John Wiley & Sons, 1977.

Mitchell, Daniel J. B. "Recent Union Contract Concessions." In The Brookings Institution, *Brookings Papers on Economic Activity,* vol. 1. Washington, D. C.: The Brookings Institution, 1982, pp. 165–201.

Mortimer, Kenneth P. "A Decade of Campus Bargaining: An Overview," in Douglas, J.M. (ed.) *Campus Bargaining at the Crossroads,* 1982, pp. 97–107.

National Academy of Engineering. "The Long-term Impact of Technology on Employment and Unemployment," Washington, D.C.: National Academy Press, 1983.

National Coal Policy Project. *Where We Agree: Report of the National Coal Policy Project.* Boulder, CO: Westview Press, 1978.

National Commission on Productivity and Work Quality. *Labor-Management Productivity Committees in American Industry.* Washington, D.C.: 1975.

New York Stock Exchange. *People and Productivity: A Challenge to Corporate America.* New York Stock Exchange Office of Economic Research, 1982.

Nicholson, Nigel; Ursell, Gill; and Blyton, Paul. *The Dynamics of White-Collar Unionism: A Study of Local Union Participation.* NY: Academic Press, 1981.

Odaka, Kunio. "Implications of Dual Allegiance in the Modernization of Industrial Relations in Japan," Proceedings of the International Conference on Industrial Relations, Tokyo: 1965, pp. 97–125.

O'Toole, James, ed. *Work and the Quality of Life: Resource Papers for "Work in America."* Cambridge, MA: Massachusetts Institute of Technology Press, 1974.

Ouchi, William G. *Theory Z: How American Business Can Meet the Japanese Challenge.* Reading, MA: Addison-Wesley, 1981.

Outten, Wayne N., and Kinigstein, Noah A. *The Rights of Employees.* Toronto: Bantam Books, 1983.

Panitch, Leo. "The Importance of Workers' Control for Revolutionary Change," *Monthly Review* 29, 10 (March 1978): 37–48.

Parsons, Talcott. *Politics and Social Structure.* NY: The Free Press, 1969.

Parsons, Talcott. *The System of Modern Societies.* Englewood Cliffs, NJ: Prentice-Hall, 1971.

Parsons, Talcott, and Platt, Gerald M. *The American University.* Cambridge, MA: Harvard University Press, 1973.

Peel, Jack. "The Future of Industrial Relations in Europe," in Torrington, D. (ed.) *Comparative Industrial Relations in Europe,* 1978, ch. 13, pp. 253–69.

Perkins, Edwin J., ed. *Men and Organizations: the American Economy in the Twentieth Century.* NY: G. P. Putnam's Sons, 1977.

Perlman, Selig. *A Theory of the Labor Movement.* NY: Macmillan, 1928.

Peters, Thomas J., and Waterman, Robert H., Jr. *In Search of Excellence: Lessons From America's Best-run Companies.* NY: Harper & Row, 1982.

Pinchot, Gifford. *Intrapreneuring.* NY: Harper & Row, 1985.

286

Bibliography

Piore, Michael J., and Sabel, Charles F. *The Second Industrial Divide: Possibilities for Prosperity.* NY: Basic Books, 1984.

Pound, Roscoe. "Legal Immunities of Labor Unions," in Chamberlin, Edward H. et al., *Labor Unions and Public Policy*, Washington, D.C.: American Enterprise Association, 1958, ch. 4.

Prondzynski, Ferdinand von. "Freedom of Association in Modern Industrial Relations," *Industrial Relations Journal* 15, 1 (Spring 1984): 9–16.

Purcell, Theodore W. *Blue-Collar Man: Patterns of Dual Allegiance in Industry.* Cambridge, MA: Harvard University Press, 1960.

Quinn, Robert P., and Staines, Graham L. *The 1977 Quality of Employment Survey: Descriptive Statistics, With Comparison Data From the 1969–70 and 1972–73 Surveys.* Ann Arbor, MI: University of Michigan Institute for Social Research, 1979.

Rankin, Thomas Donald. "Unions and the Emerging Paradigm of Organization: The Case of ECWU Local 800." Ph.D. dissertation, University of Pennsylvania, 1986.

Reich, Robert B., and Magaziner, Ira B. *Minding America's Business: The Decline and Rise of the American Economy.* NY: Vintage Books, 1983.

Reisman, Barbara, and Compa, Lance. "The Case for Adversarial Unions," *Harvard Business Review*, May–June 1985: 22–36.

Riesman, David. *The Lonely Crowd: A Study of the Changing American Character.* New Haven: Yale University Press, 1961.

Rifkin, Jeremy, and Barber, Randy. *The North Will Rise Again: Pensions, Politics, and the Power in the 1980's.* Boston: Beacon Press, 1978.

Roehl, Janice A., and Cook, Royer F. "Issues in Mediation: Rhetoric and Reality Revisited," *Journal of Social Issues* 41, 2 (1985): 161–78.

Salisbury, Robert H. "Why No Corporatism in America?" in Schmitter, Philippe C., and Lehmbruch, Gerhard (eds.) *Trends Towards Corporatist Intermediation*, 1979, ch. 8.

Sayles, Leonard R., and Strauss, George. *The Local Union: Its Place in the Industrial Plant.* NY: Harper & Bros., 1953.

Schatzki, George. "Majority Rule, Exclusive Representation, and the Interests of Individual Workers: Should Exclusivity be Abolished?" *University of Pennsylvania Law Review* 123 (1975): 897–938.

Schiemann, William A., and Morgan, Brian S. "Managing Human Resources: Employee Discontent and Declining Productivity," San Francisco: Opinion Research Corp. Strategy Briefing for Human Resource Executives, 26 October 1982.

Schlesinger, Leonard A. "Supervisory Roles in Participative Work Systems," Ph.D. dissertation, Harvard Graduate School of Business Administration, 1979.

Schmidman, John, and Keller, Kimberlee. "Employee Participation Plans as Section 8(a)(2) Violations," *Labor Law Journal* 35, 12 (December 1984): 772–80.

Schmitter, Philippe C. "Democratic Theory and Neocorporatist Practice," *Social Research* 50, 4 (Winter 1983): 885–928.

Schmitter, Philippe C., and Lehmbruch, Gerhard, eds. *Trends Towards Corporatist Intermediation.* Beverly Hills: Sage Publications, 1979.

Schneider, Leslie, and Ciborra, Claudio. "Technology Bargaining in Norway," mimeo, 1982.

Schneider, Thomas J. "Quality of Working Life and the Law," mimeo: speech to John F. Kennedy School of Government, 19 November 1981.

Scott, Bruce R., and Lodge, George C., eds. *U.S. Competitiveness in the World Economy.* Boston: Harvard Business School Press, 1985.

Selznick, Philip. *Law, Society, and Industrial Justice.* NY: Russell Sage Foundation, 1969.

Sentry Insurance Co. "A Sentry Study: Perspectives on Productivity—A Global View," 1981.

Shaiken, Harley. *Work Transformed: Automation and Labor in the Computer Age.* NY: Holt, Rinehart, and Winston, 1985.

Shapiro, Irving S. *America's Third Revolution: Public Interest and the Private Role.* NY: Harper & Row, 1984.

Shipka, Thomas A. "The Impact of Unions on Academic Standards and Accreditation in Higher Education," in Douglas, J.M. (ed.) *Campus Bargaining at the Crossroads*, 1982, pp. 33–46.

Shorter, Edward, ed. *Work and Community in the West.* NY: Harper & Row, 1973.

Slichter, Sumner H.; Healey, James J.; and Livernash, R. Robert. *The Impact of Collective Bargaining on Management.* Washington, D.C.: The Brookings Institution, 1960.

Sloan, Alfred P. *My Years With General Motors.* Garden City, NY: Doubleday, 1964.

Sloan, Alfred P. "Concept of the Organization," in Perkins, Edwin J. *Men and Organizations*, 1977, pp. 120–30.

Smelser, Neil. *The Theory of Collective Behavior.* NY: The Free Press, 1962.

Smith, Adam. *An Inquiry Into the Nature and Causes of the Wealth of Nations.* NY: The Modern Library, 1937.

Srivastva, Suresh; Salipante, Paul F., Jr.; Cummings, Thomas G.; Notz, William W.; Bigelow, John D.; and Waters, James A. *Job Satisfaction and Productivity.* Cleveland, OH: Dept. of Organizational Behavior, Case Western Reserve University, 1975.

St. Antoine, Theodore J. "The Revision of Employment-at-will Enters a New Phase," *Labor Law Journal,* August 1985: 563–67.

Stein, Maurice R. *The Eclipse of Community: An Interpretation of American Studies.* Princeton: Princeton University Press, 1960.

Stewart, Richard B. "The Reformation of American Administrative Law," *Harvard Law Review* 88 (June 1975): 1667–813.

Stieber, Jack. "Recent Developments in Employment-at-will," *Labor Law Journal,* August 1985: 557–63.

Stieber, Jack, and Blackburn, John. *Protecting Unorganized Employees Against Unjust Discharge.* East Lansing, MI: Michigan State University School of Labor and Industrial Relations, 1983.

Stone, Katherine. "The Origins of Job Structures in the Steel Industry," *Review of Radical Political Economics* 6, 2 (Summer 1974): 113–73.

Strauss, George. "Is There a Blue-Collar Revolt Against Work?" in O'Toole, James (ed.) *Work and the Quality of Life,* 1974, ch. 2.

Sturmthal, Adolf, ed. *White-Collar Trade Unions: Contemporary Developments in Industrialized Societies.* Urbana, IL: University of Illinois Press, 1966.

Sullivan, James M. "Unions in Politics: A Madisonian Faction in our Federal System," *Journal of Labor Research* 5, 3 (Summer 1984): 275–85.

Summers, Clyde. "Individual Protection Against Unjust Dismissal: Time for a Statute," *Virginia Law Review* 62 (1976): 481.

Summers, Clyde. "Comparisons in Labor Law: Sweden and the United States," *Industrial Relations Law Journal* 7, 1 (1985): 1–27.

Summers, Clyde W.; Wellington, Harry H.; and Hyde, Alan. *Labor Law: Cases and Materials.* 2d ed. Mineola, NY: The Foundation Press, 1982.

Surace, Samuel J. *Ideology, Economic Change, and the Working Classes: The Case of Italy.* Berkeley: University of California Press, 1966.

Susskind, Lawrence E., and Cruikshank, Jeffrey. *Breaking the Impasse: Consensual Approaches to Resolving Public Disputes.* NY: Basic Books, 1987.

Susskind, Lawrence, and McMahon, Gerard. "The Theory and Practice of Negotiated Rulemaking," *Yale Journal of Regulation* 3, 1 (Fall 1985): 133–65.

Thimm, Alfred M. *The False Promise of Codetermination: The Changing Natures of European Workers' Participation.* Lexington, MA: D.C. Heath, 1980.

Thompson, E.P. *The Making of the English Working Class.* NY: Vintage Books, 1963.

Toennies, Ferdinand. *Gemeinschaft und Gesellschaft.* Leipzig: Fues's Vertag, 1887.

Toffler, Alvin. *The Adaptive Corporation.* NY: McGraw-Hill, 1970.

Torrington, Derek, ed. *Comparative Industrial Relations in Europe.* London: Associated Business Programmes, 1978.

Touraine, Alain. "An Introduction to the Study of Social Movements," *Social Research* 52, 4 (Winter 1985): 749–87.

Touraine, Alain. *The Post-Industrial Society.* N. Y.: Random House, 1971.

Trist, E.L. "On Socio-technical Systems," in Bennis, W. G.; Benne, K. D.; and Chin, R., *The Planning of Change,* 1961, pp. 269–82.

Ulman, L., ed. *Challenges to Collective Bargaining.* Englewood, NJ: Prentice-Hall, 1967.

U.S. Dept. of Health, Education and Welfare. *Work in America.* Cambridge, MA: Massachusetts Institute of Technology Press, 1973.

U.S. Department of Labor. *Quality of Work Life: AT&T and CWA Examine Process After Three Years.* Washington, D.C.: 1985.

Verba, Sidney, and Nie, Norman H. *Participation in America: Political Democracy and Social Equality.* NY: Harper & Row, 1972.

Walker, Pat, ed. *Between Labor and Capital.* Boston: South End Press, 1979.

Bibliography

Walton, Richard E. "A Developmental Theory of High-commitment Work Systems," mimeo: Harvard Graduate School of Business Administration, September 1979.

Walton, Richard E. "From Control to Commitment in the Workplace," *Harvard Business Review*, March–April 1985: 76–84.

Walton, Richard E. *The Impact of the Professional Engineering Union.* Boston: Division of Research, Graduate School of Business Administration, Harvard University, 1961.

Watson, Thomas J., Jr. *A Business and its Beliefs: The Ideas That Helped Build IBM.* NY: McGraw-Hill, 1963.

Wattenberg, Ben J. "As the Dust Settles: Centrism at Work in the Participatory State," *Public Opinion,* June–July 1984: 2–6.

Webb, Sidney and Beatrice. *Industrial Democracy.* London: Longman's, Green, 1902.

Weber, Max. *The Theory of Social and Economic Organizations.* NY: The Free Press, 1947.

Weiler, Paul. "Striking a New Balance: Freedom of Contract and the Prospects for Union Representation," *Harvard Law Review* 98 (1984): 351–420.

Woodworth, Warner et al, eds. *Industrial Democracy.* Beverly Hills: Sage, 1985.

Yankelovich, Daniel et al. *The World at Work: An International Report on Jobs, Productivity, and Human Values.* NY: Octagon Books, 1984.

Yankelovich, Daniel, and Immerwahr, John. *Putting the Work Ethic to Work: a Public Agenda Report on Restoring America's Competitive Vitality.* NY: Public Agenda Foundation, 1983.

INDEX